Medieval Japan

MEDIEVAL JAPAN

ESSAYS IN INSTITUTIONAL HISTORY

EDITED BY

John W. Hall and Jeffrey P. Mass

CONTRIBUTORS

David L. Davis   John W. Hall   Kyotsu Hori
G. Cameron Hurst III   Cornelius J. Kiley
Jeffrey P. Mass   Elizabeth Sato
Prescott B. Wintersteen, Jr.

Stanford University Press, Stanford, California

Stanford University Press
Stanford, California

Copyright © 1974 by John W. Hall and Jeffrey P. Mass

First published by Yale University Press in 1974.
Reissued by Stanford University Press in 1988.

Printed in the United States of America

Cloth ISBN 0-8047-1510-6   Paper ISBN 0-8047-1511-4

Original printing of this edition 1988

Last figure below indicates year of this printing:

08   07   06   05   04   03   02   01

To Asakawa Kan'ichi
Pioneer historian of medieval Japan

Contents

List of Illustrations

Maps

Figures

Tables

Preface

The essays in this volume were prepared initially for the Yale Faculty Research Seminar on Medieval Japan held in the spring of 1972. The seminar was organized by the two editors as one of a series of such collective efforts sponsored by the Council on East Asian Studies at Yale and funded under a special grant from the Ford Foundation. Attendance at the seminar varied from week to week depending on the topic under discussion and the schedules of scholars who came from outside New Haven. While most contributors participated in several sessions, one of them, Kyotsu Hori of Hawaii, was unable to join the seminar in person.

The organizers of the Seminar on Medieval Japan feel especially indebted to Professor Toyoda Takeshi, who came to Yale from Tohoku University to serve as scholar in residence for the seminar. Professor Toyoda not only contributed brilliantly to the seminar discussion but also worked privately with several of the writers, making suggestions and giving assistance in the handling of documentary materials.

In addition to those who contributed essays and to Professor Toyoda, the following faculty attended one or more sessions of the seminar: Akiyama Terukazu (Yale), Albert Craig (Harvard), Gavin Hambly (Yale), Harry Harootunian (Rochester), Thomas Harper (Yale), Kaneko Hideo (Yale), Archibald Lewis (Massachusetts), Robert Lopez (Yale), Bryce Lyon (Brown), Barbara Ruch (Pennsylvania), Penelope Scull (New York University), Michael Solomon (Oakland, Michigan), Joseph Strayer (Princeton), Paul Varley (Columbia), Stanley Weinstein (Yale), and Yamamura Kozo (Washington). Student participants from Yale were Peter Arnesen, Miles Fletcher, and Sharon Nolte. Martin Collcutt attended from Harvard. Editors and contributors alike wish to thank the seminar participants for their part in helping to improve the essays in this volume through their comments. Richard Staubitz is thanked for preparing the index.

The editors recognize that any symposium volume such as this cannot hope to provide a complete and integrated treatment of a subject so broad in scope as the political institutions of medieval Japan. The eleven essays which comprise this volume are offered consequently in full realization of this impossibility. Each essay represents a discrete, and necessarily partial, contribution to the subject. For that reason it was not thought to be necessary to achieve an absolute uniformity of style or technical apparatus from essay to essay. Every effort has been made, however, to maintain a consistent vocabulary, and for this purpose a glossary has been provided.

JWH and JPM

Introduction

The study of Japanese history by scholars outside Japan has been concentrated first on the "modern" period (1853 to present) and then on the
"early modern" period (1600 to 1868). Medieval Japan has been noticeably neglected. Our knowledge of seven important centuries of Japanese
history, during which the military aristocracy emerged to take over
leadership of the country's political and cultural institutions, remains
sketchy and in many respects flawed. Almost no monographic studies
devoted to this period have been produced by scholars other than Japanese.
This in itself, of course, is no cause for alarm, since Japanese historians
have written extensively and with great perception on the medieval period.
Rather, the problem stems from the fact that the survey histories in English, which have been our prime source of information on this segment
of Japanese history, have generally failed to reflect the best of Japanese
scholarship. What is more unfortunate is that they have often perpetuated
outmoded clichés and biases, particularly in their interpretation of medieval Japan's basic economic and political institutions.

During the spring of 1972 an opportunity presented itself at Yale to
make a modest effort toward remedying the neglect that the history of
medieval Japan has suffered. Through a special grant from the Ford
Foundation in support of a series of faculty research seminars, it became
possible to organize a program of meetings devoted to the political institutions of Japan from the ninth to the sixteenth centuries. The present
volume is a direct outgrowth of these meetings.

The seminar was designed with several objectives in mind. First,
the organizers hoped to draw from the current group of American
specialists on medieval Japan the results of their latest research and
thinking and thus to introduce a significant body of new information into
the mainstream of American historical studies on Japan. Second, by
gathering together as many American specialists on medieval Japanese
political and economic history as could be identified and by associating
them with outstanding Japanese specialists as well as with American

scholars in related fields, it was hoped that a new and more intense interest could be generated in the premodern aspects of Japanese studies. Finally, by introducing specialists in the Japanese medieval field to one another and to other scholars in contrasting disciplines and areas of study, it was hoped that the seminar would help pose new questions for the field and suggest new approaches and interpretations for its practitioners.

All these objectives were more than fulfilled. The seminar proved a great stimulus, both intellectually and psychically, to the small but eager body of American specialists working in Japanese medieval studies. The factor of mutual reinforcement was most pronounced, for the lone scholar could take comfort in the knowledge that he was not, after all, working in isolation. Participants learned from one another, tested out new ideas, and picked up new insights in their subjects of research. The presence of well-known Japanese scholars also was a great boon to the Americans, whose control of historical data must perforce always remain somewhat limited.

One unexpected result of the seminar was the feeling of self-confidence it engendered in the American scholars. For while these historians, working in what is still for them a relatively virgin field, could hardly claim a mastery of Japanese evidence, their interpretations were listened to and often accepted by the invited guests from Japan. In fact, it became clear that American scholars, because of their open and freewheeling approach, had things to say to Japanese historians, even in the field of medieval studies.

As can be seen from the titles of the essays contained in this book, the seminar followed a chronological course from the Heian through the Kamakura and Muromachi periods, taking up the major changes in the structure of government and society from the ninth into the sixteenth centuries. A portion of the content of each study is descriptive and is intended to fill in details of medieval Japan's political organization. Thus the essays add considerably to our knowledge of the political structure of the Heian court. They help to explain the political interests that lay behind the creation of the Kamakura military government and how these interests were modified in the Muromachi regime. They contribute as well to an understanding of the land-tax systems that underlay these political structures.

More significant, however, are the new analytical insights that these essays contain. Over and over again the authors break new ground, offering interpretations and explanations quite at odds with traditional views. The following are but a few of these new insights:

1. Hurst, Sato, and Kiley present a dynamic picture of the Heian court

families and their political and economic competition. The elaborate
private administrative structures developed by these families permitted
them to stretch their influence from the capital into the countryside much
more effectively than has been generally supposed.

2. Hurst's second essay provides a thoroughly new explanation of the
position of the imperial house during the late Heian period. Rejecting the
idea of a century of "cloister government" rule, he nevertheless sees the
period as a golden age for the imperial family.

3. Mass's essays present a fresh view of both the Taira ascendancy and
Kamakura *bakufu* formation, as well as of the tension over land possession
that developed during the thirteenth century. The Taira's debilitating links
with the court are contrasted with the spirit of independence expressed
by the new eastern-based military government. Hori's study reveals that,
despite the troubles besetting Kamakura after the Mongol invasions, the
military aristocracy increased its hold over the country.

4. Wintersteen gives the first reasonable analysis of the sources of economic support that maintained the Ashikaga shogunate. These sources
turn out to be not land income from distant estates but Kyoto-based commercial revenues.

5. In the essays by Hall and Wintersteen, medieval Kyoto appears not
as a declining imperial capital, but as a vigorous commercial and cultural
center.

6. Davis questions the common view that rural populations in late
medieval Japan were on the verge of political emancipation, arguing
rather that political initiative remained securely in the hands of the
military aristocracy. Though the peasantry gained new freedoms at the
village level, it was the daimyo who managed to exploit the situation by
grasping direct administrative control over the villages.

From these essays there emerges, then, a view of medieval Japan
much more diverse and energetic than commonly portrayed. The civil
aristocracy remained a vigorous element in politics much longer than
is generally supposed. Commerce and urban life became more widespread
than imagined. And the political composition of the period was much
more complex and purposeful than we have been led to believe. As these
views become known to generalist historians of Japan, certainly much of
what has been written about medieval Japan will be revised. The essays in
the present collection offer a beginning for such a revision.

THE PROVINCES OF MEDIEVAL JAPAN

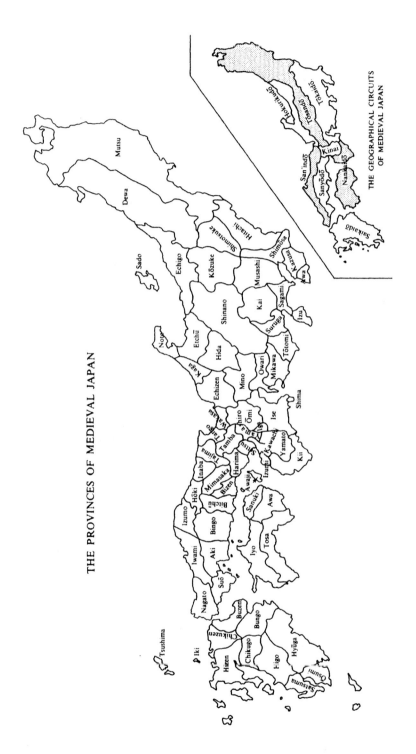

THE GEOGRAPHICAL CIRCUITS
OF MEDIEVAL JAPAN

PART ONE

Court and *Shōen* in Heian Japan

1 Kyoto As Historical Background

JOHN W. HALL

From its founding as the imperial capital of Japan in 794 to its abandonment in 1869, Kyoto served as the primary home of the old court nobility, the *kuge*. Between these dates the city held a direct and intimate relationship to the court, exemplifying in its own changing configuration the varying fortunes of the old ruling elite. Just as today the former kuge, having been stripped first of their political power, then of their wealth, and finally of their social prestige, have disappeared into the common citizenry of modern Japan, so Kyoto as a city is today several incarnations removed from the original Heian-kyō built by the Emperor Kammu.

The original city, taking its inspiration from the imperial capitals of China, was built to encompass an entire ruling class at the height of its power. With the eclipse of that power, following the rise of the provincial military aristocracy, Heian-kyō was transformed into the medieval Miyako, a city shared uneasily by the civil and military aristocracy, priests, and merchants. By the seventeenth century Kyoto had been further transformed into an appendage of the military authority concentrated at Edo. Remnants of the Heian aristocracy lingered on, but only under the watchful eyes of the then fully dominant military elite. Within the city's confines, the long history of the rise and fall of the court nobility had been played out in visible detail. It is a history for which Kyoto serves as a particularly revealing historical document.[1]

The Shaping of an Aristocratic Tradition

To say that Heian-kyō exemplified the kuge at the height of their power presupposes both an evolution in the growth of aristocratic power and in the urban design that accompanied that growth. As of 794, in other words, Heian-kyō marked the culmination of a style of city design that evolved in concert with the gradual political differentiation of the

1. With the publication by the City of Kyoto beginning in 1968 of the multivolume *Kyōto no rekishi*, a broad overview of the city's history becomes an attractive possibility.

group of noble families for which the city was built. Until the seventh century no feature of national life in Japan gave rise to an urban concentration of population except perhaps trade. It may well be that Naniwa, near the present city of Osaka, which served as port of entry for the Yamato region of central Japan, was a town of some size by the sixth century. Behind Naniwa in the inland plain of Yamato, the great land-based families that dominated Yamato politics lived in scattered rural establishments. The concept of a sedentary capital emerged only gradually and imperfectly as the rulers of Yamato, the successive heads of the family that was to emerge historically as the imperial house, achieved a more effective hegemony over their competitors. Institutions of sovereignty were clarified, and around the sovereign a "court" grew up. The name first given to this concentration of authority was *miyako* ("the palace").

Little was needed to make up a capital other than the ruler's residence and surrounding quarters for retainers and attendants. Government was decentralized, and power was diffused through a network of family relationships. As long as the distance between family headquarters was not great, the business of government could be conducted without the necessity of an elaborate administrative machine and its attendant bureaucratic offices. For these early rulers, then, the palace provided for the conduct of statecraft as well as the ritual observances by which the Yamato rulers asserted their spiritual authority over the scattered members of their family and over the other powerful families of central Japan. So long as the capital was identical with the ruler's palace the "capital" changed its location with every new ruler, since the sons of Yamato rulers each had separate establishments. During the two and a half centuries prior to 645, at which time the first public capital city was erected, there were twenty-three rulers in Yamato and thirty-one different "capitals."[2] Yet in another sense the location of these so-called capitals changed very little, for most of them were set within the southeastern portion of the Yamato Plain in the region known as Asuka. There the sweep of a five-mile radius would encompass over twenty former palace locations.

By the beginning of the seventh century the Asuka area had begun to attract a concentration of aristocratic residences, Buddhist temples, and Shinto shrines forming a denser assemblage of political and religious institutions. Administrative functions now required the periodic congregation of officials, and this presumably necessitated the construction of public buildings. Already the continental style of architecture had been introduced in the form of the Buddhist temple. Public buildings modeled after the offices and audience halls of T'ang China now began to make their appearance.

2. Yazaki Takeo, *Nihon toshi no hatten katei* (Tokyo, 1962), pp. 33–34.

What had been a slow drift toward greater concentration of political power and an increased diversity of court administrative functions was given sudden impetus by the coup d'etat of 645, the Taika Kaishin. The resulting turnover in Yamato leadership put political initiative in the hands of a court faction favoring greater centralization of government and the adoption of Chinese institutions of statecraft. Within fifty years Japan was to adopt numerous features of the T'ang system of imperial rule, taking over the rituals of imperial sovereignty, the system of official ranks, bureaucratic organization, land division, allotment, and taxation, and the division of the country into centrally administered provinces. An important part of the reform plan was the establishment of a capital city to house the new organs of government and to support the new imperial dignity.

Toward the end of the year 645, Emperor Kōtoku abandoned the Asuka region to occupy the newly built capital of Nagara Toyosaki at Naniwa. Archaeological evidence of this first effort at planned urban construction was inconclusive until after 1952, when excavations revealed that an imperial palace and public office compound of considerable size were indeed erected. Without doubt the inspiration was Chinese, and, while the outer dimensions of the city cannot be determined, the existence of a full-fledged Official Compound (Chōdōin) with an audience hall and office buildings is now archaeologically verified.[3]

After nine years, the capital at Naniwa was given up. Presumably the pull of religious bodies and influential families entrenched in the Asuka region proved too strong. Under Emperor Saimei two successive locations in Asuka were adopted and evacuated. Emperor Tenchi, who succeeded, erected his capital in 667 at Ōtsu on Lake Biwa, even farther than Naniwa from Asuka. Four years later this establishment was destroyed by fire, and shortly thereafter a war of imperial succession broke out. Emperor Temmu, who fought his way to the throne in 672, returned to the Asuka region, building on one of the sites used by Saimei. This was the capital city of Kiyomihara, best remembered as the location of the first major effort at codification of laws and institutions. Excavations of the site reveal a Ch'ang-an style plan with a division of the city into left and right halves.

But Kiyomihara was cramped, and Temmu planned a larger city somewhat farther out onto the plain. The resulting city of Fujiwara was not entered until 694, after Temmu's death. Fujiwara was obviously better situated, having more room for residential expansion and being surrounded by a more extensive agricultural region. We know a good deal

---

3. Yamane Tokutarō, "Naniwa no chōtei," in Ueda Masaaki, ed., *Asuka to Nara* (Tokyo, 1967, Nihon Rekishi Shiriizu), 2:164–67.

about Fujiwara through references in the official histories. Some thought was given to the justification of the site in terms of Chinese principles of geomancy. The city faced south and was divided into left and right halves. Seven avenues ran north and south, twelve ran east and west. The squares created by the intersection of these streets demarcated wards (*bo*) of which sixteen at the north center were reserved for the palace enclosure.[4] Fujiwara attracted twenty-four temples into its confines, and a passage in the *Nihonshoki* claims that the common residences in the city numbered 1,505 "columns of smoke," that is, 1,505 houses as counted by the smoke coming from their roofs.

Three emperors reigned from Fujiwara, but the city soon proved to be too small, and so Heijō was planned. This time a clean break was made with the vested interests of Asuka. Set in the middle of the Yamato Plain, well placed to communicate by water with the port of Naniwa and by road with the provinces to the east and west, Heijō was the boldest effort so far to create a lasting capital city. Begun in 708 and entered in 710, it was to remain the seat of government, except for a few erratic moves during the 740s, until it was abandoned in 784. Heijō had external measurements of approximately two-and-two-thirds miles by three miles. A later addition attached a mile-square bulge to the eastern side of the city, pushing its limits to the gates of the great Tōdaiji temple complex.

Heijō-kyō has disappeared except for recent archaeological excavations of the office compound,[5] but it still lives as Japan's "first permanent capital" through many surviving temples, some of which retain their original buildings from the eighth century. By the time Heijō was built there was a conscious effort to avoid the necessity of constant movement from one location to another. Every effort was made to give the city permanence and to draw to it the appurtenances of stable political power. The families of rank were assigned plots of land and induced to build residences in the city. The institutions that served in Asuka as family temples for the noble lineages were also transferred, though some left their headquarters behind and two refused to move. All told, Heijō attracted forty-eight temples. Members of the aristocracy, priests, artisans, and service personnel eventually swelled the population to an estimated 200,000 at its zenith.[6] For seventy years Heijō was the active center of Japan, its sinified specifications

4. Ōshima Nobujirō, *Nihon toshi hattatsushi* (Tokyo, 1954), pp. 46–47. Recent efforts to proceed with archaeological excavation in the face of the proposed bypass on National Highway Route 165 are reported in *Nihon rekishi* 242 (July 1967):37–40.
5. Nara Kokuritsu Bunkazai Kenkyūjo, *Heijōgū hakkutsu chōsa hōkoku II, kan-ei chiiki no chōsa* (Tenri, 1965).
6. Yazaki, *Nihon toshi no hatten katei*, p. 49. This standard estimate is undoubtedly an exaggeration.

reflecting the many features of T'ang civilization that the Japanese sought to emulate.

Yet even in Heijō the ties between the imperial bureaucracy and the foundations of political power were unstable. Between 741 and 746 Emperor Shōmu made five hasty shifts in the location of the capital. Leaving Heijō in 741 because of an armed uprising by Fujiwara-no-Hirotsugu, he first established the capital of Kuni in the hill country to the east. But Kuni was soon abandoned for political reasons, and Shōmu was again on the move. Twice Naniwa was adopted as capital, and each time principal buildings were dismantled and hauled to the site. After much uncertainty and disruption of the court, Heijō was reentered. It was Shōmu who put the final touches to the political balance of power in Nara by drawing the Buddhist establishment further into the government as a balance to court factionalism. His attraction to the Kegon doctrine and his adoption of the *kokubunji* system of officially supported provincial temples was a significant step in the effort to use Buddhism to buttress the imperial reign—a reaction no doubt to the uncertainty of reliance on court families whose interests were in competition with those of the imperial family.

This reliance on the Buddhist priesthood created problems of its own and led to the abandonment of Heijō in 784 following the near seizure of the throne by the priest Dōkyō between 766 and 770. Under Emperor Kammu the capital was removed first to Nagaoka, a site northeast of the present city of Osaka. There the arduous task of transferring government facilities and rebuilding official residences was begun. But political intrigues, the murder of the Fujiwara official in charge of construction, and the counter pulls of court interests delayed completion of the city, and work was stopped in 791. Yet another site was now proposed, namely the one presently occupied by Kyoto, and the plans for Heian-kyō laid out (see figure 1.1). Construction of the city that was at last to become Japan's enduring capital took several years and drew upon the fiscal and manpower resources of all the country's provinces. The emperor left Nagaoka for Heian in 794 despite the fact that the new Great Audience Hall (Daigokuden) would not be finished in time for the New Year's ceremony of 795. Facilities for the ceremony were completed by 796, but the government's Office of Construction was not disbanded until 805.

Heian-kyō as Imperial Capital

The new capital city was planned to fulfill the classical form of the Japanese conception of the imperial city (see figure 1.2). A great rectangle three-and-a-half miles by three miles, the entire area of roughly 6,000 acres was enclosed by a light earthen embankment and moat construction

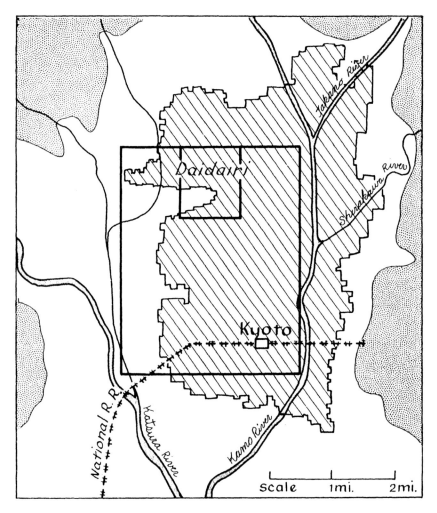

Figure 1.1   Heian-kyō and Present-Day Kyoto

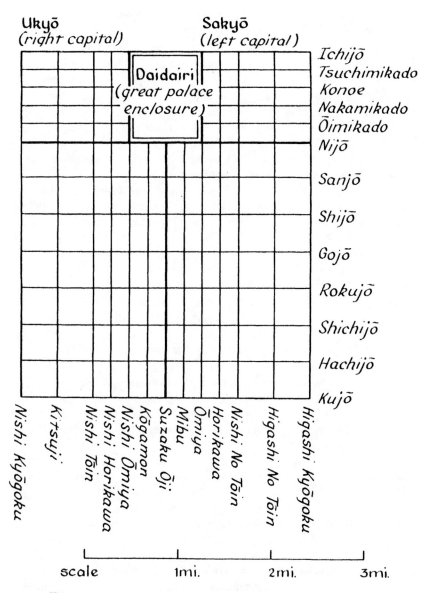

Figure 1.2   Original Plan of Heian-kyō Showing Major Streets

that served as a protection for the city. Within this outer enclosure a grid system of streets divided the city into more than 1,200 blocks of uniform size. The Great Palace Enclosure (Daidairi) was at the northern center and measured one mile by three quarters of a mile, twice the size of the present Imperial Park (Gosho). Two markets, left and right, and two temples, east and west, were provided for. (The temples of Heijō were specifically prohibited from moving into the new capital.) Provisions were made for merchant and artisan quarters, and the high nobility and other aristocratic families were allotted land for residences according to rank. Numerous court palaces, some of them occupying several blocks, or *chō* (roughly three acres), were set with ponds and gardens. Mansions of the nobility tended to cluster in the northeastern portion of the city. The Japanese aristocracy, able to settle down at long last, flowed into the city from their rural estates, making Heian the political, social, and cultural center of the country. By the ninth century it is estimated that the population may have reached 100,000, of which perhaps 10,000 were nobles and lesser officials.[7]

Heian in its first three centuries of existence encompassed an entire historical epoch. The political struggles of the previous centuries were quieted, not so much by the ascendance of a strong imperial presence as through secure domination of the court by the northern branch of the Fujiwara family. The nobility as a class was well provided for by the revenues and services from its lands. By the middle of the ninth century most functions of the central bureaucracy and the elaborate system of ministries had been bypassed, and the formal organs of state administration were serving chiefly as mechanisms for the resolution of the competing interests among the main court families. The imperial ritual and the bureaucratic routine for which the great public buildings had been erected lost all but their ceremonial and symbolic function. Yet the imposing buildings of state continued to exist. The Great Audience Hall, symbolic of imperial prestige, was rebuilt in 876, 1068, and finally in 1156 at great public expense before it succumbed to the disastrous fire of 1177 (Angen 3), which destroyed most of the Great Palace Enclosure. The Great Audience Hall was never again rebuilt, though later emperors dreamed of the prospect, and gradually the capital as architectural manifestation of imperial government lost its landmarks. Already, well before the end of the twelfth century, however, the effective political machinery of state had found a way to function independently of the public facilities of the Great Palace Enclosure.

Reflecting on the period from 645 to 1177, during which the Japanese

7. Kyōto Shi, *Kyōto no rekishi*, 1:245. Other estimates range as high as 500,000. See, R. Ponsonby-Fane, *Kyoto the Old Capital of Japan (794–1869)* (Kyoto, 1956), p. 13.

attempted to maintain a capital city on the Chinese imperial model, one can learn a great deal about the political and social process in early Japan. To begin with there is a clear relationship between the size and composition of the aristocracy and the manner in which capitals continued to be moved about even after the practice of public office construction was adopted. After the construction of Naniwa in 645, these removals must have entailed great expense, though the tearing down and rebuilding of tile roof and wooden-pillar buildings was apparently a routine process, and it was quite possible for buildings to be reused several times. Also for most moves the cost in matériel and labor was presumably shared by some faction of the nobility that had an interest in the particular move.

But the main conclusions to be drawn from the record of itinerant capitals lie in the social and political realm. First the "court," which consisted of a finite group of hereditary aristocratic families, was at the outset sufficiently small and cohesive so that it could be moved fairly easily. Also until the time of Heian, these families maintained rural establishments, so that residence at the capital was not by any means their exclusive domicile. Second, the political balance of power, comprised as it was of a relatively small group of leading families and religious establishments, was never very stable and could pull the emperor one way or another as factions developed. By the time of Heian these conditions had changed, and the aristocracy, their political activities, and cultural requirements, had grown to the point that they required a city to encompass them rather than the reverse. By that time also the machinery for local administration and taxation had been developed to such an extent that the aristocracy could live securely in the capital as absentee governors and proprietors. Thus the permanence that was seen in Heian was not the product of any overwhelming imperial power but rather the result of the willingness of the aristocracy to settle down under a stable balance of interest. The collective power of the court was reflected in the passivity of the provinces and their willingness to produce the manpower and matériel for the construction of the capital city and its public buildings.

While it took the court a century and a half to settle into its Heian base, it is significant that, once having decided on a plan for the imperial capital, the Japanese planners used roughly the same overall design from beginning to end. Japanese historians routinely claim that this design came from Ch'ang-an. But historic Ch'ang-an was different enough from either Heijō or Heian that one must assume the Japanese either had another model to follow or used an idealized version. Among the planners of Naniwa were men who had presumably visited T'ang Ch'ang-an. Yet somehow the result was quite different, not only in size but in the placement of buildings and the arrangement of functions within the walls. Nor did the Japanese appear to seek out more exact models at a later date, for once the Japanese version of the capital city plan was adopted, it was reproduced thereafter with little change other than a progressive increase in size. There was but one major exception to this uniformity of plan: while the early Japanese capitals made liberal provision for the building of temples within their confines, Heian-kyō excluded all but two temples from its plan. The reason for this was, of course, strictly political.

In contrast to whatever continental model might have inspired them, the Japanese made one noteworthy change. From the outset, they never adopted the large outer wall that could serve as a military defense. The reasons for this are not known, but we may presume it was due to lack of need. Warfare in Japan had not begun to involve sieges by masses of troops, and there were no foreign enemies against which to defend the city. To be sure, Heian was encompassed by an earthen embankment of rather modest size that necessitated the building of gates at the points where the major avenues pierced the outer wall. But today no trace of the original earthworks exists, and it would appear that they were erected principally to regulate entrance and exit from the city. When in the sixteenth century Toyotomi Hideyoshi occupied Kyoto (the medieval Heian), he threw around it a large earthen rampart and moat complex, the rampart itself being roughly sixty feet wide at the base, fifteen feet wide at the top, and fifteen feet tall.[8] But even this was not functional from a military defense point of view, and it soon fell into disrepair. This is not to say that no attention was given to the defenses of Heian-kyō. The city was flanked by mountains to the east and north and by rivers to the south and west. Such natural barriers, combined with a series of strategically placed guard points, were presumed adequate to protect against the small armed bands with which the aristocracy fought their factional battles.

Other than the outer protective embankment, walls of another sort played an important role in the organization of city life. What might be called plaster fences were everywhere used to demarcate property and protect against trespass. These were made of pounded earth or wattle and daub, the most imposing being perhaps six feet wide at the base, fifteen feet high, and tapering toward the top, where they were surmounted by tile watersheds. The various compounds into which the city was divided were all surrounded by walls or fences of this sort. The Great Palace Enclosure was so enclosed, and within it were additional compounds that held office buildings, palaces, and other facilities. Entire city blocks were walled in to contain an imperial residence (palace and garden) or the residences of high-ranking nobles. Thus shielded, the nobility lived in

8. Nishida Naojirō, *Kyōto shiseki no kenkyū* (Tokyo, 1961), p. 395.

privacy. Heian was thus a prototypical "container city," to use Lewis Mumford's apt conception: a series of walled enclosures within walled enclosures[9]. Walls were pierced where necessary by appropriately styled gates that could safeguard against intruders. But as the outbursts of violence that occurred in the twelfth century readily showed, neither wall nor gate could protect against armed force or fire.

Aside from the overall grid plan and the placement of markets and residences, which remained basically stable, when we say that the Japanese stayed with a single basic plan for their capital we are referring primarily to the Great Palace Enclosure (Daidairi) itself. At Heian this was a walled rectangular compound one mile by three-quarters of a mile (see figure 1.3). Certain obvious minor differences existed among the several previous capitals involving placement and inclusion and exclusion of facilities; but two units within the Daidairi, the Palace (Dairi) and the Official Compound (Chōdōin), were basic items common to all previous plans (see figures 1.4 and 1.5). The latter in particular, through excavations at Naniwa, Dazaifu, Fujiwara, Heijō, and Heian, is shown to have an almost identical architectural outline from early to late. A rectangular enclosure outlined by a wall and covered corridor, the main portion of the interior was occupied by the Great Audience Hall (Daigokuden) at the north and the Twelve Halls, for the gathering of various ministers of state, toward the south. (An abbreviated version of this enclosure is visible today in the remarkably faithful reconstruction at Heian Jingū in Kyoto.) North of the Official Compound, in which the great ceremonies of state were conducted, lay the Palace. In it the chief elements were the emperor's quarters, the Throne Hall (Shishinden) and the Shinto shrines for worship of the "Heavenly and Earthly deities." The rest of the Great Palace Enclosure was filled with office compounds, storehouses, depots, and stables. At Heian, a Shingon-sect chapel was set next to the Palace itself, so that the priests of this preferred sect could perform special services at the request of the emperor.

In a variety of respects the Japanese capital plan was more intimate and integrated than the Chinese plan. Even in Heijō the style of palace architecture appears to have been more modest than that of China, and imperial residences probably were roofed in thatch or wood bark rather than tile. Palace and offices were closer together, and there was less attempt to set the stage for the great public pageantry that in Ch'ang-an was such an important part of statecraft. The Reception Compound (Burakuin), built for official celebrations, was used more frequently for entertainments and

9. Lewis Mumford, "City: Forms and Functions," in David L. Sills, ed., *International Encyclopedia of the Social Sciences* (New York, 1968), 2:450.

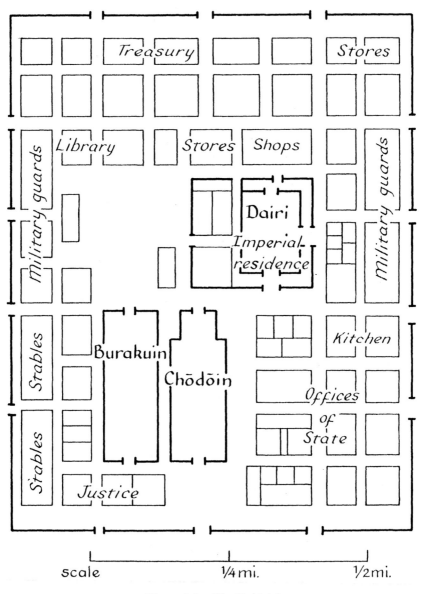

Figure 1.3   The Daidairi

contests. The religious functions of the Japanese emperor were perhaps more central to his role as sovereign and at the same time more under his private control. The imperial family itself retained its most sacred ritual objects within the palace or at shrines, such as Ise, far removed from the capital. The Great Palace Enclosure of Heian gave no sign of the powerful tension between the emperor and officialdom that characterized Chinese politics, giving rise to the grandiose and separate imperial city where the emperor husbanded his own independent sources of power (see figure 1.6).

The City of the Great Court Families

Although it was not until the fire of 1177 that the most imposing architectural evidence of Heian's imperial origin was destroyed, the uses to which the public structures of the Great Palace Enclosure were put had long since changed from their intended purposes. The organs of imperial government that necessitated the many state buildings within the Daidairi had in fact begun to atrophy almost as the city was taking shape. The routine conduct of state affairs in the presence of the emperor, for instance, which was the prime function of the Great Audience Hall (Daigokuden) of the Official Compound, was pretty much abandoned in the reign of Emperor Saga (809–23). Instead the more intimate Shishinden, the main Throne Hall of the Palace Compound (Dairi), took its place as the meeting ground between the emperor and his primary officials. The latter, the so-called *kugyō*, had by Heian times become increasingly differentiated as a recognized group having the prime voice within the court. Membership was limited to the ministers of state (joined eventually by the Sesshō-Kampaku), courtiers with third-court rank or above, and men who, though of fourth-court rank, had been appointed to the post of court councillor (*sangi*).[10] The kugyō, thus defined, numbered from between sixteen and twenty-six during the tenth through twelfth centuries. As a body they can be thought of as comprising among themselves the primary interest groups, other than the imperial family, within the Heian court. To this extent they were a court oligarchy, who when they met together served as the prime decision-making and conflict-resolving apparatus within the government. Families seeking power or security within the Heian court were obliged either to acquire the status of kugyō or subordinate themselves as clients of a family with such status. From the end of the ninth century, the highest formal level of government was thus largely restricted to meetings between the kugyō and the emperor (in the Shishinden) or between the kugyō and lesser officials (in the Giyōden). The latter building,

10. Fujiki Kunihiko and Inoue Mitsusada, *Seijishi*, vol. 1 in *Taikei Nihonshi sōsho* (Tokyo, 1965), pp. 159–61.

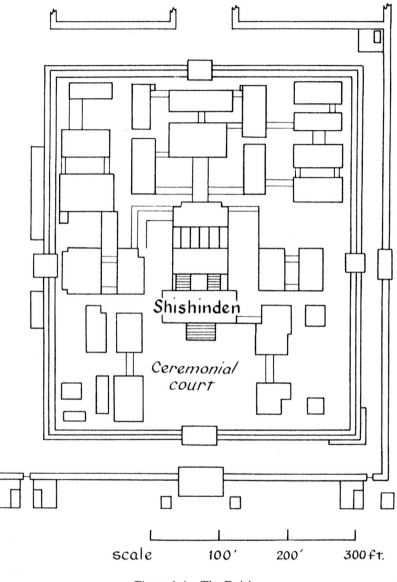

Shishinden

Ceremonial
court

scale   100′   200′   300 ft.

Figure 1.4   The Dairi

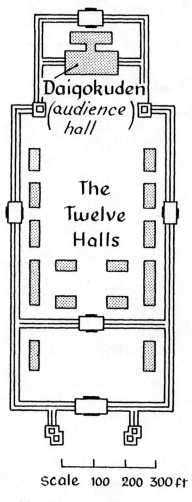

Daigokuden
(audience
hall

The
Twelve
Halls

scale 100 200 300 ft

Figure 1.5   The Chōdōin

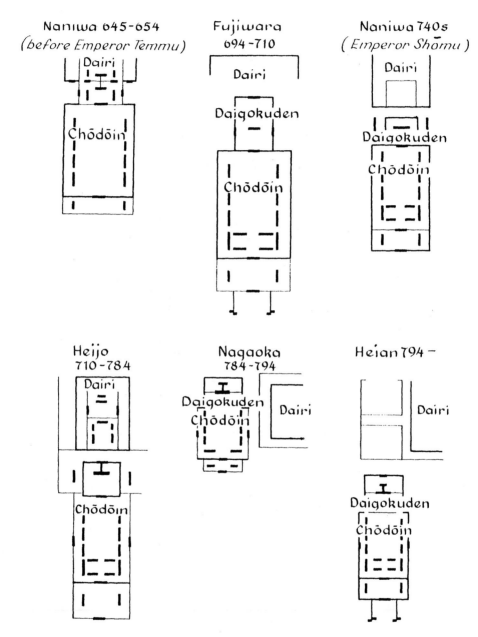

Figure 1.6   Chōdōin and Dairi in Early Capital Plans

which served as the office for the kugyō, was also located in the Palace Compound, adjacent to the Shishinden.[11]

The above abbreviation of the official routine of government reflected the increasing trend toward the privatization of political influence and the acquisition of hereditary sources of income by the court aristocracy. Court politics became a matter of regulating the struggle for position, and hence the acquisition of wealth, among the court families. "Government" served primarily as a framework within which the struggle took place and as a means of keeping it under control. Thus while the kugyō can be looked upon as representing among themselves the prime interest groups within the court, they as a body did not serve as a policy-initiating force. This came instead from the individual families themselves. Hence by the middle of the Heian period we enter an age in which political activity had become diffused into the house headquarters, or *mandokoro*, of the primary court families. Heian-kyō, as a city built around a central government, thereby became the later Heian Miyako, a cluster of palaces, mansions, and temple residences inhabited by privately wealthy and mutually competing court families and priestly organizations. At the center of this assemblage remained the emperor, symbol of the in-group cohesion by which the nobility protected its class interests. The constantly changing pattern of power-holding within the court group can be traced architecturally, therefore, by following the rise and fall of individual families as their residences flourished or decayed and by identifying the shifting locus of prime influence as it moved from one residential headquarters to another. We are taken back to some extent to the pre-Taika pattern, in which each "capital" represented a new balance of power within the elite which surrounded the emperor.

During the first two centuries after the acquisition of the regency by the Fujiwara, it was, of course, the mansion of the head of the senior Fujiwara house that became the locus of the prime influence within the court. It was there that the Fujiwara mandokoro was usually located. Also, by virtue of the common practice whereby husbands occupied residences provided by the in-law family, imperial princes frequently resided in the residences of their Fujiwara wives. Thus it was generally in Fujiwara houses that the young princes destined to become emperors were born and raised.[12] As emperors such men continued to move in and out of Fujiwara mansions, often adopting former Fujiwara houses as their own unofficial palaces (*satodairi*). The Palace served, of course, as the official residence of the reigning emperor and for all public ceremonies, so that the Palace Com-

11. Ibid., p. 163.
12. See William McCullough, "Japanese Marriage Institutions in the Heian Period," *Harvard Journal of Asiatic Studies* 27 (1967):103–67.

pound retained its public functions. But the true center of politics was to be found in the complex of private residences occupied by the reigning emperor, the ex-emperors, and the current head of the Fujiwara family.

The In and His Temple Residences

The Fujiwara hold over the emperor was broken by the growing power of the headquarters of the In, or Retired Emperor, after 1086. The resulting shift in political balance within the court community was soon reflected architecturally by a movement of the primary imperial residences eastward away from the environs of the Palace Compound. Shirakawa, the first of the politically active In, began building in 1075, while still on the throne, the temple residence of Hosshōji in the Shirakawa district of Kyoto (a section across the Kamo River to the northeast of the official palace).[13] In this general area, from that time to 1146, six temples (known collectively as Risshōji) and two imperial residences were constructed to serve the growing demands of retired emperors and their administrative personnel. Upon his own retirement, however, Shirakawa began work on yet another residential complex. This was the Toba Detached Palace begun in 1087 at a location south of the city at the confluence of the Kamo and Katsura rivers. Toba Palace was an extravaganza provided with pleasure lake and racetrack. It too became the center of a major assemblage of temples, residences of members of the In's retinue, and even streets set aside for service personnel. Simultaneously other palaces within the city, notably the Rokujō Dono and the Higashi-Sanjō Dono, were being newly built or rebuilt for use by the In. All of these building programs are illustrative of the fact that the imperial house had acquired private sources of wealth capable of supporting construction on a scale matched only by that required in building the official palace itself. But more significantly, they show that the In possessed political interests of sufficient scope to warrant such establishments. Shirakawa, who as In had achieved a status of primacy among the kugyō, was able to act out the imperial role as no other member of the imperial house since the heyday of Heian. His successors as In, Emperors Toba, Go-Shirakawa, and Go-Toba, lived up to the same role.

At the base of the new affluence that the In had acquired on behalf of the imperial house was first of all the accumulation of a large number of imperial proprietorships (shōen). Retired emperors, their consorts, or even fictive entities, such as family chapels, were now invested directly with incomes from landed estates, thus eliminating the necessity of relying on public sources of support. Added to this was a remaining semipublic

13. Kyōto Shi, *Kyōto no rekishi*, 2:118–43.

source, namely the claim that the court nobility and religious institutions had upon the tax income from the provinces. The In, along with other court institutions, were able to absorb tax revenues from the public lands (*kokugaryō*) of certain provinces made available to them as "proprietary provinces" (*chigyō-koku*). Frequent use was also made of the practice whereby the taxes from a given province were assigned on a term basis for the construction of a specific palace or temple. Under the In's authority such proprietorships would be assigned to lesser members of the court, who served as tax managers (*zuryō*) at the same time that they held what might be called a client relationship to the In. It was these court families which, receiving the taxing privileges over certain provinces, took charge of the In's construction projects.[14]

The residence-temple projects themselves point up yet another new development that the active retired emperors worked to their advantage. The relationship of the kuge to the Buddhist establishments that steadily increased along the eastern environs of the city is extremely complex and has not as yet been adequately investigated. While during the early Heian period the kuge appear mainly in the guise of patrons who supported the building of temples for purposes of spiritual benefit or for the protection of family religious interests, imperceptibly the relationship changed to one of much greater mutual benefit, both political and economic. The practice of retirement into monastic life had only the most tenuous religious significance, while the close relationship between the high priesthood and the high kuge families suggests a much greater interdependence for political and economic reasons. Thus the manner in which members of the imperial house moved into the priesthood, preserving thereby a style of life and a visibility that would otherwise have been denied them, requires the closest scrutiny. The relationship of Emperors Shirakawa, Toba, Sutoku, and Konoe with Hosshōji and the other "imperial vow" temples and with the imperial residences that adjoined the temple complexes is quite revealing. Clearly the temples were not built simply as acts of piety but as ways of protecting estate income and a certain style of life. Evidently the building of new temples could serve as a coercive device to extract support from other kuge families and to justify the use of public taxes for the benefit of members of the imperial house, the religious intent giving support to the political interest. Each of the six temples in the Risshōji complex received the commendation of specific shōen from kuge proprietors who thereby secured client relationships with both the temple authorities and the imperial house.[15]

14. Ibid., pp. 238–44.
15. Ibid., p. 127.

The intricate economic relationships that resulted from this late Heian temple construction, and the social and political implications of these relationships are yet to be fully explored. But since most of the residence-temples (*monzeki jiin*, as they were commonly called) were generally branches of larger more distant centers, there is evidence that an increasingly complicated relationship grew up between court families and the great monastic establishments, such as Enryakuji of Mount Hiei and Tōdaiji and Kōfukuji of Nara, which lay beyond the capital area. These powerful and wealthy religious centers became allies or enemies in court politics or served as refuges for politically precarious or ambitious members of the court. Thus the growth of the "imperial vow" temples of the Shirakawa area of Kyoto represented a political, if not economic, link between the In, ex-emperor Shirakawa, and Enryakuji of Mount Hiei. We may suppose, therefore, that the ascendancy of the In over the Fujiwara house was to a considerable extent enhanced by the influence that Enryakuji was able to exert through its monzeki temples on the outskirts of Kyoto.

The Taira and the Fukuhara Episode

By the time of Toba's death in 1156 political factionalism within the court had grown to such proportions that the In found it difficult to retain his position as prime arbiter. Presently another center of power, this one built up around the Taira house at Rokuhara, made its appearance. Located across the Kamo River to the south of Gojō, Rokuhara had served as residence for members of the Taira family since the time of Shirakawa. Here, after Kiyomori won military engagements in the Hōgen and Heiji disturbances, becoming court councillor in 1160 and prime minister in 1167, the Taira step by step rose to a competitive position at court. During the Heiji disturbances Sanjō Palace, the residence of the then current In, Go-Shirakawa, had been burned, forcing him back to Toba Palace. Emperor Nijō had been obliged to take refuge at Rokuhara. The Taira headquarters was becoming a new element in the struggle for control of court affairs, and Rokuhara from this time to 1333 was to remain the locus of military authority at the capital.

The rise of Kiyomori's branch of the Taira house was facilitated initially by the backing of Go-Shirakawa. Increasingly, however, relations became strained between the Taira and the In and with the great monasteries, particularly Enryakuji. The power of Enryakuji within the city had been exerted through the agency of Yasaka Shrine, situated just north of Rokuhara.[16] Conflicts arose over police jurisdiction between the shrine

16. Ibid., pp. 74–75, 573.

and Rokuhara. When in 1179 Kiyomori and Go-Shirakawa broke with each other, the Taira found themselves isolated. In 1180 Kiyomori made the decision to move the court to a new capital location.

In most political histories the ephemeral attempt of Taira Kiyomori to move the capital to Fukuhara on the Inland Sea is narrated as an unhappy but minor episode in the course of the demise of Taira power. From the point of view of the historian of Kyoto, however, it acquires more significance. In terms of the power politics of Heian-kyō, Kiyomori's act illuminates the final stage of Taira frustration as well as the extent of their actual power in hand. For Kiyomori was able to uproot not only the reigning emperor Antoku, but Go-Shirakawa (then under "house arrest") and Takakura, the active retired emperor. The plan to establish a private Taira capital, out of reach of hostile religious centers, ended in failure. In terms of urban history, the fact that Kiyomori was unable to keep the court at Fukuhara demonstrates both the pull that Heian had upon the aristocratic mind and also perhaps the difficulty that the aristocracy had in doing without the cultural symbols the old capital area could provide. One reason that is traditionally presumed to have influenced the decision to return to Heian was the discovery that no building had been built at Fukuhara capable of providing for the emperor's New Year's ceremony.

Kyoto and Kamakura

After the disruption of the Gempei War (1180–85), the city of the kuge settled back for a time into a relatively stable and prosperous condition. While politically the position of the imperial and Fujiwara houses had become more precarious and the court increasingly fragmented between competing family branches and factions, this would not have been immediately apparent to the casual observer. In 1189 Minamoto Yoritomo had been induced by Go-Shirakawa to rebuild the Palace Compound so that the imperial dignity could be restored. The In, still able to rely on income from his estates and proprietory provinces and the support of kuge clients, found it possible to live in conspicuous style. Go-Toba, the In who succeeded to this condition, in fact occupied eighteen residences within twenty-three years. While only three of these were more than casual residences, they give evidence of a remarkable flurry of palace construction in the early years of the thirteenth century.[17] By this time, of course, the scale of imperial residences had diminished to some extent, and the largest of the In's palaces, the Kōyōin, occupied a space of no more than two chō (about six acres). But construction even on this scale, particularly since it was not undertaken as part of a residential temple complex, pointed up

17. Ibid., p. 237.

the continued vigor of the proprietary province (*chigyō-koku*) system as it culminated in the upper court aristocracy. Go-Toba as In is believed to have held personally three provincial proprietorships, and in addition he had the assignment authority over some thirty-seven others.[18] It comes as no surprise, therefore, to discover that nearly all of the palaces constructed for Go-Toba were done so by members of the In's entourage who were serving at the time as provincial proprietors. The proprietary province was consequently a powerful patronage device that worked to the advantage of both patron and client.

In addition to the chigyō-koku system, Go-Toba worked aggressively to strengthen his control over private imperial proprietorships, consolidating scattered holdings, clarifying proprietary rights, and concentrating as many holdings as possible within easy reach of the capital. From these shōen Go-Toba recruited a private military guard in an effort to balance the military power base left at Rokuhara by the Minamoto.

The capacity of the kuge during the thirteenth century to continue their accustomed style of life was made possible in large part, however, by the stabilizing influence of Kamakura. Within the capital area the Kamakura presence was exercised through the military establishment at Rokuhara. Following the defeat of the Taira, Rokuhara fell into the hands of the Kamakura forces and became in 1185 the residence of a military governor, the Kyoto shugo (It is interesting to note that the term Kyoto had by now become part of the official vocabulary.) Under the shugo, Rokuhara was to serve as a force in maintaining law and order in the capital area. The military presence was several times publicly displayed, as when Yoritomo entered the capital with troops in 1190 and 1195. Yet Rokuhara remained an outpost from the point of view of Kamakura, and it was significant that the major military houses together with their troops had withdrawn from the city. The Kyoto shugo in fact shared police duties and jurisdiction with the capital guard (*kebiishi*) controlled by the court, and beyond that several military figures posted at Rokuhara became the In's clients. It is this situation, the growing group of client courtiers and military personnel and the seeming weakness of the Kamakura presence at Rokuhara, that no doubt encouraged Go-Toba in 1221 to raise a military following in an effort to restore the capital to full imperial control. Go-Toba had obviously misjudged his capacity, for the Jōkyū War, as it was called, ended in disaster for the imperial faction.

Following the Jōkyū War, Rokuhara received immediate attention from Kamakura. Because of the defection of one of the two shugo at that time, the post was abolished and a new and more weighty post, that of

18. Ibid., p. 239.

Rokuhara tandai (Kamakura deputy) was created and normally assigned to two members of the Hōjō family, which now controlled the *bakufu*. The dual appointment, which gave added importance to the post and assured loyalty, necessitated expansion of the headquarters establishment. Rokuhara now consisted of two compounds, North and South. Because members of the Kamakura guard had also joined Go-Toba, the Kyoto military guard service (*ōban-yaku*) was also modified. Military personnel, normally Kamakura housemen, were assigned on rotation for periods of three to six months presumably at six-year intervals. Thus the chance of involvement in court politics was minimized. On the other hand a much larger number of provincial military families was ultimately to have knowledge of the ways of the capital.

Rokuhara was also given increased powers: firmer police powers within the city and legal jurisdiction (as vested in the Kamakura government) over all territory west of Owari Province. The Rokuhara headquarters was increasingly an administrative as well as military center, a sort of western branch of the Kamakura shogunate. Through it, the Hōjō exercised firm control of court affairs, even interfering now in the imperial succession. Yet it is important to realize that Kamakura remained the prime center of military power. Kyoto remained a city dominated culturally, if not politically, by the kuge.

But loss of political and military power had its effect upon the court and its activities. The Jōkyū War drastically reduced the independence of the imperial house and the important kugyō, and, of course, their economic resources. One indication of this is that, as the capacity to tax became localized, the relationship between emperor, In, or Fujiwara and their clients became weighted toward the clients, who assumed more and more the role of patrons. By the end of the Kamakura period the chigyō-koku system was no longer operative. A trend was under way, and by the fifteenth century the remnants of the high court aristocracy were found living on the patronage of military houses who sought, by giving financial assistance to the imperial house or high kuge families, to gain political or social advantage for themselves.

In the decades after the Jōkyū War two other trends became noticeable in the relationship between the court and its sources of patronage. In the early years of In growth, one of the noteworthy phenomena in the environs of Heian-kyō had been the increase of residential temples under the patronage of the imperial house. During the Kamakura period another boom in temple construction occurred in the zone between the city and the hills to the east and north. These, however, were temples of a different sort, built as true religious centers and serving as headquarters for the newly popular sects: Jōdo, Shin, Nichiren, Ji, and Zen. Such temples as

Chion-in (Jōdo, 1175), Hōnen-in (Jōdo, 1206), Kenninji (Rinzei Zen, 1202), Tōfukuji (Rinzei Zen, 1236), Mampukuji (Rinzei Zen, 1261), Honganji (Shin, 1272), to name but the most outstanding, were founded at this time on the city's outskirts. Within the city, breaking the custom that had excluded Buddhist establishments in Heian, temples of the Ji sect grew in numbers, beginning with Konkōji (1286). Similarly Nichiren temples like Myōkenji (1321) and Hongokuji (1343) were built within the city.[19] The new religious institutions that thus sprang up around and within Kyoto may have added comfort to the lives of the kuge and may have served as places of refuge for priests, but they offered little by way of financial support to the court nobility.

The other trend was somewhat more rewarding to the kuge. The appearance of an independent merchant–artisan class in the city at this time follows a clear pattern of evolution from an early condition in which the kuge were very much the masters of commercial activity to one in which they became its parasitic beneficiaries. In the original Heian-kyō much of the productive work of craftsmanship was performed by state-maintained artisans. The disintegration of the imperial government was accompanied by two processes: the emancipation of state artisans into a free community of craftsmen and the conversion of some of the lower-ranking court families into hereditary middlemen between the court and various commercial and service groups. By the end of the Kamakura period the imperial house and other kuge families had begun to serve as patrons for various such groups, offering protection and receiving compensatory dues. This was the beginning of the formalized guild (za) system which proved so effective as a source of income for the kuge in the fourteenth and fifteenth centuries. A definite commercial section of the city, along Shijō Avenue, was now in the making.

The Kemmu Episode

Emperor Go-Daigo's unsuccessful attempt to revive imperial rule between 1334 and 1336 need not be described in detail. Its effect upon Kyoto was dramatic and reminiscent of the earlier Fukuhara episode. First, as prelude to a new era in the city's life, the Kemmu affair brought about the destruction of Rokuhara, and by refocusing political attention upon the capital, assured the transfer of the shogunate from Kamakura into what had been the kuge's preserve. Also, as an ill-conceived effort to regain imperial power, Go-Daigo's failure measurebly weakened the imperial house, reducing much of its economic resources and police powers within the city. The balance of power now swung sharply toward the mili-

19. Ibid., p. 321.

tary aristocracy and the priesthood, both of which were physically entrenched in the city.

In an effort to revive the lost imperial prestige, Go-Daigo placed high on his priority the reconstruction of the Great Palace Enclosure, and an order to that effect was issued in 1334. The provinces of Aki and Suō were charged with the initial construction, but no revenues were forthcoming. Neither the state powers with which the early Heian emperors had built and rebuilt their state buildings, nor the patronage powers that had supported the late Heian palace construction, worked for Go-Daigo. Heian-kyō had entered its medieval phase as the Miyako of Ashikaga times, a city dominated by the shogun and his military entourage.

The Medieval Miyako: The Shogun's City

When in 1338 Ashikaga Takauji became shogun and established his headquarters in Miyako, he assured the city's continued importance as the primary center of politics in the country. As the city in which the emperor resided, and hence the location of the symbol of residual sovereignty, and as the city of the Ashikaga shogunate, Miyako remained the focus of attention in the struggle for political hegemony. Once established in Miyako the shogun required his prime vassal lords, the provincial shugo, to build residences in the capital and to live there on a more or less permanent basis. It was as though Kamakura had been imposed on Heian. Another building boom was soon in the making, and the influx of military personnel meant that great quantities of goods and services were moved into the city from the provincial bases of the new autocracy. In medieval Miyako, however, the emperor and the remaining kuge lost all semblance of independent political power. They lived on in a political vacuum as symbols of legitimacy or objects of social and cultural emulation. Institutions of imperial government shrank to a formalized routine that could be exercised within the narrow confines of a small residence compound or in the private houses of a dwindling number of court families. Government was essentially military government, and the most impressive architectural achievements from now on were to be the product of shogunal patronage or of religious inspiration.

Medieval Miyako had visibly lost the primary purposes for which Heian-kyō had been designed, but it possessed others. No longer did the symmetry of its street plan or the overall disposition of its parts have any bearing on the nature of government or the maintenance of a centralized order. Rather, within the former confines of the city, a natural evolution led first to fragmentation and then to the clustering of functions by zones or belts according to the changing circumstances of government and cultural and economic activity. The northern part of the city continued to attract the

residences of the majority of kuge and the military aristoracy; the north-
western and southeastern portions tended to develop toward artisanship
and trade. At the base of the hills which lay to the north and east the belt
of Buddhist temples and monasteries continued to grow. No longer was
the Rokuhara area across the river to the east the exclusive province of
the military aristocracy. The Ashikaga shoguns built their residences in
close proximity to the emperor's palace. The best known of these was, of
course, the Muromachi Dono, which during the hundred years of greatest
Ashikaga ascendancy occupied a spot to the west and north of the present
Kyoto palace grounds. Built in 1378 by Yoshimitsu, and immediately
dubbed the Palace of Flowers (Hana-no-gosho), it served several times
as an imperial residence until destroyed by fire in 1476. As figure 1.7
demonstrates, the Muromachi Dono occupied at least twice as much space
as the imperial palace.

Behind the continued prosperity that medieval Miyako displayed were
a number of fundamental changes in the relationship between the various
groups that comprised the capital elite—civil, military, and religious—and
their sources of income. After the cessation of the civil war, which smol-
dered from 1336 to 1392, the shōen system of absentee proprietorship was
rapidly converted to a more direct system of land possession and exploitation. The provincial military houses are most often depicted as being the
chief gainers in the gradual "feudalization" of land tenure. But kuge
houses, and particularly religious institutions, also gained from new techniques of intensified taxation.[20] While lands controlled by the remaining
court nobility dwindled in size, the capacity to profit from them was im-
proved, in large part because they were located either within or close to the
city limits.[21] Meanwhile new commercial sources of income and the profits
from foreign trade became available. Thus at least the first half of the
Ashikaga period offers significant architectural evidence of vitality and
affluence. The shogunal villas, Kinkakuji and Ginkakuji, appear modest
in their contemporary form, but in their day they represented imposing
outlays of wealth. More obviously the result of land income and patronage
on a grand scale were the great Zen temples, the Gozen and Jissatsu, many
of which were intimately related to both the imperial and Ashikaga houses.
It was into the Zen monasteries that members of the civil and military
aristocracy now retired or sent surplus sons and daughters. Again a fairly
regular pattern of monzeki assignments became customary between these
primary Zen temples and the ranking families of Miyako. The sons of
Ashikaga Yoshimitsu, the third shogun, were placed, for instance, in

20. For an example of the latter see Kan'ichi Asakawa, "The Life of a Monastic Shō
in Medieval Japan," in *Land and Society in Medieval Japan* (Tokyo, 1965), pp. 313–27.
    21. Kyōto Shi, *Kyōto no rekishi*, 3:270–77.

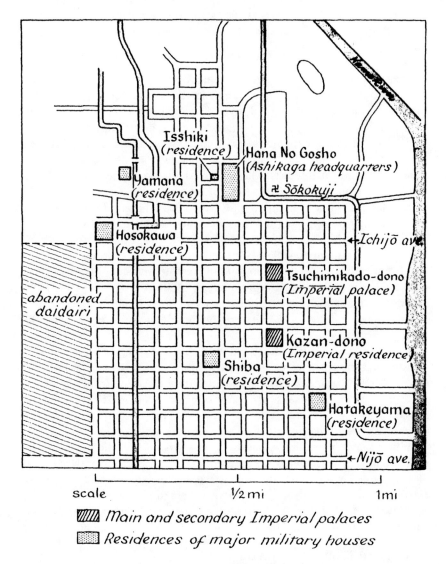

scale   ½ mi   1 mi

 Main and secondary Imperial palaces

Residences of major military houses

Figure 1.7   Northern Kyoto in 1467

Daikakuji and Ninnaji, and his daughters in appropriate nunneries.[22] It is no surprise, therefore, that the Ashikaga period brought to a high point the intellectual and artistic life of the medieval monasteries of Kyoto.

The Two Miyakos

The Ōnin War of 1467–77 proved a major turning point in the fortunes of Miyako. For an entire decade the city served as a battlefield. Most of the interior of the city was destroyed, so that today few buildings in Kyoto can be said to date from before 1467, and these are mostly on the outskirts. By the end of the war the numbers of court families had declined drastically and most of the military aristocracy had returned to the provinces to look after their local interests. The monasteries of Kyoto became ever more a refuge for the arts and letters. Miyako as a city declined dramatically in population, perhaps falling to a low of 40,000 inhabitants by the end of the fifteenth century.[23] Vacant lots occupied many of the interior city blocks, and wilderness encroached upon the fringes. But the city held on, and relics of its imperial past survived. Surprisingly, through their relationship with commercial guilds and the retention of minor landholdings in the city or in the nearby provinces of Yamashiro and Tamba, the aristocracy managed to survive in better condition than is generally supposed. But the vitality of the city was neither of the court nor of the military aristocracy.

For at least the half century between the beginning of the sixteenth century and the entrance of the great military leader Nobunaga into the city in 1568, Miyako received its identity and its vigor from the lower classes: merchants, artisans, priests of popular sects, and to some extent peasants. For a time in fact there were two Miyakos, one in the north (Kamigyō), which consisted of various artisan and service groups surrounding the few remaining houses of the aristocracy, the other to the south (Shimokyō), centered on the commercial district on both sides of Shijō Avenue. With the decline of political authority over the city and the expansion of trade, Miyako, along with a small group of other towns, such as Sakai, Hakata, and Muro, emerged as an economic rather than an administrative city. As the traditional center of fine craftsmanship in weaving, lacquer ware, pottery, and metal work, Miyako retained a reputation as the prime city in the country.

In the sixteenth century, Miyako, although still ringed by great monastic complexes, had become a city of a rising urban class. Their houses were as yet modest, and their most outstanding displays were in the colorful festi-

---

22. Ibid., pp. 52–53.
23. Ponsonby-Fane, *Kyoto the Old Capital of Japan*, p. 173.

vals that filled the streets of the city with floats and religious processions. Yet the activities of the new masters of urban Miyako gave rise to a markedly different life within the city. Commercial families organized themselves by neighborhoods for self-protection and mutual regulation, and this led ultimately to the formulation of overall commune-type organizations in both the north and south sectors. At the core of these urban communes was yet another element, a group of twenty-one Nichiren temples that had grown up in Miyako and had gained a vigorous following among both commercial and aristocratic sectors of the city.[24] Religious sectarianism had now penetrated the city, serving as a vehicle for mutual cooperation. But beyond that, the temples served as refuges in an age of physical insecurity. Temples such as Hongokuji or Honnōji, whose dimensions are known today, were enclosed by walled and moated defenses, and could be converted into armed bastions for the protection of their adherents. And the need for defense was acute. During the fifteenth century peasant mobs (tsuchi-ikki) frequently attacked the city. In the early sixteenth century it was the armed communities of Ikkō sect believers that caused the trouble. During the period from 1532 to 1535 Nichiren adherents of Miyako had to fight off desperate attacks from Ikkō groups based in Yamashina (east of Kyoto) and Ishiyama (now Osaka), mustering on occasion as many as 26,000 fighting men.[25]

Despite the unsettled condition that historians have generally assumed to have prevailed in Miyako of the mid-sixteenth century, the city apparently prospered. The Miyako seen by the early European visitors who came to Japan at about this time dazzled their eyes and led to the most enthusiastic reports. Father Luis Frois, writing in 1565, described the beauty of the palace and gardens of the emperor and the cleanliness of the commercial streets "very straight and level, all of which are closed by gates at night . . . occupied by merchants and craftsmen who weave and embroider damask and other silks and make golden fans and all other things used in this country."[26] Nor did his description of the shogun's "apartment" indicate that political powerlessness was matched by threadbare living.

> The palace is completely encircled by a very deep moat which is spanned by a bridge, and there must have been about three or four hundred cavaliers and many horses at the entrance. . . . I can assure you that I have never seen a more splendid and beautiful house built entirely of wood. The tapestries of the chamber where the *Kubo Sama* was waiting were woven in gold with pictures of lilies and birds, which made them most pleasing to the eye.

24. Kyōto Shi, *Kyōto no rekishi*, 3:543-44.
25. Ibid., pp. 554-59.
26. Michael Cooper, comp., *They Came to Japan* (Berkeley, 1965), p. 281.

The floors of the palace were covered with mats (which in this country are like mattresses) and these were elegantly adorned with a thousand decorations; and the window bars were the finest to be seen.[27]

But political and military power had long ago been withdrawn from the city. Since 1467 such power had gravitated to the provinces where locally based daimyo began to establish their own urbanized military headquarters independent of the capital. After 1570 the power centers of Japan were located in a series of castled daimyo headquarters in such places as Azuchi, Momoyama, Osaka, Edo, and half a hundred other provincial strong points. Before long the daimyo were to enter Kyoto to bring it under the control of a new generation of military leaders.

Rakuchū under Nobunaga and Hideyoshi

During the medieval period Kyoto was commonly known as Raku or Rakuchū. The practice stemmed from an earlier identification of the western half of the capital with Ch'ang-an and the eastern half with the "eastern capital" of T'ang China, Lo-yang. Since it was the eastern portion of Heian-kyō that flourished, the entire city was often called Raku-yō (Lo-yang) or simply Raku. Rakuchū referred to the portion within the city circuit; Raku-gai, the portion outside city limits.[28]

Kyoto in its guise as Rakuchū regained its political prominence during the period of national reunification between 1568 and 1590. Neither Nobunaga nor Hideyoshi, who accomplished this feat as heads of powerful daimyo coalitions, used the city as their administrative capital. For the city could be controlled but not defended. Their main castles were placed at strategic locations outside the city. Yet control of the city and the emperor was central to their plans; to them Rakuchū contained the source of legitimacy and provided the cultural appurtenances that permitted them to play the complete ruler. Nobunaga entered the city in 1568 posing as champion of the reigning emperor and Ashikaga Yoshiaki, whom he installed as a puppet shogun. He was soon at work rebuilding the imperial palace, seeing to it that the members of the court received adequate stipends.

The castle residence that Nobunaga built for Yoshiaki became the first of a new style of feudal palaces built within the city for both protection and aristocratic living.[29] Rakuchū was unified between its north and south sectors, although with differentiated treatment. The lower, or southern, part of the city with its commercial quarters was given new economic

27. Ibid., pp. 109–10.
28. Kyōto Shi, *Kyōto no rekishi*, 1:243–48.
29. Ponsonby-Fane, *Kyoto the Old Capital of Japan*, p. 188.

freedoms and protection, while the northern portion, where political opposition to Nobunaga lingered, was on occasion subjected to coercion.[30] Within the city Nobunaga did what he could to bring the Nichiren temples under control, and he diverted his military forces to contain the great Ikkō citadel at Ishiyama. His most drastic act was the destruction of the great monastic center of Enryakuji on Mount Hiei in 1571. The act effectively eliminated the independent power of the Tendai priesthood and signaled the final assertion of military authority over the city.

Hideyoshi, who succeeded Nobunaga as military hegemon, paid much more attention to the rebuilding of the city. Using Osaka as his military base and Fushimi, Kyoto's port on the Yodo River, as his residential castle, he frequently entered the city and even built a special road to facilitate his coming and going between the imperial palace and his Fushimi residence. After 1585 he ordered one of his principal vassals, Maeda Gen'i, to lay out plans for a complete reconstruction. The new plan called for an area of about half the classical Heian-kyō, occupying the eastern portion that had always been the more fully built up. Roads were laid out in grid form, but the streets were kept more narrow, and the chō were reduced in size by nearly half. The construction was completed in 1591 with the building of a large earthen rampart and moat, the *odoi*, which entirely surrounded the city, a length of about fourteen miles.[31]

Rakuchū by this time had become a feudal city; that is, it was completely dominated by the influence of its feudal military governors. The Ashikaga line of shoguns had been deposed in 1573. The emperor and other kuge were now supported by grants of stipend or land donated by the military aristocracy. A modest palace was provided for, and surrounding it land for residences of the remaining court nobility. Hideyoshi himself built on the site of the old Palace Enclosure, on a grander scale than that of the imperial residence, a palatial castle–residence known as Jurakudai, protected by imposing fortifications and surrounded by the mansions of his chief vassals. In other words he erected a small castle town in the midst of the emperor's city.

Like the castle cities that were springing up across the country, Miyako adhered to a new plan of distribution. Supreme authority emanated from the castle. Merchants and artisans were grouped by block according to specialty. Temples, except for a designated few, were removed to the fringes in three general areas. Teramachi on the east was almost entirely lined by temples so removed. Symbolic of the new military ascendancy over the priestly class was Hideyoshi's victory over the Ishiyama Ikkō

30. Honjō Eijirō, *Kyōto* (Tokyo, 1961), p. 24.
31. Kyōto Shi, *Kyōto no rekishi*, 4:294–99.

community and the removal of the Honganji's headquarters to Kyoto, where it could be easily controlled. The residences of the nobility and of Hideyoshi's military retainers were clustered to the north, in the district dominated by Hideyoshi's castle. With them the new military aristocracy brought wealth and an appetite for conspicuous consumption. A new prosperity enveloped Miyako, and its population rose to a new height of perhaps half a million (see figure 1.8).[32]

Kyoto under the Tokugawa Shogunate

Hideyoshi's death and the shift of the political center of gravity three hundred miles to the east at Edo had two important results. First, the city was largely evacuated by the military aristocracy, except for those who staffed the administrative organs of the Tokugawa shogunate. As a consequence Miyako (now more frequently referred to as Kyoto, while Edo was sometimes called Tōto, "eastern capital") again became a city of the kuge, skilled artisans, and temples. Secondly, it lost a considerable population to Edo. Under the Tokugawa shoguns the city was more strictly regulated and the noble families more completely relegated to a museum-like existence within a controlled environment. Signs of the new dispensation were seen in the great Nijō castle, which towered over the city and overlooked the newly rebuilt imperial residence, and the set of regulations imposed upon the emperor and courtiers by which the shogun restricted the kuge's activities to nonpolitical matters. Two military officials, the Kyoto Shoshidai (Kyoto Deputy) and the Kyoto Machibugyō (Kyoto City Magistrate) now asserted the shogun's administrative authority over the court and the city. Merchant freedom was a thing of the past.

By Tokugawa times the whole set of elements that had formed the "court" and "bureaucracy" of Heian days had been squeezed into a single walled enclosure. The city itself was the domain of the military hegemon. The emperor and his court were confined to a new Palace Enclosure, called Gyoen, a rectangular area about three quarters of a mile by half a mile (see figure 1.9). Within these four walls were crowded a Palace Compound, now called Kinri, with its Throne Hall (Shishinden), gardens, and the residences of about 140 kuge families. The kuge had by now lost all political power, though their social status was still respected. And the symbolic position of the emperor remained essential to the structure of legitimacy on which the Tokugawa house rested its claim to political hegemony. The entire imperial court had become a small, though ceremonially important, unit. The Palace Enclosure had come to embrace the entire court nobility who lived in seclusion behind the now carefully

32. Ponsonby-Fane, *Kyoto the Old Capital of Japan*, p. 236.

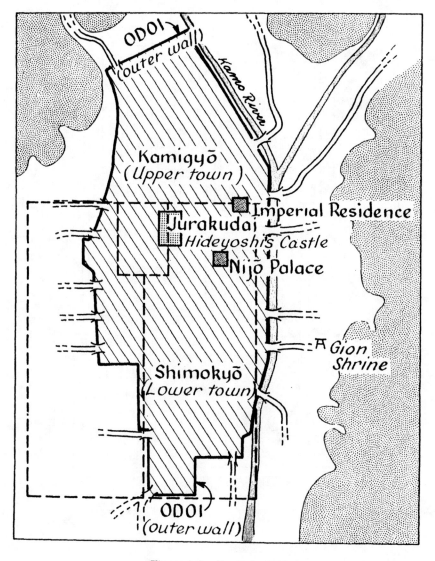

Figure 1.8   Kyoto in 1591

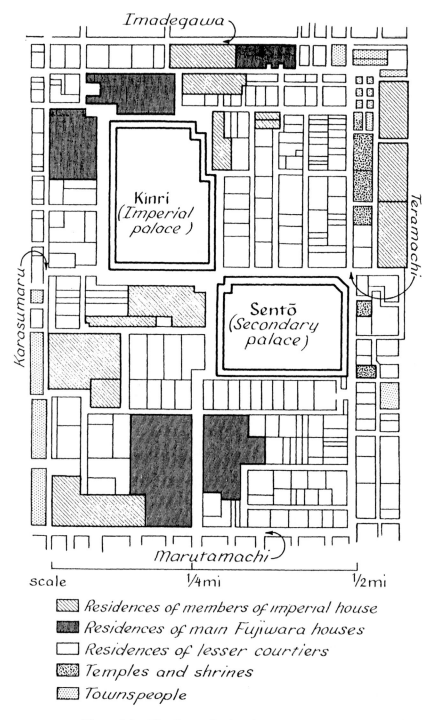

Figure 1.9   The Gyoen During the Tokugawa Era

tended walls of the Gyoen. At the beginning of the eighteenth century, income lands assigned to the court amounted to about 140,000 *koku*, equivalent to the land base of a daimyo ranking at the seventieth percentile of the then existing 243 territorial lords.[33]

Kyoto and Tokyo

As the city of the emperor, Kyoto was to have one final moment of political importance before it passed into historic memory. After 1853, when the foreign menace threatened Japan, the emperor and his courtiers were drawn into the political struggles that divided the country. When in 1862 the Tokugawa shogunate relaxed the alternate attendance requirement that daimyo and their families must live in Edo, the military aristocracy flocked to the environs of the Imperial Palace. Meanwhile, following the destructive fire of 1854, the shogunate had rebuilt the palace in its present style of restrained grandeur. From 1862 until 1869 Miyako again became the prime center of political activity. And in 1867 the land-wealth of the entire province of Yamashiro (230,000 *koku*) was assigned to the imperial house.[34]

The Meiji Restoration of 1868 thrust the emperor again into prominence, this time as a monarch in modern style. But his city had too long remained in the backwater of national politics. Edo, where the apparatus of government and the lines of trade were concentrated, had too much in its favor as a modern capital. And so in 1869 the emperor left Kyoto for good to enter Edo, renamed Tokyo, and to take up residence in the abandoned castle enclosure of the former shoguns. The kuge families were also uprooted, and their residences, except for one, were destroyed.

A full cycle had been turned. The emperor, once a true monarch, able to order into existence his own city in the imperial tradition, had step by step lost his power to become a symbolic entity controlled by others. In 1869 he was obliged to leave his city in order to add his charismatic blessing to a new form of government. Behind him he left an unoccupied palace and a spacious park where once the kuge had lived (see figure 1.10). From a capital built to Chinese specifications he transferred his residence to the foremost among Japan's "feudal" cities, where he ultimately took up residence in a palace of Western design. Yet significantly the Kyoto Palace with its Throne Hall still serves as the location for the enthronement of Japan's modern emperors. The rituals of the sinified imperial tradition are still to that extent important to the symbolism of the Japanese imperial ideology. As a final touch of mixed symbolism one may reflect upon the

---

33. Kanai Madoka, "Kyōtsū rondai 'hanseikakuritsu-ki no shomondai' o toriageru ni attatte," in *Shakai keizai shigaku* 24, no. 2 (1958):134.

34. Okuno Takahiro, "Kōshitsu goryō," in *Nihonshi daijiten* (Tokyo, 1960), 7:242.

fact that the new palace in Tokyo completed in 1968 is a modern ferro-
concrete structure designed to reproduce the essence of the classical Dairi
architecture.

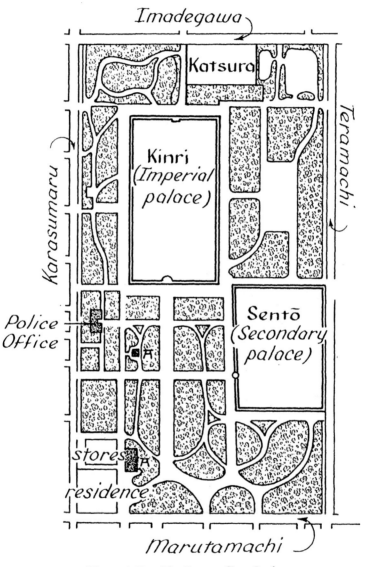

Figure 1.10   The Present-Day Gosho

2 The Structure of the Heian Court: Some Thoughts on the Nature of "Familial Authority" in Heian Japan

G. CAMERON HURST III

Throughout premodern Japanese history competition for political power has normally been a struggle among groups, usually kinship groups, rather than among individuals. The political situation in the late Heian period, for example, has been described by both Kuroda Toshio and John W. Hall as competition among a small number of powerful households, each with a strong house organization and a body of estate holdings.[1] Indeed even the political activities of the abdicated emperors beginning with Go-Sanjō in the late eleventh century are seen by both scholars as attempts to organize the imperial house so that it might compete effectively with other households for the rewards of power. Unfortunately, neither Kuroda nor Hall gives us a complete picture of either the precise nature of this competition or of how these households were organized internally. The purpose of this paper is to fill this gap by presenting a more inclusive picture of political structure within the Heian court.

Several different levels of kinship groupings can be identified in Heian Japan, and their interrelationship requires clarification. The most inclusive unit was the *uji*, or clan.[2] Each clan was divided into a number of lineages and sublineages. Among the four branches of the Fujiwara clan, for ex-

1. Kuroda Toshio, "Chūsei no kokka to tennō," in *Iwanami kōza Nihon rekishi*, vol. 6, chūsei II (Tokyo, 1963), pp. 261–302. John W. Hall, *Government and Local Power in Japan, 500 to 1700* (Princeton: Princeton University Press, 1966), p. 118.
2. The terminology for various kinship units is quite complex, even for anthropologists. I am here following the practice of Robin Fox, *Kinship and Marriage* (Middlesex, England: Penguin Books, 1967), pp. 45–50. A "clan" is a descent group in which common descent is assumed but not necessarily demonstrable. Where the actual relationship among members of the group can be demonstrated, the group is a "lineage." Thus "clan" and "lineage" refer to higher- and lower-order descent groups.

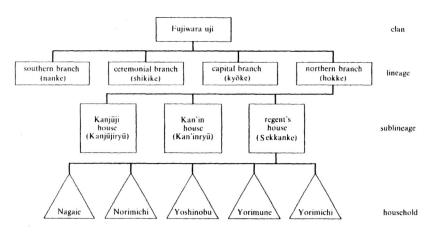

Table 2.1
Heian Kinship Organization
The Fujiwara Clan During Yorimichi's Regency

ample, was the Hokke, or northern branch, a lineage that included all the
descendants of Fusasaki, one of the four sons of Fujiwara no Fubito.
Further segmentation within this northern branch had resulted in a number of sublineages, such as the Sekkanke, or regent's house, Kanjūji
Kan'in, Hamuro, and so forth. The lowest level kinship unit was the
ie, or household, which was at any one time the basic unit of social and
political interaction (see table 2.1).

Professor Hall has suggested rather hesitantly that the Heian uji was
probably not too different from its pre-Taika predecessor;[3] but this suggestion is in need of some qualification, since the uji underwent both
structural and functional changes with the establishment of the imperial
state in the period following 645.

Prior to the Taika reform the uji was the most important functional
group in society. Japan was a loosely united federation of uji, which were
heterogeneous units bound by both territorial and kinship ties.[4] An uji

3. Hall, *Local Power*, p. 117.
4. The composition of the early Japanese uji has long been a subject of intensive
study by Japanese scholars, and various differences of opinion still exist. In particular,
scholars have differed over the degree of consanguinity among the constituent elements
of the uji. Some scholars feel that ties were largely territorial rather than consanguineous

exercised hegemony over specific territory in which it held rice lands worked by groups of producers under the leadership of the uji chieftain (*uji no kami*), who was the most important member of the main family. He led the uji members in the worship of the chief deity (*ujigami*), exercised judicial control over their activities, and was their political leader in their association with the Yamato court.[5]

The Yamato court was a federation of the most powerful uji chieftains who recognized the authority of the chieftain of the Yamato uji. The Yamato court had become sufficiently sophisticated by the sixth century to be classified as an emergent state.[6] The Yamato chieftain was recognized as ruler, but his duties appear to have been more religious than political.[7] The most powerful of the uji chieftains served as hereditary court officials, and lesser chieftains served in regional capacities. At this stage of development, however, particularistic uji interests still predominated over the universalist interests of the emergent state.

It was in order to overcome this particularism and to secure the preeminence of the Yamato uji's authority that certain of its members from the time of Prince Shōtoku (574–622) attempted to reform the Yamato state by adopting Chinese political ideology and institutions. From the Taika coup d'etat of 645 until the second decade of the eighth century the Yamato uji expended great energy to centralize the state. By 710 the

while others see kinship ties—both real and putative—as predominating. The prevalent view today is to regard the uji as a group or league of families centering around one main powerful family, with which the other families may or may not have had kinship ties. The uji are seen as territorially based groups with some political relationship with the Yamato court. See, e.g., Naoki Kōjirō, *Nihon kodai no shizoku to tennō* (Tokyo, 1964), pp. 101–11.

Naoki also has a useful review of the development of studies of the uji. For fuller information, see Tsuda Sōkichi, *Nihon jōdaishi no kenkyū* (Tokyo, 1947), pp. 590–91; Takeuchi Rizō, "Uji no chōja," in Takeuchi, *Ritsuryōsei to kizoku seiken* (Tokyo, 1958), 2:343–48; Hirano Kunio, "Taika zendai no shakai kōzō," in *Iwanami kōza Nihon rekishi*, vol. 2, kodai II (Tokyo, 1962), p. 83. Also see Herbert Passin's discussion of "Japanese Society" in *Encyclopedia of the Social Sciences* (New York, Macmillan, Co. 1968), 8:242.

5. Takeuchi, "Uji no chōja," pp. 343–48.

6. Lawrence Krader suggests a minimum set of political conditions for an emergent state, including territorial integrity, concentration of religious and secular power in the hands of the ruler, and a degree of delegation of power by the central authority. Lawrence Krader, *Formation of the State* (Englewood Cliffs, N.J.: Prentice-Hall, 1968), p. 48. By these criteria Japan would seem to qualify, although the degree of unity of religious and secular *power* is questionable. By stipulating a "concentration of religious and secular" authority and avoiding the exercise of power, we shall have no trouble classifying Japan as an emergent state.

7. Herschel Webb, *The Japanese Imperial Institution in the Tokugawa Period* (New York: Columbia University Press, 1968), pp. 14–19.

process was largely complete. A new capital city had been established at Nara; an imposing governmental structure under the authority of a Chinese-style emperor (the chieftain of the Yamato uji) and based upon detailed administrative and penal codes had been created; well-defined administrative divisions had been set up; and standardized taxation procedures had been initiated.

The state came to exercise a measure of control over the various uji. The Yamato uji, now the imperial house, succeeded in incorporating the old uji into the new state structure by eliminating their bases of power. The rice lands and groups of producers under uji control were declared imperial property in order to establish the principle of public control over what had previously been private interests. Under this new imperial state the uji were transformed both structurally and functionally. An uji was no longer a territorial unit, but now solely a consanguineous unit. It also lost most of its functional importance.

As early as 664 Emperor Tenji had established a certain hierarchy among the uji when he granted their chieftains swords of differing size to designate relative rank.[8] A few years later it was stipulated that all uji were to select chieftains who would then be recognized by imperial edict.[9] Both of these actions were intended to assert imperial control over the old uji and their chieftains. The position of uji chieftain also underwent significant change after the establishment of imperial government. The person selected as uji chieftain was to be the highest-ranking member of the uji in the new state bureaucracy. Beginning in the early eighth century, the term for uji chieftain was no longer *uji no kami*, but *uji no chōja*, a more explicit term meaning highest-ranking man within an uji. In pre-Taika times the chieftain had held a hereditary post at the Yamato court by virtue of the fact that he was leader of a powerful uji. Now the situation was reversed: a man became uji chieftain because he, of all the uji members, held the highest governmental position. Furthermore, his chieftainship was confirmed by imperial edict. Thus the uji and its members were brought within the structure of the state, and the uji chieftain served as the connecting link between the state and the uji.

Despite a Herculean effort to adopt Chinese political ideas and institutions, traditional attitudes of the old uji society were not greatly altered in Japan. The new state assumed many of the functions of the uji, but it did not try to abolish them as social units. The social features of the uji were not compatible with the requirements of imperial government, however, and the envisioned imperial state never functioned quite as intended. Over the four centuries of the Heian period (794–1185) private

8. *Nihon shoki*, in *Nihon koten bungaku taikei* (Tokyo, 1965), 2:360, Tenji 3/2/9.
9. *Nihon shoki*, 2:456, Temmu 11/12.

interests continued to expand at the expense of imperial government, a process Hall has aptly termed a "return to familial authority."[10]

Hence, although the uji continued to exist during the Heian period, they had undergone both structural and functional change. The chieftains of these uji (which can certainly be called clans by at least the Heian period) no longer exercised total control over clan members as in pre-Taika times, but they continued to play an important role in the lives of clan members.[11] First, the chieftain maintained some religious leadership over the clan members through his control of clan temples and shrines. Second, he controlled an educational institution established for the youth of the clan. Third, the chieftain had the power to secure an appointment for one of his clan members in the appointments to rank (*joi*) held at the beginning of each year. He could recommend one clan member who had not yet reached the junior fifth rank for appointment to that rank. Since one's social, political, and economic status increased markedly from the fifth rank up, this was an important power that the chieftain could exercise on behalf of his clan members.

The continued importance of the position of uji chieftain in Heian Japan is most easily demonstrated in the case of the Fujiwara. The transference of the chieftainship in this clan was the occasion for a ceremonial banquet at which the old chieftain passed the symbols of the chieftainship to his successor. These included red lacquer utensils (*sugi*) and five red lacquer tables (*taiban*) that were used in important ceremonies. The new chieftain was also given the chieftain's seal (*chōja-in*) as well as title to a group of four estates called the *denka no watari-ryō*.[12]

As imperial power waned during the course of the Heian period, the chieftainship of the uji once again came to be regarded as a purely private matter not requiring confirmation by imperial edict when it was passed from one clan member to another. Thus when a dispute arose between the brothers Yorinaga and Tadamichi over the chieftainship of the Fujiwara clan, their father Tadazane was able to remark that whereas the posts of regent (*sesshō*) and chancellor (*kampaku*) were granted by the emperor, the uji chieftainship was transferred from father to son and thus was a private affair.[13]

In somewhat changed form, then, the uji persisted as social units

10. Hall, *Local Power*, pp. 99–128 passim.

11. Takeuchi, "Uji no chōja," pp. 366–69.

12. According to Takeuchi, these estates became important as a distinct body of inheritable lands within Sekkanke estates from the twelfth century on (ibid., p. 366). For a more detailed study of the nature of the *denka no watari-ryō*, see Mitobe Masao, "Denka no watari-ryō no seishitsu," *Hōseishi kenkyū*, no. 4 (1953):238–47.

13. These two posts were traditionally held by a member of the Fujiwara clan and were the basis for the control the regent's house exercised over the emperor. Appoint-

throughout the Heian period, but they lost a great deal of their functional importance.[14] It was no longer the inclusive uji but the lower-order kinship units of the lineage and the household that became the focus of social and political interaction. Uji membership did not constitute the most important requisite of social and political association in the capital at Heian. The uji were no longer territorial units whose members lived in close proximity. Associations in the Heian period were formed not only among kinsmen but increasingly with those of similar social status. Class was a basic determinant of social and political relationships. Thus we must be extremely careful when we refer, for example, to the power of the Fujiwara during the Heian period. The Fujiwara clan was quite large, but it was only the members of a few select lineages within the clan who enjoyed this power. In fact, certain courtiers from other clans who had formed close associations with the regent's house benefited more from "Fujiwara power" than the Fujiwara courtiers of other lineages.

The segmentation of large clans like the Fujiwara was quite common. In the early Nara period (710–84), for example, the Fujiwara clan split into four lineages, the so-called northern, southern, ceremonial, and capital branches, each descended from a son of the courtier Fubito. Political misfortune befell all but the northern branch with the result that the other three branches ceased to be politically important after the Nara period. Owing to clever political maneuvering and a close marital relationship with the imperial house, the northern branch of the Fujiwara came to dominate all other kinship groups in Heian political society. Through the maternal connection (*gaiseki*) established with successive emperors from the late ninth century, certain members of the northern branch came to hold the two extralegal posts of *sesshō* and *kampaku*, jointly referred to as *sekkan*. These posts were passed on hereditarily by one sublineage within the northern branch which came to be called the Sekkanke, or regent's house, of the Fujiwara.

The monopolization of major governmental positions by members of the Sekkanke over an extended period of time meant that non-Sekkanke members of the northern branch had increasing difficulty obtaining important posts. As the latter became more and more removed from the

---

ment to either post required ratification by imperial edict. See *Taiki*, in *Zōho shiryō taisei* (Kyoto, 1965), 2:41, Kyūan 6/9/26.

14. In discussing the function of the uji in Heian Japan, Professor William McCullough points out that "its functions were primarily ceremonial and political, and it was related only tangentially to the family life of the individual" ("Japanese Marriage Institutions in the Heian Period," *Harvard Journal of Asiatic Studies* 27 [1967]:141). As I hope to demonstrate here, however, the functions of the clan were predominantly ceremonial rather than political.

Sekkanke, both in terms of genealogical distance and relative political power, segmentation into several other sublineages resulted, such as the Kanjūji, Kan'in, Nakamikado, and Kazan'in houses, among others.[15] Often it was one of these houses rather than those of other clans that provided the major threat to the monopolization of power by the Sekkanke. For example, when the Sekkanke reached the peak of its power and glory under Michinaga in the late tenth and early eleventh centuries, Michinaga's chief rival at court was another Fujiwara, the Ononomiya minister of the right, Sanesuke. Sanesuke was also a member of the northern branch although he did not belong to the main Sekkanke line.

Like the Minamoto, Takashina, Ōe, and other major clans, the Fujiwara uji was a complex unit.[16] The lineages and sublineages were made up of the extended families or households (ie) that at any one point in time formed the lowest order of kinship organization. In the dynamics of political competition in Heian Japan, it was these households that constituted the basic and most important functional units. Competition was conducted on the basis of households. Several households of a lineage might cooperate for mutual benefit, but there were few instances in which one can speak of the entire clan as a functional unit in Heian politics. These complex relationships between different levels of kinship groupings make up the "familial" basis of authority to which Kuroda and Hall both refer.

The rivalry among these familial groups was for appointment to court office and rank, or more accurately, for the acquisition of the economic and social benefits such appointments brought. The aristocratic governing class in Heian Japan, consisting perhaps of twenty thousand persons, was divided into three distinct groups according to a nine-rank system.[17]

15. Herbert Passin suggests that Japanese clans, lineages, and other such organizations tend to be functional in nature and rarely become very large. They tend toward segmentation, or fission, into smaller, more functional groups. This is in contrast to Chinese clans, for example, which seem to be able to expand unlimitedly.

16. In the Nara and Heian periods there were at least twelve uji that maintained the tradition of having an *uji no chōja* and thus at least a measure of clan unity: Ō, Minamoto, Fujiwara, Tomo, Takashina, Tachibana, Nakatomi, Imibe, Urabe, Koshiji, Sugawara, and Wake (Takeuchi, "Uji no chōja," pp. 349–66). Certainly there were many more uji than this, but by the Heian period all important political positions were dominated by members of about eight uji, and other uji names disappear from the literature. A check of the *Kugyō bunin* from the Taika reform (645) through the end of the Heian period reveals that courtiers from some fifty uji at one point held positions of the third rank and above. See Akagi Shizuko, "*Kugyō bunin* yori mita ōchō no seisui," *Ochanomizu shigaku* (June 1963): pp. 51–52.

17. Estimating the number of court officials and their family members in Heian times is extremely difficult. According to the *Engishiki*, the number of persons receiving official appointments numbered some six thousand, but adding in family members must have brought the population of the ruling class to several times that. See Murai Yasuhiko, *Heian kizoku no sekai* (Tokyo, 1968), p. 31.

The highest level of society was composed of the *kugyō*, which included those courtiers of the first through third ranks plus all those who held the office of imperial adviser (*sangi*). Courtiers of the fourth and fifth ranks constituted a second level of court society; and the lowest level was composed of courtiers from the sixth through ninth ranks, largely persons who possessed technical skills in law, medicine, and astronomy.

The kugyō households were large and consequently required considerable personnel to handle their economic, legal, and social affairs. In recognition of this fact, the Law of Household Administrative Appointment (*keryō shokuin-ryō*) was included in the Yōrō Code of 718 to provide official administrative aid for these households.[18] Five different levels of household officials were created to serve imperial princes above the fourth rank and the kugyō courtiers (see table 2.2). A steward (*keryō*) was in charge of all household matters including the direction of the other household officials. Beneath the *keryō* was an assistant (*kafu*) and an inspector (*kajū*), who was charged with investigation of household matters. Princely and kugyō households of the first rank had two inspectors and other households one. Finally, there were scribes (*shori*), who drafted household documents and kept records. Princes and officials of the top two ranks had two scribes; others had only one. Besides these officials, who served in all high-ranking households, princely households had tutors (*bungaku*). These officials were known collectively as *keryō*.

While duly recognized as officials according to the law codes, the keryō were nevertheless quite different from other government officials, and these differences largely determined the pattern of their later development.[19]

Table 2.2
Household Official System of the Yōrō Code

| Position | Rank | Household Official & Number | | | | |
		Bungaku	Keryō	Kafu	Kajū	Shori
Imperial princes	1	1	1	1	2	2
	2	1	1	1	1	2
	3	1	1	1	1	1
	4	1	1	1	1	1
Kugyō courtiers	1	-	1	1	2	2
	2	-	1	1	1	2
	3	-	1	1	1	1

18. *Ryō no gige*, in *Kokushi taikei*, rev. ed. (Tokyo, 1966), pp. 75–76.
19. Ōae Akira, "Heian jidai no keishi seido," in Okayama Daigaku, *Hōkei gakkai zasshi* 10, no. 3 (December 1960): 26. (Hereafter referred to as Ōae, "Keishi seido.")

First, their court ranks were awarded at a lower level than others of equivalent positions. Second, their semiannual allotments for rank and office were paid at a lower rate than others of equivalent status. Third, while the performance of other officials was judged by the head of their office—in which case household officials ought to have been judged by the household steward—keryō were in fact evaluated by the head of the household they served. And last, keryō were not granted the one holiday every six days to which other officials were entitled by law.

The seemingly discriminatory distinctions between keryō and other officials stemmed from the fact that their appointment was considered more private than public. The relationship between the head of a household and his keryō was unlike the superior–subordinate relationship within a government bureau: it was based upon personal, reciprocal ties rather than bureaucratic hierarchy. While keryō were publically appointed by the ministry of ceremonials (*shikibu-shō*), selections were made at the request of the household head.[20] Once appointed, a keryō could only be dismissed or transferred with the recommendation and approval of the head of his household. Moreover, the punishment of the keryō lay in the hands of the household head rather than with the government.

A further indication of the private nature of the relationship between household head and keryō is the existence of (fictive) "familial" ties binding them together. Keryō were allowed, for example, to participate in important family ceremonies along with real family members.[21] Thus, despite their public appointment, keryō were actually private officials under the control of the head of the household they served. It would appear that they were given lower salaries and fewer privileges in expectation that these deficiencies would be more than compensated for by the household head through private means. Through the public appointment of officials serving private purposes, the new state had perpetuated the proclivity for the formation of extensive leader–follower, or patron–client, relationships based upon reciprocal private obligations.[22]

After the removal of the capital to Heian, the keryō system underwent great expansion and modification in conjunction with the general growth of private, familial interests at the expense of public authority. What had originally been a very limited system of household officials established by the state for the purpose of helping households administer their affairs

20. Ibid.
21. Ibid., p. 27.
22. The tendency to form patron–client relationships in all forms of social organization appears at every period of Japanese history, from early tribal days down to and including the postwar "new" Japan.

developed in the Heian period into an extensive clientage system over which the state lost all control.[23]

The term *keishi* replaced *keryō* as the generic term for household official. Alongside the old household administrative posts established in the Yōrō Code, a number of new positions were created, the most important of which was that of director (*bettō*), who headed most of the bureaus within the household office. Not only were new positions created, but the number of persons appointed to specific household positions was greatly expanded. This expansion was brought on by the development of extensive *shōen* holdings, the construction of granaries and storehouses, residences, family temples and shrines, all of which requried increased personnel to administer. Furthermore, in imitation of the kugyō, courtiers of the fourth and fifth ranks also began to develop household administrative apparatuses that they staffed with keishi-like officials.[24]

The most important development in the nature of the household official system during the Heian period was in the increasingly personal and private ties between household head and keishi.[25] During the Nara period the system had been instituted by the state and the keryō were considered only semiprivate officials. During the Heian period, however, the last vestiges of public control over household officials disappeared, and the relationship between household head and keishi became wholly a private leader–follower arrangement. This private relationship was, as in most Japanese cases, based on increasingly strong fictive kinship relations, and keishi appear to have been treated scarcely differently from family members by the household head.[26]

The nature of the duties the keishi performed for the head of the

23. I am using the term "clientage" here in a very general sense to characterize the private dependent relationship of a lower-ranking person upon one of higher status. The client's position was not a legal one as was the case in Roman society, nor was there any sense of shame in becoming a client in Heian Japan as there seems to have been in many other societies. See, e.g., Jean Buxton, " 'Clientship' Among the Mandari of the Southern Sudan," in Ronald Cohen and John Middleton, *Comparative Political Systems* (New York: The Natural History Press, 1967), p. 229. Miss Buxton has used the term "clientship" in her description of a servile institution among the Mandari. In this society neither the chiefs nor the clients wish to admit the existence of "clientship," but such was not at all the case in ancient Japan. Clientage was *eagerly sought by both patron and client*, and the latter, far from falling into disgrace, hoped to attain a measure of political and economic mobility through the sponsorship of his patron.

24. Ōae, "Keishi seido," p. 29.

25. Ibid., p. 39.

26. Such treatment is not at all unique to clientage in Japan. See, e.g., Professor Mair's discussion of patterns of clientage among certain African tribes for this and other similarities with Japanese practices. Lucy Mair, *Primitive Government*, rev. ed. (Middlesex, England: Penguin Books, 1964), pp. 113–15.

household was largely private. They accompanied their patron on outings, visits to the family temples and shrines or the household of another courtier, and to household ceremonies. They frequently served as messengers, prepared documents pertaining to household business, and performed other miscellaneous services. A keishi could expect to be rewarded for his services by advancement in the court bureaucracy. The kugyō patron would in effect sponsor his keishi–client at court. The basis of the patron–client relationship was thus mutual need; the need of the kugyō for administrative help within his household and the need of lower-ranking courtiers for a kugyō to sponsor their interests.

The keishi held positions within the imperial government; they not only served as private household officials, but held public positions as well. They were normally courtiers of the fourth through the sixth ranks, perhaps themselves men of relatively important households. Most of the keishi of the Sekkanke, for example, seem to have been fourth- and fifth-rank courtiers, and some even appear to have become kugyō through their associations with this most powerful of Fujiwara households. The Sekkanke seems actively to have recruited middle-ranking courtiers to serve as their keishi, particularly those who were or had been provincial governors.[27] Diaries of Fujiwara nobles make frequent mention of zuryō keishi (provincial governor–household official) serving the Sekkanke. The regent's house could utilize both the administrative talents and the personal wealth of such governors in the administration of its private affairs. Provincial governors, on the other hand, might be able to reassure continued appointment to lucrative governorships if they had a powerful patron such as the regent. Other types the kugyō sought to serve in their households were those with technical skills such as document preparation, accounting, and mathematics.

There appear to have been at least three ways of entering into the clientage of a kugyō.[28] The kugyō himself could select a person, perhaps because of kinship or upon the recommendation of another courtier. The relationship could be established through the good offices of a third party, the traditional Japanese go-between. Or an aspiring keishi could request appointment directly from a kugyō.

But service as a household official was just one form of clientage in the Heian period. While keishi formed the top level of persons tied to the head of a kugyō household by personal bonds, far more numerous were the housemen (ke'nin), the retainers (samurai), and the personal servants and attendants (chōdai shijin, or toneri). Although there is debate among scholars concerning the origin of the term ke'nin, it seems clear from

27. Ōae, "Keishi seido," p. 40.
28. Ibid., pp. 43–44.

Heian documents and literature that it referred to all those private followers of a household who were not keishi, in other words, all those who did not hold titled administrative positions with relatively specific duties.[29] They were also followers or clients of the lord who entered his service for protection and/or advancement within the imperial state system. Their functions seem to have been quite diverse and unspecified, ranging from attendance in the capital to service as estate officials in the provinces. These housemen were bound to the lord by the same kind of ties as were the keishi, although the keishi were more highly ranked within the household.

There was one group within these housemen whose duties were specific, however. These were the *samurai*, or retainers, who performed military, police, and guard duties for the household. In the case of the highest-ranking households, such retainers were frequently descendants of aristocratic families or imperial lineages and leaders of large bands of retainers of their own. The Seiwa Genji, for example, served as samurai for the Sekkanke and came to be known as the "teeth and claws" of the Fujiwara.[30] In return for loyal service the Seiwa Genji became influential at court through the patronage of the Sekkanke. The retainers attached to lower-ranking noble households were more frequently called *rōdō* and tended to be men of the local landholder (*myōshu*) class. In return for military duties in the capital or in the provinces—where they might serve as private troops for their lord while he was provincial governor—they

29. Ōae Akira, "Heian jidai no rōdōsei to ke'ninsei," in Okayama Daigaku, *Hōkei gakkai zasshi* 11, no. 2 (September 1961): 154.

30. The relationship between the Seiwa Genji and the Sekkanke appears to date from the Anna Incident of 969. The incident was a successful attempt by Fujiwara no Morotada to eliminate his court rival, the minister of the left, Minamoto no Takaakira. Minamoto no Mitsunaka, founder of the Seiwa Genji line, lent his military support to Morotada. Mitsunaka's sons Yorimitsu, Yorichika, and in particular Yorinobu came to function as the "teeth and claws" of the Fujiwara.

Although this most famous of Minamoto lineages is generally regarded as descended from the emperor Seiwa, one strong bit of evidence suggests descent from Emperor Yōzei. Yorinobu attained considerable success at court because of his subjugation of the rebel Taira no Tadatsune in 1031 and also due to his close association with the regent Michinaga. In his latter years, while serving as Governor of Kawachi, Yorinobu first established the Genji link with the Shinto god Hachiman when he presented a document to the Iwashimizu Hachiman-gū. In the document, which lists his accomplishments and prays for the continued success of his house, Yorinobu refers to himself as a descendant of the emperor Yōzei. The document, discovered among the Iwashimizu Hachiman-gū documents by the Meiji scholar Hoshino Hisashi, seriously undermined the previously unquestioned belief in the ancestry of the Seiwa Genji. The reason suggested by Hoshino for claiming descent from Seiwa was the fact that Yōzei was a very undistinguished sovereign, having been deposed by Fujiwara no Mototsune. Although opinions are still divided, many scholars—Takeuchi, e.g.—lean toward a Yōzei origin (Takeuchi Rizō, *Bushi no tōjō*, in Chūō Kōronsha, *Nihon no rekishi* (Tokyo, 1965), 6:40–43.

were often able to insure the tax-free status of their lands. These samurai and rōdō provided military protection for their lord in both his public and private duties.

The lowest level of clients attached to a kugyō household included the servants and attendants, or *toneri*. Those of princely households were called *chōdai* ("within the curtain") and those of noble houses *shijin* ("resource men"). These servants were somewhat like keishi in that they were originally allotted to noble and princely households by the state according to certain legal stipulations. But they, too, soon lost their public character as large numbers of peasants absconded from their lands, fled to the capital, and entered into the private service of the great households. The motivation in the case of these peasants was to escape the harsh corvée labor service owed to the state. Since toneri were exempt from corvée labor, the practice of entering into the service of an important household became increasingly popular during the Heian period.

Thus large numbers of clients of the great kugyō households enjoyed a similar relationship with their patron. While the nature of the relationship was private, the rewards they sought for their service were in a sense public. The higher-ranking keishi, ke'nin, and samurai sought better official government posts while the toneri desired to escape harsh government corvée labors. Another similarity between these different levels of clientage was the tendency for all to become hereditary. The personal bonds that drew patron and client together continued over the generations so that one family might provide keishi for a particular kugyō household for four or five generations. The same was true for ke'nin, samurai, and toneri.

The accepted manner for prospective keishi, ke'nin, and samurai to enter into the service of a kugyō patron was to call upon him at his residence, present one's name placard (*myōbu*), and request an audience (*kenzan*).[31] After the formalization of the relationship, the client was expected to render loyal service to the patron, whom he referred to as lord or master (*nushi* or *shujin*). For his part, the kugyō was obliged to look after the needs of his client, normally by sponsorship of his career at court. Both the practices and the terminology involved in this system of clientage are quite similar to those of the vassalage relationship between Japanese

31. The *myōbu* seems to have been somewhat like the namecard (*meishi*) in universal use in Japan today. On it was written one's office, court rank, and name. While it was used to announce one's attendance at the palace and for other such formal purposes, it was frequently presented to a higher-ranking person for the purpose of entering into a patron–client relationship.

Kenzan is not the only term for such an audience, and there does not appear to have been a standard word. Frequently, a client simply "presented himself" (*mairu*) before the kugyō. There are other references to a "first audience" (*shozan*) on the part of the client. See e.g., *Gyokuyō*, (Tokyo, 1907), 3:147, Bunji 2/1/27.

feudal warriors. Indeed, these relations of clientage appear to be one source for the development of feudal relationships in Japan, much as the Roman *patrocinium* can be seen as a remote root of European feudalism.[32] True, the Heian patron's benefice did not take the form of the grant of a fief (although he was often able to secure tax-free status for the estate holdings of a client), and the service of the clients, with the exception of the samurai, was not military. Yet the binding personal relationship between patron and client expressed in terms of fictive kinship is in many ways similar to later Japanese feudal practices.[33]

During the Nara period when the imperial government had provided a small number of keryō to handle their affairs, households of high-ranking nobles had developed administrative councils (*mandokoro*) to deal with family business. When in the Heian period kugyō households came to control extensive estate holdings and to attract numerous clients, their administrative organs expanded correspondingly. The mandokoro was still the administrative apparatus for all matters, but a number of lesser bureaus were added to it.

The mandokoro of the Fujiwara regent was somewhat larger than that of other courtier households, but its organization was characteristic of Heian kugyō households.[34] It included a documents bureau (*fudono*) for handling complaints and other types of correspondence. There was also a secretariat (*kurōdo-dokoro*) modeled on that established by Emperor Saga. A retainers' office (*samurai-dokoro*) was added to coordinate the activities of the warriors in the service of the household. There was a well-staffed stable (*mimaya*), where the horses, oxen, and ox carts needed by Heian courtiers were cared for. An attendants' bureau (*zuishin-dokoro*) was established to control the attendants allotted by the court to high-ranking nobles. There was an office for court dress (*gofuku-dokoro*) to store and care for all the ceremonial robes belonging to the household. The *shimmotsu-dokoro*, or provisions bureau, handled the receipt and storage of rice and other grains, vegetables, fish, and other foods for the household's meals; and the *zen-bu* was the cook's bureau in charge of the actual preparation of the food.

32. As I have already indicated, patron–client relationships seem to have been important in Japanese social organization from earliest times, but the formalization and regularization of forms of clientage appear to date from the late Nara–early Heian period.

33. For a further discussion of this point, see Ōae, "Keishi seido," pp. 50–51. Also see Ōae, "Heian jidai no shiteki hogo seido," in Okayama Daigaku, *Hōkei gakkai zasshi* 11, no. 1 (June 1961): 13–14.

34. *Shugaishō*, in *Kojitsu sōsho* (Tokyo, 1952), p. 366, provides the outline for the organization of the regent's house administrative bodies. See also Fujiki Kunihiko, "Nara Heian-chō ni okeru kenseika no kasei ni tsuite," in Tōkyō Daigaku Kyōikugaku-bu, *Jimbun kagaku-ka kiyō*, no. 1 (April 1952): 1–20.

All these different bureaus within the mandokoro were headed by directors (*bettō*) under whose authority were a number of lesser household officials: *keishi, azukari, anju, shimogeishi,* etc. During the Heian period court officials of the fourth and fifth rank—who were frequently keishi in the service of kugyō households—began to develop their own household administrative agencies, modeled after those of the kugyō. These were normally smaller, however, and the officials who staffed them had somewhat different titles.

In the Nara period household officials had been able to issue documents (*kachō*) of a strictly private nature to subordinates within the jurisdiction of the household. Communication with any public body, which was frequently necessary, required the personal document of the household head. By 804, however, household officials, acting on instructions from the kugyō, were able to use the kachō to communicate with governmental bodies. To avoid confusion, it was required that the rank, office, and surname of the household head be clearly written at the top of the kachō and the seal of two keryō be affixed at the end. In the Heian period a number of other documents besides these *kachō* came to be used by kugyō households in the conduct of their business. These included orders (*kudashibumi*), directives(*migyōsho*), and, in case the head of the household happened to be an uji chieftain, chieftain's edict (*chōja-zen*). These various documents dealt with private affairs of the household, most frequently with its shōen holdings. This was true even of the Sekkanke, although Japanese historians often claim that kudashibumi of the regent's house actually took the place of imperial edicts.[35]

Heian court society was thus dominated by a ruling elite composed of a small number of high-ranking court nobles who were heads of powerful familial interest groups.[36] Their households had complex administrative bodies staffed by numerous clients. It was these households, not the more inclusive uji, that formed the basic units of social and political interaction.

35. Kitayama Shigeo, "Sekkan seiji," *Iwanami kōza Nihon rekishi,* vol. 4, kodai IV (Tokyo, 1962), pp. 3–20, points out that documents issued by the mandokoro of the regent's house did not replace imperial edicts but dealt almost exclusively with private house matters. He further warns against the oversimplifications that have resulted from dependence upon the concept of *sekkan seiji* (politics of the regent's house). A number of Fujiwara mandokoro documents are collected in Takeuchi Rizō, ed., *Heian ibun* (Tokyo, 1967), and in section 7 of *Chōya gunsai,* in *Kokushi taikei,* rev. ed. (Tokyo, 1967), pp. 173–94.

36. The high-ranking courtiers, or kugyō, who composed the highest echelon of court society, usually numbered between 15 and 20 from the early Heian period through the reign of Emperor Ichijō (r. 986–1011). Thereafter there were normally 25 to 30. The increase in the number of kugyō corresponds to the beginning of the domination of the Heian court by the Fujiwara regent's house.

The uji persisted in the Heian period, but as a functional unit it was replaced by the lower-order kinship group, the household. It was these powerful households, commonly referred to in the literature of the times as *kemmon seika* ("influential houses and powerful families") that bore a certain resemblance to the pre-Taika uji.

The imperial state structure formed the arena of political competition for these various households. Despite the growth of extensive private interests and the increasing "familialization" of authority, the Chinese-style state structure did not wither away and die but continued to function as the source of ultimate legitimacy. Within the imperial bureaucracy created in the Nara period, decisions of state were made by the kugyō who met in the grand council of state. The decisions reached by these courtiers were ratified, rejected, or returned for reconsideration by the emperor. Japanese emperors throughout history have normally been little more than rubber stamps for decisions made by others, but during the Nara period and early Heian, under the still strong influence of Chinese political ideas, emperors and empresses (i.e., Shōmu, Shōtoku, Kammu, and Saga) exercised considerable influence in the actual decisions of state.

Certain changes in the imperial state system during the Heian period made it more responsive to the realities of Japanese society. The complex process of drafting edicts, for example, was simplified with the institution of the sovereign's private office. Originally established by Saga in 810 as a temporary measure, the office became permanent; and it functioned as an intermediary body between the emperor and the kugyō, exercising considerable influence in affairs of state. Moreover, the meeting place of the kugyō was moved from the grand council of state offices; they most frequently met at the headquarters of the inner palace guards (*konoefu*). Here the kugyō, expanded in the Heian period with the creation of councillors and imperial advisers, met to "discuss and decide" (*sadamemōsu*) matters of state. This process was referred to as *jin no sadame*, or *jōgi*.[37] At such gatherings, the head of the controlling board (*benkan*) would review the precedents—often Chinese as well as Japanese—and have a secretary (*geki*) prepare a recommendation. Then the kugyō, beginning with the lowest-ranking imperial adviser, would express their views on the issue. The ranking member of the body, the prime minister (or the minister of the left if the former post was unfilled), would find a consensus and announce the final decision.[38] One of the imperial advisers would write up the decision and forward it to the sovereign's secretary (*kurōdo*), who

37. See Fujiki Kunihiko's discussion of *jin no sadame* in *Nihon rekishi daijiten* (Tokyo, 1959), 10:321.

38. Prime minister (*dajōdaijin*) was the highest post within the imperial bureaucracy, and the person appointed to the post was supposed to set a moral example for the rest

in turn would seek the emperor's approval and have it properly drafted in document form.

Japanese patterns of decision-making exhibit a considerable degree of continuity. Although it would be rash to overdraw the parallels, decision-making in Heian Japan bore striking similarities to its present-day counterpart. Consensus, or the appearance of consensus, rather than simple majority appears to have been of major concern then as now. Each kugyō was essentially the leader of a faction made up of kinsmen and clients whose interests he represented. Consultation and compromise, as well as bribery and pressure, were utilized to achieve a workable balance among these various interests. Before formal meetings of the whole body, individual kugyō frequently visited others at their residences to discern views on the upcoming issue, whether it be a decision over court appointments, rewards for special military service rendered to the court, or more ceremonial matters. Household officials of these kugyō often acted as go-betweens to feel out positions on various issues. These courtiers met at poetry recitations, banquets, and other social events that often functioned as arenas of political discussion, in much the same manner as Japanese leaders today meet in small, informal groups at geisha houses and cabarets to discuss politics. Alliances were formed, promises extracted, and compromises made so that general consensuses probably were arrived at before the more formal jin no sadame. The ultimate decisions were determined by the relative strengths of these courtier households, but the formalization of these decisions through jin no sadame and ultimate imperial approval was taken very seriously by Heian courtiers.

In this discussion of the nature of Heian political society, little has been said about the emperor and the imperial house, but this neglect has not been inadvertent. The emperor was the ultimate source of political authority but the emperor and the imperial house as a whole exercised little real power between the early ninth century and the latter part of the Heian period. In the Nara and early Heian periods there had been sovereigns who exercised substantial power, and certain members of the imperial uji had occupied major government posts; but throughout the Heian period the number of non-imperial kugyō, particularly Fujiwara uji members, increased.[39] Thereafter imperial princes reached the upper

---

of society. Since one's moral qualities were the determinant factor in appointment to the post, it was not supposed to be filled unless a properly qualified individual was available. Minister of the left was the second-highest post in the bureaucracy.

39. Akagi Shizuko, "*Kugyō bunin* yori mita ōchō no seisui," pp. 53–55 chart 2. Based upon her study of the *Kugyō bunin*, Professor Akaei has discovered that during the Nara and early Heian periods as many as thirty different uji produced kugyō; from the mid-tenth century on, however, all kugyō came from only eight of these uji (ibid., p. 52, chart 1).

echelon of court power only on rare ocasions, and consequently the imperial house was seldom represented in the kugyō meetings.[40]

Imperial attempts to curb the primacy of private interest had been unsuccessful. Ironically, however, by initiating and championing an imperial state system, the imperial house had eliminated its own private, familial base of power. As a result it was unable to compete effectively for power during most of the Heian period. The emperor was the symbol of public authority and was largely dependent upon public revenues for support. While other familial groups took advantage of the incompleteness of the nationalization of land and accumulated vast private estates, the emperor and his house suffered financially as a result of the development of these estates. Yet as a personification of public authority it was neither seemly nor possible for the emperor to participate in the alienation of public land.[41] Furthermore, by providing household officials and servants for the great kugyō households, the state unwittingly facilitated the development of an extensive system of private clientage. Thus the kugyō households had all developed private, familial bases of power that functioned as instruments for political competition. Only the imperial house, tied to the public structure by its own policy, was without a private base of power.

Moreover, the imperial house was somewhat different structurally from other kinship groups in Heian Japan. There was no imperial clan including all persons of real or putative common descent; neither was there a common surname uniting all imperial descendants. One lineage provided the emperor, and the members of this lineage were known as the imperial house (kōshitsu). Since emperors had several consorts and were surrounded by concubines and various female attendants, imperial offspring tended to be quite numerous. An imperial clan including all such persons could have been potentially enormous. To avoid a strain on the treasury, and to limit the number of persons eligible for dynastic succession, many princes outside the direct line of succession were granted surnames and allowed to function as other courtiers. The imperial house was thus a lineage, like the Sekkanke; but no clear picture of an imperial clan corresponding to the Fujiwara uji has thus far emerged.

Princes who were cut off from the imperial house could be granted one of two surnames, Taira or Minamoto. These two offshoots of the imperial house were considered clans, just like the Fujiwara, Ōe, Takashina, or any other uji, and they developed similar traditions. For example, all those

40. There were exceptions during the reign of Saga in the ninth century when a number of kugyō from the imperial offshoot Minamoto clan did tend to cooperate, forming what some scholars have called an "imperial faction." See Hayashiya Tatsusaburō, "Insei," in Zusetsu Nihon bunkashi taikei, vol. 5, Heian jidai II, (Tokyo, 1957), pp. 63–64.

41. Ishimoda Shō, Kodai makki seijishi josetsu (Tokyo, 1964), p. 361.

persons with the name Minamoto formed a clan. There was a clan chieftain who performed the same ceremonial functions as other chieftains. As was the case in other clans, one lineage monopolized the chieftainship; in the Minamoto case, it was the Murakami branch. The clan was composed of several different lineages, each one descended from and named after the emperor who had originally granted the surname. Thus there were lineages of the Minamoto clan, or Genji in the Sino–Japanese reading, called Uda Genji, Daigo Genji, Seiwa Genji, Murakami Genji, and so on. As in the case of other clans, the lineages were more important as functional units than the entire clan, and the immediate household most important of all; as a consequence, the clan chieftain did not enjoy extensive power.

The other imperial offshoot clan, the Taira or Heishi, were even less organized as a clan. The individual lineages were similar to the Minamoto in that they were named after the emperors who had granted the surname, but there seems to have been no tradition of chieftainship held by one of the lineages.[42] In the later part of the Heian period, when successive members of the Ise branch of the Kammu Heishi—Masamori, Tadamori, and Kiyomori—rose to political power at court, there seems to have evolved some clan solidarity under their general leadership. Even then, however, they were little different from the Fujiwara Sekkanke, working largely for the advancement of the fortunes of immediate family members and clients with little concern for the well-being of the entire clan.

The imperial house itself, lacking a private, or familial, base of power, did not function like other households. The emperor was solely a public person, constantly surrounded by officials, servants, empresses, and concubines. After the Taika reforms, early empresses had been chosen from among imperial house females, resulting in some degree of familial solidarity. In 729 this tradition was broken, however, and Fujiwara Fubito's daughter Kōmyō became Shōmu's empress. From that time on empresses and concubines were almost always selected from Fujiwara families, most frequently from the regent's house. Because of the nature of Heian marriage institutions, maternal kinsmen, particularly maternal grandparents, had a dominant influence within the household.[43] Consequently emperors were surrounded by Fujiwara mothers and grandmothers, wet nurses and female attendants.[44] Most of the women in their lives were from some Fujiwara household, usually the Sekkanke, and this

42. Takeuchi, 'Uji no chōja," p. 353.

43. McCullough, "Japanese Marriage Institutions," esp. pp. 141–47.

44. The rearing and even education of young children of aristocratic houses in Heian Japan was frequently left in the hands of wet nurses. See Wada Hidematsu, "Rekishijō ni okeru menoto no seiryoku," in Wada, *Kokushi kokubun no kenkyū* (Tokyo, 1926), pp. 182–201.

was equally true of the men with whom they came into contact. Such a situation made it difficult for the imperial house to maintain much cohesion as a separate family; the emperor was as much a member of the Fujiwara regent's house as he was of the imperial house.

In the pre-Taika period, then, the Yamato ruler had been only the first among equals. Like other uji chieftains he had both private and public roles, acting on the one hand as chieftain of his own uji, and on the other as ruler of the Yamato court. After the attempted transformation to an imperial state system, great household heads maintained joint public and private functions, between which there appears to have been minimal distinction. A man might be minister of the right in his public position, but he was also the leader of a large private social unit, including his own family members and a number of clients. The emperor, however, was different. He no longer played a private role as head of a household. His dual role was eliminated, and he functioned solely as a public figure, head of the state structure and symbol of legitimacy.

One would expect the emperor to have had a position analogous to that of the Fujiwara regent, who as highest-ranking public figure of the clan served as chieftain, head of his own extensive household unit, and patron of numerous subordinate followers. As the highest-ranking public figure among imperial descendants, the emperor should have been chieftain of the clan; he also should have been head of his immediate household with many clients in his service. But he fulfilled none of these roles. His only role was a public one, and that largely social and ceremonial. He possessed extreme prestige and ultimate political authority as descendant of the Sun Goddess and emperor, and he was the focus of Heian cultural life, but his influence in real political life was minimal.

For despite the heavy overlay of Chinese political institutions and ideas in premodern Japan, native traditions of kingship doggedly persisted. Long before the Chinese-inspired Taika reforms the duties of the ruler appear frequently to have been ritualistic and sacerdotal, "while the decision-making functions of government were exercised at a level where they were responsive to the competitive interests of the group of families that constituted a ruling oligarchy."[45] Indeed, even Pimiko, the first Japanese ruler mentioned in historical sources, held herself above the realm of actual politics while her brother handled such responsibilities. With some exceptions this has been the pattern of rule for most of Japan's premodern history: the emperor has been the symbol of authority, the "legitimizer of group consensus," as Hall puts it, while someone else among the ruling group—prince regent, regent, ex-emperor or shogun—

45. John W. Hall, "A Monarch for Modern Japan," in Robert E. Ward, ed., *Political Development in Modern Japan* (Princeton: Princeton University Press, 1968), p. 20.

has exercised real power. Both privately within the imperial house and publicly in politics, the emperor has normally been above the realm of real power.

It was also part of the Japanese tradition of kingship that only a member of the imperial house—a descendant of the Sun Goddess—was eligible for the position of emperor. Thus in political struggles the supreme goal was to control or dominate the imperial position rather than to usurp it as in so many other societies. It was, in a sense, a human chess game where the object was to capture the king—but the king could not be removed from the board. Furthermore, the most powerful tool in the game was the queen, demonstrated most forcefully by the lengthy domination of the imperial family by the Sekkanke.

Thus although the Japanese emperor was not expected to rule, his position as the sanctifier of political decisions was of overriding importance: the emperorship was the major political asset of the imperial kin group. In ancient Japan the periods of greatest imperial house weakness were those times when the imperial position was controlled by some other family or faction—the Soga clan, the priest Dōkyō, and the Sekkanke, for example. Conversely, control over this asset by the imperial house itself was the surest means of aggrandizing its own power. It was this latter phenomenon (discussed in chapter 3) that occurred during the final century of Heian rule.

3 The Development of the *Insei*: A Problem in Japanese History and Historiography

G. CAMERON HURST III

The last one hundred years of the Heian period (1086–1185), the century between the ascendancy of the Fujiwara regent's house and the rise of the *bushi* to power, was a time during which court society was dominated by the three successive abdicated sovereigns, Shirakawa, Toba, and Go-Shirakawa.[1] Although abdicated sovereigns had been quite common figures in Japanese court circles for almost half a millennium, none had enjoyed the position of Shirakawa and his successors. So great was the power and influence of these retired sovereigns that Japanese historians regard their activities as representing the emergence of a new political system, the *insei*, or "cloister government" as it is most commonly rendered in English.[2] While the term "insei" is an exceedingly comprehensive one,[3] the standard interpretation can be summarized as follows:

> *Insei* refers to the system of government in which decisions of state were made by the abdicated sovereign. He conducted politics from his retirement palace, which was guarded by his own body of warriors and in which was located the *In-no-chō*, or ex-sovereign's office. This office was the administrative agency through which the ex-sovereign conducted his rule. Staffed with personal officials of the ex-sovereign's own choosing, the In-no-chō issued documents on his behalf which possessed greater authority than those of the imperial government. This system of rule was conceived by the emperor Go-Sanjō as a means to curtail the power of the Fujiwara regents and reassert the lost power of the imperial house. Go-Sanjō died

1. Throughout this essay I employ six terms interchangeably to refer to these persons: abdicated sovereign, retired sovereign, ex-sovereign, abdicated emperor, retired emperor, and ex-emperor. I also avoid the common translation of *In* as "cloister" because of the religious connotation of the term.

2. This is a term used by Sir George Sansom, but again I avoid its use, both because of the religious connotation and because, as I shall argue here, I do not think it is entirely accurate.

3. See, e.g., *Nihon rekishi daijiten* (Tokyo, 1959), 2:126.

before he was able to realize his plan, but his son Shirakawa established the system upon his abdication in 1086. He continued to rule as retired emperor until his death at seventy-seven in 1129. Toba and Go-Shirakawa followed in his footsteps, ruling the country from abdication until the establishment of the Kamakura shogunate in 1185. All three were absolute rulers who completely ignored the emperor and the established channels of imperial government.

For Japanese historians, then, insei is a distinct political system established at a particular time in history by a certain individual with a specific motive. It has not always been so, however. "Insei" is not a term used in late Heian times to describe the contemporary political situation, but rather the creation of later historians to describe the complex set of political circumstances of that period. It was Jien, chief abbot of the Tendai sect and younger brother of the regent Kanezane, who first discussed the idea of government by abdicated sovereigns in his *Gukanshō* of 1221. More than one hundred years later Kitabatake Chikafusa elaborated on the idea in his *Jinnō shōtōki*. In 1713 Arai Hakuseki, in the *Tokushi yoron*, referred to the period from 1086 to 1185 as the "age of rule by abdicated sovereigns," and finally in 1837 in the *Nihon gaishi* Rai San'yō used the term "insei" to describe this idea of rule by retired emperors.[4]

The concept of insei was further systematized and refined by Japanese scholars after the Meiji Restoration; Wada Hidematsu and Kuroita Katsumi were particularly influential in making the term a standard one in the jargon of Japanese historians. Western historians have also adopted the concept of insei as "cloister government" in their studies of the late Heian period. Noting the similarities between the rule of the Fujiwara regents and the cloister government of the ex-sovereigns, Sir George Sansom stated that the Fujiwara *mandokoro* moved to the office of the retired sovereign. Professor Shinoda speaks of the existence of "two courts," referring to the emperor and his court and cloister government; and Professor Brownlee states that during this period sovereignty normally resided with the ex-sovereign.[5]

The standard interpretation of the insei has not escaped the assault of

4. *Gukanshō*, in *Nihon koten bungaku taikei* (Tokyo, 1967), pp. 104, 124–26, 149–50, 158, 188–89, and 332–33; *Jinnō shōtōki*, in *Nihon bungaku taikei* (Tokyo, 1965), p. 142 (It was Chikafusa who suggested the idea that *In-no-chō* documents were more authoritative than imperial documents); *Tokushi yoron*, in *Iwanami bunko* (Tokyo, 1965), pp. 37–73; *Nihon gaishi*, (Tokyo, 1907), p. 42.

5. George B. Sansom, *A History of Japan to 1334*, (Stanford, Calif.: Stanford University Press, 1958), p. 201; Minoru Shinoda, *The Founding of the Kamakura Shogunate, 1180–1185*, (New York: Columbia University Press, 1959), p. 46; John S. Brownlee, "The Shōkyū War and the Political Rise of the Warriors," *Monumenta Nipponica* 24, no. 1/2 (1969):64.

revisionism, led by Marxist historians in postwar Japan, but only a few minor elaborations have resulted. Focusing upon the acquisition of extensive estate holdings by the imperial house during the late Heian period, Ishimoda Shō has argued that the establishment of the insei was an economic necessity for the house.[6] While it was contrary to the basic spirit of the codes that formed the legal basis of the imperial state, the acquisition of estates (*shōen*) was nevertheless permissible so long as the proper legal procedures were followed. According to Ishimoda, the emperor as head of the imperial state could not effectively engage in the acquisition of shōen, but the retired emperor, unhampered by any institutional restraints, could and did seek to accumulate estate holdings for the imperial house.

Historians interested in the economic aspects of the power of the abdicated sovereigns have also turned their attention to the provincial governor, or *zuryō*, class, which appears to have provided much of the ex-emperors' economic base. The most influential of the Marxian scholars —Ishimoda and Hayashiya Tatsusaburō—as well as those of the non-Marxist school—Takeuchi Rizō and Yoshimura Shigeki—have all stressed the importance of these zuryō, though with a much different focus.[7] The question for these historians has been whether the retired sovereigns controlled the zuryō in a "despotic" fashion, or whether the zuryō were merely using the retired emperors as "robots" for their own advancement.

More recently, however, Kuroda Toshio has added perhaps the most useful refinement of the concept of insei. He sees the political structure of medieval Japan as one of competition between a number of powerful families or kinship blocs (*kemmon*) of which the imperial house was one.[8] In Kuroda's view what is important in the concept of insei is the establishment of the In-no-chō and the acquisition of shōen by the imperial house. In his commentary on the insei, Professor John W. Hall, relying upon Kuroda's work, concludes that these two developments indicate that the "imperial house itself. . . . was obliged to look to its own house organization and to assert itself as a separate kinship bloc in the contest for power

6. Ishimoda Shō, *Kodai makki seijishi josetsu* (Tokyo, 1964), pp. 366–67.
7. Zuryō is a complex term that scholars cannot agree upon, but it appears that by late Heian times it was broadly applied to anyone serving in a provincial governorship. Hayashiya Tatsusaburō, *Kodai kokka no kaitai* (Tokyo, 1955), pp. 199–200; Takeuchi Rizō, *Ritsuryōsei to kizoku seiken* (Tokyo, 1958), vol. 2; Takeuchi, *Bushi no tōjo*, in Chūō Kōronsha, *Nihon no rekishi* (Tokyo, 1965), 6:162–97; Yoshimura Shigeki, *Insei* (Tokyo, 1958).
8. Kuroda Toshio, "Chūsei no kokka to tennō," in *Iwanami kōza Nihon rekishi*, vol. 6, chūsei II (Tokyo, 1963), pp. 261–302. Kuroda expands his ideas in *Shōensei shakai*, in *Taikei Nihon rekishi* (Tokyo, 1967), 2:103–36.

at court."[9] The studies by Kuroda and Hall suggest that perhaps the activities of the abdicated emperors in the late Heian period should not be regarded as the establishment of a new political system, but rather as an organizational attempt on the part of the imperial house to reassert its own control within the existing system.

In the remainder of this essay I would like to pursue the idea that the so-called insei should be regarded as an attempt by the imperial house to establish itself as an independent kin group in the struggle for court power. Within the context of familial competition as suggested by Kuroda and Hall and as described by me in somewhat more detail in chapter 2, I would like first to outline broadly the emergence of the abdicated sovereign as a participant in the struggle for court power in the Heian period. Then I wish to examine in more detail the nature of the In-no-chō, or ex-sovereign's office, in order to determine how it was structured and staffed, and just what function it did serve.

Abdication and Abdicated Sovereigns in Ancient Japan

Although it is impossible to arrive at any sound conclusions about the activities and intentions of ex-sovereigns from Go-Sanjō's time on without understanding the role of retired sovereigns prior to that time, Japanese scholars have virtually neglected the study of abdication in the pre-insei period.[10] Imperial abdications before Go-Sanjō can be divided into three chronological periods. From the first recorded abdication,[11] that of the

9. John W. Hall, *Government and Local Power in Japan, 500 to 1700*, (Princeton, N. J.: Princeton University Press, 1966), p. 118. What I find particularly commendable about Professor Hall's discussion is his avoidance of the term "cloister government" or any other translation of the term *insei*.

10. There is but one book-length study of the insei (Yoshimura Shigeki's *Insei*), and it is slim and outdated. In virtually all of the many articles and sections of books devoted to the insei, the first paragraph or two normally mentions that once or twice before the late eleventh century an ex-sovereign exercised some power. Reference is made to Kōken and Uda, but the matter is dismissed as irrelevant. For a lengthy study of abdication see G. Cameron Hurst III, "Insei; Abdicated Sovereigns in the Politics of Late Heian Japan, 1086–1185," (Ph.D. diss., Columbia University, 1972), pp. 40–118. Hereafter cited as Hurst, "Insei."

11. Some scholars recognize Keitai as the first sovereign to have abdicated, but the textual reference is not at all clear. The term abdicate (*jōi*) is not used; it merely states that Keitai made Ankan emperor then passed away. I interpret this to mean that he simply made Ankan heir apparent. See *Nihonshoki*, in *Nihon koten bungaku taikei* (Tokyo, 1965), 2:48. There was a serious succession dispute at this time. and the history as well as the historiography of the Keitai-Ankan era is quite confusing. For more information, see Hayashiya Tatsusaburō, *Kodai kokka no kaitai*, pp. 1–39; Mizuno Yu, *Nihon kokka no seiritsu*, (Tokyo, 1968), pp. 118–39; and Inoue Mitsusada, *Shinwa kara rekishi e*, in Chūō Kōronsha, *Nihon no rekishi* (Tokyo, 1965), 1:468–519.

empress Kōgyoku in 645, through the reign of Kammu in 806 marks a distinct period during which the practice of abdication began and became well established as a means of dynastic transfer. From the reign of Heizei in 806 through the death of En'yū in 991 can be seen as a second period, during which abdication became so frequent that it was almost expected of an emperor. It was also a period during which several ex-sovereigns wielded considerable political power within both the imperial house and the entire court society. The third period, 991–1068, from the reign of Ichijō through that of Go-Reizei, was the highpoint of Sekkanke domination of the imperial house under the regencies of Michinaga and Yorimichi. During this period Fujiwara leaders kept a close watch over the matter of succession and were hesitant to allow abdications, probably because they had learned how potentially powerful an ex-emperor could be.

In the first period abdication appears to have developed in conjunction with female rule during a time of great political change in Japan. The first four sovereigns to abdicate were all female, and in conjunction with the practice of enthroning the chief consort of the deceased emperor, abdication seems also to have functioned as a means of avoiding succession disputes.[12] After abdication, sovereigns were given the title *dajō tennō* (great abdicated sovereign) and treated with considerable respect. But with the exception of Kōken, who stated in her edict of abdication that she would continue to handle major court matters while the emperor could discharge minor affairs and ceremonies, ex-sovereigns appear to have enjoyed little political or familial influence. Regardless of the familial relationships between abdicated and titular sovereign, the position of emperor was considered supreme.[13]

During the second period abdication became so common that eleven of the fifteen emperors who reigned during that time yielded the throne. More important, ex-emperors became the most venerated figures in court society, and several of them—Saga, Uda, and En'yū, for example—exercised considerable influence within the imperial house and in the imperial government. Whereas in the first period the emperor seems to have been superior to the abdicated sovereign in all aspects, during this time private, familial relationships within the imperial house came to supersede

12. Inoue Mitsusada has argued persuasively that female rulers in ancient Japan came to the throne only as stopgaps to avoid dynastic schism. The origins of abdication seem to be intimately related to this. See Hurst, "Insei," esp. pp. 42–56.

13. *Shoku Nihongi*, in *Kokushi taikei*, rev. ed. (Tokyo, 1965), pp. 287–88, Tempyō hōji 6/6/3/. In the same edict, e.g., Kōken laments the fact that she had been unable to fulfill the proper filial duties to her mother, the great empress dowager Kōmyō, because of her position as sovereign.

public positions.[14] Emperors paid formal visits of respect (*chōkin*) to retired sovereigns if the relationship was father–son, and showed great respect and deference even if the ex-emperor was an elder brother. Emperors sent epistles and requests to ex-sovereigns in the same manner that courtiers memorialized the emperor: the retired sovereign was called *heika* ("your majesty"), while the emperor referred to himself as *shin* ("your subject").[15] Although the imperial house lacked the kind of house organization that other kinship groups enjoyed, it would appear that during this period the abdicated sovereign came to function in the capacity of head of the imperial house (see chapter 2).

It was also during this period that ex-sovereigns developed a well-organized administrative apparatus to handle their private affairs. While various offices serving the needs of retired emperors had long been in existence, by at least the abdication of En'yū in 984 the term "In-no-chō" was used to refer to the whole complex. The In-no-chō was staffed by officials known collectively as *inshi*, but those closest to the ex-emperor were simply referred to as his *In-no-kinshin* (close associates).[16] Although extensive information on the types of men who served in the In-no-chō is not available, they appear to have been a rather homogeneous body. They were generally men who had long been close to the emperor, serving him as crown prince, emperor, and then ex-sovereign; they were usually men with technical skills in document drafting, Chinese language, or Confucian teaching; and they were almost without exception not members of the Fujiwara regent's house.[17]

Institutionally, an abdicated emperor had no power, no authority, and no position: *dajō tennō* was an honorific title given to one who had yielded the throne. Yet from the beginning the ex-sovereign continued to enjoy some of the powers of the emperor. Through the early Heian period, for example, ex-sovereigns issued edicts (*shō* and *choku*) in the same manner as the emperor, and it appears that these were processed in the same governmental offices as imperial edicts.[18] By the mid-Heian period, however, this confusing practice ceased as ex-emperors developed their own mechanism for issuing documents. Officials in the In-no-chō issued on

14. Hurst, "Insei," pp. 71–72.

15. Ibid., pp. 72, 82.

16. Information on the abdication of En'yū, including reference to the In-no-chō, is found in *Shōyuki*, in Tokyo Daigaku Shiryō Hensanjo, *Dai Nihon kokiroku* (Tokyo, 1959), 1:49–50, Eikan 2/10/7. For a discussion of the significance of the appearance of the term *In-no-chō*, see Hurst, "Insei," pp. 100–01. The term *inshi* appears as early as Saga's time, and several different specific titles are mentioned including director (*bettō*) and secretary (*kurōdo*).

17. Hurst, "Insei," p. 114.

18. Ibid., p. 116.

behalf of retired sovereigns *inzen* (ex-sovereign's edicts) and *kudashibumi* (orders of the ex-sovereign's office). While only one of these documents is extant, they appear to have dealt mainly with private matters of the ex-emperor or the imperial house.[19]

Since the retired sovereign had no official status within the state structure, he did not participate in politics in a formal way. But through his position as father of the emperor and head of the imperial house, an abdicated emperor could exercise considerable influence outside the formal governmental structure, particularly when a Fujiwara regent did not enjoy a stranglehold on the imperial position—as in the cases of Saga, Uda, and En'yū.[20] Such a situation was not unlike the maternal hold that Fujiwara regents had over emperors born of Sekkanke mothers. Thus, contrary to what is usually said of abdicated sovereigns prior to the insei period, they often enjoyed considerable political power.

During this second period retired sovereigns were supported economically by sustenance households (*fuko*) and annual allotments (*nenkyū*) awarded by the court.[21] Waste fields and other lands were also granted for the upkeep of their palaces, and such grants appear to have continued to support the palace even after the death of the ex-emperor. Sometime during the Saga–Junna era of the early ninth century the *goin*, or retirement palace, seems to have been established for handling such lands and other economic assets of the imperial house.[22] During his reign an emperor would select one of many palaces of the imperial house as his retirement palace, lands would be allotted for its maintenance, and officials would be appointed to handle its affairs. After abdication, the emperor moved to the palace, and it ceased to be called a goin, becoming instead

19. The single remaining document is Uda's *inzen* of the early tenth century, collected in *Tōdaiji yōroku*, in *Zoku zoku gunsho ruijū* (Tokyo, 1909), 12:160–61, Enchō 6/8/28. The edict concerns the estate holdings of the Todaiji, a temple with which Uda was closely connected. Japanese historians apparently assume that this *inzen* was the only one prior to the insei period simply because it alone is extant. I have discovered references to others, and they appear to deal with private imperial matters. See Hurst, "Insei", p. 106·

20. Fujiwara no Kane'ie, regent during the reign of Ichijō, once lamented that the "requests" of the ex-sovereign (in this case, En'yū) were "weightly and difficult to refuse" (*Shōyūki*, 1:162, Eiso 1/2/19).

21. Sustenance households were awarded to imperial family members and kugyō according to their rank and office for income purposes. Half of the rice tax of these households and all the other taxes were paid to the recipient rather than to the imperial government. Annual allotments allowed certain imperial house members and kugyō to make appointments of rank and office. They then collected an appointment fee from the appointee.

22. Hashimoto Yoshihiko, "Goin ni tsuite," *Nihon rekishi*, no. 217 (June 1966): 11–25.

the ex-sovereign's palace. The goin lands appear to have been under the control of the emperor while he was on the throne and of the ex-sovereign once he had abdicated. While in general the imperial house was unsuccessful in developing a private economic base prior to the insei period, the goin and the goin lands, which appear to have been fairly extensive, indicate that the house had begun to create one.[23]

The institutional apparatus created by ex-sovereigns—the In-no-chō, inshi, and goin lands—continued to exist during the third period (991–1068), but the potential for the exercise of political influence by abdicated emperors was seriously curtailed. This was the period when Fujiwara domination was at its height under Michinaga and Yorimichi. Control over the mechanics of dynastic succession was fundamental to the maintenance of Sekkanke power, and Fujiwara leaders, Yorimichi in particular, were hesitant to allow abdication except in the face of imminent death. This was apparently due to the experience gained during the second period when several ex-emperors exercised more influence in politics than was desirable from the Sekkanke standpoint. Fujiwara regents were well aware that an emperor could be more easily controlled than an abdicated sovereign, particularly if the abdicated sovereign was the father of the reigning monarch.

Thus even before the reign of Go-Sanjō all the elements that Japanese historians see as part of a political system consciously designed by that emperor had long been in existence: the senior position or headship of the ex-sovereign within the imperial house, the administrative office of the In-no-chō, a staff of private officials to serve the ex-emperor, and the beginnings of a private economic base. What prevented the final emergence of the imperial house as a private familial interest group was the domination of the imperial position, the chief asset of the house, by the Fujiwara Sekkanke. The accession of Go-Sanjō broke that domination and provided the opportunity for the imperial house, under the headship of the ex-emperor, to compete effectively for real power at court.

The Reign of Go-Sanjō

Although he was regent and chancellor for fifty years and a member of the kugyō for seventy, Fujiwara no Yorimichi was all too aware of the vulnerability of Sekkanke power. Its power lay in the continued control of the imperial position through strong maternal ties. Yorimichi's own position was based upon the maternal relationships of his sisters Shōshi, mother of both Go-Ichijō and Go-Suzaku, and Kishi, the mother of

23. See Hurst, "Insei," pp. 303–05 for a discussion of imperial house finances prior to the late Heian period.

Go-Reizei. Yorimichi's attempts to produce a grandson as heir to the throne were unsuccessful: his own daughter and an adopted daughter as well as the daughter of his younger brother Norimichi were all introduced into Go-Reizei's women's quarters, but no male heirs resulted from these unions. The emperor could produce only females. Thus the continuity of political power of Yorimichi and his descendants was in jeopardy.

The only possible successor for Go-Reizei was Prince Takahito, the future emperor Go-Sanjō.[24] The second son of Go-Suzaku, Takahito was born in 1034 while his father was still crown prince, and his mother, known as Lady Yōmeimon'in, was Princess Teishi, a daughter of the late emperor Sanjō. The possibility of Takahito's becoming emperor was a grave threat to Yorimichi.

When Go-Suzaku became seriously ill in the last few months of 1044, he expressed a desire to abdicate in favor of his eldest son, Go-Reizei. Yorimichi agreed to this, but Go-Suzaku then indicated his strong wish that Takahito be made crown prince at the same time: Go-Reizei himself had no male heir and Go-Suzaku felt it proper that Takahito succeed his elder brother. Although Yorimichi grudgingly consented to Takahito's appointment, he was by no means reconciled to having him as a future emperor.[25] Takahito was closely watched by Yorimichi during his unprecedented twenty-four years as crown prince, and Go-Reizei was never permitted to abdicate in his favor, despite repeated pleas to that effect. Only upon the death of his elder brother in 1068 did Takahito at last attain the throne; Yorimichi, his long struggle having been to no avail, resigned the chancellorship and retired to his villa at Uji.

Because Go-Sanjō was not under the restraint of the Sekkanke as so many of his predecessors were, he was able to participate forcefully in ruling the country. The composition of the kugyō underwent a change during his reign with an increase in the number of Minamoto courtiers in that body, which appears to have brought about what one scholar refers to as a "revival of the imperial faction."[26] Furthermore, Yorimichi's successors were unable to achieve any Fujiwara unity, with the result that

24. See G. Cameron Hurst III, "The Reign of Go-Sanjō and the Revival of Imperial Power," *Monumenta Nipponica* 27 (1972): 65–83, for a fuller dissussion of the events of Go-Sanjō's reign.

25. Traditional accounts credit Yoshinobu, Yorimichi's younger brother, with having forced the decision, and Shirakawa is even said to have remarked that neither he nor his father would ever have become emperor had it not been for Yoshinobu (*Gukanshō*, p.188).. Besides pressure from Yoshinobu, however, Yorimichi was probably influenced as much by the tradition that a crown prince should be appointed at the time of enthronement as well as by a reluctance to deny the dying wish of an emperor.

26. Hayashiya Tatsusaburō, in *Zusetsu Nihon bunkashi*, vol. 5, Heian jidai II (Tokyo, 1957), pp. 63–64.

many non-Sekkanke Fujiwara also appear to have supported Go-Sanjō. With the cooperation of several courtiers,[27] Go-Sanjō directed his major efforts toward reviving the dwindling economic resources of the *ritsu-ryō* state as well as the imperial house. His most important accomplishment was the issuance of two shōen regulation ordinances that appear to have been somewhat successful.[28] This success was a result of the fact that for the first time in Japanese history an agency was created to carry out such regulations. All previous attempts at controlling the growth of shōen had been incomplete because they had been left in the hands of provincial governors.

This time, however, Go-Sanjō established the *kiroku shōen kenkeisho* (office for the investigation of estate documents), or *kirokujo*, as it is more commonly known. Little documentary evidence of its activities survives, but what is extant suggests that the office directed efforts against the holdings of both the major religious institutions and the Sekkanke and actually did abolish many shōen.[29] At the same time Go-Sanjō turned many of the seized lands into imperial edict fields (*chokushiden*) that were virtually indistinguishable from shōen. His regulation policy thus had the dual purpose of curtailing the estate holdings of others while building up the private lands controlled by the imperial house itself.

After only four years as emperor, Go-Sanjō abdicated in favor of his son Prince Sadahito, the emperor Shirakawa. Different theories have been advanced to explain the motivation for Go-Sanjō's abdication, but it was obviously calculated to guarantee the independence of the imperial house from the control of the Sekkanke.[30] Sadahito's mother was Fujiwara no Moshi, a daughter of Yoshinobu. Although Yoshinobu, a younger brother of Yorimichi, was not the chieftain of the clan nor anywhere near the most influential courtier at the time, the possibility that the Sekkanke

27. The most notable were the "former three fusas" (*saki no sambō*): Ōe no Masafusa, Fujiwara no Tamefusa, and Fujiwara no Korefusa.

28. From an investigation of fragmentary evidence, Professor Takeuchi argues that there were two separate edicts rather than one (Takeuchi, *Ritsuryōsei to kizoku seiken*, 2:393–94).

29. See Takeuchi, ed. and comp., *Heian ibun* (Tokyo, 1968), vol. 3, docs. 1043, 1046, 1058, 1061, and 1083. Doc. 1083, pp. 1092–1107, e.g., indicates that thirteen of thirty-seven estates claimed by the Gokoku-ji of the Iwashimizu Hachimangū were declared illegal and seized.

30. Some information on the abdication is contained in *Hyakurenshō*, in *Kokushi taikei*, rev. ed. (Tokyo, 1965), pp. 33–34, Enkyū 4/12/8. For more detailed information see *Tamefusakyō-ki*, manuscript owned by Tōkyō Daigaku Shiryō Hensanjo, Enkyū 4/12–Enkyū 5/1. Some scholars suggest illness as the reason for abdication, but the *Hyakurenshō* and the *Fusō ryakki* mention the illness more than three months after abdication and say that it was sudden. Jien's theory that the abdication was motivated by a desire to institute the insei is the most frequently offered reason.

might reestablish its control over the emperor did exist. Fear of just that possibility had led Go-Sanjō to delay Sadahito's appointment as crown prince at his own succession: since one of his empresses was a daughter of Emperor Ichijō and another a daughter of Minamoto no Motohira, Go-Sanjō seemed to be awaiting the birth of an heir with no Fujiwara connection.

Eventually, however, in 1069 Go-Sanjō had to confirm Sadahito as crown prince. In 1071 Motohira's daughter Motoko gave birth to Prince Sanehito; in the next year Go-Sanjō abdicated in favor of Sadahito and had this young boy designated crown prince. His treatment of Sanehito is in marked contrast to the manner in which he had handled the crown prince appointment at his own succession, and it clearly indicates Go-Sanjō's desire to transmit imperial succession to his non-Sekkanke sons. Further evidence to support this can be found in Go-Sanjō's instruction to Shirakawa that Prince Sukehito, another son of Motoko born subsequent to Go-Sanjō's abdication, succeed to the imperial position after Sanehito.[31]

During the few short months Go-Sanjō lived as ex-sovereign prior to his death, he engaged in no activities that even suggest he was attempting to institute a new form of rule by ex-sovereigns. Like other retired emperors before him, Go-Sanjō established an In-no-chō staffed with close associates to serve his needs.[32] But absolutely no evidence of any political ambitions can be discerned from the sources. By his abdication Go-Sanjō merely sought to secure the continued independence of the imperial house. As abdicated emperor, senior member of the imperial house and father of the reigning sovereign, he could effectively block the domination of Shirakawa by the Sekkanke and guarantee the transfer of the succession to his sons by Motoko. In conjunction with all his other activities, Go-Sanjō's abdication was designed to secure the independence of the imperial house so that it might compete effectively for real power at court.

Shirakawa as Emperor and Retired Sovereign

Go-Sanjō's fears were to prove unwarranted. Shirakawa not only successfully prevented the reestablishment of Fujiwara control over the imperial institution, but he was also able to increase the power and wealth of the house far beyond what his father could have hoped for. The Fujiwara chancellors Norimichi and Morozane, lacking firm maternal connections with Shirakawa, were unable to exercise the kind of power their predecessors had enjoyed. While the heyday of Fujiwara power and glory

31. Takeuchi, *Bushi no tōjō*, p. 161, quotes the *Gempei seisuiki* to this effect.
32. For details, see *Tamafusakyō-ki*, Enkyū 4/12/21.

may have been over, the Sekkanke nevertheless remained the most wealthy and influential of the court families; but beginning with Shirakawa's reign, the imperial house, normally under the active headship of the retired sovereign, became the most influential familial group at the Heian court.

Shirakawa ruled for fourteen years in much the same manner as had his father, and the composition of the kugyō likewise continued unchanged. Sekkanke courtiers held most major posts, but the Minamoto, particularly the Murakami lineage, enjoyed strong representation. The decline of Sekkanke influence is further indicated by the fact that middle-ranking Fujiwara courtiers and even kugyō of non-Sekkanke lineages sought alliance with the imperial house.

Shirakawa was also concerned with the revitalization of the ritsu-ryō state and the imperial house, and since it was control over land that proved most problematic, Shirakawa issued another shōen regulation ordinance in 1075.[33] Despite this ordinance and repeated mention in courtiers' diaries of the emperor's concern over the growth of shōen, Shirakawa's main worry, like that of his father, was the future of the imperial house as a political force, and specifically, the matter of succession. While he was as much concerned with imperial house fortunes as Go-Sanjō had been, his father had bequeathed to him a pattern of succession that effectively cut off his own descendants: Motoko's sons Sanehito and Sukehito were to succeed him.

Lacking an heir of his own, Shirakawa was unable to alter this scheme, at least not until 1079 when his favorite consort Kenshi gave birth to Prince Taruhito. In 1085 Crown Prince Sanehito died, and Shirakawa was presented with an opportunity to divert the succession from his half brother to his son. Although Shirakawa ought to have immediately made Sukehito crown prince in accord with Go-Sanjō's wishes, he postponed the decision for almost a year. It was obviously difficult for Shirakawa to act against his father's instructions, but by the seventh month of 1086 he appears to have made his decision. Construction of a magnificent retirement palace, the Toba Dono, was begun just south of the city along the banks of the Kamo River.[34] Four months later Shirakawa abdicated in favor of his son Taruhito after first naming him crown prince. This was the emperor Horikawa.

Prince Sukehito was to be cut off from imperial succession forever; he was not made crown prince to Horikawa despite some court sentiment for

33. Not too much is known about the effect of this ordinance, but at least one document mentions the confiscation of two Tōdai-ji estates in the province of Mino. *Heian ibun*, 3:1128, doc. 1118.

34. See Murayama Shūichi, "Insei to Toba rikyu," *Shirin* 15 (1953): 56–79.

such a move. Instead the position was left unfilled for eighteen years while Shirakawa waited for Horikawa to produce an heir. To guard against the possibility of Sekkanke domination of the imperial institution once again, Shirakawa even arranged for his own sister, Princess Atsuko, to marry the emperor. While in theory the idea was a good one, the fact that Horikawa was only thirteen and his aunt was thirty-four mitigated against a congenial marriage. Indeed, the ex-sovereign's prayers for an heir were to no avail. Finally in 1098 Shirakawa arranged for the emperor to marry Shishi, daughter of a close associate, Fujiwara no Sanesue. This union resulted in the birth of Prince Munehito in 1103, and Shirakawa had the infant made an imperial prince and then named crown prince within eight months of his birth.[35] This hurried disposition of the crown prince's position after eighteen years' vacancy clearly proves that Shirakawa's intention had always been to divert imperial succession from his father's line to his own. The purpose that his abdication was designed to effect was accomplished.[36]

With the birth of Munehito (the future emperor Toba) a rare situation in the history of the Japanese imperial house came about. Grandfather, father, and son served as ex-sovereign, emperor, and crown prince. More important, none of these positions was hampered by Sekkanke maternal relations; the imperial position was totally controlled by the imperial house. It was an occasion of imperial unity and independence almost unmatched in Japanese history.[37]

Thus Shirakawa's abdication was motivated by a concern over imperial succession rather than by a desire to institute a new form of political control. This statement does not deny that Shirakawa was a major force in the politics of the period. On the contrary, he was the center of court society and a very powerful man, indeed at times the most powerful figure at court. His political participation was similar to that of previous ex-emperors: he exercised considerable personal influence through his position as senior member of the imperial house and father of the emperor. The difference between Shirakawa and previous ex-sovereigns lies more in the *extent* to which he was able to influence politics rather than in

35. The apprehension that surrounded the birth of Toba is amply reflected in the story as Toba related it to Fujiwara no Yorinaga. *Taiki*, in *Zōho shiryō taisei* (Kyoto, 1965), 1:67–68, Kōji 1/5/16.

36. Shirakawa was not entirely secure, however, and an attempt was made on the life of Toba in 1114. The incident is fully recorded in Tadazane's diary *Denryaku*, in Tokyō Daigaku Shiryō Hensanjo, *Dai Nihon kokiroku*, (Tokyo, 1960–68), 4:59–62, Eikyū 1/10/5–22. See also Hurst, "Insei," pp. 162–64.

37. Only in the Engi era had there been an analogous situation with Uda, Daigo, and Suzaku.

the *manner* in which he did so. And this in turn depended upon his control of the imperial position.

Shirakawa established an In-no-chō upon abdication and staffed it with officials from among non-Sekkanke courtiers close to him.[38] Like past In-no-chō, Shirakawa's functioned as a private house office and not as an alternate form of national government (see pp.78–83). From the sources available to us today there does not appear to have been any significant change in the political complexion of the court upon Shirakawa's abdication. He did not, as is usually suggested, suddenly emerge as sole master of the political scene, as supreme dictator who ruled from his retirement palace, issuing documents more powerful than imperial edicts. Actually, the sources show that the traditional decision-making apparatus remained intact and continued to function as before.[39]

In fact during the first fifteen years of his retirement Shirakawa does not appear to have been very active in politics at all. Morozane served as chancellor and appears to have worked quite well with Emperor Horikawa.[40] Certainly Shirakawa had influence over some members of the kugyō council, within which the Fujiwara Sekkanke had lost a good deal of its old power since Go-Sanjō's reign. But he was by no means the autocratic figure pictured in the *Heike monogatari* who could control everything in the realm except the flow of the Kamo River, the dice of the *sugoroku* game, and the unruly monks of Mount Hiei.[41]

It was only after the turn of the century that Shirakawa began to express his political desires strongly, and this appears to have been prompted more by misfortune within the Sekkanke than anything else. Morozane had become ill in 1094 and passed both the clan chieftainship and the post of chancellor to his son Moromichi. Unfortunately, Moromichi, apparently one of the most able of all the Fujiwara regents, died five years later at the young age of thirty-eight.[42] When Morozane himself passed away in 1101, the fate of the Sekkanke rested in the hands of Moromichi's twenty-four-year-old son Tadazane. It was from that time

38. For the details of the abdication and the initial appointment of In-no-chō officials, see *Yanagihara-ke kiroku*, in Tōkyō Daigaku Shiryō Hensanjo, *Dai Nihon shiryō* (1927. Reprint ed., Tokyo, 1956), ser. 3, 1:3–10.

39. Hurst, "Insei," pp. 169–71.

40. For a discussion of Horikawa's role at court, see Akagi Shizuko, "Shirakawa-in to Horikawa tennō—insei shoki no in to tennō," *Shintōgaku*, no. 53 (May 1967).

41. On at least three occasions—in 1088, 1092, and 1093—associates of the ex-sovereign were banished for improper actions. It seems unlikely that a man portrayed as the dictatorial ruler of the land would allow his associates to be treated in this fashion. See Hurst, "Insei," p. 172.

42. The *Honchō seiki*, in *Kokushi taikei*, rev. ed. (Tokyo, 1965), pp. 306–07, Kōwa 1/6/28, has a very laudatory account of Moromichi.

that Shirakawa became the elder statesman at court and began to influence political affairs significantly. For the next twenty-eight years he was the most powerful and revered figure in the land, living a life of grandeur and power that few members of the imperial house in Japanese history ever enjoyed.[43] Many of the decisions at court, particularly official appointments, appear to have been made in accord with the *In-no-ōse* (orders of the ex-sovereign).[44] Yet it is important to note that Shirakawa still operated through the established channels of ritsu-ryō government, utilizing the emperor, the regent, and the kugyō council to achieve his purposes rather than creating new institutions to replace the existing political apparatus.

The Retired Emperor Toba

Shirakawa was still active during the first six years of Toba's abdication, but following Shirakawa's death in 1129, Toba was senior retired sovereign and head of the imperial house for twenty-seven years.[45] Like his grandfather, Toba was the major political force and cultural focus of Heian court society, but he and Shirakawa were quite different individuals. In fact, many of the most serious problems of Toba's tenure as retired emperor were the direct legacy of actions taken by Shirakawa.

First of all, there was discord within the imperial house between Toba and the emperor Sutoku. Sutoku was the son of Empress Shōshi, better known by her palace name Taikenmon'in, and was born shortly after she became Toba's consort. Shōshi was described by Fujiwara no Tadazane as a "strange and unusual consort," and her life style seemed to many to disqualify her for the high honor of becoming empress.[46] She was the daughter of Fujiwara no Kinzane but had been adopted by Shirakawa, who was exceedingly fond of her. She had been involved with one courtier, and a marriage had been arranged between Shōshi and Tadazane's son Tadamichi before Shirakawa decided that she should become

43. The imperial house may have enjoyed great power in the Yamato period, but it would certainly appear that the entire house—ex-sovereigns, emperors, retired imperial ladies, and crown princes—had more influence and wealth and freedom of movement during the insei period than at any other time in Japanese history.

44 Tadazane's diary in particular is full of references to *In-no-ōse*.

45. Toba was forced into abdication while his grandfather was still ex-sovereign, and there was thus a senior–junior ex-sovereign situation. Saga and Heizei had been junior and senior abdicated emperors in the early Heian period, and the practice was not infrequent. During the insei period, the senior ex-sovereign remained the most powerful person in the imperial house. The junior abdicated emperor (or emperors) had their own In-no-chō and officials but enjoyed virtually no power and influence in real politics.

46. Quote from *Denryaku*, in Tōkyō Daigaku Shiryō Hensanjo, *Dai Nihon Shiryō*, ser. 4, vol. 18, p. 421, Eikyū 5/10/10; p. 422, Eikyū 5/11/19; and p. 428, Eikyū 5/12/20.

Toba's consort. Despite criticism of the action, Shirakawa arranged her entry into Toba's women's quarters and shortly she gave birth to Sutoku. Both the *Kojidan* and the *Hōgen monogatari* claim that Sutoku was not Toba's child at all, but the result of a liaison between Shirakawa and Shōshi.

Thus while Sutoku was legally recognized as Toba's son, he was widely rumored to be Shirakawa's son. Perhaps largely for this reason Toba never enjoyed good relations with Sutoku, particularly after 1123 when Shirakawa forced him to abdicate in Sutoku's favor. Once Shirakawa had passed from the scene, Toba was able to force Sutoku's own abdication and transfer imperial succession to the offspring of his favorite consort, Bifukumon'in. But the rift between the two men never healed, and in fact it was to become one of the sparks that touched off the Hōgen Disturbance, which broke out immediately after Toba's death in 1156.

The relationship that Shirakawa enjoyed with the Sekkanke also underwent a change during Toba's retirement years. Tadazane appears not to have accepted the fact that Shirakawa had made the imperial house into the most potent political force at court, and he struggled with the ex-emperor to preserve Sekkanke power. Eventually Tadazane voluntarily left the court and secluded himself at Uji for more than a decade.[47] Upon Shirakawa's death, however, Toba managed to persuade Tadazane to return to the capital. Now the heads of the imperial house and the Sekkanke cooperated, and Tadazane even attempted to win Toba's favor by making contributions to him in the manner of other, less prestigious houses seeking advantage.[48]

During Tadazane's long absence, his son Tadamichi had guided Sekkanke fortunes, but Tadazane reclaimed his position upon his return. This action caused great resentment on Tadamichi's part, and a serious rift developed between the two. Thereafter Tadazane began to favor his younger son Yorinaga as heir to the chieftainship of the Fujiwara clan, and the Sekkanke became hopelessly divided. This division was also to be a factor in the Hōgen Disturbance. Thus during Toba's tenure as ex-sovereign there was not the competition between the imperial house and the Sekkanke that had been characteristic of Shirakawa's years, but there were instead serious struggles within the two houses over their respective headships.

47. The immediate provocation was an argument over the admission of Tadazane's daughter Taishi into Toba's women's quarters in 1122. See Hurst, "Insei," pp. 176–77.

48. These contributions included the commendation of shōen, the offering of gold, and the construction of a new palace and Buddhist hall in the Toba Dono. See Hurst, "Insei," p. 192, n.18. The references are all found in Fujiwara no Yorinaga's diary *Taiki*, in *Zōho shiryō taisei*, (Kyoto, 1965), 2:44, Kyūan 6/10/12; 2:102, Nimpyō 3/9/17; and 2:129, Kyūju 1/7/29.

Toba worked diligently to consolidate the strong position of the imperial house established during Shirakawa's lifetime. In his In-no-chō he
continued to employ men from the same houses his grandfather had
relied upon, but he directed his attention much more determinedly toward
the economic assets of the imperial house.[49] Not that Shirakawa had
neglected economics, but he was very ambivalent about the position the
house should take toward the accumulation of shōen. He was responsible
for shōen regulation ordinances both while emperor and after abdication,
and few documents from his time testify to the establishment of imperial
estates. Toba, on the contrary, was enthusiastic about acquiring imperial
estates, and one of the largest group of holdings he created, the Hachi-
jōin-ryō, contained more than 220 separate shōen.[50]

Like Shirakawa, Toba exercised his political influence by utilizing the
existing structure and controlling the imperial institution, and it was in
the control of the emperorship that he had problems. Toba secured
Sutoku's abdication in favor of Konoe, Bifukumon'in's son, and he wished
to pass succession through Konoe's line. Unfortunately, however, Konoe
was ill and died young. Bifukumon'in and Toba then wished to enthrone
her adopted son Prince Morihito, but Morihito's father Masahito was
alive and in the prime of life. Masahito was grudgingly allowed to ascend
the throne as Go-Shirakawa in 1155, but Morihito was made crown prince
and was their real choice for emperor.[51] Toba was to die within the year,
but even before his death he foresaw a possible revolt being launched by
the frustrated ex-emperor Sutoku and his supporters to amend the succession pattern he had established. Indeed, only eight days after Toba's
death Sutoku, joined by an equally disgruntled Yorinaga, raised the
abortive revolt known as the Hōgen Disturbance.[52]

The Era of Go-Shirakawa

Go-Shirakawa became emperor only as a means to achieve the eventual
succession of his son Morihito (Emperor Nijō); but after his side's victory
in the Hōgen affair, Go-Shirakawa became a forceful emperor and dom-
ineering ex-sovereign who controlled the fortunes of the imperial house
for thirty-six years, during which time real power in Japan shifted from
the court aristocracy to the newly arisen military elite.

Go-Shirakawa remained emperor for only three years, but he was

49. Several confidants were dismissed, however, because of their differences with
Toba. See Hurst, "Insei," p. 189.
50. Ibid, p. 321.
51. The *Gukanshō*, p. 216, notes that Toba felt Go-Shirakawa to be unqualified for
emperorship.
52. The primary source recounting the events of the Hōgen Disturbance is *Heihanki*, in *Zōho shiryō taisei* (Kyoto, 1965), 2:111–26, Hōgen 1/7/15–30.

unusually vigorous for a Japanese sovereign. Aided by his associate Shinzei,[53] Go-Shirakawa set out immediately after the Hōgen uprising to revive the imperial state, which had fallen into "evil practices of the degenerate age." A new, detailed shōen regulation ordinance was issued and the kirokujo reestablished in imitation of Go-Sanjō's action of 1069.[54] At Shinzei's urging, Go-Shirakawa also reconstructed the Imperial Palace (Dairi), which had been burned repeatedly during the mid-Heian period. Shinzei himself was responsible for compiling the *Honchō seiki*, an official history designed to continue the chronicles of the country from where the *rikkokushi* had left off in the late ninth century.

In 1158, however, Go-Shirakawa abdicated in favor of his son Nijō, perhaps because Bifukumon'in had urged him to do so in accord with Toba's wishes.[55] Even though his abdication may have come at the urgings of Bifukumon'in, Go-Shirakawa intended to exercise the kind of political influence his immediate successors had enjoyed as well as to participate fully in the cultural circles of Heian court society.[56] He immediately established his In-no-chō and proceeded to control the affairs of the imperial house.

At the outset, he was perhaps not as powerful as either Shirakawa or Toba because of stubborn opposition from Emperor Nijō. Although the *Hyakurenshō* claims that Nijō and the chancellor Morozane conducted politics without consulting the ex-sovereign, other sources show that Go-Shirakawa and the retired Tadamichi did indeed exert considerable influence over their respective sons.[57] Nijō did, however, try to rule as forcefully as he could despite his father, and he was even criticized in the *Gempei seisuiki* for his lack of filial piety. On several occasions in the early 1160s Nijō was able to have associates of the retired sovereign dismissed from their court posts. Nijō was the most forceful emperor to reign during the insei period and a serious impediment to Go-Shirakawa's political influence.

Once again it was the matter of imperial succession that worsened the relationship between the two men. For the first six years of his reign Nijō had no heir, and there was no crown prince. In 1161, however, Taira no Shigeko, a lady-in-waiting to Go-Shirakawa's sister, had given birth

53. Shinzei is the priestly name of Fujiwara (Takashina) no Michinori.
54. Hurst, "Insei," pp. 217–20.
55. See ibid., pp. 205–07, for a discussion of the succession pattern conceived by Toba and Bifukumon'in.
56. Go-Shirakawa was perhaps more aesthetically inclined than his two predecessors, and he was particularly fond of the popular poetic craze over *imayō*. He often held poetry recitations attended by persons from all social strata.
57. *Hyakurenshō*, p. 73; Hurst, "Insei," pp. 226–30.

to a son of the ex-emperor's. The possibility of the future accession of this prince led several Taira courtiers, including some in Go-Shirakawa's service, to plot his accession, and for this they were dismissed from office and exiled.[58] Finally in 1164 one of the palace women in Nijō's women's quarters gave birth to a son, and when the emperor became ill in the middle of the year, he began preparations to make his son crown prince. However, Nijō's illness became serious, and he abdicated in favor of the young boy (Emperor Rokujō) even before the latter's installation as crown prince. He acted hastily with the hope that Go-Shirakawa would not attempt to remove Rokujō from the throne, as he surely would have done had the boy been crown prince.

But in 1168 Nijō's work was undone when Rokujō was forced to abdicate in favor of Takakura, the son of Go-Shirakawa and Taira no Shigeko. Although Go-Shirakawa had expected to control this emperor completely, he was again foiled, this time by the maternal relatives of the new sovereign, the Taira. Go-Shirakawa was forced at this juncture to confront the question of whether to continue cooperation with Kiyomori, Shigeko's brother-in-law and the leading Taira courtier.[59] For several years the two did cooperate and Go-Shirakawa even adopted Kiyomori's daughter Tokuko and made her Takakura's consort. But during the 1170s Taira power at court increased while Go-Shirakawa's dwindled, and finally in 1177, with the discovery of the Shishigatani affair—a plot against Kiyomori by many of Go-Shirakawa's associates—discord between the ex-sovereign and Kiyomori came out into the open. From then until the actual outbreak of the Gempei War, Go-Shirakawa was closely controlled—at one point even placed under house arrest—by Kiyomori. During the fighting and particularly after 1183 he dominated the court scene once again, but now he had to deal with a newly risen power structure, the Kamakura shogunate.

Thus Go-Shirakawa never was able to dominate the court to the extent he might have wished; but he was nonetheless successful in maintaining and even expanding the influence and wealth of the imperial house during a very difficult and tumultuous era. Particularly in the area of shōen acquisition, Go-Shirakawa continued the efforts of Toba in building up a huge landed base for the imperial house.

The In-no-chō

In the foregoing discussion of the political role of abdicated sovereigns in Heian Japan, I have emphasized the fact that they exercised headship

58. *Hyakurenshō*, p. 75, Eiryaku 2/9/5.

59. In my opinion Japanese historians have long given too much emphasis to the concept of a Taira polity (*Heishi seiken*). This view is similar to that of Jeffrey Mass as expressed in chap. 6 of this book.

over the imperial house, which had been successfully reorganized to allow it to compete effectively for power at court. I should now like to analyze in further detail the institutional basis of this revitalized imperial house: In-no-chō, the In-no-kinshin, and the imperial estate holdings.

The In-no-chō developed over the course of the early Heian period as a group of administrative bodies to serve the needs of the ex-sovereign. In the later Heian period it came to function as the major private administrative office for the whole imperial house. While the number of officials in the In-no-chō increased and its authority expanded with the rise in power of ex-sovereigns from Go-Sanjō's time, the In-no-chō remained essentially a private house organization to handle the affairs of the retired sovereign and other members of the imperial house.

Structurally, the in-no-chō resembled the household offices of other powerful families; it was in essence an imperial mandokoro, very much like that of the Fujiwara regent. Its internal offices were wholly analogous: secretariat (kurōdo-dokoro), document bureau (fudono), attendant's bureau (tsukae-dokoro), bureau for ceremonial dress (gofuku-dokoro), stable (mimaya), warrior's bureau (mushadokoro-chō), and so forth.[60] In fact, so similar were the structures of the In-no-chō and the Sekkanke mandokoro that both the Shūgaishō and the Koji ruien treat the offices and officials of both under the same category.[61]

There were three major posts in the In-no-chō apparently not attached to any specific bureau. Directors (bettō) were the senior officials in the ex-sovereign's office, but their duties appear to have been few since during the insei period most were kugyō with important posts at court. There was no fixed number of directors; upon abdication it was usual to appoint about five, but it was not uncommon for their number to rise to more than twenty. Supervisors (hōgandai) were in charge of the everyday business of the In-no-chō and were generally men of the fourth through sixth court ranks. Two or three clerks (shutendai) were in charge of drafting the documents issued by the In-no-chō. These latter were men of outstanding calligraphy and wide experience in documentation.

If the In-no-chō was primarily a house office rather than an alternate court, then the contents of the documents issued by the office should demonstrate that fact. With very few exceptions, the documents issued by the In-no-chō and those private documents issued personally by the ex-sovereign deal in one way or another with estate holdings.[62] The

60. See Hurst, "Insei," pp. 258, 260, and 328–33.
61. Shūgaishō, in Kojitsu sōsho (Tokyo, 1952), p. 366; Koji ruien (Tokyo, 1931–36), 15:94.
62. There are eighty-one extant documents of the In-no-chō and the ex-sovereign collected in the Heian ibun, which I have examined in the course of this study. See Hurst, "Insei," pp. 261–62, n.7, for a breakdown of these documents. See also Suzuki

documents concern three types of shōen: (1) those controlled by the ex-emperor himself, (2) those owned by retired imperial ladies (*nyoin-ryō*), and (3) those that belonged to associates or confidants (*kinshin*) of the retired emperor. It would seem safe to conclude, then, that the In-no-chō functioned primarily as an administrative agency for the estates of the entire imperial house, including associates who were essentially clients.

The In-no-chō issued two kinds of documents, orders (*kudashibumi*) and communiqués (*chō*). The communiqué was a document of transmission (*dentatsu monjo*), that is, it was used to communicate with nonsubordinate and unrelated offices; there was no superior–subordinate relationship between the issuing and receiving offices.[63] The In-no-chō communiqués were drafted by a clerk who affixed his seal at the end of the document; the directors and supervisors then placed their seals on the document along with a notation of their various official posts and ranks.

Most of these communiqués are addressed to provincial government offices. Their ultimate purpose was to secure the issuance of a provincial governor's order (*kokushi no chōzen*) granting provincial immunity to the shōen in question. The procedure was quite complex. The communiqué would be sent to the governor, who generally resided in the capital, who would in turn have his order drafted and sent to the provincial office along with the communiqué. The governor's order usually included some phrase such as "the communiqué of the ex-sovereign's office is attached." Messengers from both the In-no-chō and the provincial office would visit the estate in question and mark the borders with boundary stakes. Thus the immunity from taxation of an estate claimed by the ex-sovereign, a retired imperial lady, or one of the ex-emperor's clients would be recognized. It was the order of the provincial governor as a representative of the imperial government, however, and not the communiqué of the ex-sovereign's office, that guaranteed the immunity. The communiqué was clearly not more authoritative.

The orders (*kudashibumi*) of the ex-sovereign's office were similar to those issued by other house offices, by mandokoro of Buddhist temples, and by even the sovereign's private office (*kurōdo-dokoro*).[64] Drafted in the same manner and possessing the same seals as a communiqué, the surviving orders of the In-no-chō are mostly addressed to officials on

---

Shigeo, "Insei-ki in no chō no kinō ni tsuite—in no chō hakkyū monjo o tsūjite mitaru," (graduation thesis, Tokyo University, 1961). All exceptional documents are from the 1160s on, when Go-Shirakawa was ex-sovereign and the court situation was complicated by the rise of a new warrior element and the struggle between Go-Shirakawa and the Taira. See chap. 6 of this book.

63. Hurst, "Insei," p. 263.
64. See Aida Jirō, *Nihon no komonjo* (Tokyo, 1962), 1:258–300.

estates under the jurisdiction of the ex-sovereign's office. Yet many are addressed, like the communiqués, to local government officials. Indeed, so are many kudashibumi from the offices of retired imperial ladies, Buddhist temples, and high-ranking courtiers. But local officials were under the authority of the governor, not of these private houses. In actuality, the kudashibumi of the ex-sovereign appear to have functioned similarly to the communiqué: they secured the order of a provincial governor recognizing the immunity of an estate. This function is clear from the body of most kudashibumi, which direct the local officials to take action "in accord with the provincial governor's order." Such an order usually accompanied the kudashibumi or followed shortly thereafter and authorized the action. Again, it was the governor's document that legally authorized the recognition of the estate.

The ex-sovereign also issued *inzen*, or ex-emperor's edicts, which were similar in nature to *rinji*, *migyōsho,* and *ryōji,* the private documents issued by the emperor, high-ranking courtiers, and other imperial house members respectively.[65] The inzen were simple documents drafted by one of the ex-emperor's associates and were generally addressed to estate officials or heads of imperial temples, but in any event dealt with private estate business rather than with public matters.

These various documents indicate that the primary function of the In-no-chō was the administration of imperial estates, but they also indicate that the documents themselves did not possess greater authority than those issued by the legally constituted offices of the imperial government. Their greatest realm of authority was in internal affairs of imperial shōen, and while they were certainly powerful in securing immunity for estate holdings, they were not powerful enough to grant that immunity. Two examples from the documentation of the late Heian period should demonstrate this.

In 1162 the court received a request from the Daidembō-in in regard to its Yamahigashi-shō in the province of Kii.[66] It was one of five estates designated for the support of the temple when Toba established it in 1132. It received an inzen from Toba and a charter from the grand council of state confirming its immunity. Later, however, local officials had claimed that the estate and its residents owed them services and began interfering in the estate. The temple complained to the In-no-chō (Go-Shirakawa's) about these activities and the ex-emperor sent an inzen to the governor about the matter. He ordered the local officials to desist "in accord with the ex-sovereign's edict," but they continued their interference. In this

65. See Satō Shin'ichi, *Komonjo-gaku* (Tokyo, 1968), for a discussion of these documents.

66. *Heian ibun,* 7:3580–82, doc. 3234, Ōho, 2/11.

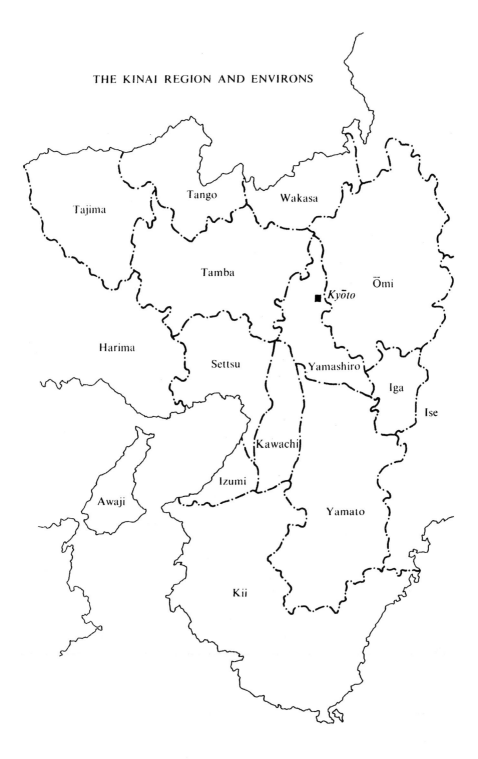

THE KINAI REGION AND ENVIRONS

document, the Daidembō-in asks for an imperial decision on the previously issued charter acknowledging the immunity of the estate. While the priests seem to be uncertain of the extent of the inzen's authority, they do state clearly that "although the charter of the grand council of state and the ex-sovereign's edict similarly derive from the imperial pleasure, eternal and unperishable documentary certification is limited to the charter of the grand council of state." They requested that another charter, reiterating the estate's immunity, be issued.

An edict of 1132 was issued to the Daigo-ji Enkō-in concerning the status of its Ushigahara estate in Echizen.[67] It seems that in 1086 the temple had claimed two hundred *chō* of empty land which had been cleared, cultivated, and recognized as immune by the governor. Successive governors, however, had alternately ignored the immunity and then recognized it again. The temple was an imperial one, having been founded for Shirakawa's beloved consort Kenshi, and thus it looked to the ex-sovereign for protection. In this edict, the court recognized the legitimacy of the original estate boundaries and ordered local officials to cease interference. Thus even imperial temples under the protection of the ex-sovereign found it necessary to secure legal imperial immunity to protect themselves. Documents from the In-no-chō or the ex-emperor were simply not possessed of the same authority as those from the imperial government.

Thus in terms of its structure, the kinds of officials it employed, and the nature of the documents it issued, the In-no-chō appears to have been little different from other private house offices, except, of course, that it was larger and more powerful. It was not a separate court, and its documents were not issued to usurp the authority of the imperial government; indeed, many In-no-chō documents were designed to effect the issuance of imperial government documents. What, then, of the men who served in the In-no-chō?

In-no-kinshin

Among the officials who served the ex-sovereign was a group of close associates or confidants who were known as *In-no-kinshin*.[68] These men were the most influential courtiers in the service of the ex-emperors, and all at one time or another were directors in the In-no-chō. This group of kinshin has been criticized both by traditional writers, like Jien, who saw them usurping much of the power and the wealth of the Sekkanke, and by modern scholars who see them as an emergent class of provincial go-

---

67. Ibid., 5:1909–10, doc. 2241, Chōjō 1/9/23.
68. Sometimes they were referred to as *In-no-kinjū* or *In-no-kōsuru tomogara*, but *kinshin* is the most common term.

vernors parasitically using the ex-sovereign to further their own class interests. A considerable amount of information about these men can be obtained and must be considered before any definitive statements about the kinshin can be made.[69]

The first and most obvious fact to emerge from a study of the In-no-kinshin is that they came from a limited number of court families which generation after generation provided trusted associates for the ex-sovereigns. There were seven of these kinshin families: the Kanjūji Fujiwara, the Takashina family, the Fujiwara descendants of Yoshikado, the Fujiwara descended from Matsushige, the descendants of Fujiwara no Michitaka, the Kan'in Fujiwara, and the Ise Taira.[70] These kinshin families are in many ways analogous to those whose members served as hereditary household officials (*keishi*) for the Sekkanke and other major courtier houses. Interestingly, some of the kinshin—Fujiwara no Tamefusa and others of the Kanjūji Fujiwara, for example—had traditionally been keishi of the Sekkanke, and it would appear that they transferred their loyalty from the regent's house to the ex-sovereign's as the latter's political fortunes rose at the expense of the former's.

Besides this hereditary clientage relationship, kinshin families tended to form marital relationships with the imperial house, and the mothers of Shirakawa, Horikawa, Toba, Konoe, Go-Shirakawa, and Go-Toba were all from kinshin families. These maternal relationships, while not threatening to take on the binding nature of those once exercised by the Sekkanke, appear to have been a major factor in determining the influence of many In-no-kinshin.[71] Kinshin families also tended to intermarry frequently, indicating that they may have formed a relatively close-knit body. Many kinshin families provided wet nurses for the emperors of this period and capitalized upon the strong emotional bond forged between the wet nurse and her ward.[72] Some kinshin were thus "breast brothers" of emperors and ex-emperors and benefited greatly from this relationship.

Another fact to emerge from studying the kinshin is that many of them not only served the abdicated sovereign, but also held administrative posts in the offices of other imperial house members: crown prince, empress, and

69. Appointments to the In-no-chō were not official government posts, and thus there is no official list of them. But courtier diaries are full of references to In-no-kinshin and their appointments, and thus with a considerable amount of digging, the names of most kinshin can be learned. By reliance upon such diaries, the *Kugyō bunin*, and the *Sompi bummyaku*, a fairly good picture of these men can be obtained. See Hurst, "Insei," pp. 271-99, 334-63.

70. Ibid., pp. 279-85 has genealogical charts for these families.

71. The exception, of course, was the case of the Taira.

72. Wada Hidematsu, "Rekishijō ni okeru menoto no seiryoku," in Wada, *Kokushi kokubun no kenkyu* (Tokyo, 1926), pp. 182-201.

retired imperial lady. In this respect, then, the kinshin can be seen as confidants or clients of the entire imperial house, rather than simply of the ex-sovereign.

A number of significant points can be made in regard to the official careers of the In-no-kinshin. First, with the exception of the Kan'in Fujiwara, the kinshin families were of only middle rank at the outset of the period but tended to be upwardly mobile over the course of the insei period, due largely to their association with the ex-sovereigns.[73] Second, virtually all kinshin served as provincial governors, many enjoying long provincial careers extending over many provinces. Finally, the kinshin tended to be appointed to posts in the capital that were politically and economically important to the imperial house—*kurōdo no tō, kura no kami, ōkura no kyō,* and *shuri no daibu.*[74]

The latter two facts point to the economic importance of the kinshin to the ex-sovereign and the imperial house. In the late Heian period provincial governors, as tax collectors, were in the best possible position to accumulate wealth. Governors (*zuryō*) notoriously misused their powers to extract wealth from the peasant population, and this wealth was frequently used to support a life style in the capital so ostentatious that it became the object of criticism (and envy) by kugyō courtiers. An alliance between the ex-sovereign and provincial governors was mutually advantageous: the zuryō could provide economic support for the retired emperor and for other imperial house members through "special contributions" (*bekkō*)[75] while the retired emperor, by virtue of his headship of the imperial house and influence at court, could guarantee their continued appointment to lucrative provincial posts or to more important positions at court.

Another reason for the retired sovereigns to seek alliance with zuryō was the authority these men enjoyed in their provinces. Cooperation with provincial governors was necessary to establish provincial immunity for estate holdings as we have seen, and indeed it seems to be no accident that the provinces in which kinshin served as governors tended to be those in which the retired emperor had extensive estate holdings.[76] Provincial governors also tended to function as go-betweens in the process of estate commendation from local landholders to important court personages such as the ex-sovereign.[77] Since the abdicated emperors, Toba and Go-

73. Even the Kan'in Fujiwara progressed politically during this period in relation to some other Fujiwara houses.

74. See Hurst, "Insei," pp. 297–98.

75. The *Kugyō bunin* even records the fact that a governor was appointed due to such contributions, referring to them as *bekkō zuryō.*

76. Such provinces were largely in western and southwestern Japan. See Hurst, "Insei," pp. 295–96, n. 16 for a breakdown of the provinces in which kinshin served as governors.

77. Murai Yasuhiko, *Kodai kokka kaitei katei no kenkyū,* (Tokyo, 1965), p. 388.

Shirakawa in particular, were interested in the acquisition of shōen for the imperial house, there was no better group of persons to whom they could have extended their patronage.

The ex-emperor could secure the appointment of his kinshin to provincial posts by exercising his influence over the kugyō council, which increasingly was constituted of courtiers close to him. His suggestions and even orders (*In-no-ōse*) were not lightly disregarded, and diaries of several courtiers indicate that provincial appointments were of particular interest to ex-sovereigns. Beyond that the retired sovereign, along with other imperial house members, was permitted under the provincial allotment (*bunkoku*) system to appoint governors to a small number of provinces.[78] These never numbered more than two or three at any one time, but over the course of the insei period a large number of kinshin were appointed governor by "allotment of the ex-sovereign" (*imbun*).[79]

If the In-no-chō was an office primarily engaged in the administration of imperial estates over which the ex-sovereign exercised control, and if the kinshin who served in the In-no-chō were intimately connected with the process of acquiring immunity for estates belonging to the imperial house as well as commending their own holdings to the imperial house, we must then examine more carefully the nature of imperial estate holdings.

Imperial Estates and Abdicated Sovereigns

While the entire court suffered from declining public revenues during the Heian period, the imperial house was more adversely affected than other families. The emperor was head of the governmental structure based upon a policy of public land, and thus it was inappropriate for him to participate in the alienation of public land as so many other houses did.[80] Aside from this institutional restraint, the emperor was hardly a free agent because of the domination of the Fujiwara regency for much of the period. And even though the ex-sovereign normally functioned as the head of the imperial house, he lacked the necessary control over the house's most important asset, the emperorship. Thus it was difficult for even the ex-emperor to operate independently to create much of an economic base for the imperial house.

It was only during the reign of Go-Sanjō and the revival of imperial

---

78. The best discussion of the provincial allotment system is Hashimoto Yoshihiko, "Ingū bunkoku to chigyōkoku," in Takeuchi Rizō Hakushi Kanreki Kinenkai, ed. and comp., *Ritsu-ryō kokka to kizoku shakai* (Tokyo, 1969), pp. 575–91.

79. Again, the *Kugyō bunin* lists them as appointed by allotment.

80. Ishimoda Shō, *Kodai makki seijishi josetsu* (Tokyo, 1964), p. 361. Public land does not, of course, mean that there were no owners. It simply means land that is taxable by public government.

power attained by breaking the dominance of the Sekkanke that the imperial house was able to compete effectively for actual court power. While attempting to curtail the estate holdings of other courtiers, Go-Sanjō also acquired private lands for the imperial house that were virtually analagous to shōen. Thereafter, under the headship of the ex-sovereigns Shirakawa, Toba, and Go-Shirakawa, the imperial house accumulated vast numbers of shōen, eventually becoming the largest landholder in the country.

Ishimoda Shō has pointed out that the retired sovereign built up the private holdings of the imperial house because the emperor was hampered by the institutional restraints of his position. This seems fair enough as far as it goes, but it does not account for the fact that virtually no imperial shōen were held in the name of the ex-emperor himself. They were nominally owned by imperial temples or retired imperial ladies. It would seem that there was still an institutional restraint working upon an ex-sovereign (importantly, one who had been emperor) as well. Somehow, direct participation in the accumulation of privately controlled lands was not an appropriate imperial activity. Even the private lands acquired by Go-Sanjō were designated *chokushiden*, and most imperial estates were usually termed "imperial holdings" (*goryō*) rather than shōen.

The most common explanation of Japanese historians for the large number of imperial house estates held by temples is that it was an expression of the deep Buddhist faith of the house during this period. Certainly it was the era of the latter day of the Law, when the construction of temples was considered a path toward salvation. Moreover, the ex-sovereigns all eventually took the tonsure and as priestly retired sovereigns (*hōō*) ranked high in the Buddhist world. But it was a pious age in which it was common to become a priest or take up residence in a Buddhist temple; the imperial house did not enjoy a monopoly on faith.

It would appear that another major reason for having temples control imperial estates was to protect the estates from possible confiscation. Large blocks of holdings belonging to a single individual were liable to be confiscated in times of crisis and rebellion. For example, as a result of his defeat and death in the Hōgen affair, Fujiwara no Yorinaga was divested of his various shōen.[81] Estates divided among numerous temples, in other words, simply appeared more secure from the threat of seizure. That these well-endowed temples of the imperial house were of virtually no importance in the history of Japanese religion emphasizes once again that they were largely social and economic assets for the house and com-

81. *Heihanki*, 2:156–58, Hōgen 3/3/29, records these holdings and declares them goin holdings.

fortable, even luxurious, residences to which ex-sovereigns, retired imperial ladies, and other imperial house members could retreat.

As pointed out in the discussion of In-no-chō documents, the ex-sovereign's office controlled imperial rights not only in temple holdings, but also in estates belonging to retired imperial ladies (nyoin-ryō). These portfolios of shōen were created for the most part during Toba's and Go-Shirakawa's tenures as abdicated sovereigns, when the imperial house came into the possession of extensive holdings and transmission of these holdings became crucial. It was as a means to provide support for imperial ladies as well as to avoid the disaster that could befall one large portfolio of holdings in case of confiscation that Toba divided imperial temples' holdings among his consorts Taikenmon'in and Bifukumon'in and his daughters Jōzaimon'in and Hachijō-in. The holdings of Hachijō-in, for example, included estates belonging to the Anrakuju-in, Kankikō-in, and Rengeshin-in as well as shōen commended directly to her.[82]

Lands that came into imperial ownership during the late Heian period are referred to in later sources as "lands pledged during the three reigns" (sandai gokishō no chi). The In-no-chō appears to have had control over imperial rights in these lands. What, then, can we say about the nature of those rights? For the most part, imperial estates were obtained by commendation (kishin) from some courtier or local proprietor. The nature of just what was commended in such cases has been a matter of dispute among Japanese historians, but it appears that the ultimate proprietor (honjo or honke) at the top of the commendation ladder could receive either a portion of the produce of the estate with no administrative rights, or both a portion of the produce and administrative control.[83] While there were a few imperial estates in which the ex-sovereign enjoyed some form of administrative control, the overwhelming percentage were ones in which he, or one of the retired imperial ladies, possessed income rights only.

Administrative control of these estates remained in the hands of the courtier proprietor (ryōke) who had initiated the commendation, and most of these men were kinshin zuryō who enjoyed a close relationship with the ex-sovereign.[84] The ex-emperor was thus in possession of a considerable amount of private income from imperial estates but enjoyed little admin-

82. Hurst, "Insei," p. 321.
83. The traditional view has been that the owner merely transferred title to a more powerful individual or institution and paid a percentage of the yield but retained administrative rights over the land. Nagahara Keiji, Nihon Hōkensei seiritsu katei no kenkyū (Tokyo, 1962), pp. 57–62.
84. There were very few instances in which local cultivators commended their lands directly to the ex-sovereign.

istrative control over them. A commonly quoted figure credits the retired emperor with control of one thousand imperial estates in fifty-nine provinces, but this figure does not indicate the amount of income or wealth the estates provided.[85]

Income and wealth from shōen were not in the form of gold and precious gems stashed away in treasure chests, but included all the necessities and luxuries for daily life. The rents and services which shōen owed to a proprietor were distributed in such a way that the central lord's needs were all provided for. In the 1191 document listing the shōen holdings of Go-Shirakawa's Chōkō-dō, for example, the contributions of ninety estates are broken down so that one can see a full year's daily allotments.[86] Every day a different shōen was to provide the various foods for the temple; warriors from a particular estate were to perform guard duty at the west gate for so many days in a particular month; another shōen was responsible for the sand to be used in a special ceremony in a certain month. Everything imaginable, from *tatami* mats and bolts of cloth for clothing to shovels and even *go* ("chess") boards, was divided up among the various holdings of the temple so that the expenses of an entire year could be totally met. Thus when Go-Shirakawa visited the Chōkō-dō for extended periods of time, he lacked nothing. This was the manner in which shōen provided income and wealth for the abdicated sovereign.

In the late Heian period the imperial house, under the active headship of successive abdicated sovereigns, reemerged as a major political force in Japan after a long period of domination by the Fujiwara regency. Crucial to this process was the attainment of independence from the Sekkanke, which allowed the imperial house to control its most important political asset, the emperorship. Beyond that, effective competition for court power required a private house administrative agency, a large body of clients among the courtiers, and a private economic base in the shōen system to make up for diminishing public revenues.

The attainment of all these assets by the imperial house came during the period from 1086 to 1185. While Go-Sanjō contributed much to the revival of imperial power and while ex-sovereigns continued to head a powerful imperial house up until Go-Daigo's time, it was essentially the hundred years covering the tenures of the ex-sovereigns Shirakawa, Toba, and Go-Shirakawa during which the imperial house enjoyed its golden age. It is this reemergence of the imperial house under the headship

85. Both Ishimoda, *Kodai makki seijishi josetsu*, p. 360, and Hall, *Government and Local Power in Japan*, p. 120, make this claim. I have been able to account for sixty provinces, and the figure of one thousand estates is now regarded as a very low one.

86. See Takeuchi, *Bushi no tōjō*, pp. 282–88.

of the ex-sovereign that the Japanese historians have tried to characterize by the concept of insei. But the concept needs rethinking. The In-no-chō should not be seen as an alternate government, and its documents should not be regarded as replacing imperial edicts. The In-no-chō, the In-no-kinshin associated with it, the vast number of shōen holdings it controlled —all these should be seen as the institutional basis of the imperial-house organization that was necessary to compete for power within the existing framework of the imperial state.

4   The Early Development of the *Shōen*

ELIZABETH SATO

By the time of the first appearance of *shōen* in the mid-eighth century, Japan had been governed for almost one hundred years by a civil bureaucracy modeled on that of T'ang China. The institutions of government were embodied in legal codes adopted in the Taihō era (promulgated in 702). These legal, or penal, codes (*ritsu*) and administrative codes (*ryō*) endured as the foundation of the country's legal system until the fifteenth century, although their force as active instruments of government eroded with time and became extensively modified by custom. The *ritsu-ryō* codes provided the legal framework within wihch the shōen was to emerge and develop as an alternative system of land administration.

The land-tenure and land-tax systems put into effect under the ritsu-ryō codes had aimed at giving the state secure and far-reaching administrative authority over the produce from the land and over the manpower that produced it. A fixed amount of paddy land was assigned to each household member. For the purposes of the allotment system, the rice land was surveyed and organized into fields of equal size in a grid pattern[1]. In addition, the allotment system established the household or residential group (*ko*) as the unit for allocating land and collecting taxes. Each member of the ko received a specified amount of land according to his status.[2] The allotment was to be reviewed every six years to allow for demographic changes. The ko was also the basic unit on which taxes were levied. The head of the ko was responsible for the taxes of all the ko members. In addition to the grain tax (*so*), members of the household were required to pay a tax in kind (*chō*), usually cloth or a special product of the area, and

1. For the details of the organization of the grid (*jōri*) system, see Iyanaga Teizo, "Jōrisei no shomondai," in Mikami Tsugio, ed., *Nihon no kōkogaku* (Tokyo: Kawade Shobō, 1967), 7: 205–21.
2. According to the provisions of the Taihō Codes, each able-bodied male over age six received two *tan* of paddy land; a female received two-thirds of this; household slaves and other persons received lesser amounts. *Nihon rekishi daijiten* (Tokyo: Kawade Shobō, 1957), 6: 286–87.

a labor tax (*yō*), which was calculated in terms of labor duty in the capital and normally paid off in cloth. The household also had to bear the costs of transporting the *chō* and *yō* to the capital. Moreover, corvée labor of sixty days a year was due the provincial government. Often all or part of this was commuted into produce.[3]

In addition to land for allotment (*kubunden*), several other categories of land were recognized under the ritsu-ryō codes. Most of these, such as rank land, office land, and imperial gift land, were subject to taxation. Land provided for the support of temples and shrines was not subject to government taxation. Other lands that were not yet fed into the allotment system were held under the direct management of the central government. These could be rented to *kubunden* cultivators as supplemental plots on an annual basis. In practice, the same fields were rented to the same persons year after year.[4]

The land system of the ritsu-ryō codes, taken in its strictest terms, offered little opportunity for land to move out of the administrative control of the state. There has been much discussion of this alleged state ownership and of what constituted public and private possession. It is not possible to treat these problems fully here, but on the basis of documentary evidence and recent studies, the position taken by C. J. Kiley seems most reasonable—namely, that the system under the codes should not be considered one of state ownership. Instead, the state's main concern was to retain administrative power over land and the power to control revenue from the land.[5]

By the middle of the eighth century, however, the amount of land not completely subject to government control began to increase. This was paralleled in the central government by what J. W. Hall has described as a "return to patrimonial authority."[6] The formal bureaucratic structure of government was gradually being superceded by extra-governmental offices controlled by powerful court families. The political process culminated in the ascendancy of the Fujiwara regents beginning in the mid-ninth century. As offices in the central government came to be held by successive generations in the same family, the lands that accompanied these offices became hereditary and were increasingly regarded as coming under the direct control of that family. At the other end of the scale,

3. Aoki Kazuo, "Ritsu-ryō zaisei," in *Iwanami kōza Nihon rekishi*, vol. 3, kodai III (Tōkyo: Iwanami, 1964), pp. 117–46.

4. Iyanaga Teizo, "Ritsuryōsei tochi shoyū," in ibid., pp. 35–78.

5. Cornelius J. Kiley, "Property and Political Authority in Early Medieval Japan" (Ph.D. thesis, Harvard University, 1970), pp. 1–10.

6. John W. Hall, *Government and Local Power in Japan, 500 to 1700* (Princeton, N.J.: Princeton University Press, 1966), pp. 99–128.

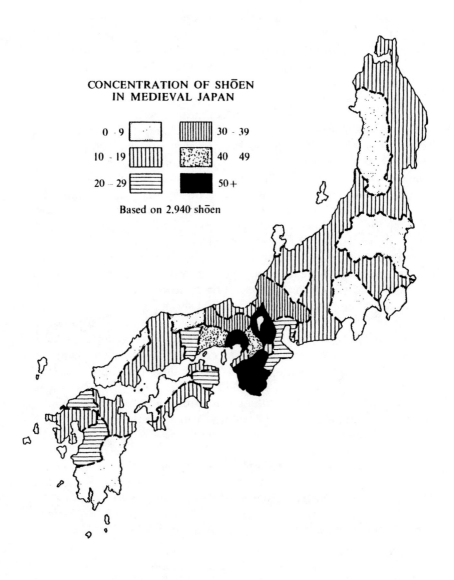

CONCENTRATION OF SHŌEN
IN MEDIEVAL JAPAN

0 - 9
10 - 19
20 - 29
30 - 39
40 - 49
50 +

Based on 2.940 shōen

plots allotted as kubunden to cultivators began to be regarded as more fully under the cultivators' control, with a consequent weakening of the government's ability to exercise uninhibited authority over the alienation of such land. The importance of property as an element of power was growing at the expense of the government's administrative authority.

Privatization was a gradual process that occurred within the context of a society still living under the general provisions of the ritsu-ryō codes. The process, at least with respect to land tenure, did not reach its culmination until the eleventh and twelfth centuries—the high point of the *kishin*-type shōen (shōen formed through commendation). Just as the offices and techniques of the Fujiwara regents stood outside the procedures for government as envisaged in the ritsu-ryō codes, so the shōen stood outside the system of landholding and taxation defined in the codes. In both instances, however, the new methods at first supplemented rather than supplanted the systems established by law.

Although the emergence of the shōen followed a process roughly contemporaneous with the lessening of the central government's control over land, this did not mean that shōen originated with the conversion of allotment land into the personal property of shōen holders. By far the major source of land converted into shōen came from yet another category—land available for reclamation. Under the regulations for land reclamation enacted in 723, newly developed land could be held by the reclaimer and treated as his personal property for two or three generations, though it was subject to the grain tax. In 743 this condition was extended to tenure in perpetuity, thus removing these lands from the allotment system. The creation of a new type of permanent tenure in which the land was regarded as the reclaimer's personal property opened the way for the development of *shōen*.[7]

As the term "early shōen" implies, the time of development is a crucial factor in any analysis of the shōen. At the time of their first appearance, shōen were quite different from what they became at a later, more "mature" stage of development. Although the term "shōen" appeared in Japanese documents from the beginning of the eighth century,[8] it was not

7. Kiley, "Property and Political Authority," pp. 6-10.
8. Originally, *shō* referred to a noble's villa or a residential park, both the term and its object being concepts imported from T'ang China. By the beginning of the eighth century, *shō* had become associated with land marked for reclamation. Documents from the mid-eighth century indicate that *shō* referred to a parcel of land distinct from cultivated land and often to the site of a building, either a storehouse for tools used in reclamation or for produce from nearby fields. As more and more land was reclaimed, the fields came to be regarded as more important than the buildings. Thus the term *shō*, now often expanded to *shōen*, was applied to the entire complex of buildings plus fields. As the final step, the buildings that served as the headquarters for the reclamation project

until the mid-eighth century that it began to be applied to discrete parcels of land with the particular characteristics that came to define the shōen form of private possession. By the middle of the tenth century, conditions under which shōen were established had changed, and the relatively simple pattern of earlier times was rapidly disappearing. Many early shōen simply vanished from later historical records, making their final appearance under the category of "overthrown places."[9] Moreover, those early shōen that did survive as productive units had acquired by the middle of the tenth century most of the characteristics of the later commendation model. More will be said of this later. What is important to note here is that it was often the individual holders of early shōen who commended their holdings to a more powerful person in return for protection from provincial authorities, thus forming the later type of aggregated domains.

A second essential feature of the early shōen was land. Although in later times rights to income from land became more important than the land itself, in the early stages of shōen development, the reverse was true: in order to produce income, land first had to be developed.[10] The land that formed the nucleus of the early shōen might start out as either completely undeveloped, "unreclaimed" land, or as land that had undergone partial development. In the latter category, developed land was purchased from the original reclaimer. In the case of unreclaimed land the shōen holder gained possession either through a gift from a ranking courtier or the imperial family, or through a petition requesting government permission to enclose and reclaim a specific area. Although a shōen holder could use either of these methods or some combination for accumulating land, most early shōen had their origins in previously unreclaimed land.

Compared to later shōen, the early shōen was quite simple in both physical and administrative structure. For the most part, the lands granted for reclamation were located within a single county, and, if several parcels were involved, they were in fair proximity to one another. This did not mean that fields brought into production were necessarily contiguous or in one enclosed area similar to a Western farm. Clusters of cultivated fields could be separated by unreclaimed tracts, since the order of reclamation often relied on the availability of irrigation and other geographical

---

were differentiated by the term *shōke*, and *shōen* referred primarily to the land. Nakada Kaoru, *Shōen no kenkyū* (Tokyo: Shōkō Shoin, 1948), pp. 43–45.

9. For examples, including Kuwabara-no-shō, see Asakawa Kan'ichi, *Land and Society in Medieval Japan* (Tokyo: Japan Society for the Promotion of Science, 1965), p. 114 (English text) and p. 137, doc. 130 (Japanese text). (Hereafter cited as *LSMJ*.)

10. That is, rice income, the measure of wealth in early Japan. Strictly speaking, timber lands or salt farms also produced income, but rice lands were the major source of wealth.

factors. Nevertheless, the early shoen was a relatively compact unit that could be handled by a simple administrative structure.

The first shōen came under the direct administration of the owner, who acted for himself and relied on his own resources to reclaim the land and bring it into production. The holder of the shōen was also the chief administrator who resided in the shōen to oversee its day-to-day functions. Thus, the early shōen did not display the complex hierarchy of functions and of rights to income that appeared in later shōen. The holder of the early shōen managed his land for his own benefit and under his own administration. This held true for the shōen of religious institutions even though the holder in this case was not a person who could reside on the shōen. Actual daily administration was handled by an official of the temple who received a salary for his services rather than a right to a portion of the income from the shōen.

A final feature of the early shōen that differentiated it from later models was the ambiguity of its liability for taxation. Most dictionary definitions of "shōen" list immunity from government taxation as one of its distinguishing characteristics. This immunity was far from complete in the case of early shōen. As will be seen in the specific examples described below, early shōen gained their tax immunities in a variety of ways, often borrowing or extending exemptions from immune lands already acquired under different circumstances. This was especially true in the case of temples, which often gained tax immunity for their newly acquired shōen by having them classified as temple land, a category not liable for grain tax under the provisions of the ritsu-ryō codes. A generally more secure method of gaining and insuring tax immunity was through a petition to the central government. When the petition was approved, the shōen holder received a charter (*kanshōfu*) issued by the Dajōkan (Great Council of State) and the Minbushō (Popular Affairs Bureau), which specified the location and area of the shōen and the extent of its tax immunity. Both lay and religious institutions used this method to gain immunity. The point to be noted here is that lands were granted for reclamation *before* they received tax immunity. Shōen holders designated their lands as shōen before any guarantee of immunity had been received—or even applied for. Tax immunity, then, was not necessarily a defining characteristic of the early shōen, although most entities that were called such by their holders eventually received at least a partial exemption from taxation. Those that did not simply failed to survive. It goes without saying that, from the viewpoint of the central government, a shōen was liable for taxation regardless of its label or the holder's protestations until it received government approval for immunity.

Let us turn now to several specific examples of how the early shōen came into being. As stated earlier, the basis for most early shōen was newly reclaimed land. The creation of new paddy fields was not an easy task as it required a large investment of labor and capital as well as local influence for negotiating boundaries and water rights. Although there were undoubtedly numerous small-scale projects by individual cultivators, the reclamation policy of the government inevitably favored the rich and powerful, who alone possessed the wherewithal to acquire tools and to hire the necessary labor.[11]

Kuwabara-no-shō in Echizen Province (present-day Fukui Prefecture) provides a good example of an early shōen that started from reclaimed land. Kuwabara-no-shō was held by the Tōdaiji of Nara, family temple of the imperial house. As the foremost institution in the system of provincial temples (kokubunji) sponsored by the government, Tōdaiji was essentially a quasi-governmental institution. In the matter of land administration, however, Tōdaiji acted independently and in its own interests. As part of the central government's patronage of Buddhism, all temples received grants of land as well as household groups of cultivators to provide income for their support.[12] Also as part of the government's land-reclamation policy, temples were permitted quotas of undeveloped land that they were encouraged to develop. Tōdaiji received permission to reclaim the largest amount, some 4,000 chō (about 12,000 acres); other temples were allowed lesser amounts, as were imperial princes and officials.[13]

In the mid-eighth century, in celebration of the completion of the large image of Roshana Buddha of Tōdaiji, major temples were authorized to acquire 100 chō for reclamation in excess of the official limits set for temple land.[14] The Tōdaiji, as it had for previous reclamation projects, immediately sent out agents to locate an appropriate site. In 755 the temple

11. Yasuda Motohisa, Nihon shōenshi gaisetsu (Tokyo: Yoshikawa Kōbunkan, 1961), pp. 19–20. For a discussion of various views on land reclamation policy, see Kikuchi Yasuaki, Nihon kodai tochi shoyū no kenkyū (Tokyo: Tokyo University Press, 1969), pp. 310–28.

12. Household groups of cultivators (jikifu or fugo) paid one-half (later all) of the grain tax and the whole of the produce taxes (yō and chō) to the temple or noble to whom they were assigned. E.g., Tōdaiji was permitted to receive income from 5,000 households; Daianji, 1,500; and Kōfukuji, 1,200. Nihon rekishi daijiten, 9:213.

13. Yasuda, Nihon shōensei gaisetsu, p. 21. At first there had been no figures set for the amounts that could be reclaimed. The limits suggest the great popularity of land reclamation. Imperial princes and court families of the first rank were allowed 500 chō; princes and nobles of the second rank, 400 chō; princes of the third and fourth rank and nobles of the third rank, 300 chō; nobles of the fourth rank, 200 chō; nobles of the fifth rank, 100 chō; nobles of the sixth rank and below, 50 chō. Among local officials, county governors (dairyō) were permitted 30 chō.

14. ZokuNihongi, Tempyō-Shōhō 1/int. 5/n.d. (749) in Kokushi taikei, pt. 1, vol. 3 (Tokyo: Yoshikawa Kōbunkan, 1956), pp. 201–02.

purchased slightly more than 96 chō (about 280 acres) in Sakai county, Echizen Province. This land was then designated as Kuwabara-no-shō and recognized as temple land. Of the total of 96 chō, 9 chō had been reclaimed by the previous holder, a member of the Ōtomo family which held lower-grade provincial governorships in Echizen throughout this period. Also included in the sale were three buildings and a few utensils.[15] In the first year after acquiring the land, Tōdaiji reclaimed 23 chō at the cost of 100 *soku* (sheaves) per chō.[16] Considering the amount of work involved in preparing paddy fields for cultivation, this cost figure is low, especially in comparison with the other expenditures on the shōen. For example, it cost almost 900 soku including wages and food for the construction of one storehouse, and 200 soku for reassembling a building.[17] In 757 ten additional chō had been reclaimed, bringing the total land in cultivation to 42 chō. Later in this year some 32 chō of unreclaimed land were sold. Unfortunately, parts of the document of sale are missing so that we do not know the particulars of this transaction. In the same year, also, Tōdaiji undertook the construction of a large irrigation project, repairing existing canals and dikes and building various new ones.[18] After 757 there is little information on further reclamation in Kuwabara-no-shō.

The documents indicate that the creation of paddy fields was not necessarily a permanent accomplishment. Parcels of land were continuously going out of production and being reclassified as wasteland. Natural disasters account for some of these instances, but by far the majority of cases were the result of local sabotage issuing from disputes among neighbors over kubunden possession.[19]

Land reclamation and irrigation projects of the scope undertaken by Tōdaiji in Kuwabara required a large investment of both capital and labor. It seems clear that the temple supplied the necessary equipment for these projects. The source of labor for both these undertakings and the later cultivation of reclaimed fields is a matter of some controversy. Since the documents are not explicit concerning the status of the workers on the shōen, there is room for a wide range of interpretation. Some scholars believe that most of the labor was supplied by slaves or corps of workers controlled by Tōdaiji.[20] While this may have been true of shōen located

---

15. Takeuchi Rizō, ed., *Nara ibun* (Tokyo: Tōkyōdō, 1944), 2:690, doc. for Tempyō-Shōhō 7/3/9 (755); and 2:690–93, doc. for Tempyō-Shōhō 7/5/3. Hereafter cited as *NI*.

16. *NI*, 2:690–93, doc. for Tempyo-Shōhō 7/5/3. A *soku* of unhulled rice equals 5 *shō* or .5 *koku* of hulled rice.

17. Ibid.

18. *NI*, 2:696–97, doc. for Tempyō-Hōji 1/11/12 (757).

19. Asakawa, *LSMJ*, pp. 96–108 (English text); pp. 80–97, doc. 91 (Japanese text).

20. E.g., Tōma Seita argues in *Nihon shōenshi* (Tokyo: Kondō Shoten, 1947) that Tōdaiji used slaves on its shōen.

near the main temple itself, the documents for Kuwabara do not indicate the presence of any such category of persons. There is a clear indication that once the land was reclaimed it was rented out on an annual basis. In this case, the renters were kubunden cultivators who held plots in the vicinity, often, no doubt, intermixed with Kuwabara plots. It is probable that these persons were also the source for reclamation labor and construction work as well, although there is reason to believe that additional labor was recruited from neighboring Asuwa *gun*. This was clearly the case in the transportation of buildings purchased there and reassembled at Kuwabara-no-shō.[21]

The management of Kuwabara was handled jointly by laymen sent out from the staff of Tōdaiji and persons appointed from among local men of influence. For the first ten years of its existence, the most important figures were Sone-no-Muraji Otomaro and Ikue-no-Omi Azumabito. The role of Azumabito in the management of the shōen illustrates how local men of influence were able to use their positions to their own economic advantage. Although Azumabito came from a well-to-do provincial family in Echizen, at the time of the establishment of Kuwabara-no-shō he held a low-ranking post in the Tōdaiji Construction Office (ZōTōdaiji-chō).[22] In fact, he was one of the group of officials who selected Kuwabara as the site for a Tōdaiji shōen. It was no accident that the place selected was near his own local base of power. For two or three years after the establishment of the shōen, Azumabito appears to have retained his position in the Tōdaiji Construction Office while at the same time serving as land administrator. In documents concerning the shōen his title is listed as *dairyō* of Asuwa county, suggesting that he also held provincial office.[23]

The specific role played by Azumabito and men like him in the development and administration of the early shōen remains open to debate. In his essay comparing the early shōen with the early manor in Europe, Asakawa Kan'ichi states that for Kuwabara-no-shō and other shōen in Echizen, management at the local level was handled by officials of the local government.[24] It cannot be denied that Azumabito and others like him held offices in the provincial government, usually at the level of county magistrate, and often signed shōen documents using these titles. It seems more logical, however, based on a study of the structure of the Tōdaiji Construction Office and its relationship to both the temple and the government, that these men in most cases held dual roles, working as officials

21. *NI*, 2:690–93, doc. for Tempyō-Shōhō 7/5/3.
22. Hiraoka Jōkai, *Tōdaiji no rekishi* (Tokyo: Shibundō, 1961), p. 43.
23. *Dairyō* is another term for *gunshi*, county magistrate.
24. Asakawa, "The Early Shō and the Early Manor: A Comparative Study," in *LSMJ*, p. 241.

of the county and at the same time working for the Tōdaiji Construction Office. This office maintained a large staff, with numerous officials who specialized in the techniques of land reclamation, surveying, and irrigation.[25] For the most part, such officials were sent out from the construction office headquarters for specific projects and did not reside for long on any one shōen. For ongoing management of a shōen, the construction office drew from within its own staff men who had local connections in the area concerned. Azumabito began his career as a scribe (shijō) in the Tōdaiji Construction Office and accompanied specialists on surveying missions before returning to his native area to administer Kuwabara-no-shō.[26] The question remains as to whether Azumabito obtained his appointment as dairyō because of his connection with the Tōdaiji Construction Office or was chosen by that office because of his eligibility for provincial office. Further research may yield the answer, but the important point here is that the administration of Tōdaiji's early shōen was at first not completely separated from local government administration.

Gradually, administrative personnel patterns were modified so that by 766 more than two-thirds of the persons holding managerial positions were priests of Tōdaiji. By this time Tōdaiji evidently felt that its position as a landholder in Echizen was sufficiently well established to preclude further need of enlisting the help of locally influential persons. It may also have been more profitable to appoint persons with no local roots, especially priests. A third explanation is offered by Kishi Toshio, who argues that the change from lay managers to priests indicated a shift in control of land administration from the Tōdaiji Construction Office to the Tōdaiji Administrative Office (sango).[27] Because the former had close connections with the central government, Kishi also suggests that Kuwabara was managed as if the fields were publicly administered land rather than temple land. His argument, though based on extensive documentation, is highly circumstantial, but it should not be totally disregarded. The Tōdaiji, as the greatest temple in the land, was a semi-governmental institution and as such evidenced no clear distinction between public and private administrative authority. More important, Kishi's argument makes clear that the techniques of shōen management were not a radical departure from established means of land administration.

The early shōen as exemplified by Kuwabara-no-shō developed from land purchased for reclamation. The recruitment of labor for the re-

25. Hiraoka, Tōdaiji no rekishi, pp. 41–42.
26. Ibid., pp. 40–45.
27. Kishi Toshi, Nihon kodai seijishi kenkyū (Tokyo: Hanawa Shobō, 1966), pp. 355–56. The sango consisted of a triumvirate of temple officials, the jōza, the terajū, and the tsuina.

clamation and administration of fields was carried out under the supervision of locally influential persons and technical experts from the Tōdaiji Construction Office. Later, administration was handled by priests sent out from the Tōdaiji. In Kuwabara-no-shō most of the cultivation was done by neighboring kubunden farmers for a rent in kind at a lower rate than the tax on government fields. The corvée duties were also less onerous than those required by the government. As temple land, Kuwabara-no-shō was not liable for the government grain tax, although several documents show that a levy equal to this was collected from the cultivators and sent to Tōdaiji headquarters in Nara. Kuwabara-no-shō thus exemplifies a type of early shōen that in its tax immunities and style of management differed very little from regular temple land (*jiden*). The administration of rent agreements with cultivators also appears to have been quite similar to that applied by provincial officials for such government land as unallotted kubunden. However, from its beginning and increasingly so after 766, it was removed from the administrative authority of the government. The power to administer the affairs of Kuwabara-no-shō lay in the hands of the officials and priests of Tōdaiji.

Ōyama-no-shō in Tamba Province (present-day Hyōgo Prefecture) provides an example of how early shōen were able to gain partial tax immunities early in their development. In 845, Tōji, a temple of the Shingon sect in Kyoto, officially purchased a total of slightly more than 44 cho (about 132 acres) from Fujiwara Yoshifusa.[28] The documents concerning this transaction do not indicate why Tōji chose this particular spot. They tell us only that the land had been purchased for Tōji by a patron of the temple somewhat prior to 845. Since Tōji had supplied the funds, the purchase by proxy was supposed to have been only a formal arrangement. However, the proxy had other ideas, and instead of donating the land to the temple as expected, the proxy began to assert his own proprietorship. In order to protect the temple's interests in Ōyama-no-shō, the chief priest petitioned the central government for recognition of Tōji's rights to the land. The request was supported with an impressive list of pious reasons why the income from the shōen was necessary for Tōji, as well as righteous indignation at the proxy's trickery. In spite of the fact that purchase by proxy was illegal, the temple's request was granted and Ōyama-no-shō was formally established as a *kanshōfu shōen*. This meant that the fields listed in its official register were recognized as immune from taxation and that

28. Documents concerning Ōyama-no-shō are collected in Miyakawa Mitsuru, ed., *Ōyama sonshi*, shiryōhen (Tokyo: Hanawa Shobō, 1964), pp. 1–2, doc. for Jōwa 12/9/10 (845). Hereafter cited as *OSS*. Fujiwara Yoshifusa (804–72) became the first Fujiwara regent to the emperor in 866. At the time of this document, he was a *Sangi* (court councillor) and a member of the Dajōkan.

the cultivators of those fields were not liable for government corvée.

According to the official register of 845, only 9 of the 44 chō had been reclaimed.[29] Unlike Kuwabara-no-shō, land reclamation at Ōyama proceeded slowly and sporadically. In fact, over the next fifty years, land went out of production faster than it was reclaimed.[30] But by 942 the total of land in cultivation had climbed back to almost 13 chō.[31] Why reclamation proceeded so slowly is difficult to determine, but there are several possible explanations. It is conceivable that Tōji was not interested at this time in promoting large projects either because of administrative difficulties or because the additional income derived from these might not have justified the investment of labor and capital. Another possibility is that there was a labor shortage in the Tamba area, so that men were not available for either reclamation work or cultivation once the land was reclaimed. A third possibility is that reclamation was largely futile, since local government officials refused to recognize the tax immunity of the newly opened land.

It is this last possibility that has the most support from documentary evidence. Beginning in the early years of the tenth century, there were repeated disputes over the status of lands in Ōyama-no-shō.[32] At first the disputes centered on the tax liability of newly reclaimed lands, but before long the local governors were claiming authority over the entire shōen. By the middle of the tenth century, Ōyama had in fact, if not in legality, lost its status as a shōen, becoming subject to taxation and control by government officials. At the start of these disputes Tōji attempted to have central government officials intercede on its behalf, but when repeated orders from the central government to the province failed to have any effect, Tōji appears to have let the matter drop. Ōyama-no-shō did gain a new lease on life when its immunities were restored in 1086 in conjunction with the construction of a new pagoda in Kyoto, but this goes beyond the period under consideration here.

The administration of Ōyama differed markedly from that in Kuwabara-no-shō. For the first fifty years or so of Ōyama-no-shō's existence, almost all of the upper ranks of the administrators (the *bettō* and *sentō*) were priests of Tōji. Priests tended to predominate also at the *tato* (land master) level, which seems rather unusual since *tato* were normally engaged in cultivation even as they supervised others.[33] That Tōji should have used

29. *OSS*, pp. 1–2, doc. for Jōwa 12/9/10.

30. *OSS*, pp. 3–4, docs. for Jōwa 12/9/10, Engi 15/9/11 (914) and Engi 15/10/22.

31. *OSS*, p. 7, doc. for Tengyō 5/4/25 (942).

32. *OSS*, p. 4, doc. for Engi 20/9/11 (919).

33. The tato is another controversial figure in early Japanese history. Some authors see the tato as identical with the *myōshu* while others see it as a distinct category. See

priests at this level may be another indication of Tamba's labor shortage. At any rate, the first layman to appear at the upper administrative level (in 938) was a dairyō of the county in which Ōyama-no-shō was located.[34] From this time on local men play an increasingly important role as shōen administrators. This was doubtless a reflection of Tōji's disputes with provincial officials and its loss of enthusiasm for running the affairs of Ōyama-no-shō.

Ōyama-no-shō, as a *kanshōfu shōen*, betrays clearly visible differences from Kuwabara-no-shō. Ōyama, at least on paper, had full immunity from tax liability based on recognition by the central government of its status as an immune shōen. This is an advance over Kuwabara-no-shō, which depended for its immunity on its classification as temple land. We know much less of the actual administration of Ōyama than we do of Kuwabara, but it is clear that in the initial stages Tōji, unlike Tōdaiji, relied mainly on its own priests dispatched to the shōen.

At least part of the difference between the two shōen can be attributed to the fact that Ōyama was established as a shōen almost one hundred years later than Kuwabara. During the course of this century, not only had the number of shōen increased, but such holdings had begun to receive recognition from the imperial government through the granting of *kanshōfu*.

Just as all reclaimed land did not become shōen, all early shōen did not have their origins in reclaimed land. Some, for instance, were formed around forest lands that might have been granted to a temple or shrine in order to supply lumber for construction.[35] Grants of this sort were ordinarily given for specific terms to cover specific projects and were not intended to become the basis for the assertion of long-term possession. But proprietary rights, once asserted, were difficult to revoke. Lands granted for the specific exploitation of one resource were often retained and used for other purposes. The creation of shōen in which forest lands served as nuclei was a slow process. Forested terrain was difficult to convert into arable fields, whether dry or paddy. Early shōen originating from forest lands were probably valued for their timber resources and beyond that as base areas from which shōen developers could extend their holdings by encroachment or purchase of nearby cultivable lands.

With these few examples of the way in which early *shōen* developed, it

Toda Yoshimi, *Nihon ryōshusei seiritsushi no kenkyū* (Tokyo: Iwanami, 1968), pp. 184–87, and Kuroda Toshio, *Shōen sei shakai*, *Taikei Nihon rekishi* (Tokyo: Nihon Hyōronsha, 1970), 2:8–34 and 67–70.

34. Miyakawa Mitsuru, ed., *Ōyama sonshi*, honbun hen (Tokyo: Hanawa Shobō, 1964), pp. 73–76.

35. For a discussion of two timberlands that became shōen, see Ishimoda Shō, *Chūseiteki sekai no kōzō* (Tokyo: Itō Shoten, 1946), pp. 1–44.

is apparent that the shōen was not yet fully established as a distinct institution for proprietary control of the land during the eighth and ninth centuries. In the case of Kuwabara-no-shō, its administration was similar to that of temple land, and what fiscal immunity it had depended squarely on that classification. Ōyama-no-shō, by possessing a *kanshōfu*, was officially recognized as a shōen but nevertheless had to struggle constantly against encroachments by local government officials.

From the early tenth century, however, the extension of proprietary rights at the local level gave rise to a new sort of landholding in which the landholder extended his control in dominial fashion over both land and cultivators. This kind of landholding was developed by local notables who had served as provincial officials under the ritsu-ryō system but could often trace their original occupancy of their lands back to special grants received after the Taika reforms. Other local notables may have emigrated from the capital, taking provincial administrative posts in hopes of improving their fortunes. Many such figures accumulated the lands of cultivators who had defaulted on repayments of loan rice.[36] In both instances, these local figures used the power and prestige of their offices to extend their landholdings, either through confiscation or by reclamation. Most important, however, their lands were held as "private lands" (*ryō*) over which they were recognized as proprietors or "lords" (*ryōshu*). This meant that the ryōshu possessed all fiscal and administrative power with regard to his lands. He was free to manage the cultivators on his lands as he saw fit and to collect revenue from them. Thus, the ryōshu took over many of the administrative functions of the government.

The small local proprietors generally held positions of some power and authority in their areas since most of them were provincial or county officials of some sort; on the other hand they were in frequent conflict with the higher officials of the provincial government. These disputes were not focused on tax immunity, as in the case of conflicts between the shōen and provincial officials, but centered on the ryōshu's assertion of fiscal authority over the cultivators. Faced with recurring disagreements with provincial authorities, ryōshu sought means of protecting their interests against government interference. The most common way of securing such protection became the practice of borrowing prestige from court nobles or powerful religious institutions. To do this, ryōshu commended their rights of ownership to some powerful figure or institution at the capital in return for political influence in securing protection. The practice of commendation of this sort marked the beginning of a new set of tenurial relationships on the land, for it resulted in the creation of a proprietary institution much

36. Toda, *Nihon ryōshusei*, pp. 116–65.

more complex than the early shōen and one that came to form the basis of what is generally thought of as the "shōen system."

To understand the structure of the late Heian conglomerate shōen we need to establish a general model. Taken in abstract form, the commendation-type shōen consisted of a hierarchy of tenures beginning at the bottom with the cultivators (*shōmin*), then the managers (*ryōshu, shōke,* or *shōkan*), and finally the *ryōke* and *honke* at the top. The ryōshu, as the person responsible for commending his proprietary holding, occupied the pivotal place in the relationships of the shōen hierarchy. In commending the title to his lands to a powerful court noble or religious institution, the ryōshu in fact lost very little in terms of actual income, though he gave up the status of "lord" to a superior authority. Although his status was usually changed to that of "manager" or "custodian" (*shōke* or *shōkan*), his function in the shōen remained essentially the same. The terms of the commendation, in other words, generally left the powers of local administration in the shōke's hands. Along with this went specific rights to the shōen's income. The court noble, known as the *ryōke,* to whom nominal possession of the land had been commended, received in fact only a right to a specified portion of the total domain income. In return the ryōke was to use his power to attain and protect the immunities of the shōen.

In the event that the ryōke found that he needed added prestige to further the interests of the shōen, he commended a portion of his rights to an even more influential courtier or religious institution, who was then referred to as *honke* (often translated as "guarantor"). As a rule, the honke took little active part in the affairs of the shōen, acting mainly as a name to lend prestige to the shōen's claims. At the upper levels of the shōen structure, both the ryōke and the honke received designated shares of the income from the shōen.

Matters regarding the transmission, receipt, and distribution of income from the shōen were handled by the shōke's *mandokoro* (administrative office), which communicated directly with the managerial office of the shōen (*honjo*). When the honjo was located on the shōen, the original ryōshu or his descendants, as shōke, were responsible for the day-to-day affairs of the shōen. These included assignment of fields to cultivators, distribution of seed and implements, regulation of water supply, collection of revenues, and, if full immunity had been obtained, administration of justice. As one of the chief officials of the honjo of the shōen, the shōke was responsible for forwarding revenues to superior proprietors.

When the honjo of the shōen was in the capital, the shōke acted as agent of the absentee proprietor, working primarily as an overseer rather than as an administrator. In some cases, special agents were dispatched from the capital to serve as officials of the shōen.

Within the context of our model the cultivators' function was to till the fields to produce crops and goods that formed the basis of shōen revenue. The question of the status of the cultivators and the degree of control the shōke had over them is one that is hotly debated by Japanese historians.[37] While it is not possible to discuss this issue in detail, it seems clear that the status of the cultivators depended to a large degree on the conditions under which they became members of the shōen. If they entered as absconding kubunden cultivators hired for reclamation work and retained as cultivators, they were, at least initially, highly dependent on the shōke. On the other hand, if they became part of the shōen by commending their own small, independent landholdings, they retained a great deal of autonomy, often being left with the right to manage their own holdings. Thus the late Heian conglomerate shōen consisted of a complex series of private agreements among these several levels of tenure over the land, and between private proprietors and the government.

As the late Heian shōen system matured, the critical practice that distinguished such holdings became the acquisition of complete immunity from taxation and entry by government officials. In the early stages of shōen growth, immunity had been limited to taxation. As was noted above, such immunities were granted through the issuance of a charter (*kanshōfu*), which listed the borders of the shōen, its area, and the area of the fields being cultivated. The winning, and protection, of such immunities had been one of the main incentives for small local ryōshu to commend their land to higher authority. The tax immunities gained at first applied only to those fields listed as cultivated in the charter and could not be extended to newly reclaimed fields within the shōen's borders. To gain immunity for new fields inside or outside the borders of the shōen required further petition by the ryōke to the central government. As time passed, new fields within the shōen could have their immunity approved by provincial, or even county officials. Immunities obtained in this way were only slightly less secure than those from the central government. The ryōke's role, therefore, did not end with the shōen's receipt of a kanshōfu, for conflict over immunities between shōen administrators and officials of the provincial government were endemic. It was frequently necessary for the ryōke to intervene at court on behalf of the shōen.[38]

A shōen's immunity was not complete, therefore, until it was free from

---

37. See Tōma, *Nihon shōenshi*, and Ishimoda, *Chūseiteki sekai no kōzō*, for discussion of the cultivators as "slaves." Kuroda views the cultivators as more independent.

38. That provincial officials repeatedly tried to collect taxes from immune lands is documented by the number of orders from the government forbidding them to do so. E.g., Ōyama-no-shō struggled against incursions by provincial tax collectors for years after the issuance of a kanshōfu in 845. *Ōyama sonshi*, honbun hen, pp. 75–77.

entry by government officials. Such freedom was acquired slowly and was not widespread until the beginning of the eleventh century.[39] Security from entry applied at first only to government surveyors and tax collectors, but it was later extended to the police. When this happened, the administrators of the shōen had gained full power of jurisdiction over both the land and the people cultivating it. They had become the true successors to provincial government in the territories that comprised their shōen.

The great strength of the shōen system of landholding was its flexibility, and it is this factor that accounted for its longevity as a functioning institution. Although the basic hierarchy of shōen land rights took the form of the shōmin–shōke–ryōke–honke pyramid, there was room for a good deal of variation within that form. Above all, it was possible for changes to take place at one level without substantially affecting other levels. For example, the honke or ryōke could change with little effect on the everyday affairs of the shōen. The reason for this was that the shōen system, as a means of economic profit from the land, was based not on direct pro-prietary control of land but rather on income from land. Total income, as defined by the goods and services provided by the cultivators, was con-ceived of as subject to allotment (or sharing) according to the relationship of each level in the shōen tenure hierarchy. These shares were defined for each shōen in terms of *shiki*, which specified the share (or amount) of revenue due each rank in the shōen hierarchy. There were, in other words, shōmin-shiki, shōke-shiki, ryōke-shiki, and so forth. Since shiki were alienable and divisible, it was possible for the income of the shōen to be widely distributed. Shiki could change hands through sale, inheritance, or donation without disturbing the function of the shōen as an economic unit.

The shōen's flexibility extended to the local level as well. It was able to absorb changes in the types of cultivator's tenure and changes in admin-istration by the shōke without altering the amount of income due the central proprietor. Thus the tendency was for higher proprietors to take little interest in how their shōen were administered at the lower levels as long as they received the agreed-upon income. At the other end, the cultivators and the shōke cared little who the higher proprietors were as long as they provided legal protection and did not make excessive demands for income.

The mature shōen proved to be an extremely successful means of secur-ing a balance between the demands of a ruling class for income, and the

---

39. E.g., Ōyama-no-shō became a kanshōfu shōen with tax immunity in 845, but did not attain immunity from entry by officials until 1042.

demands of the populace for a stable means of livelihood. As an economic system, the shōen offered advantages to all of its constituents. For the nobles and religious institutions at the ryōke and honke levels, the shōen offered a secure source of income whether or not there was an operative central government. For the local landholding class, the shōen provided revenue and a local power base that they could use to extend their influence both economically and militarily. The cultivators benefited from increased security of tenure and a less arbitrary system of taxation.

5 Estate and Property in the Late Heian Period

CORNELIUS J. KILEY

The Heian period was characterized by a gradual process of political decentralization. The government in the imperial capital slowly lost its hold over two crucial human resources, productive agricultural labor and coercive military force. By "government," however, is meant the official bureaucratic structure. The nobility in the late Heian period actually had a dual role—as participants in the official government and as private landowners. The government lost a great deal of authority; the nobility, as a class, lost somewhat less. By the tenth century tax-immune landholdings and quasi-autonomous military bands were important elements in the politics of every regional area. It was during this time, moreover, that the nobility in the capital finally abandoned ideological commitment to the authority-intensive administrative system of the earlier imperial regime, and, ceasing all real attempts to eradicate local autonomy, commenced to legitimize it in the emperor's name.[1]

Changes in the structure of local administration were accompanied by changes in the structure of the imperial court. Of these latter, the most remarkable was the institution of a permanent regency. In a very real sense, the imperial ruler was consigned to a state of perpetual minority. The exclusive claim of the dynasty to the throne, however, remained unquestioned, and the authority of the regents was founded in their ineligibility to seize the throne for themselves; their function was to provide the titular rulers with heir-producing consorts. This regency was monopolized by a single lineage, a branch of the northern Fujiwara, and became one of its special prerogatives.[2]

This arrangement is particularly noteworthy here because it embodied one of the most basic principles of the late Heian regime. The title to

---

1. Nakada Kaoru, "Nihon shōen no keitō," in *Hōseishi ronshū* (Tokyo, 1938), 2:19–69; Takeuchi Rizō, "Fujiwara seiken to shōen," in *Ritsuryōsei to kizoku seiken* (Tokyo, 1958), 2:371–91.

2. Takeuchi, "Sesshō kampaku," in *Ritsuryōsei to kizoku seiken*, 2:330–42.

authority and the power to administer it were permanently separated and kept within distinct lines of succession. This was a typical feature of land ownership in the eleventh and twelfth centuries, when ownership and possession were separated on many levels. A lord, or *ryōke*, belonging to the capital nobility might be represented on his holdings by a custodian, often called *azukari dokoro,* who held all administrative powers and whose office often amounted to a perpetual, irrevocable, hereditary agency. Estates administered in this manner, generally known as *shōen*, were a typical form of divided and shared authority.

One important similarity between the Fujiwara regency and the various land custodianships lies in the status relationships on which they were each based. The Fujiwara, although related maternally to the dynastic rulers, were of a totally distinct status. Their regency was therefore quite different from one that might be conducted by a person himself eligible for the throne. It is because the Fujiwara lacked any real parity of status with the dynasty that their regency could, beginning in the late tenth century, become a permanent standing institution. Disparity of status permitted the exercise of complementary functions. The Fujiwara could thus enjoy an "interest" in the dynasty that was unavailable to truly royal personages. They possessed what the dynastic group "owned."

The typical azukari dokoro of shōen land was a locally based aristocrat, completely ineligible for the noble status enjoyed by a capital ryōke. Ownership by such a lord meant that the holding could enjoy a considerable degree of fiscal immunity, which worked to the advantage of all who had an interest in it. As the dynasty legitimized the power of the regents, the lord legitimated the authority of the local custodian. In this arrangement, disparity of status was crucial. The lord and the custodian functioned cooperatively because neither could fundamentally challenge the other's prerogatives.[3]

Consociation between persons of disparate status was a cardinal feature of the political system. Political activity during these times was strongly marked by segmentary factionalism. In the twelfth century, factional strife resulted in armed outbreaks in the capital itself. The first of these battles, the so-called Hōgen Disturbance of 1156, involved two opposed factions, each of which included members of the imperial family, the Fujiwara regent's house, and the provincial warrior aristocracy. The uprising was determinative of succession to the imperial throne, the Fujiwara regency, and the leadership of a major warrior league. Each

3. On the question of regency, see Jack Goody, *Succession to High Office* (Cambridge, England, 1966), pp. 1–56. Class disparity as an element in factionalism is discussed in Ralph W. Nicholas, "Segmentary Factional Political Systems," in *Political Anthropology,* Marc J. Swartz et al. (Chicago, 1966), pp. 45–59.

faction was represented by members of three distinct strata, who were competing with their opposite numbers on the opposing side. One of the victors, the warrior Minamoto Yoshitomo (1123–60), had drawn away much of his estranged father's military following. His father was on the losing side and was summarily executed with Yoshitomo's acquiescence.

Factional loyalties, as illustrated above, could override family ties, particularly where issues of royal succession were involved. Yoshitomo could rationalize his unfilial conduct in terms of a loyalty relationship to the throne.[4] Alliance with royal figures who were successful in vindicating their claims on the throne justified aggression, even when directed against one's own kindred. This relationship may be compared with the tenurial bond between lord and custodian that permitted the latter to ignore the demands of provincial taxing authorities, who represented the "government."

The key positions at court were objects of fierce competition among the eligible nobles, who sought allies in the imperial house above and the provincial aristocracy below. Warrior groups could ally themselves with noble factions, which, if successful, could reward their members with official titles and immunities. Within the stratified framework of this relationship, a local warrior could bargain with a capital noble on equal terms. The social disparity therefore contributed to the solidarity of factions. Each party could aid the other to obtain a reward for which he himself was ineligible.

The relationship between ryōke and azukari dokoro involved similar elements of reciprocity and parity. In one respect, both lords and custodians were equal. The estate powers of both were equally *shiki*, a term which originally meant "office" but had come to mean any legally cognizable interest in real estate *which was the result of a private transaction* between persons of sufficiently high status. All shiki involved specific rights and duties respecting the estate. These were proprietary in nature; the relationship between lord and custodian was not a personal one, and the bond between them was not merely contractual. It resulted from the terms of the shiki they held but may not themselves have created. Both were equal in that they held cognizable interests in the same land. Shiki were regarded as titles to exploit land and not as contractual rights.[5]

The element of reciprocity is most apparent in the case of the lord's

4. Jien, *Gukanshō*, Tomimoto Ichinosuke et al., eds., *Nihon koten bungaku taikei* 94 (Tokyo, 1967), pp. 177–224. Jien paints a perhaps exaggerated picture of Yoshitomo's delight at his first opportunity to fight under imperial sanction.

5. Nakada, "Ōchō jidai no shōen ni kansuru kenkyū," in *Hōseishi ronshū*, 2:177–295, 187–96; Kuroda Toshio, "Shōensei no kihonteki seikaku to ryōshusei," in *Chūsei shakai no kihon kōzō*, Hayashiya Tatsusaburō et al., ed. (Tokyo, 1958), pp. 3–42.

shiki, which imposed upon him the duty of maintaining immunity for the holding. Only highly placed nobles could do this, so that the shiki was in fact available only to members of a restricted circle, unless it was further divided so as to preserve some interest within the noble circle. The system helped to preserve a certain minimum wealth for the nobles. At the same time, local custodians, who had the advantage of proximity to the land and its cultivators, could profit greatly from tax immunity.

There was, of course, a fundamental difference between holding shiki in the same land and membership in the same faction. Factional relationships were personal, not proprietary. Factions were also temporary, since too great a degree of success or failure would result in their immediate disintegration. A victorious faction would inevitably bifurcate when conflict over the resources won recommenced in the following generation. Shōen tenures, however, could endure for generations, although they might themselves be the objects of factional conflict. Factional ties were strictly "political," but, in the terminology adopted here, they lacked any "estate" relationship. For the purposes of this discussion, the term "estate" will be defined in accordance with the criteria established by Radcliffe-Brown:

> [A] collection of rights (whether over persons or things) with the implied duties, the unity of which is constituted either by the fact that they are the rights of a single person and can be transmitted, as a whole, or in division, to some other person or persons, or that they are the rights of a defined group (the corporation) which maintains a continuity of possession.[6]

Membership in a segmentary political faction would not form part of a person's estate as defined here. Shiki, however, were quite clearly estate rights.

As here defined, the term "estate" embraces more than property in the usual sense. Status as a noble or eligibility to become regent were also estate rights, and both involved relationships between individual holders and corporate groups such as the northern Fujiwara lineage. The corporate nature of lineage groups is well illustrated by the royal dynasty in the twelfth century, when broad powers were exercised by the senior retired emperor acting as lineage head, while the royal title itself normally reposed in a minor son or grandson. Here was another sort of bifurcation between ownership and possession. The senior member of the dynastic group "possessed" powers which the dynasty itself "owned," and in which every eligible member had a contingent interest. Similarly, heads of the Fujiwara main line could manipulate juvenile regents, thereby insulating themselves from rivals within their own group. Competition between royal and

---

6. A. R. Radcliffe-Brown, "Patrilineal and Matrilineal Succession," in *Structure and Function in Primitive Society* (New York, 1965), pp. 32–48, esp. p. 34.

Fujiwara corporate lineages became acute in the twelfth century and was a major cause of the Hōgen Disturbance. Imperial and Fujiwara house heads, who "possessed" the prerogatives of their lineages without being restrained by official protocol, were chronically at odds. In addition, each group was factionally divided, making participation by outsiders almost inevitable.[7]

Leadership of warrior groups was another sort of estate right, although the formal legal system gave it very little cognizance. These groups were of a distinctly clannish nature, all members being regarded as junior kinsmen or clients of the chief.[8] The chieftainship of such a group was quite like the lineage headship of the imperial or Fujiwara families. This was the prize that Minamoto Yoshitomo won from his father in the Hōgen Disturbance. Such a headship, being indivisible, was a scarce and unique resource, and competition among eligible candidates was therefore dynastic in character. This greatly stimulated the formation of factions that cut across these corporate groups; each candidate tended to look for support from similarly placed members of other groups.

There were therefore two major kinds of estate interest for which members of the ruling classes could compete. One of these was strictly proprietary, consisting chiefly of interests in land that could be privately created and privately conveyed. The second type was nonproprietary and included membership in the high courtier class and various sorts of lineage chieftainships, from the post of senior retired emperor on down to that of head of a local branch lineage. Such interests, unlike property, could not be passed on at the discretion of the current holder, although he could try, through marriage or adoption, to put his candidate into a favorable position. Such chieftainships were, as remarked earlier, not clearly divisible and were often the prize of the successful aggressor.[9]

Although lineage headships were necessarily unitary, so that the same person could not hold more than one chieftainship, the same was not true of property in land. One person could hold a varied portfolio of shiki. Property interests held by capital nobles tended to be distributed evenly among the owner's surviving dependents, who might include younger brothers and sisters, children and sons-in-law. This system of equal division probably reduced the tendency toward competition that already existed. Failure to acquire a chieftainship or to succeed to noble status did not mean that all was lost. During the twelfth century such devices were employed in the imperial family itself, when powerful princes who were

7. Takeuchi, "Uji no chōja," in *Ritsuryōsei to kizoku seiken*, 2:343-70.

8. Yasuda Motohisa, "Kodai makki ni okeru Kantō bushidan," in *Nihon hōkensei seiritsu no shozentei* (Tokyo, 1961), pp. 1-113.

9. Ishii Ryōsuke, *Chōshi sōzokusei* (Tokyo, 1950), pp. 59-86.

to be put aside were given extremely rich temple superintendencies that allowed them to reproduce, on a slightly smaller scale, the court of the senior cloistered emperors.

Among the nobility, the distribution of shōen interests could avert an immediate rupture of the family group by factional conflict. Proprietary and nonproprietary interests could thus balance one another. Grants of interests in land could sweeten loss of authority in capital politics.

The twelfth-century legal system tacitly acknowledged this balance in its rule that property, once voluntarily given away, could never be taken back, no matter what the relationship between the parties might be.[10] Factional segmentation in the political sphere seems to have encouraged the growth of a strong property institution. This development was related to the weakness of the state structure *as an avenue of reward distribution.* In the economic and military fields, the state commanded very small resources, but it nevertheless retained its legitimacy as the framework within which competition for vital assets could take place. In this respect, the late Heian state might be called a "judicial" rather than an "administrative" organization.

The judicial chareacter of the state was one facet of the estatist character of society in the late Heian period. It must immediately be added, however, that this state was not completely devoid of coercive or administrative authority. It did possess an extreme tolerance for autonomous groups that would have been totally unthinkable in the more classic Chinese empires, and this tolerance made outright rebellion against it quite unlikely. Such incidents as the Hōgen Disturbance, however, served to strengthen the real power of the government in Kyoto, while weakening the traditional nobility. The seizure of the central organs by members of the military class meant that Kyoto could bring more pressure to bear on the local areas, and its tolerance of immunities lessened considerably.

Despite its possession of a modicum of administrative and coercive power, the central government in the late Heian period had always to rely chiefly on its monopoly of judicial and prestige-distribution functions. The same was true of the administration of shōen. Capital temples and individual nobles were able at times to exert very strong control over certain of their privately held estates, particularly those near the capital. In other cases, their real authority was severely limited. The distinction between judicial and administrative power should here be viewed as involving differences of degree as well as of kind. There were varying degrees of autonomy that local residents of shōen could enjoy.

10. Sakanoue Akikane, *Hossō shiyō shō, maki* 2, art. 41, *Shinkō Gunsho ruijū* (Tokyo, 1931), 4:193.

Though the direct control individual nobles could exercise was slight, ultimate authority over land resources continued to be centered in the capital. The paramount tenures of the richest estates continued to reside in the nobility, which remained the ultimate source of legitimacy for the property system. The continued importance of the nobility in this sphere may be largely explained by the prevalance of a sort of commendation arrangement that I call "endowment," or *kishin*, to be discussed shortly.

Like the ruling elite in the capital, the provincial aristocracy operated within both public and private spheres. They monopolized certain key positions in the provincial administration, while privately they might be landholders in their own right or custodians of land nominally the property of others. The head of the provincial government, however, was usually an outsider appointed from the capital to collect government revenues. Such officials, called *zuryō*, were in fact tax farmers with a direct interest in the amount of revenue collected. Their administrative powers were not always clearly defined, but they were not permitted to encroach on shōen whose immunities were clear. Zuryō were likely to come into conflict with local aristocrats, both in their role as landholders and their role as public officials. In 1136, for example, a zuryō in the province of Shimōsa, attacked and dispossessed the Chiba family, a very powerful group in that area. The central government, represented by such zuryō, could sometimes make its authority felt in a very dramatic way.[11]

The Kyoto government's power to extract revenues from nonimmune areas was thus an integral feature of the entire structure. In distributing these revenues among its members, the imperial court acted as a corporate body. During the late eleventh and early twelfth centuries the head of the imperial lineage, usually a retired emperor, presided over the court as a whole, although the Fujiwara regency line never completely acknowledged their authority. It was the retired emperor, however, who controlled the zuryō class from above. The court therefore had a certain interest in preventing the proliferation of immune territories, as did the zuryō.[12]

Courtiers, however, had in their individual capacities an interest in conferring immunity on, and thereby acquiring an interest in, additional lands. As remarked above, status as a high court noble was restricted, and downwardly mobile children had to be provided for. Also, promotion

11. Murai Yasuhiko, "Kugeryō shōen no keisei," in *Kodai kokka kaitai no kenkyū* (Tokyo, 1963), pp. 373–402, esp. p. 388.
12. Estimates differ widely as to the amount of arable land that had acquired immunity by the late twelfth century. Maki Kenji believes that it reached about 90 percent of the total, while a more recent estimate by Murai Yasuhiko places it well below 50 percent. Maki Kenji, *Nihon hōken seido seiritsu shi* (Tokyo, 1933), pp. 177–79; Murai, "Shōen to kisakujin," in *Chūsei shakai no kihon kōzō*, Hayashiya et al., pp. 43–80, esp. pp. 46–47.

within the court itself was to some degree a matter of purchase. Finally, noble status demanded continued conspicuous consumption. Local landholders were willing, on certain conditions, to present individual nobles with "endowments," in other words, income-producing interests in land. The arrangement made often resulted in a lord–custodian relationship in which the original owner became an azukari dokoro and the noble a ryōke, or lord. Most local authority would be retained by the "endowing" aristocrat, and the land would become immune, on the theory that it was the capital noble's shōen. In 1119, for example, Fujiwara no Tadazane (1078–1162), the current head of the regency line and himself a former regent, proposed to "establish" a very large (more than twenty-five square miles) immune territory in the remote northeast, where actual court administrative authority was virtually nonexistent. When reprimanded by the emperor Toba (1103–56), Tadazane replied that these lands had been pledged to him by their original holders, that this was a strictly private arrangement, and that in any case the holdings of his family had to be strengthened.[13]

Within each province, there existed immune lands, partially immune lands, and totally nonimmune lands. Perfect immunity meant freedom from all economic and administrative control by the provincial officials, who were barred from entering the area. Many immunities, however, were less than perfect, and many were of uncertain legality. Disputes between local holders and government representatives were a chronic feature of the system, and such disputes were frequently settled locally, without reference to the capital. De facto immunity was enjoyed by many local owners, or *ryōshu*, and their privileges were frequently given official certification by local governors. The taxing function of the zuryō could be exercised only with cooperation from the local aristocracy, and here too there were factional cleavages.

Within each province, nonimmune lands were termed *kokugaryō*, provincial domains, which were distinct from the immune shōen, and from which local hereditary "officials" could also derive incomes. The Chiba, mentioned earlier, were officials of this sort, although they also figured as officials of shōen. Local struggles involved fiscal–administrative powers over land and cultivators, and distinctions between public and private domains provided the legal framework for the rationalization, and possible peaceful resolution, of such struggles. Although it was in the immediate interest of the zuryō to disallow claims of immunity wherever possible, he could not always do so. The zuryō, who operated on a special administrative level between the capital nobility and the local aristocracy,

13. Fujiwara Munetada, *Chūyūki*, 1119/3/26, *Shiryō taisei* 12, p. 120.

was unable to represent either side unequivocally. He too was in need of continual support from above, and this meant that he might be inclined to act as an intermediary in the negotiations between individual nobles and local holders leading to kishin and the creation of further immunities. On the other hand, if the lord of a putatively immune domain were lacking in the requisite influence, he might feel free to disallow the immunity.

It is for this reason that property relationships and factional relationships resembled one another so closely. The zuryō, although his power was chiefly administrative, exercised a large amount of purely judicial power, expressed in the recognition or nonrecognition of immunities. As in the court above, the rights and privileges of provincial notables were in a process of continual readjustment. From the late eleventh century onward, the court of the retired emperors, known as *In-no-chō*, became the forum of last resort in these disputes, as the retired sovereigns acquired the paramount authority to make zuryō appointments. Such appointments depended upon the candidate's ability to purchase favor, just as the purchase of immunity for a landholding did. Members of the high nobility were disqualified by their position for appointments as zuryō. In their efforts to dominate the court, the retired sovereigns actively promoted zuryō interests.

This growing importance of the zuryō system to the interests of the imperial house helps to explain the issuance of the famous edict of 1069, which set rather severe limitations on shōen formation. All shōen established after 1045 were declared invalid, as were all shōen that lacked clear documentation and all those that "impeded" the conduct of the provincial administration, in other words, the administration of the zuryō. In this edict, the basic rules for the exercise of the zuryō's judicial functions were set forth, and they were rapidly elaborated in a legalistic way. It was ruled in 1073, for example, that where immunity had been acknowledged by generation after generation of provincial governors, explicit documentation was not required. Again, land found as a matter of fact to be "within the precincts" of an immune local shrine required no further documentation. The zuryō was thus given a wide area of administrative discretion, and the whole system seems to have been directed toward identifying those claims to immunity that a zuryō might reasonably acknowledge. In this way, the imperial court backed up the zuryō's authority, while not upsetting well-established shōen.[14]

Shōen-limiting edicts were issued repeatedly after this, and all seem to have been directed at supporting the zuryō and the court (in its governmental function) by preventing shōen from exceeding the desirable maxi-

14. Murai, "Kugeryō shōen no keisei," pp. 384-90.

mum. None of these edicts, however, completely stopped new shōen from being established, and none was intended to do so. Retired emperors were themselves quite active in promoting the establishment of immune lands for their wives, protégés, and residential temples. The edicts strengthened the hand of the retired emperors in controlling the direction in which commendations would be made rather than in abolishing the practice altogether. Zuryō were active participants in this process and often functioned as intermediaries in kishin arrangements. The zuryō were required to make substantial contributions to the retired sovereigns' establishments in order to maintain their positions, and making new lands available for their (indirect) utilization was one way of advancing their careers.

The result of these trends was the movement of power into the hands of the zuryō and their patron, the retired emperor. The position of other courtiers, in particular the Fujiwara, was weakened. This meant that although the court as a whole was probably strengthened vis-à-vis the local aristocracy, the preexisting nobility was being displaced by zuryō in positions of real influence. In a sense, zuryō of provincial origin were beginning to "overthrow" the traditionally privileged courtiers.

The element of segmental factionalism cannot alone explain the rise of the zuryō class. The zuryō was, in large part, the representative of the local gentry vis-à-vis the capital, and his military prowess made him a formidable protector. The position of zuryō was a competitive one; the most successful tax-gatherers were in the best position to make large contributions to the court of the retired emperor, and they had to be rewarded with appointments to more and richer provinces.[15] Within the court, the ceremonially qualified courtiers were being threatened by zuryō power, and in that respect, the court was in decline. On the other hand, the court, viewed as a corporate body in control of the various provinces, was accumulating power. The retired emperor's organization was not merely a "faction." It had, particularly in its later stages, a distinct policy, which favored the consolidation of local resources within a single hierarchy, to the detriment of the Fujiwara and others. In this respect, it was not simply a faction, but a party, with implications for fundamental organizational change.

The shōen, a dominial complex that could embrace a multiplicity of shiki, was an important means of consociation in an age of conflict. It should perhaps best be regarded as another sort of "corporation" in the

---

15. Abe Takeshi, *Ritsuryō kokka kaitai katei no kenkyū* (Tokyo, 1966), pp. 560–94; Takeuchi, "In-no-chō seiken to ensho," *Ritsuryōsei to kizoku seiken* 2:392–419; Kawakami Tasuke, *Nihon kodai shakai shi no kenkyū* (Tokyo, 1947), pp. 333–66.

sense suggested by Radcliffe-Brown in the passage qu〔
thing "owned" by this corporation was the actual land o〔 〔〔.〔
shiki holder had a sort of possessory right, in that he could actively exploit the land in some way. These rights, however, were not necessarily
precarious and could be both hereditary and fully alienable. As in other
corporate groups, there was considerable potential for conflict, particularly in the exercise of rights against the land.

The term "shōen," which had been introduced from China at some time
prior to the eighth century, originally meant any landholding, whether
agricultural or residential, that was not a part of the owner's principal
residence. Shōen were the holdings of absentee owners. The term appears
frequently in eighth-century materials but never as the name of a legal or
administrative unit. It was not until late in the ninth century that this word
began to take on technical administrative significance, and it was not a
regularly employed term until several decades after that.

As the word "shōen" began to be the regular designation for a unit of
immune lands, the word "shiki" became the term for a recognized interest
in shōen lands. It had originally been applied to the deputies of the owning
noble or temple, whose duty it was to manage cultivation, keep records,
etc. By the eleventh century, these "shōen officials" had become subordinate landholders within the shōen. The cultivation rights that had
originally been given to them as compensation for their services became a
species of property. A shiki that had remained in the same line for three or
four generations was a species of property vis-à-vis the "owner," who
could not, except for serious cause, dismiss his agent.

The terms "shōen" and "shiki" had by the eleventh century become
clearly associated with the concept of immunity, and contrasted, to some
degree at least, with the administration of "provincial domains." These
terms, however, signified more than simple immunity. A shiki was a constituent unit of a shōen, considered as a corporate unit. Legal recognition
of this corporateness was quite as important as recognition of immunity.
In a very real sense, the two were one and the same: immunity was what
stigmatized the holding as a fully autonomous corporate entity.

Another concept central to the new system was that of the "ryōshu"
(lord). This term was usually applied to provincial landholders and never
to the capital nobility, who were, on account of their status, called "ryōke"
instead. A ryōke, however, was merely a noble ryōshu. Ryōshu, during
the early Heian period, was used in contrast to *jishu* (landowner) in such
a way as to indicate that the rights of a ryōshu were more extensive than
that of a jishu. The difference was that a jishu merely had power to exploit land economically by cultivating it; a ryōshu had other powers, of a
clearly "administrative" nature. He "occupied" a territory, and could

exercise discretionary control over a wide range of activities within it.[16]

These terms appeared in a context of administrative law that consciously deprecated property so as to enhance the prestige of bureaucratic office. When, in the tenth century, the term "ryōshu" began to appear, it indicated that the older distinctions between property and political authority were breaking down, since formerly only representatives of the bureaucratic state had been allowed to "administer" territories, control vacant lands, or manage irrigation facilities. A ryōshu was a landholder whose powers included what formerly had been prerogatives of the state. These were normally such powers as the allocation of plots to the cultivators, the collection of revenues from them, and the general supervision of agricultural work. Like the term "shōen", the word "ryōshu" was originally a nontechnical term and lacked any particular legal consequences. In the tenth century, to be a ryōshu was neither legal nor illegal. During these times a ryōshu was not necessarily the outright "owner" of the lands he managed; sometimes managers of temple lands were so called, if the power they wielded was sufficiently extensive. In fact, an organization such as a temple could not, because of its collective nature, be a ryōshu or have a shiki in the early Heian period. Only individuals could perform the functions implied by these terms.

By the mid-eleventh century the term "ryōshu" began to take on a different, more precise meaning for the administrative system. The term was used to rationalize shōen corporateness. All shōen holdings came to be traced to an "original ryōshu" from whom all the various shiki holders had ultimately derived their rights. The original ryōshu was to the shōen what the founding ancestor was to the clan. In the development of this concept, heavy reliance was placed on an ordinance of 743, which had ruled that land opened to cultivation at the private expense of the reclaimer would be his personal property in perpetuity.

This statute had originally meant that land privately reclaimed (with official permission) would be exempt from the system of allotment then in force and could furthermore be conveyed by the reclaimer independently of his kindred. The statute had not intended to give reclaimers the power to create divided tenures of the lord–custodian type. Nevertheless, the customary law of the late Heian period referred to this text as the basis for the creation of ryōshu rights, including the power to occupy vacant territories.[17]

16. Nakada, "Ōchō jidai no shōen ni kansuru kenkyu," pp. 181–96; Kuroda,"Shōensei no kihonteki seikaku to ryōshusei," pp. 17–29.

17. Sakanoue, *Hossō shiyō shō, maki* 2, art., 39, *Shinkō Gunsho ruiju* 4:192–93; Kuroda, "Shōensei no kihonteki seikaku to ryōshusei," pp. 21–29. A famous decree of 902, in which the government sought to forbid many sorts of "private" land control,

Ryōshu powers were undoubtedly based on reclamation projects in some cases, but in many others, certified histories of reclamation amounted to little more than legal fictions. Ryōshu powers could sometimes be acquired over an area by reducing the cultivators to a state of economic dependence and thereby acquiring control over them and their lands. In such cases, the peasant community itself became an object of "cultivation." Indeed, it had been a regular practice of the earlier imperial regime to compensate its higher officials by allowing them to exploit peasant households in this way. The early Heian term for this was *kōei*, (management-cultivation). The ryōshu of the eleventh century was doing exactly that, except that his legitimacy was based on property rather than on office. Accordingly, his powers were justified in terms of the old land-reclamation laws, whatever their original purport may in fact have been.[18]

In this way, the concept of ryōshu paralleled that of shiki. In both cases, what was originally a "public" official function had been assimilated to a system of property. The old system had strictly forbidden all sorts of divided land tenure; when officials exploited peasant villages they relied on the services of subordinate officials, and the only persons considered to have land ownership rights were the peasants themselves. The subordinate administrators of shōen, however, held shiki, which were in fact land rights. A ryōshu was someone whose rights were, formally at least, based on a land reclamation claim.

Local ryōshu inevitably came into conflict with public officials, as both sought to exercise the same sorts of authority over the inhabitants of an area. The immunity-granting process was one way of tolerating selected private holdings of this type, in a situation where official titles of authority had become restricted to a few chosen lineages. It was, in other words, a way of accommodating accumulations of wealth outside the preestablished legal system. Grants of immunity not only gave economic advantages; they also confirmed the "original reclaimer" claims on which most of these holdings had to be based.

The process of "endowment" that appeared in the eleventh century may be seen as an extention of these tendencies. The noble who received commendation and thereby became ryōke was considered the holder of a ryōke-shiki. The original holder became the "manager" under another shiki. The application of the term shiki to both interests created by the transaction shows that the relationship was a bilateral one, in which the

---

stresses the need to keep fiscal administration of territory in government hands and cites as authorities the very regulations later used to justify ryōshu rights in the *Hossō shiyō shō. Ruijū sandai kyaku, maki* 19, 902/3/13, *Kokushi taikei*, 2nd ser., 7:608–09.

18. Kuroda, "Shōensei no kihonteki seikaku to ryōshusei," pp. 21–29; Nakada, "Ōchō jidai no shōen ni kansuru kenkyū," p. 73.

parties were on a relatively equal footing. The actual degree of subordination depended on the terms of the transaction. The transaction itself, however, must be regarded as a private act, leading to official recognition of a shōen as immune (and *a fortiori* corporate) landholding. Under this legal system, both lord and custodian were considered the legitimate successors of the "original ryōshu."

Such relationships had to be periodically renewed and were undoubtedly subject to some degree of renegotiation at each new generation. If the ryōke-shiki passed into the hands of a noble too weak to maintain the immunity, he would be forced to make a further commendation to someone more powerful than himself. This might tempt him to put more pressure on the custodian for revenues and thus generate a conflict. The custodian could also repurchase the interest his predecessors had commended. In 1112, for example, a lord in need of funds made an extraordinary demand on his custodian, who complied on the condition that the payment be considered the "repurchase" price of the lordship.[19]

The shōen might, in these respects, be considered an "estate community," in which all shiki holders enjoyed a certain parity. This was well expressed by the term *shoryō* (domain). Each person holding a shiki interest in a piece of land could refer to it as his domain, ignoring all other holders. All persons deriving income from a piece of land were said to "possess," (*chigyō* or *ryōshō*) the entire holding.[20]

The corporateness of the shōen, as remarked earlier, bore some resemblance to older clan organizations and some resemblance to segmentary political factions. Late in the tenth century, when the practice of endowment had not yet fully developed, the relation between tenure and clan filiation was somewhat more explicit. During the last decade of the tenth century, for example, a landowner who had turned his title over to Fujiwara no Michinaga (966–1027) received in return a clan name that admitted him into a line of minor nobles.[21] This was apparently an earlier method of conferring "influence" on the donee, enabling him to protect his holding from provincial demands. It would seem that at that time the theory that both lord and custodian were successors to the "original ryōshu" had not yet matured.[22]

19. Murai, "Kugeryō shōen no keisei," p. 381.
20. In the event of confiscation of land from defeated "rebels," their kin could lay claim to it on the grounds of "title to possession" (*chigyō no yuisho*). If the present holder were abruptly dispossessed, inchoate "ownership" rights would immediately be claimed by competitors within his own lineage group. Ishii Ryōsuke, *Nihon fudōsan sen'yū ron* (Tokyo, 1952), pp. 28–42.
21. *Yoshimine keizu*, in *Zoku Gunsho ruijū* (Kanseikai-bon) 7A, p. 494.
22. Nakada, "Ōchō jidai no shōen ni kansuru kenkyū," pp. 98–103.

The property system of the late Heian period depended for its legitimacy on the authority of the noble caste resident in the capital. The distinction between "provincial domain" and "shōen" implied that, in the strict sense of the term, no domain was a shōen unless it had a lord whose influence could to some degree override local authorities, and this in turn almost always required noble patronage of some sort, however nominal. The most notable exception to this was the estates of large religious institutions like the Ise and Usa shrines, which could also provide the needed sanction. Not all ryōshu holdings would qualify as shōen under this definition. Many of them were unable to secure formal immunity, even though their holders might qualify as the legitimate successors of an original reclaimer and thereby be able to exercise broad administrative powers. There was always the possibility of intimidation of provincial authorities by ryōshu connected with powerful military bands, but their position was somewhat precarious, as it was subject to the vicissitudes of political and factional conflict. The tendency to acquire an immunizing lordship, and sometimes several such lordships, was therefore strong. The corporateness of the shōen protected the individual holder not only against the claims of provincial authorities, but also against his own kindred who might at any time advance an adverse hereditary claim to possession. The certification by the ryōke of one person as manager, for example, confirmed that person as the designated heir to the shiki.

This suggests that the late Heian institution of property, of the type expressed by shiki, was the product of interaction between broader estate groups. In the lord–custodian relationship described earlier, membership and nonmembership in the noble caste were vital factors. The alliance meant that each party made the facilities peculiar to his group available to the other, so that each acquired an interest in the other's "estate," which allowed him to act independently of his own group. A well-protected custodian, for example, could act autonomously with respect to the provincial government staffed in large part by his peers. A ryōke could extract income somewhat independently of his particular position in the government, in other words, privately. It is at this point that a distinction might be drawn between property and estate as above defined. Noble status was an estate right that consisted of membership in a single corporate group. Property, however, required more than this. In the late Heian period, when members of the noble group and members of local lineages could hold congruent interests in the same land, property of the "judicial" type began to appear.

The shōen as an institution was predicated on the continued monopoly of prestige distribution by the noble caste. The efforts of the retired sovereigns to centralize this function in their own courts, and their concurrent support of the zuryō class, contributed substantially to the weakening of noble caste privilege and to the increasing tension between capital and countryside. The court's administrative power was undoubtedly increased by Taira Kiyomori's dictatorship. However, its legitimating functions, and hence its legitimacy, were severely impaired, inviting an uprising from below. The turbulence of the 1180s, which resulted in the founding of the Kamakura *bakufu,* was in a sense a revolt against centralized power. It was not, however, aimed at destroying the noble caste, but rather at preserving it from the depredations of Kiyomori's clique. The Kamakura regime was committed to upholding the property system of the past and made it one of its unique assets.

The property system of the late Heian period was an important constituent of the estate system as a whole and, as pointed out by scholars of the time, was totally nonfamilial in content. Indeed, it was the principal means of affiliation (other than the simple faction) between persons of unrelated groups. Like the faction, the shōen had a basically vertical structure. It must be added, however, that two equivalently structured opposed factions, such as those which participated in the Hōgen Disturbance, appeared only rarely. Those were relatively "pure," or one-dimensional, groupings, but most factions were not nearly so pure and differed in aim and composition from their opposite numbers. The Kamakura faction, for example, pursued policies and aims quite different from those of its enemies in the capital. "Pure" shōen were probably also the exception rather than the rule, and the proprietary element in their composition, although essential, did not rule out their significance as political organizations capable of hierarchical administrative order.

Every political regime has estatist and nonestatist elements, whose relative importance may vary. In late Heian Japan, the estatist element was very important. The position of property (as narrowly defined above) within the total estate system suggests new avenues of comparison and criticism, particularly respecting the conception of Japanese feudalism. There is such a thing as an estatist political order, as seen in both France and Japan during the twelfth century. The structure and function of corporate groups in the property and political systems of such regimes should reveal a good deal about the nature of "feudal" societies.

PART TWO

Bakufu versus Court

6 The Emergence of the Kamakura *Bakufu*

JEFFREY P. MASS

The emergence of the Kamakura military government (*bakufu*) during the 1180s has long been a subject of heated debate among Japanese historians. While there is unanimity that Japan in 1190 was much different from what it had been a decade earlier, there is little agreement on the precise character of the cumulative changes, or on why they unfolded as they did at each stage. The treatment that follows is an attempt to join this debate, concentrating specifically on two areas—the originality of the warrior-government idea, and the techniques used to bring the bakufu to fruition. As I will argue, the appearance of the Kamakura military regime marked an entirely new phenomenon in Japanese history: the coming together of men of the provinces to create a locus of authority that was both physically and institutionally distinct from the capital city and imperial control. It is a view that sees disengagement and innovation as more persuasive in explaining the 1180s than continuity with the past or integration with its traditions.[1]

The Nature of the Taira Ascendancy

It is well to begin our story with an exploration into certain key features of the Taira government that preceded the Minamoto-led bakufu. Treatments of the Taira have usually divided into two basic classes. Following the Taira vs. Minamoto (or Heishi vs. Genji) motif found in the famous war tales of the period, one group has supposed that the Taira hegemony of 1156–83 was representative of Japan's first military government; the age of warrior rule began with the Heishi, not the Genji. However the Taira proved to be bad rulers, wielding their military strength as an oppressive force. And so eventually a great war broke out (the Gempei War, or Genji vs. Heishi conflict) in which the Taira as holders of power for a genera-

1. This approach, then, gently challenges the position taken by Professor Hall, who posits a "growth within the old system . . . a legal division of powers made by the court itself" (John W. Hall, *Government and Local Power in Japan, 500 to 1700* [Princeton, N.J., 1966], p. 153).

tion were replaced by their inveterate battlefield rivals, the Minamoto. The successive Taira and Minamoto regimes were different, but only insofar as the Genji with their eastern base and institutionalized forms marked an advance in warrior strength and independence over a rival polity whose headquarters had been in Kyoto.

By contrast, the other school of thought has emphasized that despite the Taira's military origin the Heishi leaders became full-fledged members of the central nobility after arriving permanently in Kyoto in 1156. (This was the date of the so-called Hōgen Disturbance in which Genji and Heishi units were called upon to settle an imperial succession dispute.) The Taira scion, Kiyomori, ascended the twin ladders of court rank and imperial office and ruled Japan from his central base as the country's ranking title-holder and landed proprietor. The Taira, it is alleged, were no different from the Fujiwara. The Heishi were Kyoto nobles, the Genji provincial warriors.

Both theories take for granted the fact that Kiyomori did indeed rule Japan, differing primarily on whether he ruled as a military aristocrat or as a central noble. In recent years, however, a new view of the Taira period has been gaining in currency. It is a view, promoted first by Ishimoda Shō, which suggests that until the coup d'etat of 1179/11 in which Go-Shirakawa, the ex-sovereign (In), was dismissed by Kiyomori, the two men actually shared authority, the In holding the more substantial voice. In other words, during much of the period of Kiyomori's supposed national hegemony the Taira leader had yet to emerge as the clear ruler even within Kyoto.[2]

The Ishimoda reinterpretation makes possible an appraisal of the Taira in entirely new perspective. For example, we can now point to and appreciate (1) Kiyomori's failure after 1156 to advance beyond his former status as a provincial protégé of the In, (2) his introduction after the Heiji Disturbance of 1159–60 into specific political organs and hierarchies in which the In needed support,[3] (3) his failure to advance quickly to full proprietor status over public and private landed estates, and (4) the Taira leader's inability, even into the 1170s, to dislodge the In from his position as patron or provincial proprietor for lands over which Kiyomori now stood as the nominal lord. The thrust of this argument, at any rate, is that it can now be shown that governance by Taira Kiyomori did not attain the level of actual hegemony until just before the 1180 outbreak of

2. See Ishimoda Shō, "Heishi 'seiken' ni tsuite," in Ishimoda, *Kodai makki seiji shi josetsu* (Tokyo, 1968), pp. 470–87.
3. The Heiji Disturbance was a series of brief skirmishes in which the Minamoto survivors of the 1156 Hōgen Disturbance were either destroyed or sent into exile by the victorious Taira.

the Gempei War. Called into question is the validity of any historical reference to a "Taira polity" (Heishi *seiken*), be it of a military shape, a traditionally noble cast, or whatever. By contrast, as we shall see, the Minamoto achievement from its very inception can legitimately be called a new government.

That the Taira failed to establish themselves as military rulers can be demonstrated variously. The limited size of their core vassal band and the absence of any concerted effort to extend sway locally are two of the clearest indicators.[4] But the Taira were equally deficient in their "civilian" program, for example, in the area of "house government." One of the hallmarks of the Heian system of rule was the issuance by major Kyoto families and religious institutions (*kemmon seika*) of general edicts of guarantee over land, public–private judicial decisions, and orders affecting some portion of the Heian corporate structure. At the summit of this assemblage of "ruling houses" in the period just before the Taira's rise was the retired emperor whose administrative office (*In-no-chō*) disseminated edicts that were second in prestige and authority only to those of the collegially controlled State Council.[5] This implies a kind of "edict hierarchy" reflecting the balance of strength within Kyoto during any given time period. In view of Kiyomori's obviously commanding presence in the capital after 1156, we are hardly prepared, therefore, for the almost total lack of documents attributable either to him personally or to his private house office (*mandokoro*). In fact, for the whole of the "Heishi period" we find only three such old records, and one of these can be dismissed immediately.[6] The two others,[7] described briefly on page 132, concern Aki Province with which Kiyomori, during an unusually long ten-year governorship, established a unique relationship. The question is thus raised as to whether these directives to Aki should be considered within the same framework as those issued to other provinces by traditional Kyoto-based kemmon seika.

While such findings by no means foreclose on the likelihood that Kiyomori was responsible from behind the scenes for decrees issued

4. For details see chap. 1 of my forthcoming *Warrior Government in Early Medieval Japan: A Study of the Kamakura Bakufu, Shugo, and Jitō* (New Haven, 1974).

5. For a comparison of In-no-chō and Imperial State Council documents see G. C. Hurst's essay on the retired emperors (chap. 3).

6. *Kōfukuji Bettō Jidai Ura Monjo*, 1156/10/13 Harima no kuni Taira Kiyomori shojō, in Takeuchi Rizō, ed., *Heian ibun* (Tokyo, 1969), 6:2352, doc. 2845, is an informal directive issued while Kiyomori was still only a provincial governor. (Hereafter cited as *HI*.)

7. *Itsukushima Jinja Monjo*, 1164/6 Gon chūnagon ke (Taira Kiyomori) mandokoro kudashibumi, in *HI*, 7:2609, doc. 3285; and ibid., 1179/11 saki no dajōdaijin ke (Taira Kiyomori) mandokoro kudashibumi, 8:2985, doc. 3891.

through normal bureaucratic channels,[8] it does suggest that the Heishi leader was never able (or did not see fit) to govern "in his own name." On this important point the Taira seem clearly distinguished from capital noble families of commensurate status. Nor was this an accident of surviving records: contemporaneous materials as well as documents from the post-1185 years refer to the great variety of decrees issued by retired emperors, great ministers, and other kemmon seika.[9] Only the Taira seem never to be cited in this all-revealing context.[10]

How are we to interpret this suspected low output of Kiyomori documents? Factors such as the Heishi's *nouveau riche* acquisition of land and office titles, and the likely difficulties encountered in creating and staffing on short notice an administrative house organization, can certainly be pointed to. But the consideration that seems clearly paramount was the ongoing, overbearing presence of the In. Put another way, areas of governance that might have become associated with the country's leading power remained instead the responsibility of the country's leading authority. The issuance of legitimizing-type land edicts—even during an age of advancing local instability—is a conspicuous case in point. Examples of such decrees can be found from Go-Shirakawa during his short reign as emperor, and then in much greater abundance from his subsequent tenure as In.[11] Similar edicts issued by the Heishi are virtually unknown.

8. And yet there are rather few specific cases in which we *know* that this occurred. The only two local agencies that can be readily cited are the Aki provincial headquarters (*kokuga*) and the government-general of Kyushu (*Dazaifu*). During this period, most of the Aki kokuga decrees and at least a portion of Dazaifu's edicts were prompted by commands issuing ultimately from Kiyomori. Control of *central* agencies seems to have come after the 1179 coup, e.g., a Grand Council (*Dajōkan*) order that was sent out to eastern (Tōkai circuit) governors at the express direction of the Heishi leader. See *Naikaku Bunko Shozō Settsu no Kuni Komonjo*, 1180/2/20 Dajōkan fu an, in *HI*, 8:2990–91, doc. 3903.

9. See, e.g., *Kōyasan Ikenobō Monjo*, 1205/5/27 Kanto gechijō, in Kōyasan Shi Hensanjo, comp., *Kōyasan monjo, kyū kōya ryōnai monjo* (Kyoto, 1936), 9:93, doc 49. Although earlier documents by (1) the successive In, Toba and Go-Shirakawa, (2) a former Left Minister, (3) the proprietor (*ryōke*) of the disputed shōen, and (4) Minamoto Yoritomo were presented in evidence in this 1205 litigation, there is no mention of the Taira.

10. Cornelius J. Kiley suggests that there was probably a large number of Taira house office edicts but that these may have been destroyed after the Heishi defeat of 1185. Even admitting this as a possibility, the virtually total blackout on references to Kiyomori documents—both before his death in 1181 and then retrospectively—still requires an explanation.

11. See, e.g., *Kanshinji Monjo*, 1157/2/12 Go-Shirakawa tennō rinji an, in *HI*, 6:2362 doc. 1271. This document is an edict of guarantee for a Kanshinji Temple estate in Kawachi Province. Even in 1178 it was Go-Shirakawa, not Kiyomori, who moved to guarantee the Iwashimizu Shrine head abbot's hereditary possession of shōen in Chi-

It was almost as if nothing had changed despite the "rise of the Taira." The absence of Heishi edicts of this type is paralleled by other, more serious deficiencies. During the very period that Kiyomori is alleged in most histories to have been finalizing his mastery over capital and country by gaining appointment as prime minister (dajōdaijin), it can be shown, significantly, that Taira kinsmen were being confirmed by the ex-sovereign in mere management positions over land. The most blatant example of this appears in a document of 1166: the retired emperor is seen authorizing that the descendants of Taira Shigehira, one of Kiyomori's own sons, possess in heredity the administrative post (azukari dokoro) over a newly formed imperial shōen.[12] Other instances can be cited as well, among them cases from 1169 and 1178. In the former, the In issued a directive to the public officers (zaichōkanjin) of Bingo Province, whose acting governor (gon no kami) is listed as a ranking Taira.[13] Thus a Taira was performing in a subordinate role in a unit area over which Go-Shirakawa probably stood as ultimate "proprietor." In the 1178 example, the retired emperor issued an edict to the government-general of Kyushu in which a certain Taira Masako and her descendants are confirmed in a hereditary managerial (azukari dokoro) post over Hizen Province's Matsuura-no-shō.[14] Evidently, Go-Shirakawa had succeeded in partially interposing his own authority between Kiyomori and the latter's own clan membership.

The In's authority did not end even here. It extended into areas which, in consideration of the Taira's military background, should logically have been under Kiyomori's jurisdiction. In 1160, for example, Go-Shirakawa prohibited lawless disturbances in Yamashiro and Kii provinces,[15] and even sixteen years later it was the In rather than Kiyomori who issued a directive to public officials countrywide admonishing them to prevent violence against Iwashimizu Shrine lands.[16] Why is it that we are able to find no comparable "peace-keeping" authorizations issued by Kiyomori?

---

kuzen, Awa, and Bizen provinces (Iwashimizu Monjo, 1178/6/12 Go-Shirakawa In-no-chō kudashibumi, in HI 7:2942–44, doc. 3833).

12. Nibu Jinja Monjo, 1166/1/10 Go-Shirakawa In-no-chō kudashibumi an, in HI, 7:2664–65, doc. 3375.

13. Kōyasan Monjo, 1169/11/23 Go-Shirakawa In-no-chō kudashibumi, in HI, 7:2749, doc. 3521.

14. Tōji Hyakugō Monjo, 1178/6/20 Go-Shirakawa In-no-chō kudashibumi, in HI, 8:2948–50, doc. 3836.

15. Ōtani Daigaku Shozō Monjo, 1160/5/5 Go-Shirakawa In-no-chō kudashibumi, in HI, 7:2498–99, doc. 3093; Kōyasan Monjo, 1160/10/22 Go-Shirakawa Hōō Inzen, in HI, 7:2510, doc. 3113.

16. Iwashimizu Monjo, 1176/6/10 Go-Shirakawa In-no-chō kudashibumi, in HI, 7:2901–02, doc. 3765.

The point of the foregoing observations is not to argue that the Heishi were simply powerless before the In; in late 1179, as we know, they simply gathered forces and succeeded in deposing their rival. Instead, what the evidence seems to suggest is that in the period before the coup we find very little indication of an independent (or even self-reliant) Heishi power. Not only had Kiyomori failed to "succeed" Go-Shirakawa as the leading political authority in Kyoto, but in certain instances the Taira scion's own housemen seem to have been as dependent on the In as they were on their own chieftain. It is only in Kyushu and in Aki Province that we find documented examples of a direct Taira involvement in a central–local exchange of titles in land for the promise (albeit implicit) of loyal service. In the 1164 and 1179 Kiyomori edicts referred to earlier (n.7), the former reveals the grant of a local management post (*gesu shiki*) in return for commended land, while the latter speaks of *jitō* posts and demonstrates Kiyomori's control over them.

Notwithstanding the Taira's energies in these two regions of long-standing association, it seems clear that in the country as a whole Kiyomori's promotion of local adherents to both old (e.g., governor)[17] and new (e.g., *jitō*)[18] offices did not proceed rapidly. At least part of the blame for this failure can be attributed to the perpetuation of an alliance between the In and Heishi that left the latter in a condition of semiclientage. By virtue of Kiyomori's failure to develop a method of governance that was institutionally and politically distinct from the In's, the entire Heishi program suffered on precisely the point from which the Minamoto movement would soon derive much of its initial success. Unlike Yoritomo, who would undertake from the outset to confirm under his own seal whatever land or office rights a vassal (or would-be vassal) claimed to be rightfully his own, Kiyomori by contrast seemed almost willing to pass on such requests to the In.

We have a situation, then, in which Kiyomori's performance as both a political ruler and vassal chieftain seems curiously attenuated. Certainly we know that the Taira did have men everywhere that it counted as followers. But one cannot help but wonder, based on the evidence at hand, how many of the lands later confiscated as "Heishi" had been in fact that,

17. Saeki Kagehiro, Kiyomori's main vassal in Aki, was made governor of that province in 1180 or 1181, in other words, after the coup d'etat. A document of 1182 shows Kagehiro in his capacity of governor. *Itsukushima Jinja Monjo*, 1182/3 Aki no kami Saeki Kagehiro yuzurijō, in *HI*, 8:3064, doc. 4026.

18. See ibid., 1176/7 Aki kokushi chōsen an, 7:2905, doc. 3772. Kiyomori, as mentioned in n. 8, is known to have controlled the Aki provincial apparatus: hence this jitō appointment through that agency. The office of jitō itself, which would shortly come to symbolize Kamakura power throughout Japan, was used by the Taira (as far as our documents reveal)only in this single province. Most scholars assume a wider usage.

in other words, rights confirmed by Kiyomori or received out of direct Taira largess.

The Taira Polity after 1179

The period 1179–80 witnessed the birth at last of an identifiable "Taira polity." This development was a direct result of a final political break between two old allies: Kiyomori's opponents late in 1179 were the In and the latter's personal entourage in Kyoto. In view of the attack that would issue in several months from the eastern-based Minamoto, this Heishi choice of enemies at court seems highly ironic. But Kiyomori cannot in fairness be faulted for his lack of prescience on this point. Since the provinces were still quiet in 1179 there was nothing as yet to indicate any goal other than to end, finally, three generations of dependent status. Thus, the emphasis of the Heishi program was even now one of surpassing in strength traditional competitors of the center. This is illustrated in several ways. First, Kiyomori's decision in 1180/6 to move the capital from Kyoto to Fukuhara in neighboring Settsu Province was due less to any perceived need to concentrate on local organization than to a desire to escape the baneful influence of hostile central religious rivals. Hence the fact that the imperial family, regalia, and other links with the past were scrupulously carried to this "new Kyoto."[19] Second, the roughly twenty proprietary provinces that the Taira were now able to gain title over were designed more for the enrichment of immediate clan members than for the gathering up of local warrior support.[20] This was made clear when a year later these supra-governorships failed to produce in sufficient quantities the men and supplies needed to wage war. This failure was partly the result of titles coming into the Taira fold too late. It should be pointed out, however, that even the few provinces that had been held by the Taira since the 1160s saw their entrenched public officers defect in short order to the Genji.[21]

In practical terms it was seemingly only at this juncture in late 1180 that the Heishi became aware that bureaucratic ascendancy was no substitute for a carefully nurtured bond of dependent vassalage. Local officials wanted confirmatory decrees guaranteeing their local authority, not governors of Heishi surname sent out from the capital. While no specific

19. See Fujiwara Kanezane, *Gyokuyō*, 1180/6/2 (Tokyo, 1966), 2:413–14. By 1180/11, Kiyomori was back in Kyoto faced with the need to galvanize support for his war effort against the Minamoto.

20. This is at variance with the traditional view, which has presumed a much earlier assemblage of some thirty of these supra-governorships.

21. This refers to Wakasa, Noto, and Echizen provinces, all in Hokurikudō facing the Japan Sea. For these three defections see *Gyokuyō*, 1180/11/28, 2:446; 1181/7/24, p. 518; and 1181/9/2. p. 525.

evidence exists to show that the Taira even now undertook any actual re-ordering of centrist proclivities that had been hardening during two decades of residence in the capital, we do see for the first time the begin-ning of a program that went beyond the mere quantification of traditional titles and offices.[22] The establishment of two new regional posts (*sō-kan* and *sō-gesu*) in the first and second months of 1181 demonstrates the germ of an awareness that large-scale recruitment and requisitioning needs could best be met by the presence of Taira agents posted to the provinces for that purpose.[23] The Taira were learning that mere proprietorship over land was not enough.

Despite these efforts, the Heishi, as we know, were defeated in the Gempei War. The historical significance of this fact cannot be over-emphasized. The Taira, who by 1180 had finally come into possession of all the ingredients of traditional hegemony, were about to be toppled due largely to the obsolescence of those ingredients; the Heishi had become, in a sense, an anachronism of the Heian system of rule.[24] Conversely, what helped bring about this demise were social and economic currents long in evidence in the provinces but heretofore impotent before a system in which authority by definition radiated out from the center. The Genji would emerge victorious in the struggle that engulfed Japan during the 1180s largely because they were better equipped than the Heishi to harness and control society's dynamic new force—the armed warrior and his demands for a more secure tenure over land. This control, as we will now attempt to show, is directly attributable to the decision not to come to Kyoto. The bakufu's greatest asset was to be its independence.

The Minamoto Drive for Power in the East, 1180–1183

There were two essential features of society in Japan's eastern provinces

22. This was not a break with the past, only a broadening from it; the desire to "possess" in large numbers was still very much in evidence. E.g., in *Hyakurenshō*, 1180/12/28 and 1181/1/4 (*Kokushi taikei*, 1901), 14:136–37, we see reference to two of Kiyomori's most infamous acts–the burning down of Tōdaiji and Kōfukuji temples, and the seizure of their estates. It would seem that along with the Taira's post-1179 piling up of public land titles through the provincial proprietorship method, it was during this same time period that the Heishi acquired most of their traditional figure of "500 shōen."

23. The *sō-kan* and *sō-gesu* are treated in Ishimoda Shō, "Heishi seiken no sō-kan shiki setchi," *Rekishi hyōron* 107 (1959), pp. 7–14; and Ishimoda, "Kamakura bakufu ikkoku jitō shiki no seiritsu," in Ishimoda Shō and Satō Shin'ichi, eds., *Chūsei no hō to kokka* (Tokyo, 1965), pp. 36–45. Kiyomori's death on 1181/int. 2/4 deprived the Taira of the leadership required to carry off bold experiments such as *sō-kan* and *sō-gesu*. The fates of both programs are unknown.

24. By hindsight it can be argued that the post-1179 Taira achieved a more com-prehensive assemblage of the symbols of traditional power than perhaps any of their

that aided the Genji in their drive to power. The first has just been al-luded to—the desire of great warrior families to acquire guarantees of land tenure that would be more secure and more permanent than any they had previously obtained from Kyoto.[25] It was this that made them recep-tive to the overtures of a great military scion like Yoritomo, who began by promising mutual security through a combination of regional coales-cence and independence from the old capital. The second feature was the existence of provincial governmental apparatuses that were staffed at the middle and upper levels by each region's ranking warrior houses. For Yoritomo this meant that he would be able to gain a director's role over an already functioning eastern governance merely by establishing himself as the guarantor of his vassals' "public functions." Persuasion that warrior lands and offices were capable of being legitimized locally by the creation of a new coordinating agency thus became the order of the day. It must have seemed a breathtaking idea.

The immediate background to the war's outbreak in 1180 is well known and requires only brief mention.[26] Yoritomo, scion of the famed military house of Minamoto, had been living in quiet exile in the Kantō since the demise of his father twenty years earlier in the Heiji Disturbance. The period 1160–80 was thus one of total eclipse for the Genji with no visible prospects of revival or amelioration. Then in 1180/4 a disaffected son of Go-Shirakawa issued an unexpected call on all warrior groups in the east both to rise up against the Taira and, implicitly, to support his own bid for the emperorship. Several months of careful assessment on the part of Yoritomo were ended in the eighth month by a proclamation to the effect that the eastern provinces, both public and private land, were henceforth to be under his own jurisdiction (*AK* 1180/8/19).[27] By this simple act of declaring independence from Kyoto, Yoritomo had launched on a course that would eventually bring him to national power.[28] He would rule from the outside looking in.

---

central predecessors. In this they represented a "final culmination" of the Heian pattern but in so doing severely upset the traditional collectivist spirit that dominated Kyoto politics. This led to deep cleavages when what was needed most was a united stand against the external warrior threat. Even the restoration of Go-Shirakawa to his former status (*Gyokuyō*, 1180/12/18, 2:453) seemed to avail little. The burnings of Tōdaiji and Kōfukuji came only several days later (see n. 22).

25. Eastern warrior society before 1180 is treated in Mass, *Warrior Government*, chap. 2.

26. A clear account appears in Minoru Shinoda, *The Founding of the Kamakura Shogunate, 1180–1185* (New York 1960), pp. 48–59.

27. The reference here is to the *Azuma kagami*, an official chronicle of the Kamakura bakufu covering the years 1180–1266 (Hereafter cited in text and footnotes as *AK*.)

28. To be sure, Yoritomo did claim justification for his action by citing the anti-

THE KANTŌ REGION AND ENVIRONS

Two days before his proclamation of 8/19, Yoritomo had ordered his followers to attack the governor's deputy (*mokudai*) of Izu. This province was a proprietary holding of the Taira as well as the site of the Genji leader's own long exile; it was appropriate that the war begin here. But this act had a larger importance since it provided a pattern for similar rebellions in neighboring areas. Responding to the urgings of Yoritomo, indigenous local officers throughout and beyond the Kantō simply moved to depose all Kyoto-sent agents.[29] This is most clearly seen in

Taira directive from Go-Shirakawa's son. The latter, however, was already long since dead, hunted down during the fifth month by Heishi troops (*AK* 1180/5/26).

29. This suggestion appears in a Yoritomo letter to Taira Hirotsune, the ranking local officer of Kazusa Province. Hirotsune was called on to rally his subordinate provincial officials and to round up and presumably eliminate any persons sent out from the capital (*AK* 1180/9/1).

Shimōsa, where the mokudai was eliminated by the native assistant governor house of Chiba (*AK* 1180/9/13), and in Suruga, where a combined Genji force proceeded to destroy that province's central deputy (*AK* 1180/10/1,13,14). Other Kantō cases are less explicit, but within months this clearly effective anti-Kyoto contagion had spread all the way into Hokurikudō, facing the Japan Sea. In 1181 we find evidence of similar local versus central confrontations in Noto, Echizen, and Echigo.[30]

In several *Azuma kagami* entries we see the converse side to this anti-mokudai policy—evidence of local officers actively coming to the support of Yoritomo. To cite only the most prominent of these cases, provincial officials from Awa (*AK* 1180/9/4), the native assistant governor of Sagami (*AK* 1180/8/20), the native acting governor of Musashi (*AK* 1180/10/2), the native assistant governor of Kazusa (*AK* 1180/9/19), and the native acting assistant governor of Shimotsuke[31] are all seen falling in behind the Genji leader. These great provincial chieftains brought more than manpower with them; they delivered into Yoritomo's hands a potential for rulership over vast territories. With an emphasis on public agencies and public land, the bond between Genji overlord and one or more of the leading official houses in each province meant an impetus toward regional governance.

What is important to recognize, then, is that even at the outset Yoritomo and his advisers had more in mind than the mere creation of a fighting force based on agreement in arms. The objective was as much political as it was military: the Minamoto scion was to be ruler of the Kantō and neighboring provinces; his major vassals were to be his provincial lieutenants. Yoritomo wasted no time in attempting to breathe actual life into his new "government." On the very day that he declared his authority over the east, he took his first step toward assuming the role of sponsor and protector of the region's leading temples and shrines. In marked contrast to the Taira, who were consistently seeking to outdo their central religious rivals in the competition for land profits, Yoritomo took it upon himself on 8/19 to seize a unit of the public domain and grant it to Izu's Mishima Shrine.[32] The form that this bequest took is of special importance. Yoritomo sought to make his act "official" by cloaking it in the guise of a public directive to the resident officers of that province's headquarters; with the mokudai of Izu now deposed, Yoritomo simply assumed for himself the authority—without the title—for that province's

30. See *Gyokuyō* 1181/7/24; 1181/9/2 and 9/9; and 1181/7/1, 2:518, 525–26, 510.
31. Koyama Tomomasa is referred to in *AK* 1181/int.2/20 as having joined the Genji during the previous year.
32. *Mishima Jinja Monjo*, 1180/8/19 Minamoto Yoritomo kudashibumi, in *HI*, 9:3782–83, doc. 4883.

governance. The last of Yoritomo's politically directed activities within this initial cluster was the creation of a coordinating agency for warrior affairs (*samurai-dokoro*).[33] When joined in 1184 by administrative and judicial offices (*kumonjo* and *monchūjo*), these three boards would come to form the bakufu's central structure.[34]

This auspicious beginning very nearly ended in disaster several days later. Highlighting the fact that Yoritomo's pretensions to overlordship for the east would have to be contested by bow and sword, there occurred on 8/23 the famous defeat of the Minamoto at Ishibashi in neighboring Sagami Province. What is of special significance here is that Yoritomo's opponents in battle were not forces recruited and sent out from the capital region by the central Taira: the army that Yoritomo had to confront was one that was entirely local in origin. This fact tells us a great deal about the nature of the initial division into "Genji" and "Heishi," and ultimately of the warfare as a whole. Yoritomo's overtures to a province like Sagami had the effect of polarizing indigenous warriors less on the basis of remembered loyalties to his own forebears than on the pivot of the current state of inter- and intrafamily rivalries in that area; how one might fight depended largely on how one's neighbors and kinsmen might fight. To a very large degree, the battle for Sagami was thus a provincial civil war. Typically the Miura, as ranking public officers, chose to fight for the Genji, and so did their relatives, the Wada, along with another major family, the Sasaki.[35] In opposition were the Ōba and their various subordinates. A clear distinction must thus be drawn between a handful of later battles, which *can* be described as involving "main force" Genji and Heishi troops, and these far more common localized confrontations among and between traditional rivals.[36]

A free selection of loyalties within the context of one's geographic placement and/or family situation was not to last long, however, at least

33. Citing *AK* 1180/11/17, most historians have claimed that it was this date during the eleventh month that marked the founding of the *samurai-dokoro*. A careful reading of this entry, however, suggests that the warrior office may have been opened during the eighth month, probably on 8/19.

34. *AK* 1184/10/1 and 10/20. These agency names were all adopted from *kemmon seika* practice.

35. The Sasaki were originally from Ōmi Province near the capital but had taken up residence in Sagami after banishment in the wake of the Heiji war. Having lived in Sagami for only twenty years they nevertheless became a power there and are one of the few families known to have developed a close relationship with Yoritomo during the latter's period of exile. For this they were richly rewarded, becoming one of the most honored of Genji vassal houses despite their non-Kantō origins. See *AK* 1180/8/9.

36. For an explicit case of division based on geographical and/or blood competition, see *AK* 1181/int.2/23, for the Shimotsuke-based Koyama choosing to fight as Genji, while their kin, the Ashikaga, elected to oppose them as Heishi.

not in the Kantō. Yoritomo's physical presence there and his success at gaining the allegiance of the provincial officer class soon made it difficult for local families to use a Heishi labeling with effect. Before long, houses that had initially opted for the Taira were seeking to reverse themselves.[37] A recorded total of 200,000 Genji by the tenth month is certainly exaggerated (*AK* 1180/10/18); but it illustrates how completely the tide had already turned in favor of the Minamoto. This was despite the Ishibashi defeat two months earlier. By the end of 1180 only the smallest residue of a "Gempei war" remained in the Kantō. Within several months after that Yoritomo's main preoccupation would become one of purging and purifying from within what was now clearly a "Genji east."

It was during the tenth month of 1180 that there occurred the only significant direct confrontation (before 1184) between main-force Genji and Heishi armies. What is of special importance concerning the famous Battle of Fujigawa is its location in Suruga Province to the west of the Kantō. The defeat of the Taira in this battle led immediately to a division of the east into de facto spheres: the ten or so Tōkai and Tōsan provinces from Suruga and Kōzuke eastward became a Yoritomo preserve virtually unmolested by any further attempts from Kyoto to revive its former influence. Correspondingly, the Taira forces that were sent out from the capital over the next two and a half years were concentrated exclusively in Hokurikudō and the area known as Chūbu located between the capital and the Kantō. This had great significance for the way the Minamoto movement developed. Reasonably secure for the time being from any danger of external attack, Yoritomo could safely turn his attention inward; however, by so doing he allowed the main brunt of the continued anti-Taira fighting to fall to "Genji" troops not immediately under his own command. One result, as we shall see shortly, was a not unwarranted 1183 claim by Minamoto (Kiso) Yoshinaka, one of the two principal Chūbu generals, that it was he who should logically be recognized as the true Genji leader.[38] A second result with even more far-reaching implications was the nearly decade-long trial that Yoritomo would be forced to suffer before these nominal Minamoto in Chūbu could be either done away with or converted into real vassals.[39]

---

37. For example, see *AK* 1180/9/30 and 12/22 (the Nitta of Kōzuke), and 1180/9/29 and 10/4 (the Edo of Musashi).

38. Yoshinaka was Yoritomo's cousin. For his activities see *AK* 1180/12/24 and 1181/9/3,4. The other commander was Yoritomo's uncle, Minamoto Yukiie. See *AK* 1181/3/10, 11/5; 1182/5/19, 5/25.

39. Perhaps it was only in Tōtomi, placed evenly between Kyoto and Kamakura, that an actual "Gempei war" was taking place between Taira from the central capital and Minamoto from its eastern counterpart. Each side wanted Tōtomi as its ultimate

Returning to the Taira's apparent readiness to abandon without a fight the Kantō region and environs, this can be further illustrated by the almost total lapse in communication between central owners and their various holdings in that part of the country. And thus while we are able to find court edicts (much as in the past) purporting to abolish local disturbances, the land units cited in such decrees seem invariably to be in regions still under central jurisdiction. A pair of directives from 1181/12, for example, sought respectively to prohibit disturbances in some twelve shōen, all in western Japan,[40] and to expedite the payment of levies and services from a total of twenty estates, only one of which was in the Kantō.[41] In another reference of 1181 we see that the "eastern provinces" were to be deliberately excluded from a general levy imposed to defray Kōfukuji temple repairs.[42] Evidently, the Taira-dominated court had determined that a quarantine of the Kantō was well worth the price of an indefinite stoppage of revenues from that remote segment of Japan.

Kyoto's landowners, however, did not necessarily share in this un-willingness to negotiate with the rebels in the east. Thus when Yoritomo, in a celebrated incident, made his mid-1181 offer to divide the country into respective Taira and Minamoto administrative spheres under overall court authority, his overture met with a divided response.[43] While central religious estate holders as well as the In[44] were not averse to granting Yoritomo the recognition he desired, the Taira, who were opposed to allowing a Genji jurisdiction to advance to the very fringes of the capital region itself, refused all consideration of the plan. Yoritomo's only contact with the court over the next two years was therefore secretive and indirect, with a handful of anti-Heishi religious institutions acting as go-between.[45]

But why, after a full year of total disregard of Kyoto, would the Genji leader now have been seeking an accord?[46] The question is a highly com-

defense perimeter, thus prompting Yoritomo in late 1180 to post to that province a fron-tier officer charged with "protection" (shugo) duties. See AK 1180/10/21; 1181/1/27, 28, 3/13, and 3/19.

40. Iwashimizu Hachimangū Kiroku, 1181/12/2 Go-Shirakawa In-no-chō kudashibu-mi an, in HI 8:3052, doc. 4012.

41. Shin Kumano Jinja Monjo, 1181/12/18 Go-Shirakawa In-no-chō kudashibumi, in HI, 8:3053–55, doc. 4013.

42. Gyokuyō, 1181/3/21, 2:496.

43. Ibid., 1181/8/1, p. 519.

44. Go-Shirakawa had been restored to active status in late 1180. See n. 24.

45. See Ishimoda Shō, "Kamakura seiken no seiritsu katei ni tsuite," Rekishigaku kenkyū 200 (1956): 8–12, for a discussion of Yoritomo's quiet overtures to Kyoto during 1181–83.

46. Indeed the dilemma may well be a false one: it is highly puzzling that AK does not corroborate Yoritomo's offer of an accord in mid-1181. The diary Gyokuyō is known

plex one but seems evidently to relate to Yoritomo's desire to expand beyond the Kantō. The major thrust of his reasoning, in other words, gives vindication to the Taira's fears regarding Chūbu. Inasmuch as the entire western half of the eastern provinces constituted a region in which Yoritomo's influence derived from his own kinsmen, it may well be that the Kantō lord's rationale in mid-1181 was a desire to be rid of the Taira in the Chūbu so as to free himself from dependence on Yoshinaka.[47] The project fell through, however, and the scenario for a Yoshinaka–Yoritomo confrontation was delayed until 1183.

Looking at conditions in this period in the Kantō itself, we have already alluded to the rapid growth of local support that Yoritomo came to enjoy during the fall of 1180. After Fujigawa, for example, we see the house of Ōba, victorious foe over the Minamoto at Ishibashi barely two months earlier, now doing a complete turnabout by abjectly offering a voluntary surrender (*AK* 1180/10/23). This development had great significance for Yoritomo: in correspondence to his gaining a release from any need to confront those calling themselves "Heishi," he would become free to devote attention to a potentially much more formidable enemy—the collateral lines of his own house that refused to honor his chieftainship.

Yoritomo wasted no time in going on the attack against his own kinsmen. Barely a week after Fujigawa, Yoritomo demonstrated his total unconcern with the Taira in the west by marching east into Hitachi Province, home region of Satake Hideyoshi, a blood relative whose family a generation earlier had refused to fall in behind Minamoto Yoshitomo, Yoritomo's father. The differences between father and son (in effect, between the 1150s and 1180s) are important. Whereas Yoshitomo had been unable to bring to heel recalcitrant Genji branches such as the Satake, Yoritomo simply used his massive military strength to force the issue; the reluctant Satake were destroyed in battle on 1180/11/5 (*AK*). In some cases prudence won out over intransigence. Thus the Nitta house of Kōzuke, which like the Satake and other branches had refused to recognize Yoritomo's Genji chieftainship (*AK* 1180/9/30), managed to escape the fate of their kinsmen by offering in the twelfth month to submit voluntarily (*AK* 1180/12/22). By contrast, a generation earlier the Nitta had simply refused with impunity to fight for Yoshitomo.[48]

---

for its reiteration of rumors, and there are some scholars who question the authenticity of the alleged 1181 peace move.

47. It is alleged by *AK* that Yoshinaka was restive under Yoritomo's chieftainship (1180/12/24). Thus it was perhaps not entirely coincidental that within several weeks of the 1181/8 overture to Kyoto, Yoshinaka is seen rushing into Hokurikudō to, in effect, stake out his claim there. See *AK* 1181/9/3,4.

48. Yasuda Genkyū (Motohisa), *Bushidan* (Tokyo, 1964), pp. 104–05.

This type of submission was no guarantee, of course, that Yoritomo would bestow full or permanent forgiveness. The example of Shida Yoshihiro, an uncle of Yoritomo based in Hitachi Province, is a case in point. Apparently to avoid being attacked by his nephew in the wake of the Satake fighting, Yoshihiro made a disingenuous offer of support to Yoritomo, finally recognizing the latter's Minamoto leadership. This was accepted at first (*AK* 1180/11/7), but soon the old suspicions and enmity came once again to the fore (*AK* 1181/int.2/20). Yoritomo wasted no time on this second occasion. He moved to destroy Yoshihiro and to distribute the latter's local holdings to deserving vassals among his own following.[49]

In addition to these localized wars against Genji relatives—a necessity due to generations of intraclan factionalism—Yoritomo took several nonmilitary steps in order to promote his rule over the east. Central to his entire program was the creation of a political seat that would be more than just a headquarters. The village of Kamakura may well have been chosen because of its strategic location and historic ties with the Minamoto.[50] But before the year 1180 was out we see predictions (although recorded much later) of Kamakura's future as a political center for the entire east (*AK* 1180/12/12). More important, still, was that Yoritomo was no longer issuing his decrees on the run, as it were. Now when he prohibited local outrages, authorized fiscal exemptions, assigned new lands, or issued orders to "public" officials, he was doing so from a stationary base area that he could call his capital.[51]

The 1181/8 overture to the court, therefore, had been amply prepared for by events close to home. Not only had internal security in the Kantō been added to the post-Fujigawa sense of immunity from outside attack,[52] but Yoritomo had succeeded in establishing a pivot point from whence he could easily govern and administer this new Genji east. With these

49. *AK* 1181/int.2/28. Extensive confiscations and land redistributions came into use from the time of the Fujigawa battle (see *AK* 1180/10/23). For the resettlement after the Satake fighting see *AK* 1180/11/8.

50. Kamakura was first suggested to Yoritomo on 9/9, but his arrival there was delayed until 10/6. For the Genji's past links with Kamakura see *AK* 1180/10/12.

51. These several activities are described (in order) in the following Yoritomo edicts: *Sonkeikaku Shozō Monjo*, 1180/10/18 Minamoto Yoritomo gechijō, in *HI*, 10:3908, doc. 5066; ibid., 1180/11/8 Minamoto Yoritomo kudashibumi, 9:3783, doc. 4884; *Kashima Jingū Monjo*, 1181/3 Minamoto Yoritomo kishinjō, in *HI*, 8:3019, doc. 3961; *Mishima Jinja Monjo*, Minamoto Yoritomo kishinjō, in *HI* 9:3783, doc. 4885.

52. This security was not yet final. We read, e.g., of bad feelings between Yoritomo and his vassal Hirotsune, the chieftain of Kazusa (see *AK* 1182/1/23). The difference now was that any further enhancing of Yoritomo's power in the Kantō would require his turning against some of his *own men*. At the end of 1183 Hirotsune would be cashiered and the latter's vassals converted into Kamakura vassals (see *AK* 1184/1/17 and 2/14).

accomplishments behind him, it was only natural that he should have begun to look outward.

Yoritomo's horizons were widened by a development that he had probably not foreseen. The rebellion of Kantō warriors had come to serve as a model or signal for similar outbursts in other parts of the country. In Kyushu's Satsuma, Bungo, and Higo provinces, in Shikoku's Iyo and Tosa, and especially in Chūbu and Hokurikudō, local families were either using the Genji–Heishi labels to fight one another, or adopting the Genji credo of refusing obedience to officials sent out from the capital.[53] Signs of an unprecedented countrywide civil war were now in the wind.

The Minamoto Expansion into Western Japan, 1183–1185

As this local fighting increased in intensity, and as Taira-directed war levies seemed only to reduce still further the land revenues reaching Kyoto, dissatisfaction with the Heishi as protectors of the capital and its interests reached new heights. Thus when on 1183/7/28 Kiso Yoshinaka and Minamoto Yukiie entered Kyoto with the Taira in flight before them to the west, the invaders may have been looked on at first with some approval. Probably these expectations were due to Yoritomo's standing offer to restore shōen rents in return merely for court recognition of the Genji. At least we can be certain that the impending arrival of Minamoto forces was related to the In's issuance on 7/17 of a type of document virtually unseen since the outbreak of war—an authorization that a central institution's proprietorship over a Kantō estate be restored to its earlier condition.[54] The court seemed ready to make peace with Yoritomo.

It was at this point, however, that the latent divisions between the Chūbu and Kantō arms of the Genji movement finally came to the surface. Within weeks after his arrival in Kyoto, Yoshinaka began to move precipitately, alienating both the In, whose authorization to pursue the Taira he was slow in carrying out, and Yoritomo, whom he eventually

53. For the struggles in Satsuma, Bungo and Higo provinces see Asakawa Kan'ichi, *The Documents of Iriki* (Tokyo, 1955), p. 95; *AK* 1181/2/29; and *Hyakurenshō*, 1181/4/14, p. 139. The struggle in Iyo was between that province's two leading public officer families, the Kōno and Nii. The two divided "loyalties" on that basis between the Genji and Heishi. See Tanaka Minoru, "Kamakura jidai ni okeru Iyo no kuni no jitō gokenin ni tsuite," in Takeuchi Rizō hakushi kanreki kinenkai, comp., *Shōensei to buke shakai* (Tokyo, 1969), p. 275. On 1182/9/25 (*AK*) a younger brother of Yoritomo, Mareyoshi, was killed by local houses in Tosa, the province in Shikoku to which he had earlier been exiled. Yoritomo's first dispatch of easterners into the west took place two months later when on 11/20 an avenging party was sent to Tosa.

54. *Tamon' in Shozō Monjo*, 1183/7/17 Go-Shirakawa Hōō Inzen, in Nuki Tatsuto, ed., *Sōshū komonjo* (Tokyo, 1970), 5:74, doc. 1831. A less detailed copy of this document appears in *HI* 8:3098, doc. 4097.

attempted to displace as Genji chieftain.[55] What is significant, however, is that even as Yoshinaka and his confederate, Minamoto Yukiie, were gathering up prestigious court titles, high provincial office, and large numbers of lands confiscated from the Taira,[56] Yoritomo, whose own imperial status had now been technically exceeded by that of vassals, did not rush to the capital either to claim his own reward or to contest theirs. There may well have been a variety of reasons behind this, some logistical, but in view of later developments Yoritomo would seem to have been holding out for an agreement with the court on his own terms. Already negotiations had been opened regarding Kamakura's role in suppressing violence within the estates of Kantō and Hokurikudō, and to that were soon added the outrages committed by Yoshinaka and his followers.[57] The result was that by the first week of 1183/9, according to one source, most of official Kyoto was already in despair over Yoshinaka and was ready to call in Yoritomo as the former's replacement.[58]

Japanese scholars have not been able to reach a consensus regarding the court–Kamakura arrangement that was finally hammered out in the tenth month.[59] For virtually all observers the arguments have centered narrowly on the amount and precise character of the authority that Kyoto was *releasing* to Kamakura.[60] That Yoritomo was already master of the

55. E.g., in *AK* 1184/2/21 we see a reference to Yoshinaka's having awarded to a warrior in 1183/8 a confirmation decree for possession (*chigyō*) of some three estates. It was a privilege that Yoritomo normally reserved for himself. By the tenth month (if not earlier) the enmity between the two Minamoto cousins had become overt, and by the end of the year a Kantō army was moving westward in pursuit of Yoshinaka.

56. Within a matter of days Yoshinaka was made Director of the Left Horse Bureau (*Sama no kami*), governor of Echigo (subsequently governor of Iyo), and possessor of some 140 confiscated land units. Yukiie was made governor of Bingo (subsequently governor of Bizen) and holder of 90 land units. See *Hyakurenshō*, 1183/8/10, 8/16, p. 144.

57. A court decree of 1183/9, e.g., refers to outrages being committed in an Echizen estate by a certain "police captain" (*kebiishi*). This person is shown to be an agent of Yoshinaka by a related document affirming that the guilty party was the "former governor of Iyo," i.e., Yoshinaka. *Ninnaji Monjo*, 1183/9/27 Go-Shirakawa In-no-chō kudashibumi an, in *HI*, 8:3102, doc. 4107; and ibid., 1184/5 Go-Shirakawa In-no-chō kudashibumi, in Tanaka Minoru, ed., "Ninnaji monjo shūi," *Shigaku zasshi*, 68.9 (1959), p. 75. (Hereafter cited as Tanaka, "Ninnaji monjo.")

58. This is graphically described in *Gyokuyō*, 1183/9/5, 2:627.

59. The agreement took the form of an authorization from the In to Yoritomo. The original has not survived but references to it appear in *Hyakurenshō*, 1183/10/14, p. 145, and in *Gyokuyō*, 1183/int.10/13, 20, and 22, 2:642, 45–46.

60. The substantive points of the edict, as well as the inconsistencies found in the several *Hyakurenshō* and *Gyokuyō* paraphrases, can be summarized as follows: (1) Kyoto proprietorship of estates *either* in Tokaidō and Tosandō, *or* in those two circuits *plus* Hokurikudō, was to be restored with Yoritomo's assistance to its prewar condition; (2) should there be any persons in those regions who fail to obey, they were *either* to be

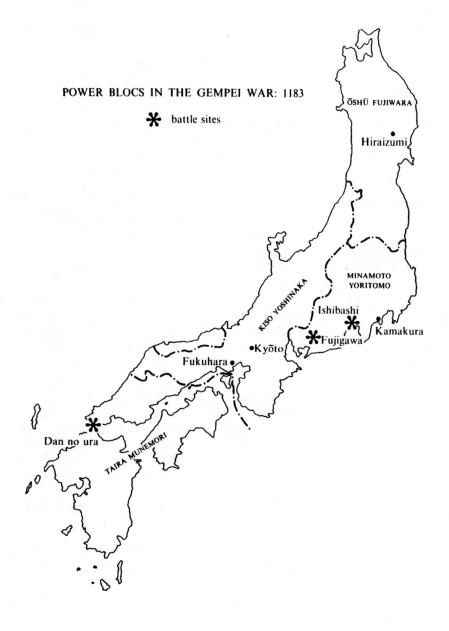

POWER BLOCS IN THE GEMPEI WAR: 1183

✳ battle sites

ŌSHŪ FUJIWARA

Hiraizumi

MINAMOTO
YORITOMO

KISO YOSHINAKA

Ishibashi

✳
Fujigawa

Kamakura

•Kyōto

Fukuhara •

✳
Dan no ura

TAIRA MUNEMORI

Kantō without this court decree, and that the Genji leader used this edict to expand his interests territorially and politically in the direction of the capital, are points that have been generally neglected. In the months after 1183/10 what we find is nothing less than a bakufu[61] push into Chūbu, Hokurikudō, and beyond, as well as a presumption by the Genji chieftain that he now possessed the right to substitute his own governance wherever conditions might warrant. Moreover, from roughly this date on, Yoritomo began to engage in an activity that had no precedent during Heian times: as a local figure he began to issue confirmatory decrees on behalf of central institutions. It was a clear reversal of past practice in which all such guarantees as well as all authority flowed outward to the provinces; and it was to mark a turning point in Japanese history. In the context of a country in crisis, writs with the force of actual power were coming to replace in importance court documents, which carried only prestige.

Therefore, the matter of how historians textually interpret the terms of the 1183/10 In decree seems much less important than how Yoritomo himself interpreted them. The bakufu would appear to have used both the 1183/10 authorization as well as follow-up edicts regarding the limits of Kamakura's police competence in the west[62] as virtually open-ended mandates for activities that often enough simply infringed on traditional Kyoto rights. At the very start we find an 1183/10 Yoritomo pronouncement in which the various lands belonging to Kamowake Ikazuchi Shrine were ordered freed from Heishi interference and resulting losses;[63] this was fully in accord with the intent of the In decree of the same month. By 1184, however, we see that Yoritomo's range of involvement in central affairs had become much wider. In the fourth month, for example, we find him actually settling a land dispute between two proprietors.[64] In the period that followed, Yoritomo is seen making high-level public official appointments in provinces where he had no authority, and shōen assign-

---

hunted down by order of Yoritomo, *or* merely dealt with by him as he saw fit. See Mass, *Warrior Government*, chap. 3.

61. The term "bakufu" itself appears only later, but I use it here to designate the government in Kamakura. In Chinese history "bakufu" had connoted the military headquarters of a person achieving the title of "captain of the guards," a designation which Yoritomo himself received from the court (and then resigned) in 1190. Although references to the bakufu appear in *AK* from about this time (e.g., 1191/3/3), this chronicle is a much later work. When the term actually came into use is not known precisely.

62. Recorded in *Gyokuyō*, 1184/2/23, 3:13.

63. *Kamowake Ikazuchi Jinja Monjo*, 1183/10/10 Minamoto Yoritomo kudashibumi, in *HI*, 8:3102–03, doc. 4109. We find in this document the increasingly common reference that an In decree had been issued but was being ignored. A little later we will see cases in which allusion to the In is simply dispensed with entirely. See n. 90.

64. *Kashiwagi Shi Shozō Monjo*, 1184/4/3 Minamoto Yoritomo kudashibumi, in *HI*, 8:3125 doc. 4147. For another example, see *AK* 1184/7/2.

ments in estates he did not own.[65] He is known also to have ignored legal channels by simply issuing directives to western province public officers completely outside his jurisdiction.[66] The court's several edicts to Yoritomo had given a measure of respectability to the new Kamakura government; the chaos into which the country was rapidly descending did the rest.[67]

The year 1184 thus saw the bakufu emerge as a national institution. This involved a somewhat confusing mosaic of simultaneous developments. In the military sphere, Yoshinaka was destroyed during the first month, thereby opening the way for the start of a consolidation drive in the Chūbu.[68] Also, for the first time Yoritomo turned his attention to defeating the Taira. No longer did the Genji chief entertain serious thoughts of compromising with his enemy. The Gempei War, which began in earnest only now, concluded barely a year later with the 1185/3 destruction of the Taira leadership at Dannoura.[69] In the political sector, we find Kamakura basing its newly inflated hopes for a permanent national presence on a policy that included the offer of Genji membership and confirmation of holdings in exchange for warrior pledges of loyalty.[70] It was a program of vassal recruitment that, much as in the Kantō, simply ignored traditional boundaries and immunities. At the same time, however, the bakufu saw obvious value in coming to the aid of individual estate owners whose

65. For a "public" appointment to the office of Iwami Province constable (ōryōshi), see *Hagi Han Masuda Ke Monjo*, 1184/5 Kajiwara Kagetoki kudashibumi, in *HI*, 8:3137, doc. 4175. Kajiwara Kagetoki was one of Yoritomo's western deputies. For shōen appointments to the officer-level posts of *gesu* and *kumon* in a central province (Settsu) estate, see *Aida Jirō Shūshū Eisha Monjo*, 1184/5/18 Minamoto Yoritomo kudashibumi, in *HI*, 10:246, supp. doc. 245.

66. For such a directive to Nagato Province, see *Nagato Sumiyoshi Jinja Monjo*, 1185/9/7 Minamoto Noriyori kudashibumi an, in Takeuchi Rizō, ed., *Kamakura ibun* (Tokyo, 1971), 1:4, doc. 5 (hereafter cited as *KI*). This document by Noriyori, a brother of Yoritomo, is directed to the Nagato resident officers (*zaichōkanjin*).

67. The pages of *AK* make this clear. Unchecked lawlessness was now rampant in many parts of the country, with the central government becoming increasingly paralyzed.

68. E.g., Yoritomo in mid-1184 moved against one of his own vassals in Kai-Suruga, Ichijō Tadayori (*AK* 1184/6/16). The objective, very likely, was to replace a ranking member of the "Kai Genji" with a houseman of his own choosing.

69. An account of the war during 1184-58 can be found in Shinoda, *Shogunate*, pp. 85-100. It is most interesting that Kamakura-period materials often speak of the "war of Bunji" (*Bunji no ran*), meaning the fighting and dislocations of 1184-86. (Technically, the Bunji period began only in 1185/9); For such a reference see *Kasuga Jinja Monjo*, 1257/12/25 Kantō gechijō, in Kasuga Jinja Shamusho, comp., *Kasuga Jinja Monjo* (Nara, 1928), 1:278-79, 23, I.4.

70. See *AK* 1184/3/1, 10/12, and 1185/1/1, for Yoritomo's offer of vassalage to western families of prominence who, despite prior Heishi associations, would now fight for the Minamoto. Not surprisingly, actual application of this policy was much more selective than the war rhetoric seemed to promise.

lands were being ravaged by indigenous lawbreakers. Despite the inherent conflict of these policies—protection of local against central interests and vice versa—the two were made to work for the bakufu's clear advantage. Men *and* land in a part of Japan far from the Kantō were now being brought within Kamakura's reach.

It was thus made clear that eastern warriors were now to be directly involved in both organizing and restraining their western counterparts. As part of this bakufu program of expansion into western Japan, Yoritomo in 1184 granted his power of attorney to four or five ranking vassals whom he designated as his deputies. Of first importance within this group was Minamoto Yoshitsune, brother of Yoritomo, who early in that year was dispatched to Kyoto for the purpose of opening an office there. In a technical sense Yoshitsune was charged with serving the court through an issuance of desist orders against warrior violence in a part of Japan still fully under central jurisdiction. In fact, however, it is possible to argue that unusual pains were taken to insure that Yoshitsune would perform in a primary capacity as Yoritomo's proxy; in none of the documents that bear his name do we see any reference to prohibitions of outlawry "in accord with an In decree." Furthermore, in all but one of these records the only signature we find is that of Yoshitsune's given name; no offices or imperial titles, as would normally have been the case for a central official, were affixed.[71] Finally, there is the content itself of Yoshitsune's directives. While all of these in one way or another seek to prohibit unlawful war tax or soldier levies in central estates, the beneficiaries were invariably great temples or shrines, not the In or other members of the court.[72] The only Yoshitsune documents not of this genre

71. The one exception is *Kasuga Jinja Monjo*, 1184/9/20 Minamoto Yoshitsune shojō an, in *HI*, 8:3149, doc. 4208, in which Yoshitsune's new guards' title of 8/6 (see *AK* 1184/8/17) is included. Yoshitsune's acceptance of this award without first seeking Yoritomo's approval marked the beginning of a deteriorating relationship between the two brothers that would have its greatest impact in late 1185. The important question here, however, is why, when several other Yoritomo vassals were receiving mid-1184 nominations for court appointments, Yoshitsune was consistently denied such a promotion. The usual explanation refers simply to Yoritomo's jealousy of his brother's military exploits and growing fame. But another reason seems to fit equally well. As I have argued, Yoritomo wished to have his deputy in Kyoto remain entirely outside the central bureaucracy. Of the remaining Yoshitsune documents issued in this capacity, four are dated from before his guards' award (between 1184/2 and 1184/5, in *HI*, 8:3116, 3135, 3137, docs. 4136, 4167, 4174; and 10:3915, doc. 5087), and the other (8:3160, doc. 4228), is dated 1185/1/22. This final document—with only Yoshitsune's personal seal as signature, *no* title—appears to have been issued just before he took to the field again in pursuit of the Taira.

72. See *HI*, 8:3116, 3135, 3137, 3149, 3160, 4136 (Kasuga Shrine), 4167 (Kōyasan Temple), 4174 (Kōya Denpōin Temple), 4208 (Kasuga Shrine), 4228 (Matsuo Temple),

show the latter attempting to secure the major public officer house of distant Iwami Province for the Genji camp.[73]

If Yoshitsune seems to have functioned primarily as a stand-in for his chief in Kamakura, this spirit of independence from Kyoto is equally in evidence for his replacements early in 1185. A pair of stylistic usages found in the edicts issued by Kondō Kunihira and Nakahara Hisatsune make clear the ultimate source of their authority. With the exception of the very earliest of their decrees,[74] all Kondō and Nakahara documents begin with the following set phrase: "The special agents of the Kamakura lord issue [Kamakura *dono otsukai kudasu*]. . . . " And second, while the two deputies, unlike Yoshitsune, do refer to prior authorizations issued by the In, invariably equal prominence is given to an edict of the Kamakura lord. The phrase thus appears as follows: "In accord with an In directive (*inzen*) and Kamakura lord directive [Kamakura *dono no ongechi*]."[75] Yoritomo evidently was not intending to *deny* the imperial polity within the latter's own reduced sphere, rather only to establish Kamakura as an independent government that could stand apart from the court.

Mentioned earlier was the bakufu's effort to make contact with and convert to vassalage the major families in non-Kantō areas. After the death of Yoshinaka in 1184/1, we find evidence, for example, of a Yoritomo deputy, Hiki Tōnai Tomomune, being sent to win control of Hokurikudō. A pair of documents from that year show Hiki securing local lords in Wakasa and allegedly making a local appointment into a shōen of Echizen.[76] While no actual proof exists of a Hiki involvement elsewhere in the Hokurikudō, such authority can be assumed both from his Kamakura-derived title of *kannōshi* and from a later reference in *Azuma ka-*

---

and 10:3915, doc. 5087 (unnamed shrine).

73. *Hagi Han Masuda Ke Monjo*, 1184/5 Minamoto Yoshitsune kudashibumi an, in *HI*, 8:3138, doc. 4177; and ibid., 1185/6 Minamoto Yoshitsune kudashibumi an, p. 3180, doc. 4262.

74. *Kinshōji Monjo*, 1185/4/24 Kantō gechijō an, in *HI*, 8:3173–74, doc. 4242. Since the disturbed area referred to in this document was the Tosandō's Ōmi Province—technically under Yoritomo's jurisdiction since 1183/10—perhaps there was no need to stipulate Kamakura's competence.

75. See e. g., Kondō and Nakahara decrees of 1185/4/28, 5/1, and 7/1, in *HI* 8:3174, 3175, 3181, docs. 4243, 4245, 4265.

76. *Jingoji Monjo*, 1184(?)/4/4 Minamoto Yoritomo shojō, in *HI*, 8:3125, doc. 4184, and *Ninnaji Monjo*, 1184/5 Go-Shirakawa In-no-chō kudashibumi, in Tanaka, "Ninnaji monjo," p. 75. Inasmuch as Wakasa's major provincial officer family, the Inaba, went over to the Chūbu-based Genji early in the war (*Gyokuyō*, 1180/11/28, 2:416), authority there may have been divided on some basis with Tomomune. After the war, and until 1196 when they were overthrown, the Inaba held the upper hand. See *Wakasa no kuni shugo shiki shidai*, in *Gunsho ruiju*, bunin bu (Tokyo, 1930), 2:107.

gami.[77] Also from 1184 we find a reference to Hōjō Muneyasu, an agent of Yoritomo (Yoritomo *no tsukai*), being sent during that spring to Echizen's Ushigahara Estate to take up residence.[78] Perhaps we can infer from this the initial stage of a settlement program of Kamakura housemen into certain parts of Hokurikudō.

But there were other approaches as well, each seemingly formulated to accommodate the special circumstances of individual areas. Thus while in Iwami and Iyo (in western Honshu and Shikoku) Kamakura succeeded in winning the support of the prominent Masuda and Kōno families, leaving each temporarily in independent command, in Sanuki a Kantō officer was sent for the purpose of organizing directly the resident officials there. Similarly, in several provinces that were closer to the capital region (Ise, Iga, and the Sanyōdō bloc from Harima through Bingo), we find bakufu officers, called *shugo* or *shugonin*, who not only performed as local recruiting agents but who assumed in their assigned areas a large percentage of the collapsed wartime governance. All of these shugo were warriors who had been sent out from the Kantō. In Kii Province, by contrast, evidence remains of a native shugo, a practice later eschewed. Finally, in Kyushu, which did not fall under extensive bakufu influence until late in 1185, we find Kantō aliens coming to exercise a share of local governance under the title "steward-in-chief" (*sō-jitō*).[79]

It will be evident from the foregoing that while the precise means of penetrating an influence varied from province to province, a common denominator did exist: independence from court-controlled hierarchies marks *every* case for which information survives. The emphasis was on obtaining de facto control of local agencies either by sending in eastern deputies or by creating a private link with a region's major family. Moreover, in those cases in which Yoritomo did accept governorships of the traditional type, they were for provinces that the bakufu already had absolute power over (for example, Sagami or Musashi) or were sooner or later dropped in favor of shugo and/or jitō (for example, Iyo).[80]

77. *AK* 1191/6/22. The term "kannōshi" is suggestive of a responsibility to promote agriculture by direct administration over farmers in public land. It was an assignment that not only seemed appropriate given the advanced dislocations brought on by the war, but that was certain to work to the bakufu's advantage. In order to carry out a a charge of this type, Tomomune was probably empowered with certain rights of control over the separate provincial headquarters (*kokuga*) in Hokurikudō. The right to dictate to these agencies of local government meant an opportunity to win the support of their resident officers. See Tanaka, "Ninnaji Monjo," p. 76.

78. See *Daigo Zōjiki*, vol. 10, in Asakawa Kan'ichi, *Land and Society in Medieval Japan* (Tokyo, 1965), Japanese section, p. 11.

79. For details on all of these see Mass, *Warrior Government*, chaps. 3, 4, and 6.

80. See *AK* 1184 6/20, 1185/8/29, and 1185/12/6 for the governor appointments made

Institutionalization of Kamakura Power, 1185-1190

It was mentioned earlier that destruction of the Taira leadership came in 1185/3. The end of the Gempei War, however, cannot be said to have resolved the major issues of the day. The warriors committing countrywide violence were under no immediate compulsion to cease these lawless activities, and a postwar restructuring of the central-local power arrangement was not as yet in the offing. Both problems were of course interlocking. Another problem involved the bakufu's need under the new postwar conditions to gain a greater control over its own legal future. Despite Kamakura's high degree of dependence on nontraditional means of obtaining and exercising power, the central polity could not simply be ignored. A way would have to be found to deny the In his freedom to prune the legal parameters of bakufu competence, while at the same time to borrow Kyoto authority to curtail armed band ravagings. Both objectives required new directions and new policies.

A break was slow in coming, however, leaving a strong impression of indecision during the spring and summer months of 1185. In truth, the real problem was one of knowing precisely what kind of decisive action *could* be taken. It was only gradually that a crisis over jitō control and a deterioration of the relationship between Yoritomo and Yoshitsune eventually showed the way. Brief comment on each of these is necessary here.

Almost parallel with the 1184 increase in local encroachments against land there developed a tendency for warrior violators to claim *both* allegiance to the Genji and possession of a noncentrally authorized jitō title. This was a very singular combination since it led to a growing identification of jitō with the Minamoto movement. To this was then added a flurry of central owner appeals that Kamakura take responsibility for stamping out these warriors-turned-jitō.[81] In this way the highly de

---

at Yoritomo's instigation. Almost all in central and western Japan went to courtiers who were considered friendly to Kamakura; where a western province governorship was assigned to a Genji vassal, such as Iyo to Yoshitsune in mid-1185, Yoritomo quickly saw the danger of such a step and moved to overturn this appointment. By 1186 the governorships that Yoritomo controlled were all in the east, with the single exception of Bungo, gateway to northern Kyushu (see *AK* 1186/3/13).

81. The jitō's 1180s development is examined in Mass, *Warrior Government*, chap. 4. Evidence of such locally authorized or self-styled jitō exists for widely separated parts of the country. E.g., for Echizen in Hokurikudo see *Ninnaji Monjo*, 1184/5 Go-Shirakawa In-no-chō kudashibumi, in Tanaka, "Ninnaji monjo," p. 75; for Tajima west of the capital, see *Kōzanji Monjo*, 1184/4 Go-Shirakawa In-no-chō kudashibumi, in *HI*, 8: 3133-35, doc. 4166; and for Kyushu, see *Itōzu Monjo*, 1185/4/22 Go-Shirakawa In-no-chō kudashibumi, in *HI*, 8:3172-73, doc. 4241.

facto jitō–Kamakura identification hardened: all that was needed for a formalization to take place was a pretext plus the awareness of the unlimited potential value of a claim to total jitō jurisdiction. "Dismissals" of self-styled jitō could then be combined with an even more momentous program of jitō "promotions." Appointment to this most sought-after of local titles would be posed as the regular reward for loyal vassal service, and the new jitō concept, connoting a secure, Kamakura-guaranteed land-management tenure, could become the major fulcrum for bakufu rewards and punishments.

What seems to have crystallized such thinking was Yoritomo's final estrangement with Yoshitsune, combined with the latter's investiture by the In as jitō for Kyushu.[82] As we have seen, Yoritomo's greatest sensitivity throughout the war was reserved for threats that issued from within his own clan. Quite predictably, therefore, when Yoshitsune began to steer a course during the ninth month that was openly rebellious, the Genji leader determined to seek destruction of his own brother. These plans went unfulfilled, however, as Yoshitsune eluded capture and induced the In to invest him with an anti-Kamakura charge. It was the third time in five years that Yoritomo had been branded a rebel. Yoshitsune did not stop there, however. As mentioned above, he received from Go-Shirakawa the special designation of jitō for Kyushu: it was a clear sign that times and conditions had changed since 1183 when Yoshinaka had demanded from the In investiture as shogun.[83] On that occasion Yoritomo's response had been swift and decisive, leading, we will recall, to a punitive expedition and greater involvement beyond the east. Now two years later a threat from an even more intimate clansman led to another sharp turn from the past.

What happened next is one of the most debated questions in all of Japanese history. While we know that an armed force was dispatched from the Kantō for the purpose of inflicting on the court a series of demands, we cannot be sure of the precise content of those demands—or of the court's response. *Azuma kagami* records that in addition to a thorough housecleaning of courtiers who had been connected in any way with Yoshitsune, the harried In was forced to agree to a Yoritomo right to appoint shugo (provincial constables) and jitō countrywide, as well as

82. An excellent treatment of the Yoritomo–Yoshitsune relationship appears in Shinoda, *Shogunate*, pp. 95–99, 122–30. This relationship had taken many turns since the first signs of strain in 1184/8, but it was only in the summer of 1185 that the estrangement began to assume break proportions.

83. See *AK* 1184/1/10. While the shogunal office merely elevated the holder to a ranking generalship, the jitō chieftainship seemed to imply both supervisory rights over territory and a command authority over all bushi. Minamoto Yukiie, Yoshitsune's ally, received a similar designation as jitō over Shikoku (referred to in *AK* 1185/11/7).

to a Kamakura levy of a standardized war tax.[84] There exists, however, considerable cause to doubt the complete accuracy of *Azuma kagami's* hindsight rendering of these seminal events. For example, a related *Gyo-kuyō* account fails to mention either shugo or jitō by name, referring only to certain undefined lands in western Japan that were now to be parceled out to Kamakura vassals.[85] How to square these two accounts has led historians into a confusing labyrinth of speculation. Several points stand out, however. While Kamakura-appointed jitō are known before 1185/11, the bakufu's countrywide program of placements began in earnest only from this juncture.[86] Second, shugo, as they came to be understood historically, did not appear until the 1190s;[87] *Azuma kagami's* account concerning their authorization in 1185 seems clearly in error. And third, the bakufu's authority during the period under review went far beyond jitō (and shugo) anyway. Evidently what Yoritomo had forced the court to acknowledge was not a range of competence that was specific, but rather one that was amorphous and embracing. Jitō were integral, but not yet everything. This is borne out by data such as a bakufu directive addressed to nonvassal warriors of various categories, and Kamakura prohibitory decrees aimed at warrior lawlessness in the different classes of land.[88]

84. The key entries here are 1185/11/28, 11/29, and 12/6. These references to shugo and jitō have long been fixed on by legal historians and textbook writers as representing the birth of feudalism in Japan. It is argued that Kamakura's right to appoint both figures countrywide constituted an official joining of vassalage with benefice, feudalism's sine qua non.

85. *Gyokuyō*, 1185/11/28, 3:119.

86. Jitō appointments had been made irregularly by Kamakura since 1180, e.g., the reference to a Shimotsuke Province district-level (*gun*) jitō appointment of 1180/11/27 in *Mogi Monjo*, 1192/8/22 shōgun ke mandokoro kudashibumi, in *Dai Nihon shiryō*, ser. 4, vol. 4 (Tokyo, 1903), p. 146.

87. While documentary evidence exists for a few "*shugo* figures" (*shugonin*) during 1184–85, these persons exercised a haphazard, emergency authority in their provinces that was very different from the tightly defined duties of the Kamakura shugo of the 1190s. I have seen only one or two fully contemporary references to shugo during the second half of the 1180s.

88. For a reference to the bakufu's jurisdiction over constables (*ōryōshi*), estate stewards (*gesu*), and resident provincial officials (*zaichō*), see 1187/9/13 Kantō migyōsho, in *KI*, 1:161, doc. 264, reproduced from *AK*. Taking only a single day in 1186, we can find bakufu desist orders issued against *bushi* outrages in (1) six *gō* units in Yamashiro, home province of Kyoto, (2) three private estates in Harima Province, (3) various sites in Suō Province, (4) a Tamba Province estate, and (5) several component units of a Kaga Province shōen. Whereas the guilty parties in (1) and (2) were only unnamed bushi, in (3) we see a reference to the unlawful acts of ranking vassal Doi Sanehira, in (4) the reference is to Hōjō Yoshitoki, Yoritomo's own brother-in-law, and in (5) one of several guilty persons was self-styling himself as a jitō. See (1) *Kamo Chūshin Zakki*, (2) *Torii Ōji Monjo*, (3) and (4) *Kamowake Ikazuchi Jinja Monjo*, and (5) *Hiramatsu Monjo*, 1186/9/5 Minamoto Yoritomo kudashibumi, in *KI* 1:106–07, docs. 167–71.

There was no immunity from the bakufu's countrywide enforcement power, save that which had been granted by Yoritomo or one of his deputies.

The significance of 1185 should now be obvious: the court had abdicated its traditional role as guarantor of last resort over the provinces. It was a development that had never come to pass under the Taira[89] and that constituted an open admission that Kamakura with its authority resting on power was now of more immediate influence than the court itself.[90] In early 1186 it might have looked very much as if the bakufu were about to claim a permanent right of interference in all public and private governance.

Such appearances, however, proved transitory. Gradually, as the Yoshitsune threat receded and as the burden of new responsibilities came to be felt, the bakufu leadership became aware that its own disorganized involvement in local affairs was contributing to the confusion and diffuseness of post-1185 jurisdictions.[91] The result was the beginning of a retreat from the advanced posture of late 1185. Deciding now to concentrate on a strengthening of its jitō jurisdiction, the Kamakura leadership undertook to return much of what it had recently seized.

If we were able to chart on parallel graphs the legal and extralegal growth patterns of Kamakura's range of competence we would see, then, roughly opposite configurations. During the first half of the 1180s the bakufu's ambitions continually outran what the court had authorized, while during the second half Kamakura is seen urging Kyoto to reassume much of its abandoned governance.[92] Besieged now by appeals for redress in cases involving nonvassal and non-jitō lawlessness, the bakufu found

89. Even in 1180 after Go-Shirakawa had been relieved of his responsibilities, we find the Heishi utilizing as a replacement the more amenable Junior Retired Emperor (*Shin In*), Takakura. This figure was permitted to issue judicial-type decisions much as in the past. See the settlement by Takakura of a suit regrading local outrages and boundary troubles for three Kōyasan Temple shōen (*Kōyasan Monjo*, 1180/12 Takakura Shin In-no-chō kudashibumi, in *HI*, 8:3010-11, doc. 3946). The appeal had gone to the office of the In, not to the Taira.

90. E.g., a central proprietor of 1186, when calling on the residents of an estate in Mimasaka Province to cease their outrages, refers only to a decree issued to that effect by Yoritomo. No mention is made of any edicts of guarantee by the In. See *Sakuyō Shi*, 1186/11/12, Shugaku Hō shinnō-no-chō kudashibumi, in *KI*, 1:114, doc. 190.

91. Yoshitsune's confederate, Yukiie, was hunted down and killed in 1186 by troops sent out from the Kantō, and by the following year Yoshitsune, now a powerless refugee, was granted sanctuary in Hiraizumi, fortress of the northern Fujiwara. He was subsequently killed by his protectors in 1189 on the eve of a bakufu invasion of the north.

92. Before 1183/7, of course, Yoritomo's governance over the Kantō was entirely beyond the pale of court-centered legality.

that it did not possess the resources to guarantee everyone's interests.[93]

On a related point, the return of authority to Kyoto was not for the reasons usually offered, namely, concessions granted out of weakness vis-à-vis the court. There was weakness, certainly, but it was the weakness of constituted authority—now meaning the bakufu—versus anarchy. Under these circumstances Kamakura's restoration of jurisdiction over all titles save that of jitō was undertaken in the hope that revitalized hierarchies would serve as the most effective counterweight to continued warrior violence.[94] Such was the impetus for restabilization that Kamakura even became aware that the jitō tenures of its own men could not be held sacrosanct; when conditions warranted, the bakufu would have to be prepared to countermand awards distributed to distinguished vassals.[95]

Given this circumstance in which many of the greatest instigators of trouble were in fact men of Kamakura, much of the bakufu's time over the next fifteen years was taken up with adding and subtracting housemen through recruitments and ongoing purges. Firming up control over the Chūbu region was a major preoccupation especially during the late 1180s, with attention turning to a jettisoning of key western housemen in the period from 1196. In both cases, and indeed for all parts of Japan, it became a basic policy of the bakufu to send out replacements chosen from within its own midst. Virtually all external jitō awards (as opposed to those of a confimatory nature), as well as all shugo titles, went to families whose origins were strictly eastern.

93. One of the clearest examples of this is seen in a bakufu judgment decree of 1205. After reluctantly assuming jurisdiction in this non-jitō case, Kamakura directed that in the event of future trouble all appeals be sent to the In. See *Kōyasan Ikenobō Monjo*, 1205/5/27 Kantō gechijō, in *Kōyasan monjo: kyū Kōya ryōnai monjo*, 9:93–94, doc. 49.

94. The local office that was closest to the jitō in terms of income and responsibility was the *gesu* post. Much evidence exists to show that the bakufu on its own volition eschewed jurisdiction over this gesu title. A series of documents relevant to Ōi-no-shō in Mino Province will illustrate this. During the period from 1210–13 a local dispute arose concerning possession of that estate's *gesu* post. An affidavit from the bakufu stated that although details of the trouble had been sent to Kamakura, the case could not be handled since an earlier jitō authority had been "returned" to Tōdaiji as proprietor. Next we see a Tōdaiji reconfirmation of its earlier *gesu* appointment, and a statement by temple authorities that after Kamakura had made inquiries concerning the matter, the latter had announced Tōdaiji's jurisdiction. See *Tōdaiji Yōroku*, 1211 Ōe Hiromoto shojō; *Tōdaiji Monjo*, 1212/1 Tōdaiji bettō mandokoro Ōi-no-shō gesu shiki buninjō; and ibid., [undated] Tōdaiji kumonjo kudashibumi an, in *Gifu Kenshi, shiryō hen*, kodai-chūsei III (Gifu, 1971), pp. 529–30, docs. 181–83.

95. E.g., Doi Sanehira's jitō post over Bingo Province's Ōta-no-shō was abolished in mid-1186. See *AK* 1186/7/24 and *Kōyasan Monjo*, 1186/7/24 Minamoto Yoritomo shojō, in *KI*, 1:87, doc. 131.

In 1190, after a successful military campaign against the Fujiwara of northern Japan, Yoritomo made his first trip to Kyoto. This was not, however, the pilgrimage of a provincial warrior seeking fame and fortune in service to the court. Yoritomo was no Taira Kiyomori. Instead, Yoritomo's triumphant visit provided final symbolic proof that Japan now possessed two governments: the worst of the 1180s crisis was now over, but the bakufu and its leader remained essentially unintegrated with the traditional system of central rule. This became graphically evident when Yoritomo, after receiving (and then selectively resigning) a handful of ranking titles from the Kyoto court, proceeded to return to his own warrior capital in the east. Even the well-known accession of Yoritomo to the post of shogun in 1192 had no immediate importance; he had been lord of the Kantō since the end of 1180, and Japan's greatest chieftain from soon thereafter.

By the time of Yoritomo's death in 1199 the bakufu could claim, therefore, not merely a birth but a history of almost two decades. It owed that history not to the imperial authority that had attempted throughout to make of eastern warrior power a growth within itself, but to the vision and efforts of a leadership that saw its greatest hope in continued independence.

7 *Jitō* Land Possession in the Thirteenth Century: The Case of *Shitaji Chūbun*

JEFFREY P. MASS

The Kamakura *jitō* can be described in several ways. He was first an appointee and vassal of the *bakufu* which claimed an exclusive jurisdiction over the office tenure of its man. Only Kamakura could appoint, discipline, and dismiss jitō. At the same time, a jitō was an appointee to a piece of land that neither he nor the bakufu held at the highest level of possession.[1] In varying degrees of reality, such authority lay with a traditional noble or religious institution, or, in the case of public domain, with a "provincial proprietor" and his client, the governor. What this meant in practical terms was that beginning in the 1180s the country's non-military absentee proprietors were forced to absorb into their estates management-level warrior–officers over whom they had no direct control. It was this immunity of the jitō as a vassal of Kamakura that set the stage for the thirteenth century's endemic central–local struggles over land.[2]

The Central–Local Power Balance before 1180

While classifiable under various systems, essentially there were two types of jitō—those who were longtime residents in their appointment areas, and those who were newly intruded from the outside. It is often suggested that confirmatory-type jitō (the former group) involved a finalization by the bakufu of a local possession that even before 1180 was often quite secure. This security issued from the fact that future jitō families commonly held their lands as shōen, the result of a transaction in which

---

1. The bakufu did come to possess directly considerable domain in the eastern provinces, especially in its base area of the Kantō. It also obtained in ownership an unknown number of estates that had been seized in the middle 1180s from the Taira. In probably the majority of cases, however, jitō assignments were made into the estates of others.

2. For a full treatment of the jitō's immunity, see chap. 5 of my forthcoming *Warrior Government in Early Medieval Japan: A Study of the Kamakura Bakufu, Shugo, and Jitō* (New Haven, 1974).

a title deed and regulated income were traded off for central legal protection against provincial levies and entrance. The essence of real authority, however, was kept in local hands.[3]

As true as this description may seem if one were to judge only from commendation and investiture documents,[4] in fact, as other records reveal, the long-term amelioration of a local lord's condition was much less certain: shōen establishment proved readily translatable into central owner gain in ways not made explicit in the original contract. In explaining this development, shōen proprietors (ryōke) were often pushed to considerable lengths to make their estates more responsive to their own dictates and needs. That is, in the face of general warrior lawlessness and the continuing plague of governor office disregard of shōen immunity,[5] there were some ryōke, especially religious institutions, who used their superior status to convert shōen into objects of greater central control. This aspect of the ryōke's potential has generally been undervalued even though a look backward from the thirteenth century makes the phenomenon clear. The ryōke's property interest, as we shall see, was not a tenuous thing; it exhibited points of real strength as well as a remarkable quality of resilience.

In the twelfth century, before the bakufu's formation, we should consider then not merely the rising power of warriors but also the jurisdictional authority of the country's leading proprietors. Central among the rights that shōen owners adroitly used were the reinvestiture of commending families with each new generation, the settlement in the capital of complex local disputes relating to shōen, and the regular examination of fields (kenchūken) preliminary to taxation.[6] The posting of central agents, and increasingly of a permanent deputy, merely sharpened the discontinuities of interest between central and local figures.

3. Minoru Shinoda, *The Founding of the Kamakura Shogunate, 1180-1185* (New York, 1960), pp. 23-25.

4. Commendation documents often made it quite explicit that the essence of shōen administration was to remain in the hands of descendants of the original donor. E.g., *Ninnaji Monjo*, 1139/11 Fujiwara Kaneko kishinjō, in Takeuchi Rizō, ed., *Heian ibun* (Tokyo, 1963), 5:2038, doc. 2417. (Hereafter cited as *HI*).

5. The violations of the Echizen governor against Ushigahara-no-shō represent an unusually clear example of this. See *Daigo Zōjiki*, 1133/6/14 Kan sen shi, in Kyoto Fu, comp., *Daigoji shin yōroku*, Jō (Kyoto, 1951), p. 196. An English translation of this document appears in Asakawa Kan'ichi *Land and Society in Medieval Japan* (Tokyo, 1965), pp.47-49.

6. For an interesting discussion of the shōen owner's *kenchūken*, see Shimada Jirō, "Zaichi ryōshusei no tenkai to Kamakura bakufu ho," in Inagaki Yasuhiko and Nagahara Keiji, eds., *Chusei no shakai to keizai* (Tokyo, 1962), pp. 241-43.(Hereafter cited as Shimada, "Zaichi.)"

In the Kantō, where the majority of the post-Heian confirmatory-type jitō held their traditional homelands, the foregoing commended-land pattern was exceeded in importance by two other models. In cases where older shōen existed, it sometimes happened that the larger among local holders (myōshu) were invested as "shōen officers" (shōshi) and charged with much of the responsibility for estate administration and protection. Presumably their modest class origins and military inclination made them ideal candidates for this role. Among the houses in this category that assumed as surnames the names of their shōen (and that later became important vassal families of Kamakura) were the Shibuya of Sagami, Shimokabe of Shimōsa, and Hatakeyama of Musashi.[7] What is important, however, is that before 1180 these "shōen officer" houses were still of only estate functionary ranking; their titles remained precarious, their lands subject to tax levies. Many of them had considerable cause to feel dissatisfied and insecure.

The second pattern is the critical one for the Kantō region. As it happened, the greatest of the warrior families of eastern Japan held most of their landed interests outside the shōen system of immunities. As duly authorized members of the provincial officer class, these houses possessed broad territories—often whole districts—that were technically part of the "public land" sector. But even these families could show a surprising vulnerability to political decisions made in the capital. The outstanding illustration of this is the 1136 confiscation by the governor of the district-level holdings of the great Chiba house of Shimōsa.[8] The latter's hereditary "provisional vice-governorship" (gon no suke), which had helped promote the family's status among local peers, was of no avail against dictates issued officially from the capital. The Chiba were compelled to either suffer the indignity of confiscation in silence, or become outlaws and risk being cut adrift permanently.[9]

The result was a readiness on the part of warriors who possessed horses and men but not the legal power to resist central superiors to participate in the bakufu's new system of locally based land confirmations. They avidly sought and received in return for pledges of loyalty an authorization making them jitō, and thereby acquired at last a total immunity

---

7. Yasuda Genkyū (Motohisa), Nihon shōen shi gaisetsu (Tokyo, 1966), pp. 134–35.

8. Details of this incident can be found in Ichiki Monjo, 1146/8/10 Shimōsa no kuni Taira (Chiba) Tsunetane kishinjō, in HI, 6:2187–88, doc. 2586.

9. Reinstatement came a decade later after the Chiba heir had paid a large indemnity to the provincial governor's office. (Ibid.) His family's inheritance, however, was still insecure and in 1160 he lost it again. (Ibid., 1161/4/1 Shimōsa gon no kami Taira [Chiba] Tsunetane shinjō an, 6:2527–28, doc. 3148.) Reinstatement this time came only after the launching of the Minamoto movement in 1180.

against centrally inflicted punishments or dispossessions. This was a revolutionary development, although it did not yet imply full "local proprietorship." Jitō investitures did not, ipso facto, require the withdrawal—
at least from shōen—of the proprietary agents and administrators who
might still be present. In view of Kamakura's willingness to allow some
eastern shōen to survive intact, a stage beyond the receipt of a jitō title
was sometimes found necessary. The arrangements that emerged were
called *ukesho* and involved a negotiated contract to the effect that the jitō
would exercise a full local administration merely in return for regular
tax transmissions. Eastern shōen coming under such agreements now
became "jitō proprietorships" in all but name.[10]

The Eastern Jitō in Western Lands

If jitō title-holders in the east had now as a group traveled much of the
way toward excluding from their homelands most central authority, this
was far less true for the other great class of jitō, the easterners who, as
rewards for valor, were appointed into the confiscated lands of western
enemies. Strictly speaking, what had been confiscated was not territory
but the rights in land of the person (or family) being dispossessed. Not
only was the top layer of proprietary authority left intact in most cases,
but since most of these exchanges were taking place in a region of Japan
where ownership and administration were still largely fused, the recipient
jitō found themselves in a relatively disadvantageous position. In a very
real sense they were expected to perform as their predecessors might have
performed—as obedient officials to a central owner. As jitō, they were
immune from summary dismissal by Kyoto. But their duties and income
levels in an alien part of Japan made it clear that theirs was a legacy
that was in fact quite modest. Expected to continue in the tradition of
Heian tax managers and policemen for centrally owned shōen, there
were many jitō who gradually undertook through violence to convert
these new holdings into possessions on the eastern model. The basic
clash of interests that highlights the thirteenth century thus became one
between Kantō-born jitō and central proprietors of western province
estates.

This contest was made the more inevitable by the presence in domains of
resident deputies called *azukari dokoro*. While in earlier times such
figures tended to be indigenous local magnates,[11] we have already noted

10. For early ukesho in the Kantō see the case of Musashi Province's Kawagoe
Estate, a holding of Shin Hie Shrine located in Kyoto. *Azuma kagami* (*AK*) 1186/7/28
and 8/5. See also *AK* 1192/12/25 for a bakufu-arranged jitō ukesho over Yoshida-no-
shō in Sagami, a holding of Enman-In temple

11. *Azukari dokoro*, which literally means "custodial office," was the title that a major

that in the twelfth century proprietors began working to replace these with experienced administrators of their own choosing. The start of the Gempei War seems to have accelerated this process, so that by 1200 we find centrally posted azukari dokoro in many parts of the country. The powers held by these figures were substantial, and lay in areas that would be of major concern to jitō.[12] In addition to the azukari dokoro's supervision over tax collection and general estate administration, he assumed a dominant position vis-à-vis native shōen officers. Evidence of the latter comes in his growing role as an on-the-land proxy for the proprietor: azukari dokoro began to issue the reinvestiture decrees usually required after each generational change.[13] Similarly, it was this figure who now might perform as mediator in disputes involving the content or validity of testamentary documents.[14] When placed alongside the introduction of proprietor-controlled granaries, warehouses, labor levies, and irrigation projects, the impression was reinforced that shōen really were the domains of their central owners.

It was into this milieu that the first eastern-born jitō came either as replacements for those of the native officer class who had fallen victim in the wars, or as new managers in estates that were either troubled locally or whose proprietors had themselves been guilty of anti-bakufu indiscretions during the Gempei conflict and aftermath.[15] Not surprisingly under these diverse circumstances, it proved very difficult for Kamakura to carry through on its policy of maintaining continuity with local precedents. In those cases, for example, in which a simple one-for-one jitō–native officer exchange did not take place, local officials (as well, perhaps, as the estate proprietor) were now constrained to squeeze from their own perquisites an "inheritance share" for the incoming jitō. In at least some of these instances the induced sacrifices of those both on and over the land were still considered inadequate. Easterners, as mentioned earlier, were accustomed to broad income and authority levels over their domains.[16]

commending family might be invested with on the occasion of a shōen's formation. See, e.g., *Ninnaji Monjo*, 1134/int.12/15 Taikenmon'in no chō kudashibumi an, in *HI*, 5:1956, doc. 2310.

12. Yasuda, *Nihon shōen*, pp. 154–56.

13. E.g., see *Tōnan'in Monjo*, 1183/8 Ōi-no-shō azukari dokoro dōshō gesu shiki buninjō, in *Gifu Kenshi, shiryō hen*, kōdai-chūsei III (1971), pp. 506–07, doc. 139. This practice became even more marked during the Kamakura period.

14. See, e.g., *Tōdaiji Monjo*, 1180/10 Yamashiro no kuni Tamai-no-shō azukari dokoro kudashibumi an, in *HI*, 8:3003, doc. 3930.

15. For details, see Mass, *Warrior Government*, chap. 5.

16. On the occasion of a dispute over Sasakibe-no-shō in Tamba Province, the jitō complained that in 1200 "the *jitō* income share was only a name, not a fact." Quoted in *Higashi Monjo*, 1238/10/19 Rokuhara gechijō, in *Kamakura saikyojō*, Ge, p. 10., doc. 7.

The discontent on all sides over the size of the jitō allotments was not, however, the primary cause for concern. The jitō's intrusion as a management-level officer who was not strictly within the shōen hierarchy made estate administration immediately prone to disruption. On the one side the jitō as an easterner and appointee of Kamakura was not technically beholden to anyone in the shōen chain of command; it was the bakufu, not the azukari dokoro, who renewed the jitō post after each generational change. And on the other side, members of the native officer class, despite their ranking in all cases at a level below the jitō, were nevertheless commonly excluded from the latter's jurisdiction.[17] It was a fundamentally unstable arrangement, bound to arouse resentments and to lead to a jitō's attempting to bring his authority abreast of that of the estate deputy, the azukari dokoro.

Thus, with the 1180s appearance of the Kamakura jitō, the power relationships of many shōen were radically transformed. As a general rule, original commending families were further reduced in potency, emerging now as pawns in a developing contest between the jitō or his deputy[18] and the azukari dokoro. At first it was probably the proprietary interests that gained an advantage from this development: the common incidence of jitō-induced violence tended to force a greater reliance on the azukari dokoro, and we have numerous examples of both the traditional officer and actual cultivating classes appealing for redress and assistance to the estate deputy.[19] Ultimately, however, this balance began to turn.

For it was the bakufu which held sole jurisdiction for the settlement of all such jitō-related disputes. This meant that the central owner would have to submit the case to Kamakura, trusting in the equity and efficiency of the latter's justice. As is well known, Kamakura did seek to impose settlements that were in conformity with local precedents. But the extensive delays involved in gathering evidence, the leverage used by jitō to force the signing of favorable affidavits by local personnel, and the freedom of many jitō simply to ignore negative judgments, all took their toll.[20] Gradually there developed a condition in which estate authority

---

17. See n. 24 and 63 for examples that show the variation on this point from one shōen to another.

18. Eastern jitō made regular use of deputies (jitōdai) in the management of their western province holdings. The house heads (sōryō) themselves remained in the family's Kantō homeland area. Thus when we speak of jitō activities in western lands, we are often referring to what was done by proxies, usually kinsmen.

19. See e.g., the anti-jitō complaints of local residents (including officers) in Wakasa Province's Kunitomi-no-shō. Recorded in *Mibu Monjo*, 1207/12 Kantō gechijō, in Kanaishō Toshoryō, comp., *Mibu shinsha komonjo* (Tokyo, 1930), pp. 48–50.

20. The 1207 incident cited in the foregoing note will suffice to show all three of these flaws in the bakufu's vaunted system of justice. Concerning delays, in a 1216 replay of

came to be seen largely in terms of what was possessed either by the jitō or by his azukari dokoro rival. Nothing else counted politically, meaning in effect that the traditional hierarchy of more or less vertical tenures had now flattened out and divided into two roughly parallel tracks of authority. Both the jitō and the proprietor possessed their "spheres."[21]

The Division of Authority between Central Owners and Jitō

To illustrate this phenomenon of divided authority we can point to areas such as tax sharing, segmentation of the officer corps, percentage sharing of the spoils from police confiscations of runaways and criminals, and a division of general responsibility over the non-grain producing parts of a shōen. To a certain extent landed estates by their very nature as congeries of graded tenures had always exhibited a sharing of perquisites. For example, tax officers long had retained a percentage of the annual receipts. But as the following examples relevant to the jitō will show, such sharing had now largely equalized and become based on a condition of mutual power or tension.

The annual tax (nengu) had long been symbolic of central proprietary privilege. It is most interesting, therefore, that the mid-thirteenth century Kohayagawa jitō house of Aki Province's "former" and "new" (hon and shin) Nuta Estates received from each, percentage shares of the annual tax equaling about one-third and two-fifths respectively.[22] Examination of the land surveys from both domains shows very clearly that the productive output of these estates was meant to be shared between jitō and ryōke: for the majority of itemized tax-yielding regions we see specific reference to jitō and ryōke shares, and at the end of one of these two registers we find the total income for each.[23]

the 1207 dispute we find that the suit had been filed with the proper Kamakura authorities seemingly during the first month; it was only now midway through the eighth month that the dispute was being judged. Second, regarding the jitō's use of pressure to acquire signed affidavits, we see a reference in this 1216 edict to peasants and at least one local officer being seized by the jitō in 1209 and forced to write such documents. Finally, the fact itself that we are witnessing in 1216 a partial duplication of the original 1207 suit gives clear indication that the jitō had simply ignored the earlier judgment. See ibid., 1216/8/17 Kantō gechijō, pp. 51–55.

21. Yet the jitō was still conceived of as a shōen official, while the ryōke was considered proprietor. For a schematic expression of these dual tracks of authority, see Yasuda, Nihon shōen, p. 176.

22. Yasuda Genkyū, Shugo to jitō, (Tokyo, 1964), pp. 156–57. The specific totals were 203.49 out of 686.76 koku for the Nuta hon-no-shō, and 126.89 of 337 koku for Nuta shin-no-shō. In addition, the jitō held tax-exempt salary fields (kyūden) in each estate amounting to 12 chō and 5 chō respectively (1 chō = 2.94 acres).

23. Kohayagawa Ke Monjo, 1243/2 Aki Nuta shin-no-shō kenchū mokuroku, in Dai Nihon komonjo, iewake 11, (Tokyo, 1927), 1:556–77; and ibid., 1252/11 Aki Nuta

As for segmentation of the officer corps, we are able to find instances in which a jitō lawfully controlled such shōen officials as the *kumon* or *sōtsuibushi*, as well as other cases in which this kind of authority became the object of bitter contention in the courts.[24] To take only one example of the latter, in a law suit of 1293 between a Satsuma Province jitō and azukari dokoro, more was at stake than merely the right to dictate to these native officials. Ultimate authority over their persons (meaning the appointment and dismissal privilege) as well as jurisdiction over their lands and rights were the objects of competition. In this dispute a power over the *gesu* holder and one *myōshu* post was acknowledged as belonging to the azukari dokoro, while three other *myōshu* titles, plus the posts of *kannushi, kumon, tadokoro,* accompanying rice and dry fields, and residence areas, were all recognized as belonging under the jitō.[25]

When we come to percentage divisions of the local confiscation privilege, ratios of one-third to two-thirds (either way) or fifty–fifty are common. Thus in an Awaji Province estate we find a two-thirds share for the ryōke, in a Wakasa Province shōen an evenly divided percentage, and in an Echizen domain a total authority on the jitō side over confiscations.[26] Finally, concerning the products from mountains and rivers, the standard division was fifty–fifty, as in the Awaji shōen just cited.[27]

The lesson to be gained from these examples is that the jitō and azukari dokoro had now become rivals, the one depending on his bakufu-derived immunity, elite military standing, and the constant pressure he could bring to bear locally, the other utilizing as his major support the authority

---

hon-no-shō, kenchū mokuroku, pp. 578–82. Few registers of such clarity have survived. (Hereafter cited as *DNK, iewake.*)

24. See, e.g., the bakufu's 1227 judgment to the effect that the *kumon* post of Ōta-no-shō in Bingo Province was properly under the jitō's control. *Kōyasan Kōzanji Monjo,* 1227/7/7 Kantō gechijō, in *Kamakura saikyojō,* Jō, p. 54, doc. 59. Regarding estate constables (*sōtsuibushi*), the Kohayagawa jitō house of Takahara-no-shō in Aki held jurisdiction over this post. *Kohayagawa Ke Monjo,* 1223/6 Aki Takahara-no-shō jitō tokubun chūmon, in *DNK, iewake 11,* 1:543–44. For a case in the same province and from the same year in which the *sōtsuibushi* was under the proprietor's authority, see Kumagaya Ke Monjo, 1223/3/18 Taira bō seibaijō, in Saitama Kenritsu Toshokan, comp., *Kumagaya ke monjo* (Urawa, 1970), p. 29, doc. 9. The estate in question was Miri-no-shō. This kind of local variation can be found in all parts of Japan.

25. *Shimazu Ke Monjo,* 1293/1/13 Kantō gechijō, in *Kamakura saikyojō,* Jō, p. 255. doc. 193.

26. *Iwashimizu Tanaka Ke Monjo,* 1287/11/27 Kantō gechijō, in ibid., pp. 223–27, doc.166; *Tōji Hyakugō Monjo,* 1247/10/29 Kantō gechijō, in ibid., p. 81, doc. 79; *Hōon'in Monjo,* 1243/7/19 Kantō gechijō, in Asakawa *Land and Society,* pp. 25–27 (Japanese section), doc. 48. This confiscation privilege and accompanying police authority was known under the term *kendanken.*

27. See *Iwashimizu Tanaka Ke Monjo,* 1287/11/27 Kantō gechijō, in ibid., pp. 223–27, doc. 166.

still adhering to central proprietary status. From this condition there developed during the middle decades of the thirteenth century practices such as "compromise" (*wayo*), ukesho (now in western province estates), the division of shōen by units of production (*tsubowake chūbun*), and finally the physical division of undifferentiated territory (*shitaji chūbun*). All were clearly expressive of both the new power of jitō and the retreat and/ or shift in emphasis of central title holders. Seeking to salvage their domains first by one method, then another, it soon became clear that Kyoto's proprietors had now gone on the defensive.

The Techniques of Settlement and Compromise in Mid-Thirteenth-Century Japan

Early in the Kamakura period the bakufu was quite assertive in its claim to jurisdiction over all disputes involving jitō. By the 1220s the bakufu had even begun to create a body of laws to be applied in those cases in which the "precedents" (or documents) of a local area did not supply a ready solution. Such an urge for complete control in all jitō matters, however, soon fell victim to the needs and limits of practicality. The divided-inheritance system insured that with each generation the number of jitō (technically, fractional jitō = *ichibu* jitō) would increase geometrically, and this, combined with the tendency toward bolder local action, meant an unrelenting rise in judgment cases demanding attention.[28] Perhaps inevitably the bakufu began to grow more amenable to allowing litigants to settle their own differences—even if this meant a "change" in an area's precedents or a resolution that was not in accordance with the letter of bakufu law.[29] While the sacrifice of jurisdiction in return for peace was the obvious objective here, we can easily imagine that many jitō chose to interpret this new policy in quite an opposite way. A program of carefully orchestrated pressure on the local level would create the conditions for compromise (*wayo*).[30]

The range of wayo cases is enormous and includes a clear majority of the ukesho and chūbun agreements examined below. Wayo was not a

28. The classic case of a fragmenting jitō family and its embroilment in constant litigation both internally and against the shōen proprietor is that of the Miyoshi jitō house in Bingo's Ōta-no-shō. For the bibliography on this shōen, see Yasuda, *Nihon shōen*, bibliog. p. 38.

29. Kamakura made clear its official position on this matter in an edict of 1247. In cases where a compromise settlement might be worked out, the bakufu's laws regarding jitō income and authority were not to apply. See Satō Shin'ichi and Ikeuchi Yoshisuke, eds., *Chūsei hōsei shiryōshū* (Tokyo, 1969), 1:162, *tsuikahō* 295. (Hereafter cited as *CHS*.)

30. In the words of Professor Bark describing Europe, "What started out as an abuse became a custom and eventually was claimed as a right" (William Carroll Bark, *Origins of the Medieval World* [Garden City, N. Y., 1958], p. 120).

mode of settlement adhering to any specific pattern but merely an expression of détente on any issue of long-standing dispute between jitō and ryōke. Thus, for example, an Awaji Province wayo document of 1278—one of the longest in this genre—actually sought to resolve some twenty-seven contended points. Every conceivable category of dispute is represented, including even the jitō's regular confiscation and sale of peasant-owned cows and horses to defray the costs of excursions to Kyoto.[31] As was standard in most wayo cases involving jitō, the bakufu reviewed this document and issued an edict of confirmation.[32] Evidently, Kamakura wished to retain a residual jurisdiction over its jitō appointees but hoped to avoid embroilment in the resolution of their disputes. This was not, however, always realistic: less than ten years later the bakufu was called on to resolve directly a flaring up of many of the same disagreements that had been "settled" by wayo a decade earlier.[33]

Turning next to ukesho arrangements, the aim was to guarantee regular tax receipts by contractually obligating jitō to transmit clearly itemized amounts. In return, the ryōke would renounce all involvement with the shōen in question, withdrawing his agents and closing his local office as part of the agreement.[34] Two points are noteworthy. In the first place, it must be made clear that these were ukesho in which the jitō were essentially foreigners, that is, eastern warriors in western lands. And second, these natives from the Kantō were now, by virtue of their ukesho contract, giving final displacement to whatever similar arrangements had been made at an earlier date by original commending families. If a scenario for two hundred years of history could be reduced to a sentence or two, the following synopsis might seem appropriate: at a point subsequent to the original commendation of lands, and then incorporation as a shōen, real authority came to be absorbed into a central proprietorship. However, after two or three generations of jitō pressure, a return of such powers to the land itself took place, only now with a nonindigenous Kamakura jitō as beneficiary.

Let us sample several of these ukesho agreements. One of the clearest examples comes from a component unit, Jibi-hon-gō, within Bingo Pro-

31. *Iwashimizu Monjo*, 1278/12/8 Awaji no kuni Ukai betsugū zasshō-jitō wayojō, in *DNK, iewake 4*, 1:413–20, doc. 216.

32. Ibid., 1279/1/20 Rokuhara gechijō, pp. 420–23, doc. 217.

33. Ibid., 1287/11/27 Kantō gechijō, pp. 423–30, doc. 218.

34. Professor Toyoda Takeshi suggests that in the wake of an ukesho the agents of the ryōke were denied involvement with the tax process only; intercourse with shōen did not cease regarding other matters. I do not agree with this interpretation, as will become clear shortly. Evidence relating to ukesho in Jibi and Okuyama estates (discussed below) demonstrates that proprietary involvement of any kind was specifically denied for both shōen.

vince's larger Jibi Estate. The settlement is dated 1308/2 and can be summarized as follows: (1) full authority for that gō was henceforth to be under a Yamanouchi family-head jitō ukesho; (2) entrance by any agent of the proprietor (ryōke) was now prohibited: (3) the jitō was to pay the ryōke forty-five *kanmon* of cash per year in installments of twenty-five and twenty respectively; (4) in the event of crop losses due to an act of nature, a special ryōke deputy would be sent to ascertain the extent of the loss, with appropriate tax reductions made if warranted; (5) should the ryōke violate in any way the terms of this agreement, the obligated ukesho amount was to be halved; and finally (6) should the jitō fail to pay as stipulated, the ukesho was to be revoked with full authority returned to the estate deputy (*zasshō*).[35]

It is not certain whether in the years that followed any opposition to this arrangement arose on either of the two sides. Clearly there was room for disagreement since the zasshō and jitō remained rivals who were in close proximity to one another. The Yamanouchi continued to serve as jitō over the whole of Jibi Estate even after gaining an ukesho for the hon-gō region, while the zasshō remained as deputy for Jibi minus only the hon-gō area, which had now gone under jitō control. It is interesting that when troubles did develop—at least those that are documented —they came as a result of antagonisms within the jitō house itself. In a document of 1317 a "fractional" (*ichibu*) jitō claimed that the house chief was not to interfere with that portion of the forty-five kanmon for which he himself was responsible; his share would be delivered directly.[36]

Taking as a second example an ukesho arrangement of 1240 for Oku-yama-no-shō in Echigo Province, we find that the jitō had obligated him-self to transmit either 100 *koku* of rice or 600 *mon* cash for each *koku*, plus an unrecorded *ryō* amount of cotton for clothing or 800 *mon* cash for each 10 *ryō*. The azukari dokoro was not permitted to enter the shōen or to conduct business of any kind with Okuyama Estate. The jitō, finally, was not to increase the labor burden on local residents merely to expedite transport of the annual tax.[37]

---

35. *Yamanouchi Ke Monjo*, 1308/12/18 Jibi-no-shō hon-gō sōryō jitō-zasshō wayojō, in *DNK, iewake 15*, pp. 13–14, doc. 13. The payment of taxes in coin increased with great rapidity during the Kamakura period. For a discussion of the equivalent values and efficiency of money and rice see Shinjō Tsunezō, *Kamakura jidai nō kotsū* (Tokyo, 1967), pp. 24–25. We find the calculation that while one horse could carry only. 6 *koku* (2 *hyō*, or 90 kilograms) of rice, the same horse could transport about 30 *kanmon*.

36. *Yamanouchi Ke Monjo*, 1317/5/6 Bingo Jibi-no-shō hon-gō sōryō jitō-ichibu jitō wayojō an, in *DNK, iewake 15*, pp. 16–18, doc. 15. Intrafamily quarreling was endemic for the entire period and served to complicate the effort of a house head to wrest control of a region from a central owner.

37. *Chūjō Ke Monjo*, 1240/9/27 Okuyama-no-shō azukari dokoro Fujiwara Naonari

Within a mere four years, we find the jitō and the azukari dokoro already disputing over the central owner's desire to conduct an estate-wide land survey (kenchū). In the lawsuit that developed, the jitō argued that a proprietary investigation would disrupt the agreed-upon inviolability of his ukesho; clearly he was attempting to seal permanently the estate's boundaries and to freeze the tax at the originally stipulated rates. On the other side, the azukari dokoro's position can only be interpreted as an acknowledgment of having made a bad bargain. Evidently he now hoped to compromise Okuyama Estate's new jitō-held immunity and to gain at least the potential of rate or bulk increases through a survey of that domain's fields. The bakufu upheld the initial contract of 1240, thereby confirming the jitō in his newly acquired rights.[38]

The most common causes of central owner dissatisfaction with an ukesho was the jitō's failure to pay the amounts agreed upon. In these cases we often read of huge sums that the ryōke now claimed as being in default; attempts at renegotiation sometimes followed. The helplessness of a proprietor in this situation is revealed in a document of 1327. A jitō ukesho had been in existence since 1211 for Tomita Estate of the central noble Konoe family. Over the years tax losses had accumulated and there had been numerous appeals. In 1283 the Hōjō family as jitō had commended its Tomita authority to Kamakura city's Engakuji Temple, but the losses had continued. Finally, in 1327 the Konoe sought to offer both a cancellation of all past complaints and an end to its plea for an estate-wide land survey. In return, the Engakuji jitō holder was to see to it that a revised annual tax, now only 110 kanmon, was sent to Kyoto during the eleventh month of every year. The document ends on a note of total unreality: should there be any continuation of tax violations, the original suit was to be revived and the payment schedule made to conform to the agreement of 1211."[39]

In this instance the refusal of the Hōjō-controlled bakufu to uphold "justice" worked to the clear and ongoing disadvantage of a central owner. The bakufu did have laws concerning ukesho—one of 1268, the other of 1299—and these must be mentioned; but they were no more than guidelines. The earlier of the two averred that ryōke attempts to overturn ukesho agreements were illegal beyond the usual statute of limitations,

wayojō, in Niigata Ken Kyōiku Iinkai, comp., *Okuyama-no-shō shiryōshū* (Niigata, 1965), p. 98.

38. Ibid., 1244/7/21 Kantō gechijō, p. 100.

39. *Engakuji Monjo*, 1327/5/18 Owari no kuni Tomita-no-shō ryōke-zasshō keijō, in Kamakura Shishi Hensan Iinkai, comp., *Kamakura shishi, shiryō hen* (Kamakura, 1956), 2:130–31, doc. 74. Within a few short years, Tomita would fall subject to a shitaji chūbun. See n. 104.

twenty years.[40] Presumably this meant that Kamakura would at least *hear* petitions for ukesho cancellation in advance of the two-decade deadline. The emphasis, at any rate, was on preserving those ukesho that had been in existence since before the late 1240s. The 1299 decree signified a partial adjustment in bakufu policy. It stipulated that while the earlier edict had in effect guaranteed all ukesho from before the 1240s, henceforth any contracts postdating 1221 and not arranged by the bakufu were to be under the proprietor's discretionary control.[41]

This shift in Kamakura's policy—granting Kyoto owners the *option* of retaining ukesho agreements regardless of the statute of limitations—is generally interpreted by scholars as being one part of a 1290s Hōjō program to revive central authority. The basic objectives were to provide a counterweight to the advance on the land of Kamakura housemen and to lighten Kamakura's judicial load by establishing ryōke jurisdiction over privately agreed-upon ukesho.[42] Unfortunately, it is difficult to gauge the effectiveness or meaning in practice of this 1299 law. In 1304, for example, we see the bakufu rejecting a ryōke appeal for abrogation of an ukesho that had been in existence since 1240. What makes this case interesting is a reference to confirmatory documents of 1240 and 1244,[43] as well as other evidence showing a demonstrably private origin for this ukesho (see n. 37). Here was a pattern that was probably much duplicated, and that suggests a limited application of the 1299 law. The bakufu's "return" of jurisdiction to ryōke appears to have affected only those ukesho whose jurisdiction was never entirely out of central hands anyway. Conversely, those ukesho possessing bakufu approval documents simply continued as before to retain full validity.

Shitaji Chūbun in Japanese History

It has generally been thought that the failure of an ukesho often led in time to a further stage or strategy, that of *shitaji chūbun*, or the territorial division of shōen. Here we encounter problems on a number of important points. For example, scholars have been unable to agree on why some estates proceeded to the threshold of a chūbun, while others did not; on whose interests were being promoted by a chūbun agreement; and on the appropriate place chūbun should hold in the larger sweep of Japan's

40. *CHS*, 1268/4/25 *tsuikahō*, 1:334.
41. Ibid., 1299/2 *tsuikahō*, 1:303.
42. For an example of an ukesho contract that had been entered into "privately"—that is without the use of bakufu "good offices"—see the case of Ategawa-no-shō in Kii Province, a Kōyasan holding. *Kōyasan Monjo*, 1276/7 Ategawa-no-shō jitō Yuasa Munechika chinjō an, in *DNK, iewake 1*, 5:711, doc. 1152.
43. *Chūjō Ke Monjo*, 1304/12/26 Kantō gechijō, in *Okuyama-no-shō shiryōshū* p. 108.

institutional history.[44] Perhaps most intriguing of all is the question of whether these land divisions served to convert affected jitō into Japan's first medieval fief-holders.

Certain preliminary data will be useful. First, there are some seventy-odd chūbun cases that have been identified,[45] about 80 percent from Kamakura times. The great majority of these are clustered in the final third of the period, with the earliest known example coming in 1237.[46] Second, all but a handful of the known chūbun cases occurred in either western Japan or Hokurikudō; both the Kantō, where Kamakura (and therefore jitō) power was dominant, and the central provinces (Kinai), where ryōke possession of land was still largely intact, are almost wholly excluded.[47] Finally, it has been hypothesized that a majority of chūbun cases probably occurred in estates that had received eastern jitō in the period after 1221 (the date of the Jōkyū War).[48]

It will be useful to make clear as well that we are referring to three types of land division and two methods. They are (1) equal division, (2) unequal division, and (3) component sharing on the so-called tsubowake format. Of twenty-five known cases of (1) and (2), thirteen were equal and twelve unequal, the latter ranging from a six-sevenths share favoring a jitō to a two-thirds share favoring a ryōke.[49] It can be assumed, therefore, that no institutional significance attaches to the precise fractional division of each chūbun case.[50] The two "methods" are much more important. Chūbun came about either by a compromise agreement (wayo, thirty-three known

44. E.g., Hirayama Kōzō has seen chūbun settlements as demonstrably the "final solution" to long-standing jitō–ryōke disputes. As a result of these divisions, he has argued, there emerged two independently held estates where only a single estate under a dual authority had existed before. In contrast to this view, Inagaki Yasuhiko has interpreted shitaji chūbun settlements as being the result of two wholly different programs and intentions for the land now divided. While the ryōke side was desirous merely of gaining absolute security over revenue (halved, to be sure, but now free from jitō peculation), the jitō wished to establish himself as a full local owner. Summarized in Yasuda Genkyū, "Shitaji chūbun ron," in Yasuda, Jitō oyobi jitō ryōshusei no kenkyū (Tokyo, 1961), p. 426. Yasuda's own views will be discussed later.

45. See a list of sixty-eight in Shimada, "Zaichi," pp. 221–23.

46. Ibid.

47. In Kinai, in fact, there is only one known Kamakura period chūbun case, two in all. (Ibid., pp. 222 and 224.) A full fifty-three out of Shimada's assemblage of sixty-eight are in western Honshu, Shikoku, and Kyushu. (Ibid., p. 218.)

48. Nagahara Keiji, "Namboku-chō nairan," in Iwanami kōza, Nihon rekishi 6, chūsei 2, p. 56. Actually, only four cases can be proven through documents. (Shimada, "Zaichi," p. 286.)

49. Ibid., pp. 273–74.

50. Technically, then, we should not be calling these "chūbun" since that implies equal shares. For that reason some scholars prefer to use "bunkatsu," meaning a division that is not necessarily equal.

cases), or by a one-sided petition on the part of the ryōke (six known cases). We find *no* instances in which a jitō appealed to the bakufu for a shitaji chūbun ruling.[51]

One immediate conclusion is therefore possible. Among the several defensive strategies that ryōke commonly came to initiate in the later Kamakura period, chūbun settlements were not necessarily the most desirable from the vantage point of jitō. This is made explicit in a 1303 incident in which, on the occasion of an ukesho agreement, the jitō is warned that a chūbun judgment would be levied against him should he fail to meet his annual tax commitment of 130 kanmon.[52] Clearly, a land division is being posed here in the form of a punishment. There are other cases that show only a slight variation on this theme. Referring once again to Okuyama-no-shō in Echigo, we find the proprietor of this estate actively seeking to impose a chūbun on an unwilling jitō. It will be recalled that in 1304 the ryōke of Okuyama had suffered rejection by the bakufu on his appeal for an ukesho dismissal. In the very next clause of the judgment edict we see that a chūbun petition had also been filed, probably as an alternative settlement possibility. In the ryōke's mind an ukesho cancellation was the desired end, chūbun a fall-back solution. Both requests were denied (see n. 43).

Miri and Ōyama Estates: Two Examples of Shitaji Chūbun

With the foregoing as background, we can now turn our attention to two actual chūbun case studies. In Miri Estate in Aki Province the jitō office was originally granted as a 1221 Jōkyū War award to Taira (Kumagaya) Naotoki.[53] From the start the Kumagaya came to exercise an extensive authority due to a rich legacy from the former jitō, who had been dispossessed. Not only did the Kumagaya hold a 100 percent share of the confiscation privilege for criminals and runaways,[54] but out of the eighty-four *chō* of rice land composing Miri he exercised the "executive privilege" (*shinshiken*) over all but an estimated thirty-seven. These latter fields, exclusively farmer-level *myō* units (*hyakushō myō*), constituted the full extent of the proprietor's jurisdictional area.[55]

The quarrels that developed soon after 1221 between jitō and ryōke

51. Shimada, "Zaichi," pp. 273–76.
52. Quoted in *Kasuga Jinja Monjo*, 1303/9 jitō Fujiwara Hidetsuna ukebumi, in Kasuga Jinja Shamusho, comp., *Kasuga Jinja monjo* (Nara, 1928), 1:405, doc. 348.
53. *Kumagaya Ke Monjo*, 1221/9/6 Kantō gechijō, in *Kumagaya ke monjo*, p. 26, doc. 7.
54. Ibid., 1223/3/18 Taira bō seibaijō, p. 29, doc. 9.
55. Shimada, "Zaichi," p. 246. Even at that, the jitō's police and confiscation authority was shōen-wide, meaning that the ryōke's hold over the thirty-seven chō was not immune from jitō interference.

were dwarfed in importance by the cleavage that occurred within the Kumagaya house itself. In 1235 the bakufu resolved a dispute between Naotoki and his brother, Sukenao, in a most interesting way: it ordered a parceling of the family's jitō post over Miri-no-shō. On the model of later *tsubowake chūbun* cases, a one-third approximation of everything possessed in Miri by Naotoki was given to his estranged brother.[56] This meant that salary fields, residence areas, local shrines under Kumagaya jurisdiction, and other perquisite sources, were all divided under a unit-by-unit format that could only be cumbersome and unsatisfactory.[57]

We hear nothing further for almost thirty years but then witness in 1264 an extraordinary development. So bitter had the internal family dispute now become that the bakufu moved to consummate a territorial division of Miri Estate between the two contending jitō factions themselves.[58] It was almost as if that shōen belonged to the Kumagaya rather than to its proprietor in Kyoto. In the following year the *bakufu* adopted a final bold measure in this matter: it ordered its deputies in the capital (the so-called Rokuhara *tandai*) to send agents to Miri for the purpose of striking actual boundary markers.[59] How the ryōke reacted to these developments, and how the latter's interests were affected, have unfortunately gone unrecorded. Surviving documents covering the next two decades refer only to the still-unresolved Kumagaya family feud. Finally, however, in 1299 we encounter something quite unexpected—a compromise division (wayo chūbun) between the jitō possessor of the two-thirds share of Miri and the estate's legal proprietor, Shin Kumano Shrine. It is recorded in the bakufu's confirmation edict for this settlement that the ryōke's share was only eight chō.[60] Hence the easy calculation that the jitō had now garnered some forty-eight chō, or six-sevenths of his two-thirds portion of Miri-no-shō.[61]

The episode continues beyond 1299, but we have already seen enough to draw some tentative conclusions.[62] The special advantages of the

56. *Kumagaya Ke Monjo*, 1235/7/6 Kantō gechijō, in *Kumagaya ke monjo*, pp. 35–36, doc. 15.

57. Ibid., 1235/11/12 Aki Miri-no-shō jitō tokubun denpata tō haibun chūmon, pp. 37–45, doc. 16.

58. Ibid., 1264/5/27 Kantō gechijō, pp. 50–53, doc. 20. The number of disputed items leading to this one-third–two-thirds division is a full twenty-two.

59. Ibid., 1265/5/10 Kantō migyōsho, p. 54, doc. 21.

60. Ibid., 1299/10/12 Rokuhara gechijō, pp. 62–63, doc. 28.

61. These figures are based on Miri's eighty-four chō total and the jito's twō-thirds share, i.e., fifty-six chō. A bare eight chō out of this the fifty-six were left to the ryōke.

62. Shortly thereafter the two jitō sections of Miri Estate came to be designated as separate shōen. The two-thirds portion was called the "former estate" (*hon shō*), the one-third part was called the "new estate" (*shin shō*). See Shimizu Masakane, ed., *Shōen shiryō*, Ge (Tokyo, 1933), p. 1967.

Kumagaya jitō can be dated from the time of first appointment to Miri in 1221. Although we know that the proprietor possessed jurisdiction over at least two local officers within Miri,[63] it is clear that the Kumagaya were much more fortunate in their "inheritance" than other easterners receiving awards in western Japan. By the same token, however, the very richness of this legacy served to sharpen the competition between the two Kumagaya brothers for possession of the entire package—all to the ryōke's detriment. While Miri had been listed as a Kumano Shrine holding for more than a century, the proprietor's authority over that estate was obviously quite fragile.[64] We can thus appreciate why Kumano was evidently willing to accept a chūbun arrangement that left it in possession of only eight chō, a one-seventh interest. An eight-chō share immune from jitō interference was better than a much larger estate that produced no income.

If the Miri case is illustrative of a chūbun decision highly favoring the jitō side, the case of Ōyama-no-shō in Tamba Province is representative of something quite different—a ryōke-induced division of whose merits the jitō had to be persuaded. A domain with a history stretching all the way back to the ninth century, Tōji-owned Ōyama Estate did not receive a jitō until 1221.[65] In 1241 an ukesho was negotiated, and registers from both that year and 1266 show the extent of the jitō's obligation.[66] This agreement, however, seems not to have ended the temple's direct involvement with Ōyama. Not only do we fail to find the usual written prohibition against ryōke dealings with an estate under ukesho contract (see n. 34), but several Tōji-issued tax documents suggest that the jitō's range of authority was something less than complete.[67] Perhaps it was inevitable, then, that difficulties would eventually forge to the surface: in 1287 we find Tōji moving to challenge the very validity of the original contract. The arguments in the resulting litigation can be summarized as follows.

63. *Kumagaya Ke Monjo*, 1233/5/28 Shingen Hosshi ukebumi, p. 34, doc. 14.

64. See Miri's inclusion in an 1181 register of Kumano holdings: *Shin Kumano Jinja Monjo*, 1181/12/8 Go-Shirakawa In-no-chō kudashibumi, in *HI*, 8:3053–54, doc. 4013. Miri was the only Kumano estate in Aki Province.

65. Most of the surviving documentation for Ōyama has been gathered into a convenient volume edited by Professor Miyagawa Mitsuru, *Ōyama Mura shi, shiryō hen* (Tokyo, 1964). Ōyama's 1221 receipt of a jitō is made clear in ibid., 1287/12/10 Kantō gechijō, pp. 64–66, doc. 71. No records survive for the critical period 1135–1240.

66. Ibid., 1241/5 Ōyama-no-shō ryōke nengu ukebumi an, pp. 59–60, doc. 62; 1266/12/14 Ōyama-no-shō ryōke tokubun chūshinjō an, pp. 60–61, doc. 63; and 1266/12/14 Ōyama-no-shō jitō Minamoto (Nakazawa) Motosada ukebumi an, pp. 61–62, doc. 65. These registers are very detailed and show that in addition to rice obligations of various kinds, other grains as well as special products were included. In the second of the two 1266 documents we see a reference to a collated total of 200 koku.

67. Ibid., 1267/8/18 Tōji mandokoro kudashibumi, p. 62, doc. 66, and 1280/12/7 Tōji kudashibumi, pp. 62–63, doc. 67.

The estate deputy (*zasshō*) claimed first that a scattering of peasant documents between 1242 and 1265 made clear that he, not the jitō, had been exercising general competence (*shōmu*) in Ōyama.[68] What the jitō had negotiated, he continued, was merely a "private ukesho" with a former shōen deputy, but this was clearly illegal. For these reasons both the ukesho and jitō title should be revoked, with full authority reverting to the temple proprietor. If that were infeasible, the estate itself should be divided (*shitaji o chūbun serarubeki no yoshi*). In his rejoinder the Ōyama jitō, Nakayama Motokazu, argued that the jito post had been held since the Jōkyū War with an ukesho in force since 1241. The status quo should be maintained. Motokazu then submitted a 1241 bakufu edict proving that an ukesho had indeed been agreed to. With such overwhelming evidence on his side, the jitō was awarded victory.

The next part of the dispute concerned ryōke claims that the land register on which the ukesho and tax amounts were based was not being observed by the Nakazawa. The jitō disagreed. The bakufu judged that while the deputy was repeatedly citing a register from the year 1150, the original of that document had not survived; the 1266 register would be continued as the ukesho standard. The deputy then went on to complain that the jitō had reneged on tax payments amounting to 560 koku over the period 1280–84. The jitō answered by presenting his receipts for 1280–82. The bakufu ordered the Nakazawa to make all payments due from the missing two years.[69]

This 1287 litigation illustrates clearly the case of a jitō who preferred an ukesho to a territorial division of his shōen. This can only be because the status quo with its estate-wide powers promised a greater range of authority than a half share under a chūbun. At the same time, we see that the absentee proprietor was primarily concerned with tax receipts. This interest would be crucial in the next stage of the controversy.

Before proceeding to the revived legal battle of 1294, it is noteworthy that a year earlier the bakufu had issued a decree encouraging more *wayo*-type chūbun settlements.[70] Henceforth chūbun were deemed permissable for both well-endowed jitō who had "inherited," upon appointment, considerable local powers (*hompo jitō*), and "no legacy" jitō for whom the bakufu had had to create income and privilege regulations in

---

68. As we have seen (n. 20), forcing peasants to sign affidavits was a common practice during a period in which the possession of documents was the sine qua non for victory in a lawsuit.

69. Ibid., 1287/12/10 Kantō gechijō, pp. 64–66, doc. 71. Two other minor items were also resolved.

70. *CHS*, 1293/5/25 *tsuikahō*, 1:288–89.

the period after 1221 (*shimpo jitō*).[71] The objective, clearly, was to promote a jitō receptiveness to wayo by warning that the bakufu would begin issuing punitive division orders without regard to either a shōen's history or a lawbreaking jitō's desires.[72] The outcome of this legislation was mixed, however. While an increase in the number of wayo chūbun is unmistakable, there was a corresponding upsurge in lawsuits calling explicitly for land divisions. Absentee proprietors, after all, now had some reason to expect that what they could not accomplish by wayo, they might be able to gain by direct appeal. This is what seems to have dictated the next stage of events in Ōyama-no-shō.[73]

In a complaint lodged by the Ōyama deputy in 1294, the latter now admitted the legitimacy of his rival's ukesho, asserting only that the Nakazawa's refusal to pay the full complement of taxes had continued unabated. There should thus, he argued, be a judgment calling for a "paring off" of land.[74] The jitō replied that in fact the taxes had been paid every year, and that therefore the deputy's suit was groundless. He added, however, that should the bakufu decide to hand down a "paring off" judgment anyway, he, the jitō, would not object; insuring the regularity of the absentee owner's taxes *was* an important goal. Such reasonableness on the part of the Nakazawa led to a quick termination of the suit. Foreseeing an amicable settlement, the bakufu simply issued the order for the land transfer.[75]

In seeking an explanation for the jitō's apparent change of heart, the key factor seems to have been Tōji's shift in strategy. The temple had ceased calling for a territorial division (chūbun) and was now petitioning

71. I discuss in detail the *hompo–shimpo* jitō problem in "The Jōkyū War: Origins and Aftermath" (Paper prepared at Yale University, 1971). In a literal sense *hompo* means "originally appointed" and *shimpo* connotes "newly appointed." These translations, however, have little to do with their actual meaning.

72. To the extent, i.e., that the hompo and shimpo legalisms were still expressive of real differences (a questionable hypothesis), the former were a group for which, according to Professor Shimada, we find no proprietor-induced chūbun in the period before 1293; "compelled chūbun" were foisted only on jitō of the shimpo category since they, because of their constitutional weakness, would have profited by such a division. (Shimada, "Zaichi," pp. 275–76.)

73. Whether or not the Nakazawa were considered hompo or shimpo is unclear. While we know that they received their appointment as a post-Jōkyū reward, it is uncertain whether their perquisites were considered an "inheritance" from a former shōen officer— the point on which the hompo and shimpo distinction depended. In view of the bakufu's 1287 rejection and then 1294 acceptance of a ryōke's chūbun plea, perhaps the Nakazawa were considered hompo jitō.

74. The term used is *kiri watasu*, and, as we shall see in a moment, this meant something quite different from *chūbun*.

75. *Tōji Monjo*, 1294/10/23 Kantō gechijo an, in *Ōyama mura shi*, pp. 66–67, doc. 72.

merely for disengaged tax lands.[76] It is to be noted also that the details of the settlement had not yet been worked out; the bakufu was authorizing a land separation, not stipulating its shape. A year later we find that actual implementation was left largely in the Nakazawa's own hands. With the chief objective (according to the bakufu's edict) that of creating a ryōke enclave of sufficient size to guarantee desired tax levels, a paring of certain fields from the jitō's ukesho competence was now carried out. Assigned to the temple in full authority (*ichien sata*) were twenty-five chō of paddy land, five chō of dry land, and a variety of undisclosed forest areas. Henceforth the Nakazawa were to have no involvement in tax or other service matters relating to the proprietor's reduced sphere.[77]

Accompanying this statement from the jitō was another document, a detailed register showing the unit-by-unit location in three specific village areas of the thirty chō of rice and dry fields.[78] Evidently the Nakazawa were overseeing not the partitioning of Ōyama Estate into exclusive territorial sectors, but rather only a division on a limited tsubo-wake basis.[79] So foreign in fact was the notion that a territorial chūbun was now being implemented that we do not even know how large the jitō's share was; neither that nor Ōyama-no-shō's full totals is recorded. Our conclusion, therefore, is that the jitō was simply creating in 1295 an owner's preserve of sufficient yield to meet the 200 koku tax figure of his ukesho contract.[80] In return for this largess—in effect a jitō's posting of boundaries for an absentee proprietor's demesne-type lands—the Nakazawa gained both a release from all duties to a higher authority, and an unhindered (though untitled) lordship over the rest of Ōyama-no-shō.[81]

Before leaving this estate, a word must be added about the fate of this limited division settlement. It seems clear that what the ryōke was seeking

76. A second possibility is that the Nakazawa had been apprised—based on the 1293 law—of the bakufu's intention to order the division; the jitō's defense posture merely reflected the inevitable, albeit now made more palatable by the Tōji's reduced demands.

77. Ibid., 1295/3/8 Ōyama-no-shō jitō Nakazawa Motokazu ukebumi an, p. 67, doc. 74.

78. Ibid., 1295/3/8 Ōyama-no-shō jitō Nakazawa Motokazu bunden tsubowake chūmon, p. 68, doc. 75.

79. That it was "limited" is made clear in other *tsubowake* cases in which virtually everything within a shōen is itemized and divided. See, e.g., the several registers relating to Kanaoka Higashi Estate in Bizen. *Gakuanji Monjo*, 1323/5/7, in Yanagizawa Bunko Semmon Iinkai, comp., *Yamato Kōriyama shishi, shiryō hen* (Kyoto, 1966), pp. 110–13, docs. 23–27. Separate registers were prepared for each of the jitō's branch lines, with individual fields and cultivators listed.

80. The figure 200 koku is found in the documents of 1266 and 1287. See nn. 66 and 69.

81. To reiterate, we are not talking about exclusive spheres since the ryōnke's "new" lands were mixed in with those held by the jitō.

were guaranteed tax receipts from carefully stipulated units of land; territorial possession was not considered critical.[82] Even this limited objective, however, was to remain largely out of reach: a fierce intra-temple factionalism developed over what had already been reduced in size.[83] Beyond that, there is evidence that the Tōji's share of Ōyama Estate became afflicted from another source. In the year 1300, we read of fifty lower-class persons commandeering the rice tax,[84] and thirteen years later of "evil bands" (akutō) violating the shōen under the pretext of being agents of one of the faction's deputies.[85] Incidents of this type are increasingly easy to find in the source materials of the early fourteenth century. The fate of the jitō in his Ōyama sector is not so well documented, although he, too, probably felt the effects of this rising local unrest.

The Meaning and Range of Application of Shitaji Chūbun

In other shōen when tsubowake settlements were found lacking, advancement to a territorial division was sometimes tried.[86] This was the case, for example, in a portion of Ōno-no-shō in Kyushu's Bungo Province. An unsatisfactory unit-by-unit parceling of 1292 was replaced in 1314 with a chūbun agreement that halved this territory by imposition of a simple north–south boundary.[87] The main issue here, as in many other "total" chūbun decisions, was a deterioration of the jitō–estate deputy relationship to the point of total exhaustion and breakdown. For a chūbun threshold to be reached, in other words, both sides had to recognize that continued coexistence within the same administrative unit was no longer possible. Diversionary compromises would no longer avail when the objective, after generations of mutual antagonism, had become one of eliminating each other.

82. This is the general argument of Professor Yasuda regarding any proprietor's opting for a tsubowake rather than a territorial chūbun. (Yasuda, "Shitaji," p. 450.)

83. A document of 1298 shows a division of the temple's thirty chō between these two factions. Tōji Monjo, 1298/9/19 Ōyama-no-shō bunden jō, in Ōyama mura shi, pp. 70–71, doc. 80.

84. Ibid., 1300/5/25 Tōji shigyō Gen'i shojō, p. 73, doc. 85.

85. These akutō represent a rising lawlessness that was in opposition to all constituted authority, whether ryōke or jitō. From the 1260s and 1270s we begin to see rather numerous references to these criminal bands, and Japanese scholars have interpreted their appearance as marking the real beginning of a disintegrating local order. Ibid., 1313(?) 12/13 Hokkyō Engi bugyō shittatsujō an, p. 93, doc. 138.

86. We have already seen an instance of this sequence in regard to the Kumagaya factional rift within Miri-no-shō. The more normal pattern was for the phenomenon to occur in a jitō versus ryōke context.

87. See Shiga Monjo, 1292/5/10 Kantō migyōsho, in Wakita Manabu, ed., Hennen Ōtomo shiryō (Kyoto, 1942), 1:549–50, doc. 641, for the tsubowake division; and ibid., 1314/5/28 Ōno-no-shō zasshō wayojō (Kyoto, 1946), 2:14, doc. 18, for the chūbun.

While chubun resolutions never emerged as the dominant mode of
settlement between jitō and estate deputies, the final Kamakura decades
did exhibit a marked increase in land divisions.[88] The bakufu's continuing
encouragement of central–local compromises undoubtedly contributed to
this phenomenon, and by the period's end we even begin to find chubun
settlements in non-jitō cases. This is an indication that Kamakura appointees were no longer alone as the elite of provincial warrior society.
The ravages of the divided inheritance system and the vagaries of bakufu
policy had produced a less exclusive, less protected class of jitō. As a
consequence we now begin to see holders of the *gesu* post, a ranking
land-management title traditionally under central jurisdiction, achieving
a level of challenge that could induce a chubun resolution.[89] Two examples will suffice to show this. In 1327 a gesu family of long residence in
Kii Province's Wasa-no-shō is recorded as being principal to a chubun
agreement. The stated objective was to preclude all future dissonance over
taxes (*nengu*) and land administration (*shitaji shomu*).[90] Similarly in Bizen
Province in 1324 we find the gesu of one shōen and the deputy (*zasshō*)
of another deciding to compromise and divide four villages between
them.[91]

It was argued earlier that exclusive territorial divisions were the result
of a bilateral decision to end a long-standing professional relationship.
For the jitō the permanent removal of the estate deputy and the elimina-
tion of the annual tax meant that the jitō himself now stood as the highest
authority over a lawfully recognized unit of territory. He was still called
"jitō," only now that title had come to mean something akin to fief-
holder.[92] We can illustrate this by observing what happened in the wake

88. It is probable that a majority of these were only partial in nature, e.g., a chubun
involving mutually claimed mountain and forest areas in an estate in Ise Province. East-
west boundary markers were set just as if an entire shōen were now being divided. See
Ōtomo Monjo, 1300/8/3 Fujiwara Kagetada wayojō, in ibid., 1:582–83, doc. 686. Chūbun
such as these did not involve a termination of the relationship between jitō and zasshō.

89. In terms of function jitō and gesu were very much alike. The difference was that
the bakufu claimed appointment and dismissal jurisdiction only for jitō. See chap. 6, n.
94.

90. *Kangiji Monjo*, 1327/9/3 Wasa-no-shō zasshō-gesu wayojō, in Sonoda Kōyū, ed.,
Kangiji monjo (Osaka, 1968), pp. 28–29, doc. 37.

91. *Ani Jinja Monjo*, 1324/4/19 Bizen no kuni Kashinobu-no-shō gesu-Toyohara-no-
shō zasshō wayojō an, in Fujii Shun and Mizuno Kyōichirō, eds., *Okayama Ken komonjo
shū* (Okayama, 1956), 3:105. The location of the four villages and the reasons for this
dispute between officers of neighboring shōen (though under the same proprietor) are
unclear.

92. Since all vassal-related chubun gained validity through a bakufu writ of confirmation, retention of the jitō title may have been conceived as symbolizing the continuing
link with Kamakura. To that limited extent the jitō's new holdings can be considered as
a "fief" held of higher authority.

of a 1262 chūbun in Higo Province's Nohara-no-shō. Some thirteen years after this division, at the time of the Mongol wars, the jitō head, who until now had retained his eastern homeland as the family's base area, went with his kinsmen to Higo in Kyushu. The western sector of Nohara Estate became the family's new homeland, with the several branch lines each converting a component *myō* of the halved domain into its own residence area.[93] From this denouement we can see the optimal advantage of a land-division settlement for a jitō house.

Equally interesting is the chūbun context on the central owner's side. Professor Yasuda has offered the most compelling general explanation. Under conditions of rising local unrest, he has argued, the securing of taxes and other services involved more than just confrontation with a jitō. Direct administration over the cultivator and local officer classes, not merely governance from afar, was now increasingly essential. To achieve such local power, estate deputies were constrained to become themselves like jitō, that is, thoroughly indigenized and militarized. Only at this stage, Yasuda concludes, would both sides be ready for a full chūbun.[94]

Professor Inagaki Yasuhiko has turned this Yasuda thesis fully upside down. Instead of a condition in which a jitō–estate deputy competition for local power served as *prerequisite* to a territorial division, Inagaki posits a deputy's movement toward feudalized authority only as the *result* of a chūbun. While the Yasuda view seems generally more tenable, in fact evidence can be adduced on behalf of both arguments.[95] Beyond that, it can also be shown that estate deputy efforts to achieve greater local control represented a development that considerably exceeded the mere handful of known chūbun cases. The need to contain akutō-type unrest was a general phenomenon of the late thirteenth century; it neither led to nor resulted from a chūbun experience in anything approaching a set pattern. As before, individual shōen and individual encroachment cases required particularized settlement.

Such observations are not intended to minimize the importance of the Yasuda and Inagaki speculations. While the former has succeeded in deflecting our attention away from the jitō exclusively, shifting the emphasis instead to the increasingly militarized deputy, the latter forces us to look at developments posterior to a chūbun resolution. The implementation of land divisions often created new and unexpected problems.

Taking one of the more obvious forms of difficulty, the division of a

93. See Kawai Masaharu, "Chūsei bushidan no ujigami ujidera," in Ōgura Toyobumi, ed., *Chiiki shakai to shūkyō no shiteki kenkyū* (Kyoto, 1963), p. 14.

94. Yasuda, "Shitaji," pp. 450–57.

95. Described in ibid., pp. 452 and 450.

shōen, which for generations or centuries had composed a single territorial unit, commonly neglected the topography of an area while cutting across natural social communities and irrigated rice fields. In Yano Estate in Harima, for example, a chūbun settlement of 1297 left some 63 of the total 109 farmer-level myō in that domain in a condition of obligation to both sides. Such artificial segmentation of myō made misunderstandings in the future almost inevitable.[96] In a somewhat analogous case in Satsuma's Isaku-no-shō, a 1324 north–south chūbun left the estate's main administrative office in the jitō sector, and the jitō's office plus residence structures belonging to retainers in the deputy's sphere. A cumbersome transfer and reconstruction of buildings, including even a local shrine, thus became necessary.[97] In this sense the shōen as a natural product of geography and history tended to "resist" easy divisions.

An incident of 1287 concerning Kumazaka-no-shō in Kaga Province provides intimate detail on another kind of problem—the post-chūbun "violations" of a local family excluded from the land division's benefits. Partitioning between the estate deputy and jitō had taken place in 1273.[98] Several years later the non-Kamakura gesu of a shrine in one of the two shares asserted possession over the scattered rice fields traditionally associated with that shrine. He then proceeded to harvest their yield. The bakufu's judgment in this matter was simple and direct:

> Because that person [the gesu] is not a vassal and does not hold certain documents, there is not to be a separate "possessor" [ryōshu] aside from the ryōke[99] and jitō.... He [the gesu] has used the pretext of his Sugoo Shrine gesu title to violate many chō of temple land.... His outrages are prohibited.[100]

In Kamakura's interpretation, the 1273 chūbun arrangement had created two exclusive spheres. Ryōke and jitō were to be dominant even to the point of absorbing the rights of traditional residents.

The point to be drawn from this is that a chūbun settlement to be

96. Miyagawa Mitsuru, "Harima no kuni Yano-no-shō," in Shibata Minoru, ed., *Shōen sonraku no kōzō* (Osaka, 1955), pp. 82, 89 ff.

97. *Shimazu Ke Monjo*, 1324/8/21 Satsuma Isaku-no-shō narabi ni Hioki kita-gō ryōke-jitō wayojō, in *DNK, iewake 16*, 1:558–63, doc. 550.

98. Limitations of space do not permit a detailed study of the unusual confluence of forces in this shōen. Here was an estate over which the bakufu stood as patron (*honke*). Both the estate deputy and jitō were its appointees, and yet a chūbun between them eventually became necessary. (For this information and that in the next note see the document cited in n. 100.)

99. In 1280 the bakufu "commended" the ryōke title to Tōfukuji Temple in Kyoto.

100. *Sonkeikaku Bunko Shozō Monjo*, 1287/10/11 Kantō gechijō, in *Kamakura saikyojō*, Jō, pp. 221–23, doc. 165.

effective required full implementation—and full acceptance—of its terms. In this particular case the temple ryōke, recent recipient of bakufu largess, had only the flimsiest of roots in Kumazaka Estate. Forced to confront local intransigence, its sole recourse was to appeal for assistance to Kamakura. It is important to note that this lawsuit had indeed issued from the ryōke and not the jitō. Although the gesu, as is clear, had claimed jurisdiction over some jitō fields as well, the gesu's actions had been directed exclusively against the absentee proprietor. The reasoning seems obvious. The ryōke was simply more vulnerable than a thoroughly militarized jitō who was in residence.

If local officers and aroused members of the myōshu class were beginning to assert themselves in shōen lacking a tradition of strong central rulership, similar opportunities existed for ambitious jitō. There was nothing—save the threat of bakufu justice—to prevent a jitō from encroaching on an unprotected proprietor's share of some newly divided estate. Ōyama-no-shō provides a clear case in point. Jitō violations are recorded in 1318 against the land units established two decades earlier as Tōji's exclusive private enclave.[101] In other instances a jitō who was dissatisfied with a division arrangement might appeal his grievance directly to the bakufu. This is what happened concerning the earliest known chūbun case—a 1237 public-land (gō) partitioning in the Kanto's Hitachi Province. Some sixty years later we find the descendants of the original jitō claiming that it had been a jitō deputy who had unlawfully entered the 1237 settlement. The present holder thus averred that he was entitled to possess in full (ichien ryōchi) the entire area. As compensation to the ryōke, he promised to deliver all regular tax payments.[102] Although the bakufu rejected this claim, underscoring its support of the status quo, it is worth noting that a full circle had now, in a sense, been traversed. A jitō whose family had enjoyed an unencumbered chūbun sphere for six decades was now being turned down in his appeal for an ukesho over an *entire* unit.[103]

---

101. *Tōji Monjo*, 1318/5/6 Ōyama-no-shō sata zasshō kishōmon, in *Ōyama Mura shi, shiryō hen*, p. 103, doc. 146. For further trouble, see ibid., 1325/4/7 Shami Zenshō ukebumi, p. 113, doc. 167.

102. *Ōnegi Ke Monjo*, 1298/2/3 Kantō gechijō, in Kashima Jingū Shamusho, comp., *Kashima Jingu monjo* (Kashima, 1942), p. 686, doc. 16.

103. And thus scholars have been unable to agree on the proper sequence of ukesho and shitaji chubun. Whereas Takeuchi Rizō, basing himself on one set of data, has argued that ukesho *predated* the recourse to chūbun, Makino Shinnosuke has adduced examples showing precisely the opposite effect—ukesho emerging from continued chūbun violations. In fact, as Yasuda Genkyū makes clear, both sequences were possible for different shōen. (Yasuda, "Shitaji," pp. 449–50.)

Shitaji Chūbun in Muromachi Times

A final word must be added concerning the character and frequency of shitaji chūbun settlements in the post-Kamakura age. The most important new development in the period after 1333 was the rapid growth of *shugo* to positions of provincial hegemony. This meant that in place of the bakufu as the legitimizing or authorizing agency for chūbun decisions, we now begin to find shugo performing that function. For the brief duration of the Kemmu regime the emperor Go-Daigo had evidently involved himself in at least some chūbun disputes.[104] Within months of that government's demise. however, it was the shugo who loomed as the guarantors of land divisions. In 1336/7, for example, the Ashikaga's military appointee to Chikugo ordered his personal deputy (*shugodai*) to enforce a violated land division in one of that province's shōen.[105] Some thirteen years later the evidence of shugo power in chūbun cases is even more explicit. In an incident of 1349, a compromise land division was reached between the estate deputy of a *ho* unit in Hōki and that province's shugodai himself.[106] Evidently, the stage was now at hand when jitō as independent forces on the land were giving way to shugo and their followers.

With the promulgation from 1352 of a series of bakufu laws relating to a new institution, *hanzei* (see chapter 10), shugo were now granted the right to award to retainers temporary half interests in the yields of shōen still legally under central ownership. It seems quite logical, therefore, that when hanzei grants became all but indistinguishable from permanent, chūbun-type arrangements, the earlier Kamakura denomination and pattern should have become dispensable. After the Muromachi bakufu's 1368 law in which hanzei were given final countrywide application, we find only two more cases of "shitaji chūbun."[107]

The very last known example, relating to Kii Province's Minabe-no-shō, provides a fitting end to an institution identified from its origins with jitō. We see in this incident the utter dominance by this juncture of shugo— even over a territory in which ostensibly the principals were still a ryōke

---

104. An imperial edict of 1334 shows Go-Daigo canceling an earlier chūbun in two Owari Province estates, Tomita and Shinoki. See *Engakuji Monjo*, 1334/7/11 Go-Daigo tennō ringi an, in *Kamakura Shi shi, shiryō hen*, 2:140, doc. 83. The chūbun in Tomita at least was a recent one as evidenced by the fact that as late as 1327 an ukesho was in force there. See p. 168 and n. 39.

105. *Jōdoji Monjo*, 1336/7/22 Isshiki Noriuji kakikudashi an, in Seno Seiichiro, ed., *Chikugo no kuni Minuma-no-shō shiryō, Kyushu shōen shiryō sōsho* (Fukuoka, 1966), 14:73–74, doc. 56.

106. *Sampōin Monjo*, 1349/int. 6/17 Hōki no kuni shugodai—Kuninobu Ho zasshō wayōjō, in *Shōen shiryō*, Ge, p. 1589.

107. Shimada, "Zaichi," p. 223.

and jitō. Minabe, a Kōyasan estate under a jitō ukesho for more than 150 years, was divided by exclusive order of the Ōuchi, shugo-holders of Kii, after a temple petition in 1393.[108] This authorization by the shugo, however, appears to have been merely a prelude or pretext for permanent self-involvement with Minabe. As guarantor of the 1393 chūbun, the shugo was now in a position to establish his own supervisory control over (at least) the original appellant's sector of the divided estate. In this way a new ukesho came to be organized: the shugo had succeeded to rights formerly held by the jitō. By 1441 the contracted annual remittance figure of 250 koku had shrunk to only 30 koku actually received.[109]

As there was no longer any need to compromise with or serve capital estate owners, so there was no further need for shitaji chūbun. Already made obsolete by the rise of shugo and hanzei, formal land divisions between estate deputies and jitō now fell into disuse.

108. *Kōyasan Monjo*, 1393/9/8 Ōuchi shi bugyōshū hosho an, in *DNK, iewake I*, 5:499, doc. 986.

109. Yasuda, *Nihon shōen*, pp. 215–16.

8 The Economic and Political Effects of the Mongol Wars

KYOTSU HORI

The Problem of War Rewards

In the wake of the second Mongol attack of 1281, the *bakufu*'s two major problems were the launching of a workable rewards program and the maintaining of a viable defense line against an expected third armada. Both involved Kamakura in the most strenuous search for compensation lands, after a military engagement that had left no spoils. Peculiarities in the bakufu's recruitment and defense policies merely compounded the difficulties. Since Kamakura had raised no armies in the east—merely ordering those with Kyushu land parcels to proceed to the invasion site and join the battle—the claimants for reward were primarily Kyushu natives. Consistent with this, and in order to avoid dispersal of a hoped-for permanent Kyushu guard, the bakufu determined that there should be no award lands granted beyond the boundaries of that westernmost island.[1]

The scarcity of land available as reward for military service, along with the bakufu's refusal to grant any such reward outside Kyushu, meant that the allocation of war rewards was unduly delayed. Existing documents show that it began in 1286 and continued until as late as 1307, twenty-six years after the second invasion, and they show that grants were made piecemeal as rights in land became available. For instance, it is believed that the rewards in 1286 were made possible largely because the holdings of Adachi Yasumori, *shugo* of Higo Province, and those of his followers in Kyushu fell into the hands of the bakufu after that clan's downfall the

This chapter is adapted from chapters 7 and 8 of Kyotsu Hori, "The Mongol Invasions and the Kamakura Bakufu," Ph. D. dissertation, Columbia University, 1967.

1. The standard treatment of the Mongol invasions and their aftermath in Japan is Aida Jirō, *Mōkō shūrai no kenkyū* (Tokyo, 1958).

previous year.[2] Yasumori's principal supporters in Kyushu were his son, who served as his deputy in Higo, and Shōni Kagesuke, brother of the Kyushu shogunal commissioner (*Chinzei bugyō*), Shōni Tsunesuke. Both men perished, and their holdings were immediately confiscated. After granting a percentage to those responsible for subduing these rebels in 1285, the bakufu distributed the remainder as rewards to those who had participated in the Mongol defense of 1281.[3]

On several occasions after 1286, the bakufu made further grants in recognition of meritorious services rendered in 1281. An analysis of documents concerning these later grants shows that they were made out of either land rights that fell into the bakufu's control through confiscation (for lack of heirs or violation of law) or holdings within six bakufu estates located in northern Kyushu.[4] Since there was no repetition of the incident of 1285, which had enabled the bakufu to assume control of new territory, the bakufu was forced to divide whatever happened to be available. It did so by parceling stewardships (*jitō shiki*) into several shares or, as in the case of Kanzaki-no-shō in Hizen Province, into as many as four hundred units.[5]

It has long been supposed that the bakufu, harassed by legitimate and spurious claimants alike, increasingly refused to listen to them, forbade their direct appeal to Kamakura, and finally in 1294 announced that no further rewards would be made.[6] Recent studies do not support this contention; grant lands were parceled out well into the fourteenth century. The popular misconception on this point seems to have arisen from a misunderstanding of an excerpt from an official bakufu chronicle:

> On the 29th of the sixth month [in 1295] the Council of State decreed that both rewards and punishments concerning the Kōan War [Kōan Gassen] would be terminated. On the 25th of the eighth month the Council members fixed their signatures on a joint pledge.[7]

Since the second Mongol attack took place during the Kōan era (1278–88), it was generally assumed that "Kōan Gassen" referred to the war of

2. Generally known as Kōan Gassen or Shimotsuki-no-ran (an incident of the eleventh month); discussion follows on p. 196.

3. A document, which is believed to be a roster of the recipients of rewards in 1286, indicates that many holdings granted that year were in fact former holdings of Kagesuke and others who most likely perished with him. See *Hishijima monjo*, 1286/int.12/28, in *Fukuoka ken shiryō* (Tokyo, 1932–39), 10:63–67. (Hereafter cited as *FKS*.)

4. Aida Jirō, *Mōkō shūrai*, pp. 296–97.

5. Ibid., pp. 282–90.

6. E.g., see George Sansom, *A History of Japan to 1334* (Stanford, 1958), pp. 455–56.

7. *Kamakura nendai-ki* (also known as *Hōjō kudai-ki*), 1295. The question is discussed in Aida Jirō, *Mōkō shūrai*, pp. 292–96.

defense against these invaders. Documents of the period, however, make
it clear that the anti-Mongol effort was known at the time as either
"Ikoku Gassen" (war against foreigners) or "Mōko Gassen" (war against
the Mongols). In other words, the decree in question had nothing at all
to do with the Mongols but was concerned instead with the 1285 incident
involving Adachi Yasumori.

If warriors had been the only group of people who clamored for rewards and compensations, the task of the bakufu might have been sur-
mountable. However, there were Buddhist and Shinto religious institutions
that also claimed credit for victory over the Mongols. For this, Kamakura
itself was partly to blame. From the beginning of the threat—and continuing well into the fourteenth century—the bakufu petitioned the country's great shrines to perform services for the purposes of "repelling
the enemies and safeguarding the imperial house." The final known reference to this type of appeal for divine assistance came in 1311.[8]

As an example of the converse side to these petitions—the rewards that
the bakufu felt compelled to grant—we may cite an official decree donating
a stewardship to the Usa Hachiman Shrine in Kyushu's Buzen Province.
The edict, dated two and a half years after the second invasion, clearly
states that Kamakura believed the typhoon of 1281 to have been the
work of the gods.[9]

Chief Priest, Usa Shrine   1284/2/28

> Enclosed is the patent signifying the donation of the stewardship of
> Muratsuno Beppu in the province of Hyūga. We had offered a stewardship
> in the first year of Kenji [1275] for the purpose of repulsing enemies, as a
> result of which all enemy ships were wrecked or sunk in the fourth year of
> Kōan [1281]. Now, because it is rumored that enemies may come to attack
> us again, we would like to make a donation similar to the one given before.
>
> We request that you say your prayers with the utmost sincerity. On order
> of the Shogun,
>
> Governor of Suruga Province (Hōjō Naritoki)
>
> Governor of Sagami Province (Hōjō Tokimune)

This simple and crude faith of Japan's medieval warriors seems to have
been cultivated by Buddhist and Shinto officials, who rushed to claim that
it had been their prayers and ceremonies that had produced the *kamikaze*.
Merely to extract better rewards, priests and monks made up highly
imaginative stories giving full credit for the destruction of the Mongol

8. Aida Jirō, *Mōkō shūrai*, pp. 97–122.
9. Cited in *Usa-gū engi*, in Yamada An'ei, *Fukuteki hen* (Tokyo, 1891), pt. 5, pp.
27–28. (Hereafter cited as *FTH.*)

armada to the intervention of their own deities. While many of these efforts demonstrably failed in their purpose,[10] it is nonetheless most noteworthy that Kamakura should have arranged its priorities during the 1280s to accommodate religion first. Reference was just made to the case of Usa Hachiman Shrine in 1284. On the very same day the Hachiman Shrine of Kyushu's Ōsumi Province was awarded a jitō shiki, and toward the end of that year the Niu Shrine on Mount Kōya was given a stewardship in nearby Izumi Province.[11] As was noted earlier, it was not until 1286 that the first grants to warriors were made.

The Economic Plight of Housemen

The problems of war rewards—and the maintenance of defenses against future attack—were exacerbated by the general economic difficulties of Kamakura vassals. The bakufu did not, or perhaps could not, formulate an overall policy to correct these difficulties, but in 1284 it did issue several decrees clearly aimed at placating dissatisfied Kyushu warriors and religious institutions at the expense of "commoners and moneylenders" (*bonge* and *kariage*). Two ordinances issued by the bakufu in that year stipulated that the holdings of certain important Kyushu shrines and temples that had been lost through sale or foreclosure should be restored to their original owners, even if the transaction in question had taken place more than twenty years before.[12] The bakufu had formerly specified a twenty-year period as sufficient to establish one's rights in land, even if those rights were subsequently found to be legally faulty.[13] This rule, which had originally been issued for application in Kamakura houseman disputes, was now enlarged so as to include land rights once held by important Kyushu religious institutions. Any such domains that had fallen into the hands of others were to be returned without compensation, no matter how long it had been since the sale or foreclosure had taken place.

10. E.g., as late as 1309 the chief priest of the influential Takeo Shrine in Kyushu appealed to the bakufu saying that despite his continuing efforts to gain a reward he had not as yet received one. He added that at the time of the first invasion the god of his shrine had shot arrows from its sanctuary, and that again in 1281, three purple banners on top of his shrine had pointed toward the Mongol ships just before the great storm struck them. *Takeo Jinja monjo* 3, "Hizen no kuni Takeo Jinja dai-gūji Fujiwara Kunikado tsutsushimite gonjō su" (*FTH*, pt. 6, p. 16); Satō Shin'ichi and Ikeuchi Yoshisuke, *Chūsei hōsei shiryō-shū* 1, *Kamakura bakufu-hō* (Tokyo, 1965), pp. 464–65. (Hereafter cited as *CHS*.)

11. *Shimazu monjo*, 1284/2/28 Kantō Migyōsho, in *FTH*, pt. 5, p. 27. Niu Shrine stewardship referred to in *Kōyasan monjo*, 1293/3/28, "Dajōkan Kongōbu-ji ni chōsu" (*FTH*, pt. 5, pp. 61–64).

12. *Shin-shikimoku*, art. 19, 1284/5/20 (*CHS*,1, pt. 2, docs. 491–528) and *Shimpen tsuika*, art. 165, 1284/6/25, "Chinzei ni sōtaru shinryō no koto" (*CHS* 1, pt. 2, doc. 544).

13. Jōei Code, art. 8.

Additional evidence suggests that this legislation was not limited to
Kyushu; its application may have been countrywide. Two decrees of the
bakufu in this same year assert that (1) "the holdings of shrines and
temples be restored, and [the funds derived from them] be devoted to
religious performances and to the repair of old buildings, rather than to
the erection of new ones," (2) "henceforth the construction of new temples
and shrines be stopped and the religious activities of state-supported
shrines and temples in various provinces (*shokoku kokubun-ji ichinomiya*)
be encouraged."[14] The term "various provinces" (*shokoku*) is vague but
probably meant every province, or at least was not limited to provinces
in Kyushu. This assumption is supported by the fact that only a few weeks
earlier the bakufu had ordered the state shrines and temples of various
provinces, including a shrine in the province of Kii, to report their histories and current conditions.[15] It is further supported by documents
concerning subsequent lawsuits brought by religious institutions, not
necessarily in Kyushu, demanding restoration of their former holdings.[16]
The stated purpose of the legislation was the encouragement of religious
activities in some of the more important shrines and temples, undoubtedly
for the purpose of frustrating any further invasion attempts by the Mongols.

At the same time the bakufu decided to show special favor to its vassals
in Kyushu by confirming their rights in land (*myōshu-shiki, kumon-shiki,
tadokoro-shiki*), including rights that had been lost within the last twenty
years.[17] That is to say, if a vassal in Kyushu had sold his holdings or had
failed to bail them out before foreclosure within the past twenty years, he
could claim their restoration without compensation to the present holder.
There are no documents giving a reason for this action of the bakufu, nor
is there any information concerning those who were to be its victims.
However, considering that it was Kyushu housemen who bore the chief
burden of the war against the Mongols and that it was the class of people
called "commoners and moneylenders" that was gradually gaining the
upper hand economically, it is reasonably clear that the bakufu was simply
supporting its own men against all commercial outsiders.

These measures in favor of religious institutions and Kyushu warriors

14. *Shin-shikimoku*, arts. 1 and 20, 1284/5/20 (*CHS*, 1, pt. 2, docs. 491–528).
15. *Kōyasan monjo*, 1285/9, "Chūshin, Kōyasan chinju Ōno-sha Kii-no-kuni ichinomiya no koto" (*CHS*, 1, pt. 2, supp. doc. 8). This document states that the order was
issued on 1284/5/3.
16. *Shimpen tsuika*, arts. 173–77, 181–83 (*CHS*, 1, pt. 3, docs. 80–84, 87–89).
17. *Shin-shikimoku*, art. 24, 1284/5/20 (*CHS*, 1, pt. 2, docs. 491–528) and *Shimpen
tsuika*, art. 214, 1284/9/10, from Hisatoki (?) to Akashi Yukimune (*CHS*, 1, pt. 2, doc.
562).

were in all probability intended to serve as reward and compensation at the expense of those who had not directly contributed to the anti-Mongol effort. It was an easy device for the bakufu, which was so lacking during the 1280s in reward lands for distribution. But these measures can also be seen as forerunners of the more sweeping (and much better known) *"tokusei"* regulations of 1297. The latter, which explicitly nullified countrywide almost all transferals of rights in land originally held by Kamakura vassals, served additionally to cancel all debts.[18] It was a further advance in the bakufu's policy of support for financially pressed housemen.

The question that immediately arises is the extent to which this entire trend was influenced by the Mongol wars. In this regard, clear signs of financial insolvency among Kamakura vassals had been in existence since the mid-thirteenth century. Traditional explanations for their plight, advanced by Taira Masatsura, a bakufu official in the early fourteenth century, were rising living standards (which he branded as luxury) and the parcellation of holdings through inheritance.[19] Modern scholars in fact reiterate the first point when they stress the basic incompatibility of a feudal system, based upon a self-sufficient land economy, and an exchange economy, which was gradually developing with increased agricultural and industrial productivity. The importation and increasing use of money (mostly copper coins) from China signaled another structural tension between society and economy.[20]

Masatsura's second point, the parcellation of rights in land through inheritance, is well demonstrated in documents of the time.[21] As with the first point, however, it is possible to ask why such developments should have been a problem only for Kamakura vassals. If divided inheritance was a custom of the time, others too must have suffered from the practice.

There are other possible causes for vassal insolvency, such as the economic burden of services and contributions required and the loss of their

18. This was with the single exception of debts incurred in pawnshops. "Kantō on-kotogaki hō," 1297/3/6; "Kantō yori Rokuhara ni okuraruru on-kotogaki hō," 1297/7/22 (*CHS*, 1, pt. 2, docs. 657–64). This act of 1297 (Einin no tokusei) is discussed by Delmer Brown in his article "The Japanese Tokusei of 1297," *Harvard Journal of Asiatic Studies* 12 (1949).

19. *Taira Masatsura kansō*, in *Kaitei shiseki shūran*, 27.

20. For the phenomenon of economic development during the period, see Toyoda Takeshi, *Zōtei chūsei Nihon shōgyō-shi* (Tokyo, 1952); Obata Atsushi, *Nihon kahei ryūtsū-shi* (Tokyo, 1930), chap. 1; Sasaki Gin'ya, *Chūsei no shōgyō* (Tokyo, 1961).

21. While not perhaps an appropriate example due to the enormous wealth of the Ōtomo family, the scion of that house, a shogunal commissioner for Kyushu, had his inheritance divided among eight sons. *Shiga Monjo*, 1240/4/6, in Takita Manabu, ed., *Zōho teisei hennen Ōtomo shiryō*, vol. 2, doc. 191.

positions at the displeasure of estate holders. It should be pointed out, however, that feudal dues before the time of the Mongol invasions were not very large, with the most important obligation, guard duty at Kyoto, requiring only several months service in a lifetime. Still other scholars have maintained that those who became impoverished were warrior–farmers who failed to keep up with technological improvements in agriculture. However, to argue in this fashion is to suggest that there must have been some Kamakura vassals who, contrary to the general trend, actually flourished. This division into prosperous and pressed warrior groups has not yet been sufficiently researched.

It is a commentary on the way the bakufu dealt with the economic dislocations of its men that sumptuary legislation and restrictions on transactions in land rights took the place of bold policy initiatives. Thus, for example, several times during 1239 and 1240 the bakufu placed a ban on the practice of appointing monks, merchants, or moneylenders to the position of deputy steward.[22] In 1240, transactions involving shiki were further limited when the bakufu put a ban on the sale of *shiryō* (also called *honryō*, meaning literally the original holdings of housemen as against *onchi*, which were holdings granted by the bakufu) to commoners, moneylenders, and nonhousemen. At the same time the mortgaging of onchi was also prohibited.[23] These decrees constituted a stricter application of the forty-eighth article of the Jōei Code, which simply prohibited the sale of onchi and did not say anything about shiryō.

A generation later in 1267 (a year before the first letter of Kublai Khan reached Japan), the bakufu took an important step by issuing an order that, like its later counterpart in 1284, was in some respects similar to the tokusei edict of 1297. It prohibited the sale or mortgaging of both shiryō and onchi by a Kamakura houseman, even to another houseman, and ordered that those *shiki* that had been sold or foreclosed be restored upon payment of the principal without interest. At the same time the bakufu strictly prohibited the assignment of shiki as "gifts" to anyone other than one's posterity, thus preventing the sale of holdings under the guise of gift-giving.[24] However both orders of 1267 were canceled in a few years, perhaps because they were not enforceable.[25] In 1273 the bakufu took a new step and ordered that the holdings of housemen that had been mortgaged were to be restored to their original owners even though the principal

---

22. *Shimpen tsuika*, arts. 284 (1239/7/26); 285 (1239/9/17); 35 (1240/5/25); 275 (1240/6/11), reprinted in *CHS*, 1, pt. 2, docs. 116, 126, 145, 150.

23. *Shimpen tsuika*, arts. 35 (1240/5/25); 63 (1240/4/20) in *CHS*, 1, pt. 2, docs. 145, 139.

24. *Konoe-ke bon tsuika*, arts. 93, 94 (1267/12/26) in *CHS*, 1, pt. 2, docs. 433, 434.

25. *Konoe-ke bon tsuika*, arts. 105, 106 (1270/5/9) in *CHS*, 1, pt. 2, docs. 443, 444.

of the loan had not been repaid, except for transactions that had already been confirmed by the bakufu.[26] This was one year before the first Mongol invasion. The issuance of such a decree makes clear that the war effort that followed cannot alone be considered responsible—as some scholars have implied—for the famous tokusei decree of 1297.

How, then, did the Mongol crisis affect bakufu economic policy? As has been shown, rewards for wartime service continued long after 1294, and the order banning free travel by Kyushu men did not deny them an opportunity to send along their petitions. Beside making direct grants of whole and partial stewardships, the bakufu sought to use tokusei and other similar orders as an indirect means of reward and aid. The decree of 1284 ordering restoration of the former holdings of certain religious institutions and Kyushu housemen falls directly within this context. Perhaps the related edicts of 1273 and 1297 were also at least partly aimed at providing economic aid to those western province housemen whose services were considered indispensable. Yet the bakufu's efforts were largely fruitless, principally because its resources in land were limited, and its approach to the whole problem basically unsound. As a result, the rewards and compensations were far from satisfactory, and the economic plight of the very men who bore most of the burden of the defense was left unresolved.

Changing Patterns of Inheritance

While the growing insolvency of Kamakura's vassals was eroding the economic basis of the houseman system, the moral foundation of the system was also crumbling. To a large degree, the Kamakura houseman system was organized on the basis of the sōryō-sei, a practice of eastern warrior society in which the head of a family group, or house, acted as the group's leader in both peace and war. As the decades passed, however, the solidarity of this group gradually weakened. The control of house members and their holdings, when both were scattered throughout the country, was no longer the easy task it had once been (during the twelfth century) when the members and domains of these houses were concentrated in the Kantō region. Moreover, the practice of divided inheritance helped to weaken the authority of the clan head over members of his clan. Although the head of the house retained the ultimate authority over all properties, these latter were more or less equally divided among all children, including daughters, at the time of the death of a family head. The economic independence of house members thus tended to discourage their dependency on the head for moral guidance. This was especially true after house property had been parceled out to such an extent that further divi-

26. *Shimpen tsuika*, art. 70 (1273/7/12) in *CHS*, 1, pt. 2, doc. 452.

sion was all but impossible. To take one example, in the 1190s the Sagara house moved from the eastern province of Tōtomi to its new holdings in the Kyushu province of Hizen. Four generations later, in 1311, Sagara Nagauji (Rendō) recorded in his will that henceforth the family's holdings should not be divided because "it would be difficult for the next house head to make ends meet."[27]

The increase in functions and powers of the shugo during the late Kamakura period also undermined the authority of the clan head. Originally the shugo was simply an administrative officer on the provincial level, and there was no superior–inferior relationship between him and the housemen in his province. However, his involvement in local affairs— administrative, judicial, and police—helped him to emerge gradually as a major provincial power. The Shimotsuki Incident of 1285, in which Adachi Yasumori and his faction perished, may serve to illustrate this development. A number of Kamakura vassals in the province of Kōzuke, where the Adachi house had held the shugo post for three generations, fought for this scion and died with him.[28] This fact clearly differentiates the incident from similar occurrences in previous years; when the Wada and Miura houses were destroyed by the Hōjō in 1213 and 1247, respectively, they fought and were destroyed as houses. By contrast, the authority of the Adachi chieftain, Yasumori, was no longer restricted to his own family and immediate retainer group.

The gradual weakening of family solidarity and the emergence of new power groups were given further impetus by the threat of foreign invasion. It had been a general practice of the Kamakura military regime that whenever services and contributions were needed, these would be requisitioned from the various heads of retainer houses, who in turn would allocate levies keyed to the size of his kinsman's holdings. The long period of defense against the Mongols, however, provided unusually rich opportunities for branch families to establish themselves through military distinction as independent shogunal vassals. For example, the Sata family of Ōsumi Province in Kyushu was a branch of the Nejime house. But by 1283 the former was serving its defense duty directly under the shugo, having already won a patent of confirmation from Kamakura.[29]

At the same time, the bakufu appears to have been making some effort to stem this trend by strengthening the authority of the house head in

27. *Sagara-ke monjo* 1, in *Dai Nihon komonjo*, 1, doc. 39, 1311/2/25 Sagara Rendō (Nagauji) okibumi.
28. Taga Munehaya, "Kōan hachinen Shimotsuki Sōdō to sono hamon," *Rekishi chiri* 78, no. 6.
29. *Nejime monjo*, 1283/10/22 Chiba Munetane (shugo) to Sata Yakurō (*FKS*, 10, p. 51); ibid., 1283/11/18 Chiba Munetane saikyo gechijō (*FKS*, 10, p. 52).

regard to houseman services and contributions owed to Kamakura. In 1284 and 1292, for example, it authorized the lineage head to collect double payment from those members who had neglected their share of services and contributions; in extreme cases, it was ordered that the holdings of recalcitrants could be taken back by the head of the house.[30]

Although we cannot say that the emergency caused by the Mongol crisis alone was responsible (analogous to economic difficulties) for the decline of the authority of house heads, the unusual situation over a sustained period certainly accelerated this trend. Thus when the bakufu in 1286 issued an order that Kyushu housemen not bequeath holdings to a female as long as defense against the Mongol Empire was needed,[31] this had the effect of undermining an established practice within the sōryō-sei. The system of division of property within the kinship group had been increasingly unsatisfactory even before the Mongol invasions and probably would sooner or later have come to an end anyway. Yet, by issuing such an order, the bakufu was adding its own encouragement—however tacit—to this major shift from divided to single inheritance.

Hōjō Control of the Bakufu

As is well known, this was also the period when Hōjō control of the bakufu was becoming increasingly authoritarian in nature. Especially during the shogunal regency of Tokimune (1268–84), informal meetings at the private home of the head of the Hōjō house began to absorb from the Council of State (Hyōjōshū) the highest decision-making functions of government. According to the 1277 diary entries of a high bakufu official, the regent frequently called these meetings (known as *yoriai*) to discuss matters of the highest importance.[32] Those who attended were important members of the Council of State, ranking members of the Hōjō house, and private vassals of Tokimune.

Most certainly it was the climate of emergency (rising from the threat of the Mongols) that was causing this hitherto private family meeting to be transformed into a quasi-public organ of state. As the Mongol crisis never formally ended, the yoriai also became permanent; by the later years of the Kamakura regime appointment to its membership had become one of the most prestigious of all distinctions.[33]

30. *Shimpen tsuika*, arts. 324 (1284/10/22), 325 (1294/7/5) in *CHS*, 1, pt. 2, docs. 566, 649.
31. *Shimpen tsuika*, art. 260 (1286/7/25) in *CHS*, 1, pt. 2, doc. 596.
32. Miyoshi Yasuari, *Kenji sannen-ki*, in *Gunsho ruijū*, buke-bu.
33. *Kyūshū Kanazawa bunko komonjo* 2, doc. 621, cited in Satō Shin'ichi, "Kamakura bakufu seiji no sensei-ka ni tsuite," Takeuchi Rizō, ed., *Nihon hōken-sei seiritsu no kenkyū* (Tokyo, 1955). The document is a letter written by Regent Kanazawa (Hōjō)

As this Hōjō house council assumed ever greater importance as a decision-making body, its formal counterpart, the Council of State, gradually
lost prominence and became a mere rubber stamp of the Hōjō chieftain.
This is borne out by the changing nature of Hyōjōshū membership.
Especially after the Mongol crisis arose, the number of Hōjō in the council
grew steadily while their ages declined. Though no Hōjō was in formal
attendance at the first council meeting in 1225, nearly half of that body's
members were Hōjō some fifty years later. It was also only after the Mongol crisis began that men under twenty years of age came to be appointed
to council membership.[34]

Hōjō Sadatoki, who assumed the regency following the death of his
father Tokimune, abolished the Coadjutor Institution (Hikitsukeshū)
in 1293 and took over sole responsibility for making final decisions in
houseman lawsuits. Although the Board of Coadjutors was soon reinstated,
it never again assumed its former importance, and Sadatoki kept for
himself the authority to make ultimate decisions on important cases. His
retention of this power may have been justified by the need for quick
decisions in a time of national crisis, but it brought about change from a
system of joint deliberation to one of increasingly authoritarian rule.

The shift of power from the Council of State to the private meetings of
the Hōjō family signified the replacement of the shogunal regent as chief
administrator by the head of the Hōjō house (called *tokusō*). We find,
therefore, that while there were eleven regents after Tokiyori, only three
of these were at the same time tokusō.[35] It was inevitable in this situation
that private vassals of the Hōjō chieftain, who were called *miuchi* (meaning
kinsmen) to distinguish them from vassals of the bakufu, should have
assumed prominent roles in government. They served as regular members
of the yoriai, acting headships of the Board of Retainers, bakufu commissioners of various types, and in the important capacity of censors.

While the Hōjō family concentrated its power at Kamakura, it also
took over more and more of the shugo offices.[36] It is believed that the Hōjō
had only two such offices during the early years of the Kamakura regime;
in later years it held nearly half of them. Although the beginnings of this
trend had long been apparent, the greatest increase in Hōjō shugo posts
took place during the years of the Mongol crisis. The official explanation
for this was the bakufu's need to establish a streamlined defense system

---

Sadaaki (r. 1326), to the effect that the invitation extended to him (to join the *yoriai*)
was an honor beyond his expression.

34. Satō Shin'ichi, "Kamakura bakufu seiji," p. 115; Satō Shin'ichi, *Kamakura
bakufu shugo seido no kenkyū* (Tokyo, 1948), pp. 184–85.

35. See n. 33. for what this came to mean in practice.

36. Satō Shin'ichi, "Kamakura bakufu seiji."

in Kyushu and western Honshu. Much more was at stake, however. During the final two decades of the thirteenth century, the Hōjō came virtually to monopolize ranking military offices in the threatened part of Japan.

In 1282 the bakufu established a new office of Defense Commissioner at Meihama (Meihama bugyō) near Hakata in Kyushu. The new commissioner, a member of the Hōjō house, took over from the Ōtomo and Shōni the overall command authority for Kyushu. Two years later the office of Chinzei bugyō (jointly held until now by the Ōtomo and Shōni) was reorganized to permit a sharing of power among three new commissioners sent from Kamakura, and three Kyushu constables, the Adachi, Ōtomo, and Shōni.[37] The duties of the Ōtomo and Shōni were diminished still further in 1293 when Hōjō Kanetoki and Tokiie were sent to Kyushu as the new bakufu deputies (tandai) for that island.[38] From that point until the demise of the Kamakura regime, members of the Hōjō family monopolized these twin posts.

But that was not all. The highest office under the newly established deputy in Kyushu, namely the head of its Hyōjōshū (counterpart of the Council of State at Kamakura), was also always held by a Hōjō. The first of the three leading members of its Hikitsukeshū (Coadjutors) was likewise a member of that family, with the second and third members coming respectively from the Shōni and Ōtomo. Finally, private vassals of the deputy are conspicuous in the lists of Hikitsukeshū, along with dignitaries belonging to the Shōni, Ōtomo, and Shimazu.[39]

The posts of shugo in the provinces of Nagato and Suō at the western tip on Honshu met entirely the same fate. The two offices, which had been held, respectively, by the Nikaidō and a family named Fujiwara, were now combined in the person of Hōjō Muneyori, the younger brother of Regent Tokimune. Available evidence suggests that from this time until the end of the regime the two shugo offices were always occupied by a Hōjō, whose responsibility was to defend the coast of western Honshu. As a consequence, the holder of this dual office exercised an unusually broad authority, gradually coming to be called "deputy for the western provinces" (Nagato or Chūgoku tandai).

The domination of government agencies by the Hōjō was accompanied by a power struggle within the family itself. Since the tokusō relied more

---

37. *Shimpen tsuika*, art. 165 (1284/6/25); art. 166 (1284/11/25); art. 214 (1284/9/10) in *CHS*, 1, pt. 2, docs. 544, 569, 562. There is a theory now prevalent among some scholars that the notion of a joint chinzei bugyō authority into the 1280s is inaccurate anyway.

38. *Shimazu-ke monjo*, 1293/3/21, migyōsho (*Dai Nihon komonjo*, 1, doc. 34); Satō Shin'ichi, *Kamakura bakufu soshō seido no kenkyū* (Tokyo, 1943), chap. 5.

39. Satō Shin'ichi, *Kamakura bakufu soshō*, p. 325; Kawazoe Shōji, "Chinzei hyōjōshū, dō hikitsuke-shū ni tsuite," *Rekishi kyōiku* 11, no. 7.

and more on his own vassals and on his close in-laws, rather than on ranking members of his house, those who were eliminated from the center of
power naturally tended to harbor resentment. Numerous examples can be
cited of the main Hōjō line's dependence on private followers. The acting
headship of the bakufu's board of retainers (*samurai-dokoro*), for instance,
eventually became hereditary within the Hōjō vassal family of Taira.[40]
The office of manager of the tokusō line itself was also held by a vassal,
as were a number of shugo and shugo deputy positions.

It was during the general period of the Mongol threat that these vassals,
working their influence through representation on the yoriai, began to
exert major governmental power. Two pillars of Tokimune's regency
were his father-in-law, Adachi Yasumori, and Taira Yoritsuna, a ranking
vassal who combined in his person both the acting headship of the Board
of Retainers and the headship of the tokusō's family office. Adachi Yasumori was the chieftain of a powerful eastern warrior house and was also
the shugo of two provinces, one in Kyushu, the other, Kōzuke, in the
Kantō. No sooner had Tokimune died than a bitter enmity developed
between Yasumori and Yoritsuna, probably over which of the two was to
have ultimate control over the powers of the new regent and tokusō, the
fourteen-year-old Sadatoki. This dispute ended in 1285 when Yasumori,
as we have noted, was killed in battle. The brief civil war marking this
incident is generally considered a turning point in the history of the
Kamakura bakufu. From this date until the end of the period the dominant
power at the eastern capital was securely in the hands of private vassals
of the main line of the Hōjō house, rather than in the hands of vassals of
the Minamoto or even certain ranking Hōjō kinsmen.

The Advance of General Bakufu Jurisdiction

Other changes were brought on, directly or indirectly, by the climate of
crisis during the period of the invasions. For example, the bakufu increased
its competence in the general area of foreign relations. In Kyushu, until
the office of tandai was formed in the early 1290s, the shogunal commissioners, or Chinzei bugyō, had acted concurrently as presiding officers
over the imperial headquarters at Dazaifu. In this capacity they possessed
supervisory authority over general Kyushu governance, and functioned as
foreign ministers for the imperial government at Kyoto. Despite the fact
that the bakufu from early days had taken control of Dazaifu by placing
its own men in the top offices, final authority on matters of foreign relations remained in fact in the hands of the imperial court. Thus, for instance, when the first letter of Kublai Khan arrived in 1268, it was referred

40. The Hōjō's own leadership of the *samurai-dokoro* dated back to the year 1213.

not to Kamakura but to the court in Kyoto, which decided to ignore it. Later on it was the bakufu that made decisions on how to handle such foreign correspondence. Perhaps it is significant in this regard that the office of shogunal commissioner, which functioned also as the foreign ministry for the imperial government. disappeared when the tandai post, which was purely military, came to replace it.

In another area, we have already mentioned that the bakufu in 1284 decided to confirm the shiki rights of Kyushu vassals and to restore holdings that had been sold or foreclosed within a twenty-year period (see n. 17). Most Kyushu housemen did not have shogunal patents of confirmation, and their sources of income were mostly under the control of civil estate proprietors. This meant that the decision of the bakufu concerning confirmation was a blatant intrusion on the rights of shōen owners; Kamakura was underwriting landed privileges for which it had no direct legal access. Needless to say, this kind of infringement on traditional authority must have evoked a storm of protest from those so damaged. Yet as long as the threat of a third invasion existed, i.e. indefinitely, the bakufu could cite as justification the court's consent (granted earlier) to the mobilization of nonhousemen. The latter were simply being rewarded now for their military services.

Third, as a result of the bakufu's heavy reliance upon divine power, the eastern regime came to exercise an increasing influence over many of the country's religious institutions. Until this time, with the exception of Kantō and perhaps Kyushu, where the bakufu was dominant, state-supported shrines and temples (kokubunji and ichinomiya) were uniformly under the control of the imperial government. During the Mongol crisis, however, many if not all of these were transferred to Kamakura jurisdiction.[41] It is noteworthy concerning this development that the first two articles of the Jōei Code specifically limited bakufu authority to "provinces and estates" already under its own control. When Kamakura drew up a more elaborate code on religion in 1261, its application was still limited to shrines and temples within Kantō's sphere.[42] However, when in 1284 the bakufu ordered restoration of the holdings of certain important religious institutions, the directive was no longer limited to a specific part of the country (see n. 17).

There was a similar expansion of the bakufu's authority in the matter of tax levies for the Great Thanksgiving service of the imperial court (daijō-e), and for the dedication of new shrines at Ise. Before the invasion, Kamakura levied and collected these taxes only in response to orders

41. Ishii Susumu, "Kamakura bakufu to ritsuryō kokka," in Ishimoda Shō and Satō Shin'ichi, eds., Chūsei no hō to kokka (Tokyo, 1960).

42. Azuma kagami, 1261/2/29.

received from the court, and then only in areas "under shogunal control."[43] A document dated 1311, however, suggests that the bakufu now controlled this competence for the entire country.[44] Exactly when this change took place is not known, but it is reasonable to conjecture that, as in so many other areas of expanding bakufu activity, the Mongol crisis was largely responsible.

In sum, even as Kamakura was expanding its authority into new jurisdictional areas, it was simultaneously narrowing its own base of support. The result was a mixed legacy of strength in some areas, weakness in others. Whether all of this added up to an acceleration of the pace of bakufu decline is uncertain. It is only clear that in the wake of the invasions the imperial court had lost ground once again. Rule by warriors over the country had taken another step forward.

43. Ibid., 1241/9/10.
44. *Tōji hyakugō monjo, na* (hiragana) 11–15, 1311/6, "Tōji-ryō Aki-no-kuni Shin-chokushi-den zasshō Yoriari tsutsushimite gonjō-su" (*CHS*, 1, pt. 3, doc. 37).

PART THREE

The Age of Military Dominance

9 The Early Muromachi *Bakufu* in Kyoto

PRESCOTT B. WINTERSTEEN, JR.

Until the violent entrance of the warriors into central politics in the Hōgen and Heiji disturbances of the twelfth century, Kyoto was in the main a metropolis of and for the aristocrats and households affiliated with the emperor and his court. It was the hub of the civil government, and the warrior *bushi,* even after Yoritomo had set up the *bakufu* in Kamakura, could not afford to ignore it. They remained tied to Kyoto because they needed the formal recognition and desired the cooperation of the civil government, which alone could endow the bakufu with legitimacy. During the Kamakura period, when the military houses took the initiative away from the aristocrats in Kyoto, the bushi governed eastern Japan from Kamakura and established a secondary office in Kyoto to oversee western Japan. Contrarily, during the Muromachi period, Kyoto became the site of the bakufu and an outpost was established in Kamakura. But the Muromachi bakufu was not merely the old bakufu relocated in Kyoto, for the Muromachi government availed itself of economic and political opportunities left untouched by the Kamakura government, with the result that its organizational evolution reflected its changed circumstances.

The leading powers in Kyoto had been there for some time before the Ashikaga established the new bakufu in the 1330s. Included were the court —imperial family and high nobility—and the Buddhist institution on Mount Hiei, the *sammon,* who derived much of their income from absentee proprietorships and from commercial groups for whom they acted as patrons. With the extension of administrative powers over the city and its consequently growing responsibilities there, the bakufu became by stages the economic competitor of the court and sammon. The economic advantages that Kyoto eventually afforded the bakufu may not have been important originally in bringing the Ashikaga there, but declining revenues from distant estates made the development of nearby, reliable sources of income mandatory in the long run. By the end of the fourteenth century, the Muromachi bakufu was an organization firmly tied administratively and economically to Kyoto.

An understanding of the Muromachi bakufu requires a knowledge of its involvement in Kyoto affairs. The following pages will describe some facets of the bakufu's move into Kyoto as an administrative, police, and judicial power and its gradual displacement of the court and sammon as the primary powers there.

From 1336, when the bakufu promulgated its basic legal formulary, the *Kemmu shikimoku*, it was manifest that the Ashikaga intended to stay put in Kyoto. Clearing up the problems created by the recent military action there and coming to grips with other essential matters associated with restoring its security were regarded as such vital subjects that they found a place in the formulary itself. Here is a summary of what it said:[1]

Article III: There must be a guard to put down and prevent constant acts of violence, housebreaks, armed robberies, slaughter, and holdups—"the screams of whose victims are incessant."

Article IV: The seizure and destruction of private residences must be stopped.

Article V: Vacated land (*akichi*) within Kyoto must be returned to the original owner.[2]

Article VI: Mutual financing associations (*mujinsen*) and pawnbrokers (*dosō*) which have been forced out of business through thefts and inordinate taxes must be revived since they are essential to the livelihood and security of high and low alike.[3]

Articles III and IV are relevant to the exercise of the powers of the *samurai-*

1. The text of Articles III–VI is in Satō Shin'ichi and Ikeuchi Yoshisuke, *Chūsei hōsei shiryō shu* (Tokyo, 1969), 2:4–5 (hereafter cited as *CHSS*). For a complete (but not altogether reliable) translation of the *Kemmu shikimoku*, see J. C. Hall, "Japanese Feudal Laws: The Ashikaga Code," in *Transactions of the Asiatic Society of Japan*, 1st ser. 36 (1908): 3–25.

2. *Akichi* means "vacant land" ordinarily, i.e., land that has no structure on it or is not otherwise in use. Here it refers apparently to land left unoccupied by the courtiers who fled the city with Go-Daigo and that now, as Professor Satō suggests, had been taken over by the *bushi* for encampments. (Satō Shin'ichi, "*Muromachi bakufu ron*," in *Iwanami Kōza Nihon Rekishi* [Tokyo, 1967], 7:35.) Another interpretation is that it means land that is now "vacant" because the structures formerly there have been razed in the fighting: the very purpose in returning the land is to have rebuilt the "more than half" of Kyoto that was then *akichi*.

3. J. C. Hall, "Japanese Feudal Laws," p. 14, is incorrect because he does not treat *mujinsen* and *dosō* as separate items; the former were "cooperative," to be sure, but were not "building clubs for the erection of substantial fireproof buildings." The *mujinsen* was a kind of mutual financing association in which all the members paid dues into a fund that was awarded to one of the group by lot; when each member had received the "pot" once, the association was dissolved. *Dosō* were pawnbrokers, who did often keep their goods in fireproof buildings; but such buildings were used only for this purpose.

dokoro, since they involve general policing duties and the protection of property. Article V, which implies the implementation of a judicial decision in returning land to its owners, would probably be the concern of the samurai-dokoro also. Article VI deals with the economic revival of Kyoto by encouraging the restoration of certain basic financial institutions; the pawnbrokers later became the object of regular taxation by the bureau that handled the bakufu's finances, the *mandokoro*. These four articles constitute a compact statement of what the bakufu felt needed taking care of most urgently in Kyoto. It was this kind of concern that shaped the course of the bakufu's institutional development in later years. As a commercial center, and therefore as a potential source of tax revenues, Kyoto played a significant role in determining the functions of the Muromachi bakufu's bureaus.

There were two principal obstacles between the bakufu and its full control of Kyoto. The first was the court, the traditional locus of civil authority and law both in Kyoto and out. The second was the *honjo*, the aristocratic families or religious institutions who, as patrons, used their influence to protect certain commercial groups in return for dues in cash or kind. By the later part of the century the bakufu's status vis-à-vis these two interest groups advanced from that of interloper to recognized, legitimate civic authority, equal or superior to the others. The right to govern Kyoto was not an automatically assumed prerogative.

From the late 1330s to the early 1360s the balance between the bakufu and the existing Kyoto powers was slow in changing, but the inexorable growth of bakufu competence can be seen in the samurai-dokoro's dealings with Kyoto patrons. At first the bakufu did not have the right to handle or even to take part in lawsuits in Kyoto not involving military men, but the samurai-dokoro did pursue criminals to bring them to trial. When such pursuit meant trespassing on the properties of the Buddhist honjo establishment on Mount Hiei, however, the sammon was strong in its resistance. The sammon also claimed that there were certain cases that were immune by precedent from bakufu mediation. Nonetheless, the samurai-dokoro shortly came to play a part in cases in which it was appealed to by the injured party.[4] Later on, the bakufu began making claims with regard, for instance, to the disposal of lumber remaining after the destruction of criminals' houses.[5] In 1352 the samurai-dokoro contested the disposal of such lumber by a Kyoto shrine: it said that according to a recent bakufu law the materials ought to have been handed over to the samurai-dokoro

4. Haga Norihiko, "Muromachi bakufu shoki kendan shokō," in the volume in honor of Prof. Hōgetsu, *Nihon shakai keizai shi kenkyū: Chūsei hen* (Tokyo, 1967), p. 84
5. The razing of dwellings as partial punishment for criminals was common and a frequent source of reusable building materials.

for use in repairing the jail facilities.[6] The bakufu, through the samurai-dokoro, in these instances, was whittling away at the legally privileged status of the properties of the honjo.

The lumber incident suggests that the bakufu was moving ahead into the realm of the court's prerogatives as well, since the need for renewing or enlarging the facilities used by the samurai-dokoro implies that the role of the kebiishi-chō, the police arm of the court, was declining. So much was the kebiishi-chō in eclipse by the 1360s that for its annual ceremonial release of prisoners it had to ask the samurai-dokoro to supply some![7] Even twenty years earlier the kebiishi-chō had been unable to carry out a sentence of exile, and the samurai-dokoro had had to step in. As one courtier noted, "In recent generations the kebiishi-chō has not banished the exiles—the military [bakufu] have expelled them to the provinces."[8]

The course of the bakufu's progress against the court and honjo can be charted fairly readily from the 1360s, when it began to issue supplementary laws (tsuika-hō) covering a variety of Kyoto matters. Since in the process the bakufu effected nearly complete police, judicial, and administrative control over the city, let us consider next some of the principal laws, for they indicate the general direction of the bakufu's "urban" policy as it was taking shape in that period.[9]

With the increase in the amount of goods being carried in and out of the city as a result of the growth of guilds, as well as with the increased volume of sales due to the swollen number of Kyoto residents in the mid-fourteenth century, toll barriers were lucrative. They were usually operated by members of the patron (honjo) class, but their erection was subject to the permission of the court. In 1363, however, when a certain temple petitioned the court concerning the establishment of a new toll barrier, the court said that the bakufu would have to approve it.[10] Not only had the power to grant such permission been transferred from the court to the shogun, but the bakufu itself then came to derive income from Kyoto toll barriers in future years. Barriers were of course permitted after 1363, but the bakufu's authority over their establishment and maintenance (or

6. Gion shugyō nikki, entry for 1352/9/30, quoted in CHSS, 2:171, (40).

7. Haga, "Muromachi bakufu shoki," p. 78; the source is Moromori-ki, entry for 1366/10/22. Busei kihan, a fifteenth-century description of bakufu administration, has the supplying of such prisoners as one of the regular duties of the samurai-dokoro (CHSS, 2:389).

8. Kōmyō-in shinki, entry for 1345/6/24, quoted in Haga, "Muromachi bakufu shoki," p. 78. For further background, see Moromori-ki, 1345/6/23, 24 (Shiryō Sanshu ed. [Tokyo, 1969] 3:120–23).

9. See Satō, "Muromachi bakufu ron," pp. 35–37 on the following examples; four are well known, being tsuika-hō, but two are from other sources.

10. Ibid., pp. 35–36; his source is Moromori-ki, 1363/int.1/24. A related entry for 1363/11/26 is quoted in Shinano shiryō (Nagano, 1969), 6:398–99.

destruction) was recognized by the court. Hitherto, the honjo had suffered as they lost control over their scattered landholdings; now the bakufu's authority came between them and even their toll barriers in Kyoto.

Throughout the era of the divided court several unusual circumstances put the bakufu in a strong position in Kyoto. One was the fact that the northern court, owing its existence to bakufu support, looked to it for approval even of matters such as the toll-barrier question. This resulted at the least in de facto, if not yet de jure, direction by the bakufu and it could subsequently acquire the force of precedent. The other fact is that until the court was unified in 1392, in theory a state of war existed. Kyoto was recaptured from the bakufu several times before 1363, and the bakufu may well have regarded barriers and other items pertinent to the civil administration of Kyoto as being militarily important to the security of the city and therefore necessarily open to bakufu control. In combination, these factors no doubt aided the growth of bakufu power in this one-time preserve of the aristocracy.

The usual means of announcing regulations to the townspeople of Kyoto in the Muromachi period was to set up notice-boards (kōsatsu). The earliest one whose contents are known dates from 1369 and has five articles.[11] They restricted the use of certain types of clothing and ornaments, outlawed gambling, and prohibited the sale of certain items and peddling in Shijō-machi. This is the first instance we have of the bakufu's using the regulation of dress or activities where money changed hands to assert control over the general populace of Kyoto.[12] The order was signed by Toki Yoshiyuki, the head of the samurai-dokoro.

The notice-board's third article (no. 101) marks the bakufu's initial step toward managing the commerce of the city, both in terms of goods and the location of sales. Emperor Go-Daigo had had visions in the 1330s of using the Kyoto markets as a source of regular income for his new administration. He had given up the lands attached to his branch of the imperial family and had been looking for new sources of revenue. The situation of the Muromachi bakufu from the late 1360s was in some respects analogous, since it too turned its attention to Kyoto as a source of income. Thus, the samurai-dokoro's order concerning some areas of the city's commerce and the public in the notice-board of 1369 had fiscal as well as administrative overtones.

11. *CHSS*, 2:44–45, (99–103), 1369/2/27.
12. There were, however, previously issued regulations or guidelines that were probably intended for a more limited audience, such as the *buke* alone. For examples, see *Kemmu shikimoku*, art. 1 (*CHSS*, 2:4); *CHSS*, 2:25–26, (44–50), 1346–50; *CHSS*, 2:41, (86–90), 1367/12/29. Although the 1369 *kōsatsu* is similar in its sumptuary content to these earlier *tsuika-hō*, we know by its wording that the present one was meant for a more general audience.

Among the city's most thriving commercial enterprises in the early decades of the fourteenth century were the brewers and the pawnbrokers. It has already been noted that the pawnbrokers were singled out for assistance in the bakufu's 1336 formulary because of their special role in the economic life of the city. The Buddhist establishment on Mount Hiei, the sammon, was the patron for most of the several hundred Kyoto pawnbrokers. The aristocrats were among the most frequent customers of these places and were constantly plagued by the debt collectors sent out by the pawnbrokers. In 1370, at last, the highly provoked court issued the following statement:

> The sammon collectors, using the excuse of collecting payment, have caused misery throughout the city. Moreover, having no respect for the extreme proximity of the residences of the emperor and the retired emperors, they burst into the homes of the nobles and commit all manner of evil acts. Accordingly, the abbot [of the sammon][13] was advised of the situation. Strict action ought to be taken, but he has done nothing at all. Surely it is impossible [for the collectors] to avoid the penalty for violent disturbances and disobeying an imperial command! Hereafter, the bakufu will arrest the culprits and punish them for their crimes.[14]

With these words, the court authorized the bakufu to control the excesses of the debt collectors who worked for the sammon's pawnbrokers. This step acknowledges the inability of the court's own police, the kebiishi-chō, to protect the nobles. But more was involved here than merely obtaining protection for the nobles. For the bakufu it amounted to a concession of authority over a segment of the Kyoto business community, namely, the agents of the most profitable of the sammon's operations in the city.

It is ironic to consider that the court itself may have been to blame for the immediate outrages that prompted this statement recognizing the new bakufu powers. Two months before, Emperor Go-Kōgon had decided to abdicate, and the pawnbrokers well knew that the ceremonies for that occasion as well as the enthronement and accession ceremonies for his successor would be paid for by a special levy on them. The pawnbrokers may therefore have been scrambling faster than usual to collect payment in anticipation of the coming tax, which, as it turned out, was indeed ordered early the next year by the bakufu.

---

13. I.e., the Tendai *zasu*, or head of the Tendai sect on Mount Hiei, the Imperial Prince Takamichi.

14. *CHSS*, 2:45–46, (105), 1370/12/12. There is some question as to the date of promulgation. Cf. Kuwayama Kōnen et al., "*Kaei sandai-ki oboegaki*," *Chūsei no mado* 11 (1962): 8.

The kebiishi-chō did, however, retain certain administrative functions in litigation involving land within Kyoto as late as 1381. In 1384 there are signs that the samurai-dokoro had moved into this area, too, since it was now enforcing judicial decisions having to do with land in the city.[15] Whether this in itself is sufficient to prove that the samurai-dokoro had taken over all related administrative and legal powers from the kebiishi-chō is open to doubt, but the bakufu was moving in this direction. One dimension of this is the fact that during Ashikaga Yoshimitsu's years as shōgun (1368–94) a bakufu office (the *jikata*) that dealt with the confirmation of holdings (*chigyō no ando*) of land in Kyoto came to function regularly.[16]

By the 1380s the initiative in Kyoto lay with the bakufu, not with the court. It has already been related that the bakufu acquired a measure of delegated authority over the rowdy bill-collectors sent out by the sammon's moneylenders in 1370. In 1386 the bakufu showed that it had reached the stage of being able to act without specific authorization from the court, as the following announcement demonstrates:

Item: Concerning the bill collectors of the sammon and the various shrines

In many cases the bill collectors of the sammon and the various shrines, leading a numerous body of men, trespass and are disorderly, saying they are there to press for repayment. Some time ago a law was promulgated to deal with this[17] and there was an end to such carryings-on, but in recent years reckless disorders have begun again. . . . In short, if bill collectors should have a notion to take matters into their own hands and not go through regular legal procedures, their claims will be permanently discarded even if they have merit. As regards the collectors themselves, the samurai-dokoro will be ordered, according to precedent, to take them into custody and detain them.[18]

---

15. Satō, "*Muromachi bakufu ron*," p. 36.

16. Cf. *Buke myomōku-sho*, 1:278–79. It is interesting to note that this work quotes a passage from *Kaei sandai-ki*, 1379/8/25, which lists a certain Nikaidō as in charge of the jikata. Only a month before this date Ise Sadatsugu had taken the place of this man as head of the mandokoro and ended the Nikaidō family's long incumbency in that post. But it was the Nakahara family who, under Yoshimitsu, came to hold the jikata post hereditarily (ibid). Until Go-Daigo's time, a Nakahara family (the same one?) had long been associated with the management of the Eastern Market in the city. Does this indicate that the bakufu either had been unable or unwilling to have *bushi* handle land cases in Kyoto and left them to families of long standing in the city? The impression is that the bakufu still could not do without some cooperation from the aristocrats.

17. Perhaps a reference to the previously cited 1370/12/12 edict.

18. *CHSS*, 2:59, (145), 1386/8/25.

Superficially, this is an order stopping the forcible collection of bebts by the agents of the pawnbrokers. The aim (as stated in the full text) is to preserve the "good name" of the sammon by having the collectors act with propriety, and thereby to bring peace and order to society. But the implications are broader than this. Although the debtors at court would not object to the order, since they stood to benefit from its implementation, it did help to confirm the legal status of the samurai-dokoro's policing activities in Kyoto. The court's ability to perform with practical authority in its own capital had by now all but vanished. The kebiishi-chō had been supplanted by the samurai-dokoro.

The sammon's credibility as a reliable patron of pawnbrokers and others was no doubt impaired by this order. It was an encroachment into the traditionally privileged area of the activities of religious establishments, and both debtors and bakufu had something to gain by it. Debtors stood to benefit because the pawnbrokers relied on the borrowed spiritual authority and traditional exemption of such patrons to allow them to carry on as they pleased. If the bakufu could exert effective control over the collectors, these advantages would be negated. Whereas in 1370 the court had given the Muromachi bakufu the power to arrest and punish the sammon's men, the present instance is indicative of a much increased authority: the pawnbroker's claim would be canceled if he attempted to collect from a recalcitrant debtor by any means but legal appeal to the bakufu. The bakufu had now accumulated both police and judicial controls over the sammon and their pawnbrokers.

If the foregoing order of 1386 was of potential advantage to debtors because it placed restraints on debt collectors, it may have conjured up an image, for various commercial groups, of a bakufu which might be a surer patron than either the sammon or the court. After all, the bakufu was now in a position to offer immunities on its own. In fact, in 1393 the bakufu did issue a statement that offered a degree of immunity. Here are two clauses from it:

> Regulations concerning levies on pawnbrokers (dosō) and brewers (sakaya) in Kyoto and scattered in the outlying area:
> *Item: Concerning the men affiliated with the various temples and shrines as well as those who perform services for the powerful*: They are all to lose their privileged status and be treated like everyone else.
> *Item: Concerning the taxation of 6,000* kan *of money for the expenses of the mandokoro's annual operations*: Collection will occur on a monthly basis. Even in cases of urgent (mandokoro) need, pawnbrokers and brewers shall hereafter be exempted from special taxes designated for temples and shrines, and the bakufu.[19]

19. The text of the entire document may be found in *CHSS*, 2:59–61, (146–50), 1393/11/26, but only 146 and 148 are quoted here.

By refusing to grant exemptions to brewers and pawnbrokers, who had hitherto enjoyed the protection of patrons among the religious establishments and aristocratic houses, the bakufu significantly reduced the advantage of having a patron. With the absence of exemptions, the reason for the continuation of the client–patron relationship was compromised.

On the other hand, the bakufu's announcement contained good news for the brewers and pawnbrokers: their taxes would be regularized and limited. Until then, taxes had been imposed, according to need, in an unscheduled fashion as "special taxes." Thus, the exemption from "special taxes" was really an exemption from the only kind the brewers and pawnbrokers had been paying. They would henceforth pay taxes systematically (which in itself implies further bakufu institutional development) while being guaranteed immunity from "special taxes." The bakufu showed the commercial world in Kyoto that it, like the traditional kind of patron, was capable of granting protection. Now that the old privileges had been outlawed, the bakufu was in effect fitting itself into the patronage system, wielding its accumulated police and judicial powers. The 6,000 *kan* mentioned in the second article above may be considered analogous to the dues that the protégé group had once paid in to its patron. The bakufu could tax and offer protection to commercial interests just as had been the case with the original Kyoto patrons, but it could do so as a governing body now, free from the necessity of competing with them on equal terms.

By the end of the fourteenth century the Muromachi bakufu was recognized as the Kyoto government in most police and administrative areas. It had become a Kyoto power in its own right. The samurai-dokoro and the mandokoro eased into roles performed by organs of the civil government before them. That it took over half a century to bring about this state of affairs bears witness to the fact that the transmission of authority from the court to the bakufu was not a sudden concession made under duress. It is likely that the bakufu had no intention at first of taking over the running of Kyoto from the court. Until the 1380s the bakufu's advance as a Kyoto authority came about largely as a convenience for the court by agreement with the bakufu. By Yoshimitsu's heyday, however, the economic advantages to be derived from Kyoto were regarded with increasing interest. It was then that the bakufu's status began to assume a new importance. The resultant control of Kyoto and its environs, with its resources, provided in no small measure the stability to which the vigorous bakufu of the late fourteenth century owed its power.

10 The Muromachi *Shugo* and *Hanzei*

PRESCOTT B. WINTERSTEEN, JR.

One of the weaknesses of the bakufu system of government in the Kamakura and early Muromachi periods was its dependence on land to cement
ties between superior and subordinate. In the late thirteenth century, for
instance, the Kamakura regime ran into trouble when there were insufficient lands with which to reward its men for service during the Mongol
invasions. The hope for more land was also a factor in persuading military
houses to join with Emperor Go-Daigo against the bakufu in 1333, and in
inducing these and other warrior families to fall in behind Ashikaga
Takauji's rebellion in 1335. The Ashikaga, however, possessed no private
territorial resources with which to lure potential allies, nor did the bakufu
that Takauji established in 1336 inherit any special financial or other
reserves from its Kamakura predecessor. There were only the lands that
had been confiscated from enemies and the areas requisitioned for army
use during the prolonged hostilities between the northern and southern
courts.

With land at a premium, private estates (*shōen*) continued to suffer
during the north–south court era (1336–92), just as they had in the previous century. Absentee proprietors had tried over the years to work out
compromises with the stewards (*jitō*) placed on their domains by the Kamakura bakufu. They tried dividing the land (*shitaji chūbun*) or allowing these
stewards to run an estate in return for the jitō's promise to render a fixed
annual income (*jitō-uke*). Under the first three Ashikaga shoguns, disruption of estates worsened as the new bakufu contended with the allies
of the southern court and strove to marshal regional forces under the
shugo. The shogun relied on the shugo as the bakufu's ranking administrative and military representative on the provincial level.

In the Kamakura period, the shugo's duty had been to maintain peace
within his province and to supervise and coordinate the shogun's men
(*go-ke'nin*) there. The go-ke'nin's superior was, in a military sense, the
shugo, yet he owed his ultimate, personal loyalty to the shogun. The
shugo's role changed markedly in the Muromachi period, however, as he

became the nucleus of provincial forces bound personally to himself. This was due in part to the considerable degree of autonomy that the shugo acquired both militarily and through explicit bakufu authorizations during the 1340s and 1350s. The stronger the shugo grew in his capacity to handle local issues and to dispose of land, the easier it was for him to attract men to his side. By the same token, the bakufu's structure became sounder as reliable shugo sank their roots more deeply into their provinces.

For the absentee proprietor, the shugo was a new force to reckon with. When the shugo abused his authority he posed a more formidable threat than had the jitō because his powers were province-wide. This led to attempts by proprietors to stop or slow the shugo's incursions by reaching an accommodation with him as had been done with the jitō—giving over management of an estate in return for a guaranteed income (*shugo-uke*). If the shugo lived up to his side of the agreement, it relieved the proprietor of the worry of dealing with recalcitrant peasants who withheld estate revenues or absconded with growing frequency. Shugo-uke was known in the 1340s but did not reach its peak until well into the fifteenth century. As time passed, however, the incidence of nonpayment by shugo increased. Absentee interests were set back once again.

In consolidating his control over a province, the shugo found his powers to allot confiscated and requisitioned lands to be of the greatest value. The two basic forms that this distribution took came to be called *hyōrō-ryōsho* and *hanzei,* and scholars divide on how they should be understood. One group maintains that hanzei (the major form) was basically a policy espoused by the Muromachi bakufu in order to protect the interests of its conservative backers, the absentee proprietors.[1] The other group points instead to the negative effects that hanzei had on the estate system.[2] The present study proposes another line of treatment. It will deal with the historical development of hyōrōryōsho and hanzei and then inquire into the extent of central bakufu initiative. It will also examine the role that these two institutions played in the bakufu's relative stability during the late fourteenth century.

Hyōrōryōsho

When Ashikaga Takauji fought his way back to Kyoto from Kyushu in 1336 to establish the bakufu, the security of his base, the Kyoto area, was of immediate concern to him. Those in the vicinity who responded to his call for assistance against his rival, Nitta Yoshisada, were rewarded with one-half jitō rights to the *myōden* they worked and were allowed to enter

1. Shimada Jirō, "Hanzei seido no seiritsu," *Shichō,* no. 58 (1956): 1–24.
2. Nagahara Keiji, "Shōen sei kaitai katei ni okeru Nanbokuchō nairan ki no ichi," *Keizaigaku Kenkyū,* no. 6 (1962): esp. 400–06, 451–61.

the ranks of the shogun's men (go-ke'nin).³ Takauji also made an offering
to the influential Tōji temple of the jitō-shiki of nearby Kuze-no-shō,
as well as regranting Engakuji and Nanzenji all the properties confiscated
from them since the Genkō year period (1331–33).⁴ In Kii Province, Hatakeyama Kunikiyo, one of Takauji's generals, was also handing out rewards
for recent assistance in the form of jitō- and ryōke-shiki.⁵ By conferrals
such as these, the Ashikaga and their allies attempted to attract support.

The earliest documentary evidence of the establishment of hyōrōryōsho
(grant areas for the support of troops in the field) dates from the second
month of 1337. This bestowal was authorized by the bakufu's enemy, the
southern court.⁶ On the bakufu's side similar grants were probably being
made,⁷ since a 1337 supplementary article (tsuika-hō) to the Muromachi
bakufu's law code, the Kemmu shikimoku, seems to refer expressly to this
practice:

> During the disturbances, generals and military provincial governors (shugo)
> in the various provinces have temporarily entrusted (azuke-oku) their forces
> with properties of the provincial civil government (kokugaryō) and ryōke-
> shiki as necessary. Now, there are complaints that the bakufu order to put
> the administrative agents of the owners (zasshō) of those ryō . . . back in
> control has not been carried out. . . . the land (shitaji) shall be immediately
> transferred to the zasshō. . . . If a shugo is recalcitrant in this, he shall be
> replaced; if it is a general or soldier, he shall be punished and not given any
> reward, though he may deserve it.⁸

The bakufu's concern here was not that emergency measures had been
taken to establish sources of supply, but rather that the temporary nature
of hyōrōryōsho was being ignored. If some control were not attempted,
the estate system would be rapidly eroded, costing the bakufu the support
of the great landholding religious institutions and others. Unauthorized
grants by the shugo would surely proliferate, weakening the chain of Ashikaga military command.

From 1338 on, examples of hyōrōryōsho authorized by the bakufu are

3. Dai Nihon Shiryō, VI (Tokyo, 1901), 3:599–601 (hereafter cited as DNS). Cf.
Sugiyama Hiroshi, Shōen kaitai katei no kenkyū, pp. 17–21 for details. Although Sugiyama loosely terms this "hanzei" simply because one-half of the absentee proprietor's
rights (ryōke-shiki) is involved, we shall see below that this is a questionable usage.

4. Nochi Kagami, in Shintei Zōho Kokushi Taikei (Tokyo, 1929), 1:137 (1336/7/1);
1:151 (1336/9/15); 1:151 (1336/9/17). (Hereafter cited as NK.)

5. DNS, VI,   3:753–54 (1336/9/17).

6. Ibid., 4:100 (1337/2/29).

7. However, the first recorded bakufu case comes more than a year later. Cf. DNS,
VI, 4:737, 754 (1338/3/7, 11).

8. Tsuika-hō of 1337/10/7 quoted in Satō Shin'ichi and Ikeuchi Yoshisuke, Chūsei
hōsei shiryō shū, rev. ed. (Tokyo, 1969), 2:11, (no. 1). (Hereafter cited as CHSS.)

numerous. Let us look at several of these to gain an idea of their scope. The standard form of the authorizing document was roughly as follows:

> Concerning [name of property or *shiki* in question]: you are being entrusted (*azuke-oku*) with the above as a source of military provisions (*hyōrōryōsho*). Continue to perform faithful service.
>
> [monogram]
>
> [date]
>
> [address]

Within this general framework considerable variety was possible. For example, the authorizing party was sometimes the shogun or his deputy, although more frequently a shugo. Likewise, the initiative in establishing a hyōrōryōsho might lie either with higher military authority or with the party who stood to benefit. In the latter case, a petition was sent to the shogun or shugo naming the place or rights desired and including the grounds for making the request, such as loyal military service, the scarcity of provisions for one's men, and so on. If the petition were granted, the shogun or shugo then issued a document similar to that above, itemizing the name of the place or rights involved, the special conditions, if any,[9] and closing frequently with an exhortation to continue to perform faithful service.

While it was the intention that land so assigned revert at some later date to the previous owner, it became exceedingly difficult to dislodge a donee from holdings newly received. The previously quoted 1337/10/7 bakufu tsuika-hō bears witness to this. Less than a year later, the bakufu was blaming the shugo for letting matters deteriorate:

> The intention in appointing shugo is to pacify the provinces and calm the people. Men of virtue are named to this office; if they do not serve the interests of the province, they ought to be replaced. Yet there are those shugo who have done nothing but accumulate rewards or who, claiming "hereditary rights" (*fudai no shiki*), have seized the properties (*ryō*) of nobles (*honjo*) and shrines and temples, have taken over (*kanryō*) the stewards' rights (*jitō-shiki*) of many places, have entrusted (*azuke-oku*) their warriors [with hyōrōryōsho, etc.] and made grants (*ate-okonau*) to their housemen (*kenin*). This is exceedingly improper. Shugo are firmly to uphold the articles of the *Jōei shikimoku* [the basic military legal formulary, dating from 1232], and not interfere in areas outside the *Taihon sankajō*.[10]

9. E.g., "to be shared among your family (*ichizoku*)": *DNS*, VI, 4:737 (1338/3/7); 19:71–72 (1354/6/1); 21:303–04 (1357/6/11).
10. I.e., the original definition of the shugo's responsibilities: chastising rebels, pursuing and apprehending murderers, and enforcing guard duty. Tsuika-hō of 1338/int. 7/29, quoted in *CHSS*, 2:11–12 (no. 2). Art. 3 in the above document stipulates that any

Within two years of the bakufu's founding, the shugo had already become an obvious source of difficulty; they were abusing their powers by making improper grants and by failing to enforce withdrawals from hyōrōryōsho in newly stabilized areas.

Despite the many complaints that were raised against the shugo, the bakufu does not seem to have gone to the trouble of making explicit the the length of time hyōrōryōsho authorizations should remain in force. An obvious reason for this is that Takauji was attempting to build a strong following and was willing to recognize claims to land from military men on whatever pretext. Indeed the matter of reversion after stipulated periods does not appear in bakufu documents until the 1350s. This contrasts with hyōrōryōsho authorizations coming from the southern court, to wit, an excerpt dated 1338: "Ōta-no-shō, Yamato Province: you are to manage (chigyō) this place to provide this year's military provisions (tōnen hyōrōryō no tame). . . . "[11] The same limitation of "this year" appears in a 1346 document.[12] It would be hazardous to argue solely from these two documents that the southern court was more interested in preserving the old estate system than the bakufu was, but there are other hints that the respective viewpoints did differ somewhat. In 1343, for instance, a hyōrōryōsho was assigned by the southern court with the provision that "after the war this jitō-shiki will be exchanged for another"; while in 1360 we find the assignment of hyōrōryōsho lands in exchange for lands that may or may not have been serving that purpose.[13] It is certain, then, that the exchange of lands in the case of the southern court did take place on occasion.

Thus far we have seen that both the bakufu and its adversary to the south authorized the establishment of hyōrōryōsho; that their content included both property and shiki; and that these transactions tended to involve whole units, in other words, a whole jitō-shiki or unit of property (ryō).[14]

Hanzei

In the main, the bakufu's early hyōrōryōsho policy was permissive but not calculated to create more than a limited dislocation of ownership

income already received from the holdings (shoryō) of shrines and temples, nobles (honjo), or military houses was to be returned, under threat of punishment. Presumably this was meant to apply to those cases that were either illegally granted in the first place or whose necessity as a provisioning place for the military had now passed.

11. *DNS*, VI, 4:900 (1338/7/26).
12. Ibid., 9:883 (1346/4/7).
13. Ibid., 7:615 (1343/4/17); 23:180 (1360/6/5).
14. Fractional units, though less common, are not unknown. For instance, one-seventh of a *gō* (provincial administrative unit) appears in ibid., 6:952 (1341/10/20); one-half of a *ryōke-shiki* in ibid., 12:50 (1348/10/27).

based on the realities of local power politics. It was decidedly not a policy that meant to do fundamental damage to the estate system itself. Within bakufu councils, however, there were those who held more radical views. The Kō brothers, for example, were in favor of doing away with both the imperial house and the estate system. Ashikaga Takauji's brother, Tadayoshi, who handled most of the judicial and administrative affairs of the regime, advocated a more tolerant position. By the late 1340s the differences between the Kō brothers, backed by Takauji, and Tadayoshi began to have political repercussions; their feud broke out into war. The advantage passed from one side to the other for a time, but in 1351 the Kō brothers and their kin were assassinated, and the next year Tadayoshi died —some say he was poisoned by Takauji—following a brief reconciliation. The southern court sought to make good use of this split in the ranks of the bakufu and managed to recapture Kyoto briefly in 1352.

In the seventh month of 1352 a supplementary law was issued, repeating a familiar theme:

> *Item: Concerning the properties* (ryō) *of shrines, temples, and nobles* (honjo). . . .
> Due to the disturbances in the provinces, the desolation of shrines and temples and the impoverishment of nobles has increased severalfold in recent years. However, there are even some peaceful provinces in which indiscriminate actions on the part of the *bushi* have not yet ceased. Therefore. . . . [the shugo] shall convoke the *jitō-go-kenin* in his province and, heading without delay for [troubled] areas, pacify them, and place the administrative agent of the owner (*zasshō*) back in control of the land (*shitaji*) as originally. . . .[15]

What followed, however, was new:

> Next, concerning a one-half share of the properties (*ryō hanbun*) of honjo [here probably meaning lands for which shrines, temples, and nobles acted as patrons] in the three provinces of Ōmi, Mino, and Owari: The shugo have been notified that a one-half share of this year's crop (*tōnen issaku*) from these properties shall be entrusted (*azuke-oku*) to the armed forces as a hyōrōryōsho. Half of the crop must be given to the honjo. If the military assignee (*azukari-nin*) makes excuses and fails to deliver it, full control of the property shall be returned to the honjo (*ichien ni honjo ni henpu subeshi*).[16]

At last the bakufu had made an official statement about hyōrōryōsho: it had standardized the procedure to cover all the properties of the non-military class in three provinces near Kyoto. All were now made liable to

15. *CHSS*, 2:28–29 (no. 56), 1352/7/24.
16. Ibid.

categorization as hyororyosho. On the other hand, the statement did specify a limitation on the area, length of time, and proportion of the yield involved. The very next month the bakufu issued an expanded version that already revealed changes:

> *Item: Concerning the properties of shrines, temples, and nobles. . . . concerning the properties of patrons* (honjo) *in the eight provinces (Ōmi, Mino, Ise, Shima, Owari, Iga, Izumi, Kawachi) where armed forces are in the field:*
>
> On a previous occasion it was established that this year's crop in the properties serving as hyōrōryōsho should be equally divided (*kinbun*) between the patrons (*honjo*) and the military assignee. But there are reports that half-payment (*hanzei*) has been claimed in addition to what the military assignees have already received (*sennobun o nozoki*) and that enforcement of half-payment has been abused in their desire to take in everything. This is very much out of line. In short, when both honjo and assignee agree to the amounts, the proportions of the income need not become an issue. When this is not the case, obstructions can be avoided by ordering the administrative agent (*zasshō*) to prepare a document dividing the land itself (*shitaji setchū no chūmon*), and having the military assignee choose one of the parts.[17]

In less than a month after the original order allowing a halving of one year's yield in three provinces, the number of provinces was nearly trebled, and the possibility of dividing the land (*shitaji*) to avoid difficulties was officially raised. This was the beginning of a new state in shugo encroachments.[18]

Comparing hanzei authorizations with the hyōrōryōsho that preceded them, the latter embraced a broad range of content and included assorted fractional divisions; "one-half" (*hanbun*) was among them. On the other hand, the texts of hanzei grants continued to use as their rationale the pretext of establishing a hyōrōryōsho. Hanzei grants were all hyōrōryōsho, but not all hyōrōryōsho were limited to the assignee's receiving only a one-half share. The differences between the two institutions were therefore more of nomenclature than of fact: hanzei, embodying a 50 percent division, represented a standardizing of hyōrōryōsho; it was not a totally new invention. Within the context of the times, however, hanzei does suggest a new emphasis in land policy.

Etymologically, *hanzei* is composed of two elements: *han*, meaning "half," and *zei*, meaning "payment." Hanzei thus means one-half payment

---

17. Ibid., 2:29 (no. 57), 1352/8/21.
18. The appearance of the term "hanzei" in the second of these two orders appears to be the term's earliest known usage in either a bakufu hyōrōryōsho authorization or in a tsuika-hō. The earliest documentary use of "hanzei" dates from the next year, 1353. *DNS*, VI, 18:157 (1353/6/20).

of something to someone, but who pays whom? The expectation was that the military assignee, who after all was on the land, should deliver to the actual owner the one-half share of income not requisitioned. Rather than to say, therefore, that hanzei allowed the bushi recipients to hold back half the income, the emphasis was on getting these warriors to see that the owner received his half. In other words, the authorization granted was actually no more than official recognition that the assignee was *already* in control of what he was asking for. The 1352 hanzei orders indicate, then, that the halfway stage in shōen takeovers had been passed in enough places to warrant adoption by the bakufu of an official position on the matter of hyōrōryōsho.

An unexpected result of the 1352 orders was that the bakufu at a stroke had now opened to hyōrōryōsho virtually all land in the eight provinces designated. As evidence of this, we need only note a quotation from the diary of a court noble dated just a few days before issuance of the first hanzei order in 1352:

> There is a rumor that the *buke* are about to order *hanzei* in Yamashiro. There are properties (*ryō*) of governmental bureaus (*ryō*) there. What will happen to them with *hanzei*?[19]

There was good reason, no doubt, to fear what would happen. Ten years later the Regent Konoe Michitsugu, lamenting severe losses, expressed the hope that the hanzei status of Mino and Owari might be revoked. He admitted, however, that his wish was probably forlorn:

> *Hanzei* is no illegal act (*ranbō iran no gi ni arazu*), but is authorized by the bakufu. It is difficult for court nobles to pass judgment on it. There are no precedents to go by. All we can do is complain directly to the bakufu.[20]

The effect, in other words, of the hanzei tsuika-hō was to make the hanzei form of bushi incursions legal, but hardly to make them any less injurious.

Although the 1352 orders established guidelines, as it were, for encroaching on estates, they were not enforced by the central bakufu. This was left to the shugo, whose interests did not always coincide with the letter of the new laws. Many shugo had been important regional military leaders before joining with Ashikaga Takauji. It was through their assistance and cooperation that Takauji was able to found the bakufu, and its continuation depended largely on their goodwill. This is why the Muromachi bakufu is often described as consisting of a shogun supported by a liaison of friendly shugo. The Ashikaga house, even with all its cadet

19. *Entairyaku*, entry for 1352/7/8, quoted in *CHSS*, 2:171.
20. Nagahara Keiji, "Nanbokuchō nairan," in *Iwanami Kōza Nihon Rekishi* (Tokyo, 1967), 6:77.

branches, would have been hard pressed to defend itself had the other shugo turned against it.[21]

From the very start of the hyōrōryōsho in the 1330s, both shogun and shugo had authorized such grants. In theory, of course, it was ultimately the shogun's prerogative. In practice, the granting or recognition of hyōrōryōsho was a valuable asset for a shugo as he built up his local band of allies. As we have seen, the shugo were cited repeatedly in tsuika-hō for violations of the spirit of the wartime hyōrōryōsho. A considerable gulf, however, separated exhortation by the bakufu from punitive action. In 1346 a tsuika-hō records an increment in the shugo's powers: he became authorized to arrest marauders who entered fields and made off with crops (karita rōzeki); and he was empowered to enforce land transfers resulting from litigation (shisetsu jungyō).[22] This gave the shugo an extended legal basis for operations within his province. It also made him the natural proponent and judge in matters involving hyōrōryōsho and hanzei hyōrōryōsho. With the possible exception of the late fourteenth century, it is fair to say that policy set by the central bakufu could not be implemented without shugo compliance.

Once hyōrōryōsho had been linked in the tsuika-hō with the principles of half payment and province-wide application, the prospect of dividing the land itself became a reality.[23] Further concessions, or rather, subsequent recognitions of the deteriorating state of the shōen, were not long in coming.

In 1355 the bakufu issued a tsuika-hō to the effect that while hanzei was permissible in provinces not at peace, the administration of land (shōmu) was to remain in the hands of the absentee proprietor.[24] Control of the land itself was fast becoming an issue. Two years later an equal division of the land (shitaji o kinbun shite) was recognized in cases where there had been outstanding battlefield service or great military necessity; the remaining half share was to be returned to the owner's administrative agent (zasshō).[25] Evidently, the lands "completely held" (ichien ni) by traditional proprietors were being violated because they, too, were ordered returned to their central owners.[26] As an inducement to restore such prop-

21. The Ashikaga, astonishingly, did not themselves hold any shugo posts at all; only their relatives and hereditary followers (hikan) did. There are no shugo recorded with the Ashikaga surname.

22. CHSS, 2:23 (no. 31), 1346.

23. It is not clear whether this was to be requested by the owner or by the military assignee. By analogy with the Kamakura period practice of shitaji chūbun, one would expect that the owner would have the right to request it.

24. CHSS, 2:37 (no. 78), 1355/8/22.

25. CHSS, 2:38 (no. 79), 1357/9/10.

26. A "completely held land" (ichien-chi) was one whose jitō-shiki and ryōke-shiki

erties, the bakufu held out the vague promise that they would be replaced "later."

The most telling feature of the 1357 tsuika-hō lies in one of its later articles, which reads:

Item: Concerning half-payment land (hanzei-chi)

Shugo who divide land up without shogunal permission, and recipients of hanzei grants who take more than their share, are guilty of misconduct.[27]

In the two year's time since the 1355 directive, the bakufu had shifted its position in favor of the new status quo: now, with the shogun's approval, shugo division of the land itself was officially countenanced. Another item which had changed was the fact that war and peace no longer figured in the authorization of a hanzei grant. The pretexts had almost all fallen away.

The last pronouncement the bakufu made on hanzei was by far the most comprehensive. It was promulgated a decade later, in 1367, a few months before the young Yoshimitsu became the third Ashikaga shogun. Since it gives a definitive form to the earlier, more amorphous hanzei orders and is the Muromachi bakufu's last major piece of legislation concerning land, the main parts bear extensive quotation:

Item: Concerning the properties of shrines, temples, and nobles:

Properties of the emperor and retired emperor, the *ichien* properties of the shrines and temples, and the hereditary properties of the imperial regents are different from other properties. Hanzei is not to apply to them. . . . But aside from these lands, patronage properties (*honjo-ryō*) in the various provinces shall be divided in half temporarily (*shibaraku hanbun o ai-wakete*) and the [remaining one-half of the] land shall be given over to the *zasshō*, who shall hereafter have full control of it. Should the recipient of the grant (*azukari-nin*) cause trouble for the *zasshō* or take more than his share, the land so divided shall be returned in full (*ichien ni*) to the patron (*honjo*). . . .

Next, concerning lands of nobles (*honjo*) which have been managed with full title (*ichien chigyō-chi*) since the time of the previous shogun:[28] these may not be touched by using the law of *hanzei* as an excuse. . . .

Next, concerning the *jitō-shiki* managed by courtiers: inasmuch as *jitō-shiki* are assigned to the courtiers as an expression of favor by the bakufu,

---

were both held by the proprietor. The possession of the *jitō-shiki* would presumably preclude a second, conflicting appointment by the bakufu.

27. *CHSS*, 2:39 (no. 83).

28. Ashikaga Yoshiakira, second Ashikaga shogun, 1330–67 (r. 1358–67).

these are not to be confused with patronage properties. There must be no *hanzei* with them.[29]

This order places lands belonging with full title (*ichien*) to the imperial house, religious institutions, and the houses of the imperial regents (Fujiwara) outside the realm of hanzei application. Ichien properties of court nobles as well as jitō-shiki that they received from the bakufu were also designated as immune from hanzei. Everything else was to be halved "temporarily"; the fiction of reversion was maintained to the end.

It is no wonder that the 1368 hanzei order was the final major statement concerning land to be made by the bakufu. The premise for granting hanzei authorizations had been cast aside, with wartime necessity no longer mentioned.[30] The true object of hanzei now emerged as land, not merely its fruits.

I have tried to show in the preceding pages that hanzei and hyōrōryōsho were closely related. Both were justified on the basis of the necessity of provisioning troops in the field; both involved the appropriation of resources from the religious institutions and court in the name of the bakufu; and both followed the same administrative pattern of authorization. I have argued further that authorization generally followed a request from someone already in control of what he wanted. Hanzei was never a "system" in the sense that this implies orderly administration of a program by a central authority; the shugo as a group were too intractible for that. The bakufu's statements on hanzei were thus the belated taking of an official line on hyōrōryōsho, and a tacit admission that the shōen as a central proprietary institution was now irrevocably in decline. To the extent that shōen had not been overrun by the military by 1352, hanzei, far from protecting them, exposed them to encroachment on a province-wide basis. In a sense, the 1368 order had finally caught up with reality: it gave legal recognition to the seizure and possession of land by bushi, a situation that had prevailed since the inauguration of hyōrōryōsho some three decades before.

29. *CHSS*, 2:43 (no. 97), 1368/6/17.
30. It is interesting to note that the southern court was still making use of the term "hyōrōryōsho" in its grants; e.g., see *DNS*, VI, 31:61–62 (1369/10/3).

11 *Ikki* in Late Medieval Japan

DAVID L. DAVIS

The study of the role of *ikki* in Japanese history has given rise to a certain amount of contention, some of which, unfortunately, is based on misconception. Part of the trouble lies with the term itself, or at least with its modern connotations. A standard modern dictionary defines *ikki* as "a riot; a rising; an insurrection; a revolt"—a definition that obscures the vital fact that in medieval usage an ikki was not an event but rather an organization, especially one formed for military purposes. Since these ikki were distinct from—and often in opposition to—the dominant feudal forms of organization, they gradually came to be associated with the idea of rebellion. By the eighteenth century the earlier meaning was lost, along with the original ikki form of organization. The use of the term continued, however, only now in reference to the peasant revolts (*hyakushō ikki*) of the Edo period. The hyakushō ikki were scarcely more than peasant mobs rioting as an expression of general or specific discontent; yet all too often they have been taken as models for the medieval ikki organizations.[1]

This study will focus on the two most important types of medieval ikki: the widespread local *tsuchi-ikki*, which attempted with considerable success to dominate the farming areas surrounding Kyoto from about 1428 until well into the sixteenth century, and the *Ikkō-ikki* (a type of *kuni-ikki*) formed in Kaga Province in 1474, which dominated the political life of the province between 1488 and 1580.

A consideration of the role of these ikki in Japanese society throws light on the transition between what historians have decided to call the medieval and early modern periods, or in more political terms, between the era of the Muromachi bakufu of the fourteenth and fifteenth centuries and that of the Edo bakufu founded at the beginning of the seventeenth. Recent work on this period has focused on the transformation of the daimyo institution from the shugo daimyo of the Muromachi period through one or two stages (depending on whom one follows) to the "modern" daimyo

---

1. Aoki Kōji, *Hyakushō-ikki no nenjiteki kenkyū* (Tokyo: Shinseisha, 1966), is an exhaustive treatment of the subject.

of the Edo period.[2] The roughly parallel development of ikki organizations, formed by men trying to evade daimyo control, provides a view of the same social transformations, if not from the very bottom of society, at least from a point considerably below the top. The tsuchi-ikki were intimately connected with the decay and collapse of the shugo institution, and the Kaga Ikkō-ikki and similar movements elsewhere with the emergence of the new forms of daimyo organization.

There remains a third type of medieval ikki, of lesser significance in itself, but to some extent ancestral to the others and related to the rise of the shugo in the fourteenth century. Thus before discussing in greater detail the tsuchi-ikki and Ikkō-ikki, it would be well to touch briefly upon this earlier type.

The Origins of Ikki

The word *ikki* is derived from a literary Chinese term meaning "of one goal" or "in agreement." In fourteenth-century Japan this meaning was narrowed to specify a band of warriors linked by agreement rather than by ties of blood or vassalage. The fourteenth-century chronicle *Taiheiki*, for example, offers a fine series of concrete illustrations showing the evolution of the term and of the ikki form of organization.

When Ashikaga Takauji rebelled against the Emperor Go-Daigo at the end of 1335, he was faced with the task of expanding his personal following of vassals and relatives into a national army. In some areas influential local leaders with their own followings declared for him, and he appointed them shugo of their provinces with the mandate to raise still more troops. Akamatsu Norimura of Harima Province is one example. More typically, though, Takauji was forced to dispatch various relatives and close supporters into areas where they were strangers, to try to raise armies for him. For example, in 1336 he sent several members of the Hosokawa family, a rather poor Ashikaga branch from Mikawa Province, to Shikoku, where no local Ashikaga leaders had emerged. Many of the recruits who then came forward were only small *bushi*, with a handful of retainers or perhaps none. They were grouped into ikki, at first temporarily on the occasion of a battle and later more or less permanently.[3]

The new Ashikaga armies won an important series of battles in 1336, 1337, and 1338, and Takauji was able to gain the upper hand in the country and proclaim a revived bakufu with himself as shogun. The new

2. John W. Hall, "Foundations of the Modern Japanese Daimyo," in *Studies in the Institutional History of Early Modern Japan*, ed. John W. Hall and Marius B. Jansen (Princeton: Princeton University Press, 1968), pp. 65–77.

3. Miki Yasui, "Nambokuchō nairanki no ikki—Taiheiki o chūshin ni," *Nihon rekishi* 276 (May 1971): 42–77.

bakufu, however, was unable to win a final victory over its opponents, and for another twenty-five years the country was torn by a peculiar civil war waged on three levels. First, supporters of Go-Daigo's branch of the imperial family continued to maintain substantial field armies, which the bakufu often defeated but could not eliminate. Second, throughout the country the new Ashikaga shugo faced tenacious local resistance to their control on the part of men who welcomed what support they could get from the southern court party but were not really part of it. And finally, the bakufu attempted to establish a degree of control over the nation and particularly over the shugo that was comparable to that enjoyed by the Kamakura bakufu over its go-ke'nin—a policy that the shugo resisted by occasionally deserting the bakufu for the southern court and even by encouraging warfare within the Ashikaga family itself.

Of these struggles the one of special relevance to the ikki phenomenon is the effort of shugo to win control over their provinces. The shugo had legal authority, granted by the bakufu, to levy troops for national service from every proprietorship within their territories.[4] In practice, they preferred from the beginning to rely as much as possible on armies composed of their own followers, and the recruitment of men became their most important political task. Local resistance to this occurred on many levels, all gradually suppressed by the shugo. In the early years of the new bakufu many warriors sought to become its direct vassals and thus remain out of the control of the shugo. Others resisted by affiliating themselves with the anti-Ashikaga Yoshino court, either independently or as members of vassal organizations rival to those of the shugo. The former group pioneered the ikki as a nonfeudal method of local organization.

As the shugo armies became vassal armies the original battlefield ikki tended to disappear. However, the small local gentry who had been enrolled in them on a temporary basis while on campaign saw a new potential in this kind of unit and began to form local, geographical ikki on a semipermanent basis. In this way they could band together to defend their common interests without the sacrifice of independence demanded by membership in a vassal organization.[5] Instead of hierarchy, the ikki was based on pledges of mutual loyalty, often expressed in a written oath. Some of these documents have survived, and among them many have the signatures arranged circularly so as to indicate the equality of the signatories, none coming first and none last.[6]

4. Nagahara Keiji, Nihon hōkensei seiritsu katei no kenkyu (Tokyo: Iwanami Shoten, 1961), pp. 357–66. A general discussion of authority of shugo under the Ashikaga bakufu.
5. Miki, "Nambokuchō nairanki no ikki"; Satō Shin'ichi, Nambokuchō dōran, vol. 9 of Nihon no rekishi, 26 vols. (Tokyo: Chūō Kōron Sha, 1965–67), pp. 357–60.
6. Satō, Nambokuchō, p. 360, gives a photograph of such a document.

Resistance to the shugo, whether organized feudally or nonfeudally, was not very successful. Nonetheless, the development of ikki marked the first move taken by warriors away from feudal organization and was therefore of great importance. In this regard it is surely no coincidence that ikki among warriors were appearing simultaneously with matching organizations in the agricultural villages over which warrior-gentry held some power. Yet however much the two movements might have influenced each other, there was as yet no tendency toward common action. The village governments (sō-mura) were concerned with winning administrative autonomy and economic concessions from the shōen proprietors of Kyoto and Nara, and far from resisting the shugo, they welcomed them as allies against the proprietors. Warriors as well had good reason to value the assistance the shugo could give them in achieving their own economic objectives with respect to the central owners. It was the role of these shugo in the fourteenth century as champions of local economic interests that earned them the local support that permitted their domination of the political situation.

After the death of Takauji in 1358 the bakufu managed to achieve a measure of stability that lasted for about a century, but only at the cost of a considerable deviation from the form of government originally envisaged by its founder. For one thing, the pressures of the civil war had forced the shogun to restrict his sphere of active interest to about half of the country. There had been a separate headquarters at Kamakura from the beginning, but after the death of Takauji this became an independent government under his second son Motouji (1340–67) and his heirs. Kyushu was simply abandoned during the height of the civil war, and although an expedition was sent in 1370 to force it to acknowledge the suzerainty of the shogun, no attempts were made to interfere with its shugo once they met that single requirement. Within the remaining area, central and western Honshu and Shikoku, the bakufu surrendered direct administrative control except over the city of Kyoto and the home province of Yamashiro. With respect to the rest of the country it functioned primarily to regulate interactions among the shugo.

In 1367 at the death of the second shogun, Yoshiakira, his successor Yoshimitsu (1358–1408) was a minor, and the senior bakufu official, Hosokawa Yoriyuki (1329–92), became regent. Yoriyuki was the most powerful single shugo and a forceful individual, and his enemies accused him of attempting to repeat the achievement of the Hōjō family in the previous bakufu by establishing a Hosokawa dictatorship. Once the shogun became old enough to grow restive under Yoriyuki's tutelage, however, it proved quite easy to organize the other shugo to throw the regent out (1379). This pattern was followed again in later years: should the shugo

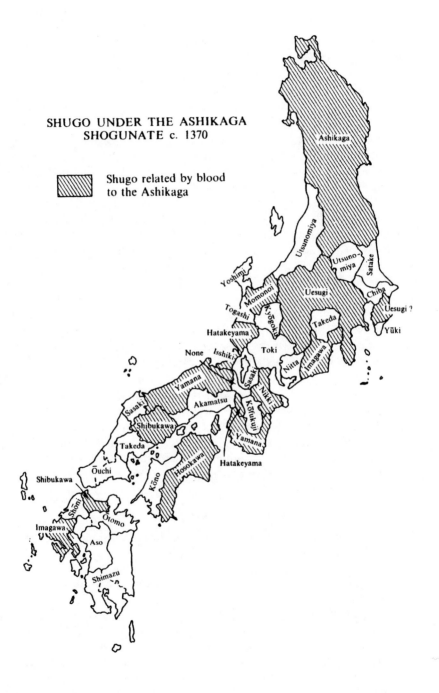

SHUGO UNDER THE ASHIKAGA
SHOGUNATE c. 1370

Shugo related by blood
to the Ashikaga

Ashikaga

Utsunomiya

Yoshimi

Utsuno-
miya

Satake

Momonoi

Uesugi

Chiba

Uesugi ?

Togashi

Kyōgoku

Takeda

Yūki

Hatakeyama

Toki

None   Isshiki

Nitta

Imagawa

Yamana

Sasaki

Akamatsu

Nikki

Sasaki

Kōfukuji

Shibukawa

Takeda

Yamana

Kōno

Hosokawa

Hatakeyama

Ōuchi

Shibukawa

Shōni

Otomo

Imagawa

Aso

Shimazu

at any time collectively become convinced that one among them was threatening to become too powerful, they could rally around the Ashikaga house to defeat him.

The nature of the shugo domain was such that it was next to invincible on its own ground but very difficult to expand successfully. The strength of the shugo depended on the strength and loyalty of his vassal organization, but such an organization took a long time to construct. Each shugo had one or more "home" provinces in which he normally had continuous tenure, these being the provinces where such powerful vassal organizations existed, and it was almost impossible for outsiders to dislodge a shugo from such a province. When Hosokawa Yoriyuki was expelled from the government, he fled to his home provinces on Shikoku, and although the bakufu ordered them invaded, there were no shugo willing to obey the command. Confronted with this reality, Yoshimitsu soon moved to pardon Yoriyuki. On the other hand, it was very difficult for a shugo to establish his authority in a newly acquired province. When Ōuchi Yoshihiro (1356–99) rebelled against the shogun in 1399, he was shugo of six provinces, but only the vassals from his "home" areas of Suō and Nagato gave him loyal support. In particular, the unreliability of his troops from Iwami, where he had been shugo for fourteen years, and Izumi, from which the campaign was launched, made the revolt a fiasco. The same problem hamstrung the Yamana in 1390 and the Akamatsu in 1441.

These factors are the key to both the stable balance of power that emerged in the 1360s and lasted for a century and the success of Yoshimitsu in manipulating the situation so as to establish his own family's primacy within the revived bakufu. The system ultimately failed, but only after the internal disintegration of several important shugo domains had first upset the balance of power and then rendered it meaningless. Among the symptoms of this disintegration were the tsuchi-ikki.

Tsuchi-ikki

At about the time that the first ikki organizations were being developed by minor bushi, the peasants of central Japan were creating similar political organizations for the purpose of waging their own struggle against shōen proprietors. This struggle was carried on in two ways. First, the new peasant political associations, forerunners of the characteristic village governments of the Edo period, aimed to assume all essential governmental functions relating to the daily life of the peasantry. These involved such matters as the management of projects requiring communal labor, but most important, the transfer of adjudication of peasant disputes over land ownership and other vital matters from a shōen's headquarters in Kyoto to the village itself. This led to an enhancement of the average peasant's security of tenure.[7] Second, the village government provided the unity and discipline necessary for direct confrontations with the shōen administration and its local agents. So long as the shōen proprietor was the principal opponent, such confrontations were normally limited to a single shōen, and wider peasant organizations or uprisings were quite rare during the fourteenth and early fifteenth centuries.

In 1428, however, a massive uprising swept Kyoto and the surrounding countryside, and as if this constituted a signal, more than a hundred similar rebellions followed before the end of the century. Nearly all these were larger than any of the ten or so recorded regional uprisings of the previous century.[8]

The year 1428 was a very difficult one for the peasants, a year of both famine and epidemic. In the eighth month, petitions for a debt cancellation edict were sent to the bakufu from various quarters. On 9/18, the commoners of Daigo, an agricultural suburb of Kyoto, rioted and burned debt records, and the bakufu had to send several hundred troops to the area to restore order.[9] At the end of the month there were demonstrations in the city itself. Again in the eleventh month there were about three weeks of rioting, during which many pawnbroker's and moneylender's premises were broken into.[10] The bakufu found it necessary to issue a proclamation forbidding "the vassals of various [daimyo] houses to cooperate with the tsuchi-ikki" and requiring the taking of oaths by those accused of such behavior. Disturbances were recorded in such provinces and cities as Uda, Yoshino, Kii, Izumi, Kawachi, and Sakai, that is to say, throughout the Kinai region.[11] This rather confused and apparently spontaneous run of disturbances was the beginning of a sequence of about thirty such incidents in the next century that involved organized peasant invasions of Kyoto. A considerable number of others occurred in the nearby countryside.

The third of these invasions of Kyoto (in 1441) was the greatest and most successful of all. In strong contrast to the 1428 disturbances, this later incident showed signs of careful planning over a period of weeks and months. The shogun Yoshinari was murdered by Akamatsu Mitsu-

7. Ibid., pp. 381–95.

8. Nakamura Kichiji, *Tokusei to tsuchi-ikki*, Nihon rekishi shinsho, supp. ser., no. 58 (Tokyo: Shibundo, 1966), pp. 225–36. A convenient chronological list of ikki of all types.

9. *Manzai jugō nikki*, Zoku gunsho ruijū, 2 vols., supp. no. 1 (Tokyo: Zoku gunsho ruijū kanseikai, 1928), 1:525, 530, 532.

10. Nakamura Kichiji, "Shoki no tsuchi-ikki," *Shakai keizai shigaku* 2, pt. 3 (December 1933): 21–22, quoting the diary of Nakayama Sadachika; p. 22, quoting bakufu edict.

11. Nagahara Keiji, *Gekokujō no jidai*, vol. 10 of Nihon no rekishi, p. 70, quoting Sadachika's diary; Nakamura, "Shoki no tsuchi-ikki," p. 26, quoting *Shatō no shonikki*.

suke in the sixth month of that year, and because his heir was a sickly child, the bakufu was thrown into great confusion. The next year was marked by a power struggle between Hatakeyama Mochikuni and Hosokawa Mochiyuki, and it was at the height of this contest (a time when most bakufu troops were in Harima on a punitive expedition against the Akamatsu) that the ikki struck, early in the ninth month. There were several days of excitement while the ikki forces gathered around Kyoto. On 8/28 there was a clash at Kiyomizu between ikki columns and troops belonging to the Kyōgoku family, with fifty-three casualties on the Kyōgoku side and ten or so on the other.[12] On 9/3 there was rioting and arson in scattered areas on the outskirts of the city.[13] The full weight of the ikki was felt only on 9/5 when armies of thousands of ikki members marched on Kyoto from all sides, seizing strategically located buildings and blocking all access to and from the city. Tōji, on the southwest corner of the city, was one of the places occupied, and its chronicle reports:

> The ikki from east of the road that descends from Toba and Kisshōin occupied Tōji. There were about two or three thousand of them. On the same day the Tamba-guchi ikki seized Imanishinomiya with about one thousand men. Nishihachijōji was seized by the "five shō" force with about one thousand men. Two or three thousand men of the Nishioka force seized the Kanchō, the Jingikan, Kitano, and Utsumasa. They have ringed the city with camps at Izumo-guchi, Kawasaki, Shogunzuka, Kiyomizu, Fukuhara, Amidamine, Tōfukuji, Imaotagi, and Mokōji. Every day they raid into the center of the city.

Another source reports for 9/7 that the ikki was "blocking the seven exits, and consequently there is no traffic and nothing in the markets."[14]

The diary *Kennaiki* records on 9/12 that earlier the bakufu had offered a debt cancellation edict that would apply to commoners only but that the ikki had refused this. Now on the twelfth an edict was issued that specifically included *kuge* and *buke*.[15] With that, the main uprising ended, the ikki having forced the bakufu to surrender to their demands exactly one week after the beginning of the blockade. Though there is no direct report of bushi participation, the insistence of the ikki that buke be included in the debt cancellation and reports of the use of bows in the pitched battle with Kyōgoku troops suggest their presence.

None of the later invasions of Kyoto quite matched the scale of the ikki

12. Narushima Ryōjō, ed., *Nochi kagami*, Shintei zōho kokushi taikei, 60 vols. (Tokyo: Yoshikawa Kōbunkan, 1964–66), 3:16, quoting *Tōji shugyō nikki*.

13. Narushima, *Nochi kagami*, 3:17, quoting *Tōji shugyō nikki*. Manrikoji Tokifusa, *Kennaiki*, Dai Nihon kokiroku, 9 vols. (Tokyo: Iwanami Shoten, 1963–), 4:67.

14. Narushima, *Nochi kagami*, 3:18, quoting *Tōji shugyō nikki* and *Kōmei kōki*.

15. Manrikoji, *Kennaiki*, 4:73.

action of 1441 but several were nevertheless quite impressive. In 1457, for example, battles took place between ikki members and mercenaries hired by moneylenders. The ikki afterward fought and routed a bakufu army of eight hundred men.[16] An incursion of 1480 was also very serious, involving the defeat of another bakufu army.[17]

One of the most striking facts about this long series of Kyoto-centered risings by tsuchi-ikki, the last of which was in 1549, is that once the basic pattern was established it did not change. The first, last, and nearly all those in between were concerned primarily with the matter of debt cancellation. The 1480 incursion was directed toward the abolition of toll barriers, where duties were levied on goods moving into the city.[18] Another in 1499, a famine year, demanded a moratorium on land rents.[19] Thus all were directed toward alleviating the immediate economic problems of the farmers of the surrounding countryside. In this they followed closely the pattern of the small rural uprisings characteristic of the fourteenth century, differing principally on the point that satisfaction was now sought from the bakufu as city government in Kyoto, rather than from individual shōen proprietors. Conversely, in this situation the simple village government no longer sufficed as the basis for action, and regional ikki came to be formed. Whereas the village government had political action as only one of its many activities, the ikki had no other purpose and did not become the basis for a regional administration.

There is much controversy concerning these tsuchi-ikki, particularly on their social composition, leadership, and main beneficiaries. The term *tsuchi-ikki* is derived from contemporary sources, but the modern tendency would be to read it as *do-ikki* and to consider the term a contraction of *domin-ikki*.[20] Contemporary records make it plain that the members of such ikki were of the social class called *domin*, "people of the soil," but we get no sense from these of the social boundaries of this designation. The line of least resistance in respect to fifteenth-century documents is to consider the term as including all persons residing in agricultural villages. This would mean the bottom stratum of the gentry class in addition to simple farmers and their dependents. Until this time, no sharp distinction had been maintained between farmer and warrior, but this began to change

16. Tsuji Zennosuke, ed., *Daijōin jisha zōjiki*, 12 vols. (Tokyo: Kadogawa Shoten, 1964), 1:261.
17. Nakamura Kichiji, "Ōnin-Bummei nenkan no tsuchi-ikki to tokusei," pt. 2, *Shigaku zasshi* 45 (July 1934): 34–59.
18. Ibid.
19. Nakamura Kichiji, "Sengoku jidai zenki no tsuchi-ikki to tokusei," pt. 2, *Shakai keizai shigaku* 4 (February 1935): 54–62.
20. Nakamura, *Tokusei to tsuchi-ikki*, pp. 39–41. Discussion of "*do-ikki* or *tsuchi-ikki*" question.

with the increasing complexity of economic life and the appearance of a discrete agricultural interest group. This latter group showed hostility not only to the merchants and moneylenders but increasingly to the shugo as well. With the development of this phenomenon, the local gentry were eventually forced to choose between life as a full-time farmer, or life as a full-time warrior–vassal, or samurai.

And thus came a spectacle difficult for the bakufu to comprehend— lower-level erstwhile vassals participating in ikki uprisings. A prime example is seen in the region of Nishioka just southwest of Kyoto, which was a particular focus of ikki activity during the 1450s and 1460s. Certain disturbances raised by the Nishioka ikki in late 1465 caused the bakufu to issue the following orders, the first dated 1465/11/1:

> Tsuchi-ikki and others have been causing riots in nearby areas for the purpose of agitating for debt cancellations. This is intolerable. Let it be known that it is our intention to immediately confiscate the property of any of our own vassals who join with them. Therefore, if any of our vassals should by chance discover those among them who have made such a decision, let him report their names. . . .

Another followed on the twelfth:

> Although firm orders were just issued against tsuchi-ikki uprisings, it is reported that once again the men of the Nishioka region are so doing. Our intention has been announced to exercise the strictest control over any who might seem to be obstinately sympathizing with them, and so it is ordered that all vassals [of Nishioka] remove to the city and remain there until the above-mentioned disturbances have been pacified.[21]

In the Kinai region there were no strong shugo organizations, and the ikki (as mentioned above) directed their complaints and demonstrations against the bakufu. In the provinces the main enemy became the shugo, who had largely succeeded by the end of the first quarter of the fifteenth century in displacing the shōen proprietors as the primary beneficiaries of the shōen system.[22] As the shugo did so, they ruptured the bond of common economic interest that had helped forge the ties of loyalty between themselves and their vassals. For from this point on, the shugo became committed to the defense of what remained of the shōen system while their vassals, as before, hoped for its destruction. For a long time the only overt resistance to the shugo was in the form of tsuchi-ikki.

Just a few months after the first great tsuchi-ikki uprising in Kyoto, and

---

21. Narushima, *Nochi kagami*, 3:407–08, Ninagawa Chikamoto's diary, citing bakufu document dated Kanshō 6/11/1; Nagahara, *Gekokujō*, pp. 97–98, quoting Chikamoto's diary.

22. Nagahara, *Hōkensei*, pp. 357–66.

possibly inspired by it, there was a similar explosion in Harima Province, the "home" province of the very powerful Akamatsu Mitsusuke (1373–1441). For some months various local ikki had been agitating for debt cancellations; then in the first month of 1429 there was a massive province-wide rebellion whose slogan was reported to be "There shall be no samurai in the province," meaning no Akamatsu vassals. In order to turn the tide against these rebels, Mitsusuke was forced to lead his household troops from Kyoto back to Harima.[23] Perhaps because of the decisive defeat of the rebellion on this occasion, there was no repetition, but there were innumerable local ikki that resisted the authority of the shugo in many ways, principally by refusing to pay dues and by expelling unpopular agents.

The basic political tool of the ikki was the *yoriai*, a mass meeting of the members, a direct derivation from the village government. The following document, though rather late in the history of tsuchi-ikki, is illustrative of the nature of such movements. It is dated 1468 and pertains to Niimi-no-shō, a shōen in Bitchū Province, still generally under the control of Tōji:

> You asked why the shōen officials have not collected the rents. The situation is that they are not [being collected] anywhere. As a part of Lord Hosokawa's domain there are ten gō. [There] the commoners have been conducting large yoriai since the seventh month of last year. Ōbayashi [Hosokawa's agent] tried numerous tactics but was unable to cope, and on the first day of the tenth month he crossed the sea and fled to Sanuki. . . .[24]

Although Niimi-no-shō was under the control of Tōji rather than a shugo, events there are especially useful for demonstrating the attitude of the bulk of local officials at this time. The author of the above letter was Kaneko Hirauji, actual ruler of the estate for many years. A Tōji document of 1461 noted that of 3,000 *kamme* (strings of cash) owed over the last twenty years (150 per year) only 799 had been paid. Tōji's correspondence with Kaneko and other "officials" in the shōen makes it clear that the latter were cooperating with the villages and granting them remission of dues on their own authority, and that as a consequence Tōji determined to send an agent directly from the temple. The inhabitants of the shōen then dispatched a statement to the effect that they would welcome the agent but would tolerate no change in the status quo.[25]

While the tsuchi-ikki movements directly involved only the lower levels

<hr/>

23. Kishida Haruyuki, "Shugo Akamatsu-shi no Harimakuni shihai no hatten to kokuga," pt. 1, *Shigakukenkyū* 105(October 1968): 62, n.22, quoting relevant documents.

24. Fujii Shun, ed., *Bitchū-no-kuni Niimi-no-shō shiryō* (Okayama: Setonaikai Sōgō Kenkyūkai, 1952), doc. 325, pp. 291–92.

25. Ibid., doc. 178, p. 186; docs. 164–66, 177, pp. 180–86; doc. 170, p. 183.

of vassal organization, their existence also placed great pressure on the higher levels. The growing opposition to the economic demands of the shugo naturally affected those vassals charged with enforcing these levies, such as the unfortunate Ōbayashi mentioned earlier. The locally resident vassals, chief of whom generally served as *shugodai* (deputy shugo), found their interests at odds with those of their shugo lords who remained in the capital. Their own incomes were dependent on the maintenance of good relations with the agricultural villages under their jurisdiction, and to the extent that shugo demands endangered this, the tendency was not to obey the shugo. Also, the displacement of all but the most powerful provincial familes by the shugo greatly limited the opportunities of the former to expand their holdings. As a result, their loyalty to the shugo, which was the basic cement of the vassal system, began to lessen and they searched for political alternatives.

The highest ranking vassals, whose power and influence were by that time heavily dependent on their positions within the vassal system, began to convert into personal followings those parts of the network that they commanded on behalf of the shugo and to struggle with other vassals similarly placed. This threat had existed from the very beginning of the shugo organizations, as most of the shugo realized, but previously the ambitions of shugodai and other chief vassals had been checked by the commitment of the vassals at large to the shugo system. By the middle of the fifteenth century, the superior ability of the shugodai, on the scene and aware of changing local conditions, to protect the interests of his followers, led many vassals to transfer their support from shugo to shugodai. Local warfare increased as these burgeoning local magnates began to struggle among themselves, often under the cover of a "succession dispute" within the shugo family. The basic issue, however, went beyond the matter of succession. What was at stake was the viability of the shugo system itself.

The first open civil war within a shugo domain occurred between 1445 and 1447 in the Togashi domain of Kaga. It was fought by rival candidates for the position of shugodai and made possible by a severe internal bakufu struggle between the Hosokawa and Hatakeyama families.[26] When the latter dispute was resolved, the Kaga civil war ended in compromise, with the province being split between the two claimants. It was an ominous precedent for the integrity of shugo regimes. Another even more significant example was the virtual collapse of the Shiba family domain in Echizen Province a few years later. The shugodai of Echizen Province, Kai Tsuneharu (d. 1459), created a personal following so forbidding that

---

26. Nagahara, *Gekokujō*, pp. 252–53. A brief summary of this episode.

in 1452 he was able to refuse with impunity to recognize the position of the shugo, Shiba Yoshitoshi. Also, in 1455 rival bands of vassals began an interminable war over the succession of the Hatakeyama family.[27]

The dismemberment of the Shiba and Hatakeyama domains destroyed the political system created by Ashikaga Yoshimitsu, one which relied on the maintenance of a balance of power among the shugo through a carefully established three-way rivalry among the Shiba, Hatakeyama, and Hosokawa families for the highest bakufu office.[28] Now, in order to balance Hosokawa Katsumoto (1430–73), the shogun Yoshimasa (1436–90) had to rely increasingly on Yamana Mochitoyo (1404–73), a man barred by law and custom from the highest office and thus willing to try to eliminate Katsumoto through warfare. The Ōnin War of 1467–77, which concentrated in Kyoto the energies of most shugo, allowed local claimants for power to come out into the open. The war ended not in victory for one side or the other, but in the withdrawal of the various participants to their provinces in order to save what they could of their home territories. The Hosokawa, whose domain held up for another generation, were left in undisputed control of the capital city and its environs.

With the collapse of the shugo system and of shugo attempts to dominate the economies of whole provinces, large-scale provincial (as opposed to Kyoto-centered) tsuchi-ikki died out. There were very few after the Ōnin War, and none after the first decade of the sixteenth century. The tsuchi-ikki had never been directed against the local gentry, but against higher authority, and with the fragmentation of such authority the need for large-scale rural agitation ended. The new rulers of the countryside, the incipient daimyo who took over the pieces of the shugo territories, were fully accustomed to working through the village organization and not against it. The shōen system, under which each farmer theoretically had his own distinct legal relationship with the holders of higher tenures, was forgotten and replaced by the village system in which the village and not the individual became the fundamental agricultural unit in dealings with the upper classes.

Kuni-ikki

The new feudal regimes that began to appear in the provinces as the shugo organizations collapsed one by one were themselves highly unstable and usually short-lived. Without the stabilizing factor of membership in a larger political framework, each stood or fell on its own merits. The

27. Ibid., pp. 253–54, 257–58.

28. Tokyo daigaku shiryō hensanjo, *Dai Nihon shiryō*, ser. 7, vol. 3 (Tokyo: Tokyo daigaku shiryō hensanjo, 1912–), p. 276. Bakufu edict of 1397 given in citation from *Nampō kiden*.

personal ability of a leader to dominate his vassals and maintain their loyalty was the key to success and was seldom transferable. The first such post-shugo feudal regime to emerge, that of Kai Tsuneharu in Echizen, began to fall apart immediately upon his death. During the sixteenth century, nearly all families that had been prominent during the previous hundred years either disappeared or changed beyond recognition. It was under these conditions that the true daimyo, the local feudal ruler, came into being.

The main problem faced by a would-be daimyo was that of securing the loyalty of the upper-grade local gentry (often called *kokujin*, or "provincials"), who made up the bulk of the military aristocracy of the territory to which he aspired. The weakness of the early daimyo was in large part a product of the independence of these kokujin families whom the daimyo were required to recruit as vassals. Each was ensconced in his own hilltop wooden castle, filled with ambition to become a daimyo himself, with innumerable temptations to better himself by playing feudal politics. The average post-shugo daimyo (usually referred to as "Sengoku daimyo," after the traditional name for this period) aimed for nothing more than the military domination of as large an area as possible. Any capable man with the ability to recruit an army of his own might in turn hope to displace him.

If the daimyo had trouble securing the submission of the military competitors in their areas, the kokujin were themselves insecure at their level. Even as the Ōnin War still raged, a few men of shrewd political insight, among both the new and old daimyo, perceived the nature of this insecurity and moved to exploit it. They sought to bind the kokujin to their service in a way that had never been achieved before, but that subsequently became the basis of "early modern" society, namely, a new kind of vassalage system. What they did was to take advantage of the changes in rural society that were giving rise to the autonomous village and the tsuchi-ikki. With the growth of peasant autonomy, the kokujin and their immediate retainers no longer had the strength to dominate villages on their own. The reasons for this were two. First, considerable numbers of their former followers, who could be classified as *jizamurai* ("village samurai") began to identify with their own private landed interests and with the newly independent village society, becoming village leaders rather than bottom members of the vassalage system. Second, as a result of the weakening of the kokujin's local power, the daimyo found it possible to bypass them and deal directly with the villages, cutting off the kokujin from the men who grew the food they ate and threatening their status as rural gentry. The kokujin, under such circumstances, were under great pressure to join the daimyo's vassal band to become full-time professional soldiers or officials in the service of the daimyo.[29] Many, in fact, gave up local residence for assigned quarters in the daimyo's castle.

The ultimate perfection of the new set of institutions that took advantage of this situation would require another two centuries, but even in their early imperfect form they proved of great advantage to those daimyo who began to apply them. The first Sengoku daimyo to develop the institutions of direct village control was Asakura Toshikage (1428–81), who put together an organization that won Echizen from the Kai family after the death of Tsuneharu and that survived for a full century. His testament to his descendants emphasized the principles that vassals should never be allowed their own castles but should live in unfortified houses surrounding the daimyo's castle, that the daimyo should be concerned for the economic health of the domain as a whole, not simply that of his own treasury, and that he should exert himself to see that there was equitable government throughout.[30] Toshikage took for granted that it was possible to deprive vassals of their military autonomy. He succeeded, and his descendants developed and expanded the system with equal success. The spread of similar systems throughout the country was slow and met with much resistance, but it was sure, for in addition to greatly enhancing a daimyo's security, it had the advantage of increasing the military power of his domain, enabling him to control and use a much greater percentage than ever before of the potential economic and human resources of his area. In earlier times the wars were fought by a mounted elite of vassals; in the sixteenth century they came to be fought by village levies of infantry, with vassals serving as officers. This development was possible in large part because the direct taxation of villages gave the daimyo, for the first time, the wealth to feed and equip such armies, and the administrative apparatus to organize them.

While many kokujin welcomed or did not resist such developments and prospered by serving the local daimyo, others valued their independence too highly to give in without a struggle. Those in hilly regions, away from the agricultural plains where the new system worked best, were able to resist daimyo power for generations without much difficulty. Throughout the country men continued to join forces and form old-style feudal bands, but others devised a new form of resistance, the warrior ikki, based upon the political institutions developed by their social inferiors.

The Yamashiro kuni-ikki, while not the first warrior ikki of which we have record, was the first to achieve a measure of success in forming a

29. Hall, "Foundations," pp. 71–77.

30. Asakura Toshikage, Asakura Toshikage jushichikajō, Shinkō gunsho ruijū (Tokyo: Naigai Shoseki, 1930), 17:452–53.

government that resisted the imposition of daimyo authority. Established in the twelfth month of 1485,[31] it emerged from the chaos created first by the Hatakeyama family civil war that had begun in 1455, then by the Ōnin War (1467–77) and the continued fighting that went on in the capital area into the next century. The two protagonists in this continued warfare were Hatakeyama Masanaga (1447–93) and Hatakeyama Yoshinari (1455–94). The fighting came to center on Yamashiro after Masanaga was appointed shugo of that province in 1482. Yoshinari invaded it in 1484, having defeated Masanaga's troops in neighboring Kawachi. Yoshinari was doing well in Yamashiro until a crucial vassal changed sides in the eighth month of 1485, producing a stalemate. The armies sat facing each other for over three months, preventing agricultural activity and consuming great quantities of food extracted from the local population. The kokujin of the region withdrew from the two armies, forming a fortified camp of their own, from which they issued an ultimatum on 12/10 embodying three demands: both armies were to withdraw from the area immediately, shōen were to be restored to their proprietors, and toll barriers were to be prohibited. Within two weeks Masanaga and Yoshinari had both withdrawn.

Early the next year the ikki held a mass meeting at which its policies were further elaborated. Descriptions of this meeting make it clear that what was meant by "restoration of shōen" was that the outsiders imported by central owners to manage them were to be removed and replaced by ikki members, with all payments to proprietors to be determined by the inhabitants of the shōen.[32] As for the shugo, they decided they could get along without one, and they created an office called the sōkoku (province general), headed by an ikki member (who would appear to have been rotated monthly) to take care of such essential government business as the punishment of criminals.[33] The ikki did not control the entire province but only a section in the south along the Uji River and the border with Yamato. Later the inhabitants of another district to the northwest invited it to expand, but this still made for a rather limited area.

The provision in the ikki "constitution" demanding that no toll barriers be erected was of course a direct appeal to the interests of the peasants, who presumably supported or assisted the ikki at first, though there is no direct evidence of this. On the other hand there occurred at least one local peasant uprising shortly after the establishment of the

31. Yanagi Mototsuru, "Muromachi bakufu hokai katei ni okeru Yamashiro kuni-ikki," Chūsei no kenryoku to minshū (Osaka: Nihonshi Kenkyūkai Shiryō Kenkyūbukai, 1970), pp. 259–85.

32. Tsuji, Daijōin jisha zōjiki, 8:418.

33. Yanagi, "Yamashiro kuni-ikki," pp. 280–85.

sōkoku, and it would seem that the ultimate dissolution of the ikki after only seven years was due in part to peasant opposition. In 1492 the sōkoku felt it necessary to raise revenue by establishing toll barriers of its own, and this decision prompted an immediate and massive peasant uprising.[34] A substantial segment of the ikki membership decided then to accept the legal shugo of the time, Ise Sadataka, and with their support he defeated the remaining diehards early in 1493.[35]

The success of the Yamashiro ikki was due to a number of advantages its leaders were able to exploit. It need hardly be said that the bushi of the area must have had considerable familiarity with the ikki principle of organization, living as they did in a region that had been a hotbed of peasant ikki for over fifty years, so that internal organization was not a problem. In the city of Kyoto itself, aristocratic shōen proprietors were so delighted at the prospect of a resumption of income, however slight, from estates they had lost control of years before, that they put their remaining political influence squarely behind the ikki. Moreover, the leading figure in the bakufu, Hosokawa Masamoto, was not indisposed to seeing Hatakeyama Yoshinari prevented from controlling the Yamashiro area. Finally, it seems likely that Yoshinari was considered a highly undesirable ruler by court aristocracy and rural gentry alike, for he was known for the particularly ruthless policy he applied to territories he had conquered. In order to suppress the independence of vassals and firmly establish his own control, he freely abolished shōen and apparently confiscated the lands of gentry as well.[36] In other words, while there is insufficient information about him to say so with assurance, it is quite likely that Yoshinari had aspirations toward the creation of a "modern" centralized regime in his domains. On the other hand, Ise Sadataka, who ultimately became shugo, lacked the kind of personal military power necessary to threaten the autonomy of the kokujin. Yoshinari was the last daimyo to attempt to build a powerful domain within the Kinai. Later daimyo who dominated the region did so from bases elsewhere, and kokujin-ikki of various kinds continued to play a major part in the affairs of the Kinai until its final conquest by Oda Nobunaga, without aspiring to de jure rule through a sōkoku organ, but acknowledging weak figureheads.

The Kaga Ikki

Unquestionably the most important kuni-ikki, or warrior ikki, was the one formed in Kaga Province about 1474. It was widely imitated in other

34. Ibid., p. 290.
35. Tsuji, *Daijōin jisha zōjiki*, 10:312.
36. Yanagi, "Yamashiro kuni-ikki," pp. 263–66.

provinces of the central region of Japan and played a major role in the wars of unification of the last part of the sixteenth century. It has attracted more attention from modern historians than all other ikki combined. In many ways its origins were similar to those of the Yamashiro ikki, that is, it was first organized during the turmoil produced by a civil war among branches of a shugo family, the Togashi. It differed from the Yamashiro case, however, in that the Togashi house was itself of Kaga origin, and the ikki emerged from the ruins of what had once been a very strong vassal organization, rather than in reaction to outsiders.

The Togashi can be traced back to at least the twelfth century but became prominent only when Togashi Takaie became one of the earliest supporters of Ashikaga Takauji and was made shugo of Kaga in 1336.[37] The family never achieved much political power within the bakufu, but it did succeed in creating a strong vassal organization.[38] In the 1440s, however, this vassal organization began to break up, leading to civil war between vassal factions during 1445-47. This disturbance resulted in the division of the province in 1447, with the northern part controlled by a vassal family named Motoori, the southern part by the Yamagawa family. The Togashi, still nominal shugo, remained in Kyoto, powerless to affect affairs in Kaga.[39] In 1458 the Motoori organization of northern Kaga itself broke up. No concrete information exists concerning the political development of that region for many years, but it is certain that no one family emerged to take charge.

The year 1467 marked the beginning of the Ōnin War, and Kaga Province inevitably became involved. Togashi Masachika (d. 1488), whom the Yamagawa organization ackowledged as shugo, allied himself to the Eastern Army of Hosokawa Katsumoto. The warriors of northern Kaga, who recognized at that time a younger brother of Masachika as shugo, naturally supported the Western Army of Yamana Mochitoyo, and promptly invaded and conquered the south. Masachika was now cut off completely from Kaga. But Asakura Toshikage, the ruler of neighboring Echizen, switched from the Yamana to the Hosokawa side in 1471, thereby offering the prospect of military support. Masachika consequently left Kyoto for Echizen to plan the reconquest of "his own" province.

37. Hioki Ken, ed., *Ka-Nō komonjo* (Kanazawa: Kanazawa Bunka Kyōkai, 1944), doc. 264, pp. 144-45.
38. *Meitokuki*, Shinkō gunsho ruijū, 26 vols. (Tokyo, 1928-38), 16:161-214,. References to the Togashi family (pp. 164, 197) indicate position at the time of the Yamana rebellion.
39. Existing accounts of this and related events in the history of the Togashi family are unsatisfactory. For further details see David L. Davis, "The Kaga Ikkō-ikki" (Ph.D. diss. in progress, University of Chicago), chap. 4.

Masachika's first problem was to find allies in Kaga. One clear opportunity was to look for them among those members of the local warrior class who had joined the so-called Ikkō sect, more properly, the Honganji sect of Jōdo Shinshū. The head of the sect, Rennyo (1415–99), was then in residence in Echizen, and a continuous stream of believers came to visit him from the surrounding region, including Kaga. As a Honganji source describes the situation in 1473:

> In that period Togashi Jiro Masachika was at war with his younger brother Kochiyo, and since Rennyo was then in residence at Yoshizaki, while Jiro was waiting in exile in Echizen he [Jiro] came and granted various fiefs and promised that if he returned to his province those of the believers who were loyal to him would not remain in their present poverty. Jiro was then invited to come from Echizen by the believers and went to Yamada in Kaga, and they were victorious in battle. Kochiyo was expelled and Jiro took control of the province.[40]

Thus the Kaga *Ikkō-ikki* came into being to assist Masachika's conquest of Kaga. Its members had formed it in the expectation of economic reward, presumably from the property of the defeated. Early the next year, however, there was a falling out between Masachika and the Ikkō-ikki because, according to the same source, Masachika had not adequately fulfilled these expectations. In the third month of 1474 the ikki membership rebelled and was quickly defeated, demonstrating that it was only one part of the coalition that had brought Masachika back to power.[41] The significance of this requires elaboration.

It has already been seen that the peasants of central Japan were prone to taking very direct measures to advance their economic interests; the peasants who joined the Ikkō sect were no exception. This sect had been the first of the Buddhist groups to reach the ordinary peasant in any significant way.[42] Other sects were concerned primarily with aristocratic or gentry patronage and demanded from their followers practices that were impossible for people without wealth or leisure. The Honganji taught salvation by simple faith and made its prime appeal to commoners, especially the peasantry. Its local priests were drawn from the village upper class, and in regions where its emissaries were particularly successful, it became inextricably intertwined with the secular village organization. As a consequence there was a tendency for its religious enemies, as

---

40. Inoue Toshio, *Ikkō-ikki no kenkyū* (Tokyo: Yoshikawa Kōbunkan, 1968), p. 336, quoting *Jitsugoki shūi*.
41. Ibid.
42. Akamatsu Toshihide and Kasahara Kazuo, eds., *Shinshūshi gaisetsu* (Kyoto: Heirakuji Shoten, 1963).

well as shōen proprietors, to blame it for the unruliness of the peasantry and to demand its suppression. Rennyo was very much afraid of a bakufu edict banning the sect and devoted much energy to urging his followers to be law-abiding, but to no avail. As he pointed out in one pastoral letter:

> Our sect has from ancient times been widely considered "strange and perverse." . . . It is forbidden to forget this even momentarily in dealings between our sect and others. They say that because our sect does not practice abstinence according to the Buddhist law, shall we not similarly be disrespectful to other sects and the civil authorities? We must be especially respectful. . . .[43]

Rennyo was nowhere more successful in converting the peasantry than in Echizen and Kaga. Moreover, given the strength of the peasant political institutions and the necessity for kokujin to accommodate themselves to these, considerable kokujin conversion also took place. Rennyo welcomed this at first but was soon dismayed at the political consequences. In later years the Honganji required central clearance of all warrior converts, in an attempt to weed out those whose motives were not religious. The spread of Ikkō-ikki, however, continued unabated.[44]

After their defeat in the third month of 1474, the Ikkō-ikki members were forced to flee to Etchū Province to the north. In order that they might return home, messengers were sent to Yoshizaki asking Rennyo to intercede on their behalf with Masachika. A certain Shimotsuma Rensu, a kokujin from Echizen and leading adviser to Rennyo, took it upon himself to order them to carry on the war and issued in Rennyo's name an order to the peasant believers of Kaga to rise in support of the ikki. This occurred in the sixth month of 1474 and was a complete failure.[45] It was the only occasion when the Honganji attempted to order its peasant followers to rebel, and the only time peasants played a significant, if passive, part in the affairs of the Kaga Ikkō-ikki. Masachika apparently did not take all of this too seriously; the sect was not banned, and the ikki members were allowed to return home.

Between 1445 and 1473 Masachika was faced with the necessity of trying to create a new political and economic organization for Kaga. His methods are not known, but it can be seen that he ran into serious resistance among warriors of that province. Judging from surviving shōen records, the level of small-scale rural violence in Kaga was very high during this period, and Masachika was completely unable to control it.

    43. Inoue, *Ikkō-ikki no kenkyū*, p. 339.
    44. Kasahara Kazuo, *Ikkō-ikki no kenkyū* (Tokyo: Yamagawa Shuppansha, 1962), pp. 130–41.
    45. Inoue, *Ikkō-ikki no kenkyū*, pp. 347–57. Honganji shiryō kenkyūsho, *Honganji shi*, 4 vols. (Kyoto: Jōdo Shinshū Honganji-ha shumusho, 1961—), 1:330–38.

In 1487 Masachika did a very curious thing. He left Kaga with a large army and proceeded to Ōmi Province in response to an order from the shogun Yoshihisa, who wished to restore the prestige of the bakufu by suppressing the robber baron Rokkaku Takayori. What made Masachika's action so unusual is that he was the only distant shugo to comply with this order.[46] In light of what followed it would seem that Masachika knew he was in serious trouble in Kaga and hoped that his aid to the shogun would be rewarded with military assistance against the unruly inhabitants of his domain. At any rate, the Ikkō-ikki, taking advantage of his absence, rebelled in the twelfth month of 1487. Masachika immediately returned and apparently won some successes against the ikki forces. But he displayed a premature determination to try for the complete subjugation of the province. A number of Togashi vassals now joined the rebellion, putting up Masachika's uncle, the ex-shugo Yasutaka then in Kyoto, as an alternative shugo to justify their defection. Faced with certain defeat in 1488, Masachika committed suicide in the flames of his burning castle.[47]

Though it is conventional to date ikki rule of Kaga from this time, Masachika's death did not bring an end to shugo rule in Kaga. Yasutaka, the choice of the rebels, actually became shugo and even went to live in the province in 1493. He died about 1504 and was followed by a son, Taneyasu, who continued as shugo until 1531, when he was expelled by the ikki after another civil war.[48] The dating of ikki rule from 1488 is based on remarks made in Kyoto courtier diaries, and the assumption that the rebels were peasants and religious fanatics who exterminated or drove away the gentry. In fact the political life of the province became very complicated. The rebels against Masachika included a number of important vassal families with important feudal followings of their own, specifically including both Motoori and Yamagawa, who were as upset at his ambitions as were the ikki members.[49] The ikki bloc was led by the leaders of the Honganji organization in Kaga, three sons of Rennyo, (Rengo, Renkō, and Rensei) who were included in the new "establishment" under Togashi Yasutaka.[50]

In the early years of this complex balance of power the ikki component was comparatively weak; it was only after the death of Yasutaka in 1504

46. Narushima, Nochi kagami, 3:827–42.
47. Inoue, Ikkō-ikki no kenkyū, pp. 357–72.
48. Hioki, Ka-Nō komonjo, doc. 1110, p. 472, establishes presumed date of the death of Yasutaka.
49. Identified from references in various documents included in Hioki, Ka-Nō komonjo.
50. This is actually an inference from a situation that existed in 1531. See n. 55.

that its influence began to increase until finally in the early 1520s it became paramount. The civil war of 1531, which resulted in the abolition of the office of shugo, was in fact a civil war among factions of the ikki, which found the heads of the three temples fighting on the losing side along with Togashi Taneyasu.

Legal documents relating to Kaga in this period show that until 1504 the bakufu and the shōen proprietors regarded Togashi Yasutaka as the prime legitimate authority of Kaga; that between 1504 and 1521 they were uncertain; and that after 1521 they routinely sent legal papers to the Honganji headquarters just outside of Kyoto, thus recognizing it as de facto shugo.[51] The political and military history of Kaga in this period also supports these conclusions. In the period before 1504 Kaga was involved in several military campaigns, all of which were related to the political ambitions of Togashi Yasutaka rather than those of the Kaga ikki. Yasutaka was an ally of Ashikaga Yoshitane who had been deposed as shogun in 1493 by Hosokawa Masamoto, at which time Yasutaka was forced to flee to Kaga, and Yoshitane accompanied him. Yoshitane tried several times to regain the capital with the aid of Togashi and others, and Yasutaka also invaded Echizen twice, in 1494 and 1504 as a part of the same war, invasions in which there is no indication of ikki participation.[52] In sharp contrast the Kaga ikki went to war twice in the years just after Yasutaka's death in 1504, fighting in Etchū in 1506 in alliance with the ikki of that province, and in Echizen in 1508 in support of an ikki rebellion against the Asakura. In neither case is there any indication of involvement of the old feudal families.[53]

By 1531 the Ikkō-ikki had become so dominant that a factional struggle within the Honganji leadership engulfed the entire province in civil war. To summarize this complicated affair, a Honganji faction came to power that year headed by Renjun, a son of Rennyo, who was hostile to the heads of the three "Kaga temples" mentioned above.[54] When Renjun attempted to enforce a greater degree of control over Kaga from the Honganji headquarters, a coalition of interests that included local Honganji priests, the Togashi, and a number of their foremost vassals, decided to defy him. Renjun was supported in Kaga by still other priests and ikki members. When civil war broke out, the main Honganji faction gained the upper hand by sending in troops from Mikawa Province, another ikki stronghold.[55] The 1531 civil war cleared Kaga of shugo authority and

51. Hioki, *Ka-Nō komonjo*, docs. 1077, 1098, 1114, 1117, 1125, 1135, pp. 455–81.
52. Tsuji, *Daijōin jisha zōjiki*, 10:407, 411–12. Inoue, *Ikkō-ikki no kenkyū*, pp. 400–02.
53. Inoue, *Ikkō-ikki no kenkyū*, pp. 387–405.
54. Honganji, *Honganji shi*, pp. 406–17, 427–28.
55. Inoue, *Ikkō-ikki no kenkyū*, pp. 452–53, quoting *Shirayama-gū shōgun kōchū kiroku*.

most of the shugodai-type military families, for while the lesser members
of the coalition that fought against Renjun were allowed to return to
Kaga, the leaders were not. In their place the ikki became the only political
force in Kaga.

One important result of the civil war of 1531 was that the Honganji,
through confiscation, gained control of a great deal of land in Kaga. Much
of this was returned to the members of the defeated faction, but as fiefs
granted by the temple. Moreover many others in Kaga and elsewhere
voluntarily commended their lands to the Honganji.[56] Thus the Honganji
became a major economic power within Kaga, able to intervene regularly
in the political affairs of the province. By 1546 its responsibilities in Kaga
had become so great that it created a permanent agency to manage them,
the Kanazawa Midō. For another forty years the Midō served as the
primary governmental headquarters of the province, and the community
that grew up around it became the nucleus for the modern city of Kanazawa.[57]

The loose cooperative association of the Kaga ikki was now transformed
into a complex but effective system of government. Under the Midō there
were four district organizations of prominent local bushi called *hatamoto*.
Each hatamoto was commander of a group (*kumi*), of which there appear
to have been twenty in all. Under the kumi were smaller regional groupings of the local bushi and heads of the village communes.[58] The result was
a powerful, integrated domain, much like that of a daimyo, that was able
to fight the powerful Uesugi Kenshin of Echigo to a stand-off and block
his access to the capital, even while sending strong assistance to the
Honganji in the Kinai area. Later, the domain was able to resist the armies
of Oda Nobunaga for five years after the catastrophic defeat of its main
army in 1575.

From the foregoing survey of Kaga history, it is clear that although ikki
domination of Kaga is conventionally dated from 1488 to 1580, the ikki
in fact avoided making itself the formal government of Kaga until forced
to do so by pressure from the Honganji in 1531. This reluctance to take on
formal governmental responsibility was repeated elsewhere, for only in
Kaga did an Ikkō-ikki ever become the basis on which the government of
an entire province rested, despite the fact that strong ikki had established
themselves in most provinces of central Japan.

The ikki movements of the fifteenth century were dedicated to the principle of maximum decentralization, in a way quite at odds with the trend
in organization of the time. However much the activities and ambitions

56. Ibid., pp. 491–98.
57. Ibid., pp. 545–52.
58. Ibid., pp. 479–91.

of feudal leaders might have contributed to the decentralizing trend at any given time, the efforts of the shugo in the fourteenth century or those of their chief vassals (the shugo daimyo) in the fifteenth, were directed toward achieving the strictest possible control over their vassals and dependents. No sooner had the ambitions of local feudal leaders and the conditions that gave them scope destroyed the Muromachi order than various of them began to devise the military and administrative devices that became the foundations of daimyo centrism. As an example, Asakura Toshikage, whom we mentioned earlier, had already by the time of his death in 1481 moved far toward establishing greater central control: he had carried out a policy that all leading vassals should be deprived of private castles and forced to live in the shadow of the daimyo's fortress, with their families as permanent hostages. Further pursuit of such policies not only put an end to the independence of local gentry of the type that had been the backbone of the various ikki movements, it forced them out of existence entirely.

Probably the biggest factor in the success of the new daimyo organizations in subordinating their vassals and subjecting them to rigorous discipline was their ability to co-opt the peasant movement for their own purposes. They did so by coming to terms with the desire of the peasantry to control their own lives: they granted the peasantry almost complete autonomy as long as they paid their taxes, and enlisted village leaders into their own rural administrative systems. By working out a system of direct communication with the peasantry, the daimyo forced the bushi to sever their close connections with the land and to move into their castle headquarters to become little more than mercenary soldiers. For that section of the gentry fully committed to the military way of life, this prospect might even have been welcome. But the lesser gentry who had always resisted inclusion in feudal organizations found the prospect less attractive. Toward the end of the sixteenth century in most places, such local families were literally forced to choose whether they would yield their swords and become peasants or yield their land and become soldiers. In either case they would be obliged to give up their independence and submit to stringent administrative controls imposed by the daimyo.

The Kaga Ikkō-ikki rebelled against Togashi Masachika precisely because he was attempting to end the general anarchy of Kaga and force the province to submit to a measure of discipline. It was content to live with Togashi Yasutaka and Togashi Taneyasu as shugo once it had won its point against Masachika. The ikki members apparently preferred to have someone else take on the burden of such minimal government as was unavoidable, rather than to give up their own independence by permitting an ikki leader to serve as hegemon. The ikki only became the actual

government of Kaga when outside pressure forced defensive recentraliza-
tion among the local kokujin, and this was achieved only by accepting an
outside agency, namely, a shugo substitute in the form of the Kanazawa
Midō.

The political organization of the ikki proper, if it can be separated for
the moment from the political organization of the Honganji, never tran-
scended the level of a committee of hatamoto. There were about twenty
kumi in Kaga, and these were the largest permanent ikki organizations.
Important political matters were discussed and settled at meetings of their
leaders and the chief local Honganji priests. Because these meetings were
held irregularly and were normally on the county rather than the province
level, the average gathering might be assumed to consist of only five
hatamoto and one or two priests. It is thought that the business of the
kumi was conducted similarly, except that the voice of the hereditary
leader, the hatamoto, would carry great weight in kumi meetings.

Since the central purpose of the Ikkō-ikki was the defense of kokujin
against the centralizing ambitions of a daimyo, it is not surprising that it
was loath to give its leaders sufficient scope to emerge as daimyo themselves. On the other hand, why should the ikki have allowed the Honganji
to establish a comprehensive daimyo-like government in Kaga? The period
between the expulsion of the shugo in 1531 and the establishment of the
Midō in 1546 was one of great instability. Antagonisms continued between the victors and losers of the 1531 civil war. The province was
threatened from outside by the Asakura to the south and the Uesugi to
the north. These conditions required unified action among the Kaga
kokujin. Since the ikki members would not permit one of their own
number to emerge as leader of the whole province, they could only welcome the appearance of a disinterested outsider able to mediate their
disputes and lead the province against their enemies. Ironically the necessities of the increasingly fierce struggle to maintain Kaga against the new
daimyo (who, unlike the shugo, had organizations that could quickly
absorb new territory into their own vassal systems) forced the Ikkō-ikki
to accept a form of government under the Midō, which increasingly came
to assert the kind of control they sought to avoid.

The Honganji-led and ikki-based organization that controlled Kaga
from 1546 was finally destroyed by Oda Nobunaga in 1580. It is interesting
to speculate what would have happened had Kaga been able to retain its
independence into the Tokugawa period. There is little indication that the
Kaga ikki had fashioned a radically new political order. Indeed, given the
fact that Honganji priests held heritable positions and were free to marry,
Kaga would probably have become largely indistinguishable from other
Edo period daimyo domains except for the peculiarities of its political

nomenclature. The Tokugawa daimyo normally governed their territories through councils of leading vassals in a manner similar to that used by the Midō, who deployed hatamoto. It is not surprising, then, that Kaga adapted well to the imposition of daimyo rule after 1580. Under the Maeda family, which organized the province between 1583 and 1600, Kaga became one of the country's most prosperous and contented domains.

The study of the development of Japanese society during the fourteenth, fifteenth, and sixteenth centuries finally reduces to an analysis of the beginnings of Japan's modernization. By modernization I mean the transformation of society from one exclusively based on agriculture to one in which there appeared a broad variety of socioeconomic roles and functions. In early medieval Japanese society every social class, from hereditary servants to the highest court nobility, depended for its income upon rights to a share of the produce from specific parcels of land, and the shōen system emerged as the legal expression of this reality. Everyone either possessed some specific shōen right, served as the personal dependent of one who did, or starved. Modern society by contrast is characterized by a market system that enables substantial segments of society to specialize in other socially useful tasks and obtain sustenance without any direct connection with agriculture or ownership of land. At the same time the remainder are freed from nonagricultural tasks and transformed into agricultural specialists, with a consequent rise in efficiency all around.

The progress of modernization may be measured in any number of ways; the classic approach is to trace the development of the market system and the emergence and growth of a specialized merchant class, and somewhat later a specialized financier class. In Western society the transformation of political institutions that accompanied modernization was heavily influenced by these groups, and it is quite useful to make this aspect of modernization the central focus of historical treatments of the whole process. In Japan, however, the attempt to explain modernization through an analysis of the commercial class and its political self-consciousness has not been very successful. For by Western standards, the political influence of merchant–financier groups remained quite limited. It is this fact that has led some observers to conclude that modernization in Japan can only be dated from the nineteenth century. For most Western scholars such reasoning makes little sense. For them, the economic, social, and cultural, if not political, role of merchant–financier groups seemed quite noteworthy in Japanese society since at least the sixteenth century. The problem of motivation for political modernization still remains, however.

It is one of the conclusions of this paper that a new perspective on this problem can be gained by taking into consideration the ikki phenomenon of the late medieval period, particularly the tsuchi-ikki. For while the ikki failed to demonstrate the capacity to form an alternative political system to that created by the daimyo, they were symptomatic of the strong local pressures for change to which the daimyo had to accommodate. Thus it is possible to suggest that the greatest source of pressure for political modernization came in fact from the activities of specialized agriculturalists. It was this group that forced the ruling classes to begin a reshaping of their political institutions. Of the three types of ikki considered above—(1) the early, small-scale ikki of the lower segments of warrior society, (2) the tsuchi-ikki, which combined the political and military forces of groups of autonomous villages, and (3) the kuni-ikki formed by warriors in partial reaction to the tsuchi-ikki—it is the second that is most significant in demonstrating the nature of the pressure involved. Even though the objectives of the tsuchi-ikki were restricted to economic matters, the endurance and enterprise of these organizations cut the ground from under the existing pattern of relationships between peasants and warriors, forcing new power arrangements and new standards, and above all making possible the system of direct daimyo administration of semi-autonomous villages that formed the essence of Tokugawa local government.

The society that emerged in the late sixteenth century was nominally feudal as far as relationships among the ruling class were concerned. But the warrior elite presented an absolutist–bureaucratic face to the rest of society, much in the manner of European governments at a similar stage of development. It is not unreasonable to suggest that if Japanese modernization is taken on its own terms, that is, if proper place is given to the role of the agricultural classes and ikki in the political modernization of Japanese society, many of the seeming anomalies that trouble historians of the Tokugawa period will begin to disappear.

Epilogue

JEFFREY P. MASS

The eleven papers included in this volume have dealt with topics spanning more than seven centuries. During this long cycle Japan moved from a polity dominated by courtier scions of great noble houses, to one in which civil and military (central and local) interests competed with one another for the wealth of the country, and finally to one in which almost all governance had become local, exercised by warriors who had the power to grasp and wield military force. Viewed from the top, this story is one of a slow erosion of transcendant authority, of a gradual unraveling of the tightly symmetrical imperial system of the eighth century to a point in the early sixteenth when virtually all power had become fragmented locally. It is the theme of decentralization in Japan's medieval institutional development that serves as the main focus—and connecting thread—among the diverse papers offered here.

The initial stage in this lengthy process of decentralization occurred during the early Heian period and resulted from a resurgent competitiveness among those situated near the summit of the social and political pyramid. Public authority came to be parceled out among the court and religious elite, gradually privatized, and thus shorn of part (but not all) of its original legitimacy. The burdens of government (but not its major rewards, titles, and ranks) came to be broadly diffused, with central figures demonstrating a willingness to delegate responsibility outward and downward.

The essays by Hall, Hurst, Sato, and Kiley contribute to a telling of this story in new perspective. The creation of competing patronage blocs, as described by Hurst, suggests that bureaucracy, despite the elaborate administrative codes adopted in the eighth century, was never the primary locus of power; nor did the political system operate entirely by hereditary succession. Within the limits of one's status in the social hierarchy, fortunes were won and lost by dint of individual ability as well as family connection. Court politics remained the essence of Heian government, and headship over, or membership in, client groups was the sine qua non for receipt of emoluments and even "public" offices. Civil service in Heian Japan was intimately bound up with private patronage.

Yet despite these potentially divisive factional tendencies within the Heian court, there were two features of the system that helped to bind it together. First, there was an explicit sense of collegiality among the court families. This was exemplified by the manner in which the Kugyō Council, consisting of the heads of ranking noble lineages and their chief clients, met and functioned as a regular governing body. Through the institution of the council a certain esprit de corps and sense of playing by accepted rules permeated the entire noble class. Second, while competition was severe within the court, the vertical arrangement of factions permitted rivalry only between peers and thereby minimized social mobility. In his important contribution to an understanding of Heian politics, C. J. Kiley has demonstrated how the concept of hierarchy in land rights was paralleled by hierarchy in the service relationships among men of different status levels. What made the system workable, even efficient, was that since local land managers, for example, were unable to aspire to membership in the high nobility, a factional alliance between them and the court proprietors was both possible and desirable. Each participant in such an alliance worked to the advantage of the others. Those at the local level provided commended income and military and other services, while persons at the top arranged for duly authorized legal guarantees. A premature break between capital and countryside was thereby prevented.

A great deal has been explained by the use of these new conceptions, including the unusual length of the Heian polity. Inasmuch as the mid-Heian "rise of the *bushi*" occurred within a framework in which the private interests of the court-based nobility and the provincially based military aristocracy were essentially joined, the advancing power of fighting men did not immediately lead to a new system of authority. Not until the late twelfth century would the idea emerge that men of the provinces might contest the authority of Kyoto and dispute the absentee rights over land of the court nobility. Only gradually did the provincial aristocracy conceive of the idea of coalescing regionally and creating an autonomous governmental structure of their own.

The political history of the last hundred years of the Heian period has been explained traditionally in terms of the appearance of powerful regimes headed successively by the retired emperors and the Taira. Hurst and Mass have questioned the appropriateness of a periodization that puts undue stress on the distinctiveness of these regimes. Abdicated sovereigns, as Hurst suggests, neither emerged suddenly during the eleventh century, nor created a form of government that was institutionally different from that over which the *kugyō* had presided for several generations. What did distinguish the period of active retired emperors was that under them the imperial family joined the competition for hegemony at court by seeking to dominate the council and by creating its own massive house organization and estate portfolio. The significance of emperors being "retired" and yet still "active" was that, once freed from the restraints of the throne, they could serve as actual power-holding heads of the imperial house. Over a domain originally conceived as an imperial realm, retired emperors eventually became the country's leading private landlords.

In order to recapture its past glory the imperial house was forced to undergo a fundamental change in its original character. The Taira too, before their final demise, were confronted by the need to change their basic character. As provincial clients of retired emperors for three generations after 1100, their experience in managing men and land had been entirely different from that of the high nobility in Kyoto. When the Taira scion Kiyomori was promoted in rapid fashion into that nobility, he possessed no well-staffed administrative house office and no lands over which he was absolute proprietor. Thus, while his personal rise was spectacular, he did not succeed, as some have claimed, immediately to "rule Japan." This was especially so since, in addition to his deficiencies as a court noble, he exhibited little comprehension of the local support he might have used to govern as a warrior overlord. It had taken the imperial house much time and extensive reorganization to escape the sway of the Fujiwara regents. It could not be expected that the Taira would have been able to break immediately from their condition as clients of the ex-sovereign. The creation of an identifiable Taira hegemony did eventually take place, but only during 1179–80, barely several months before the outbreak of the Minamoto's historic rebellion.

In Mass's treatment of the Gempei War of the 1180s, he argues that the fighting was an economic and social upheaval, not merely a confrontation between two rival warrior leagues. Provincial warriors across the country directed violence against their private enemies—neighbors and relatives who were rivals, and absentee proprietors who remained at court. Out of this chaotic condition, and representing the collective interests of the top level of provincial society, there emerged the *bakufu*, Japan's first political regime to enjoy a physical and institutional existence apart from "central authority." This new warrior government was based in the eastern town of Kamakura but extended its influence, by means of the tie of vassalage, into almost all parts of the country. Henceforth, a vassalage relationship with the new military hegemon would serve as the basis for a revolutionary form of land protection: those enrolling as "housemen" were eligible for appointment as *jitō*, a managerial title carrying immunity from dispossession by central proprietors. By distributing these jitō offices to its men, the new regime became the guarantor for a powerful sector of the provincial warrior elite.

The bakufu served another purpose; it was an instrument for the return of the country to stability. This involved both a political accommodation with Kyoto and a willingness, where necessary, to exact harsh discipline against warriors. Here was a military regime devoted essentially to orderly government. The difficulty was that Kamakura's own constituents—now a uniquely favored warrior aristocracy—were the group most apt to abuse the legal structure. The bakufu thus became, in addition to its other functions, the most important judicial agency in the land. As both Hall and Mass have noted, the pattern of patronage that in Heian times had flowed from capital to provinces now began to be reversed: the political initiative was shifting dramatically to the provinces. Much the same was true regarding control over land. *Shitaji chūbun*—the physical division of estates between competing central and local interests—was only the most conspicuous of several dispute resolution patterns that moved the jitō closer to full local land possession.

The two papers by Wintersteen sketch in much new detail on the early Muromachi bakufu. Of particular interest is his description of the gradual shift in the Ashikaga power base to a concentration in Kyoto and surrounding provinces. The new regime absorbed away the capital administration's remaining powers until by Yoshimitsu's reign as shogun this second bakufu had become Japan's new "central government." The Ashikaga's *hanzei* policy expressed the converse side to this development—the degree to which control of the countryside had now passed from the court into the hands of the rising provincial magnates called *shugo*. But the capital region retained its historic importance. Despite the general trend in society toward localism, Kyoto lived on and prospered in ways not previously realized. With civil and military aristocrats now living side by side in the capital, the prestige of the former and power of the latter did not always prove antagonistic. This was especially true in the economic sphere, as the shrunken world of provincial estates produced less and less land revenue for those who resided at the center. The story of Kyoto's survival during the medieval era thus centers increasingly on the home provinces' commercial development. Both old and new nobility, civil and military, became highly dependent on a revised tax structure in which the traditional sources of income—produce and services from the land—were de-emphasized in favor of trade and commercial endeavor. The political reach of the capital city may have atrophied noticeably, but the social and economic composition of Kyoto became infinitely more diversified as merchant and artisan groups joined with religious orders and the civil and military aristocracy to maintain a highly sophisticated level of cultural activity.

That a new mix of class interests marked the rural areas as well during the Muromachi age is revealed by Davis in his study of the *ikki*. Alongside the often-cited rise of daimyo as local military hegemons was an important, though as yet little studied, social development among the various groups living closer to the soil. Both at the level of cultivating peasants and lower military gentry strenuous efforts were made to disengage from all forms of absentee authority. Having passed through successive stages in which local warriors and peasants sought the patronage and protection of the Heian court, the Kamakura bakufu, and finally the various shugo, these groups now came to rely increasingly on themselves. The dominant illustration of this reaction against supralocal authority is of course the shrinking of the unit size for effective governance to a point during the fifteenth century when the power of the sword became the prime legitimizer of political influence. The daimyo of the Sengoku age were able to assert their authority only over those men and lands for which they could exercise coercive influence.

By the first part of the sixteenth century the institutions of transcendent authority had all but disappeared, and Japan had ceased to be the sum of its component parts. Diversity was everywhere: "medieval cities," province-wide ikki organizations, strong and weak daimyo, all existed together within the same realm. War seemed constant, yet violence in one part of the country did not necessarily mean that adjacent regions were disrupted. It was out of the multiple institutional possibilities of this age of maximum fragmentation that the ingredients of the sixteenth-century unification were drawn. Military power and political invention were combined into a new polity over which a new bakufu presided. The cycle from centralization to decentralization back to centralization found its premodern completion in the establishment of the Tokugawa shogunate.

The essays contained in this volume have sought to illuminate the political cycle that ran its course from the ninth through fifteenth centuries. In themselves these essays can reveal only a small portion of the work being done by their authors. Seven of our eight contributors (the exception being Professor Hall) have either recently completed or are in the process of completing dissertations on medieval Japanese institutions. As these more extensive studies find their way into print we can expect that our knowledge of medieval Japan will be further extended. There still will remain, however, large gaps in our understanding, and it will be useful to take note of some of these. Much remains to be explained with regard to the workings of the Heian court. While Hurst has provided us with a close examination of the imperial house, we need to know more about the Fujiwara, their landholdings and family organization. Beyond that, there are the other high-ranking noble houses whose names constantly appear in the historical records but about whom we know very little. The composition of the Minamoto and Taira *uji* and the role of the nonmilitary lineages within these large kin organizations also need study. The link between the regent's line of the Fujiwara house and the Seiwa Minamoto is referred to in many history surveys but is never described in detail. Finally, there remains to be investigated the obviously close relationship between the high nobility and the high Buddhist priesthood.

There are numerous aspects of the land-tax system that require further examination. How, for example, did the "allotment" and "proprietary" provinces function? What was the process of shōen incorporation and subsequent proprietary expansion? What was the nature of shōen administration under various types of proprietors? Through what stages did the changing character of the public land sector pass? Sato and Mass have presented partial insights into the history of the Tōji-owned estate of Ōyama, but we are still awaiting portraits in full of individual shōen. The possibility exists for such studies, for there are shōen in most parts of the country for which sufficient historical materials survive. The general condition of the lower levels of rural society is another topic that demands consideration. How, for example, should the peasants of late Heian times be treated? As slaves, serfs, or relatively independent small landholders? Historians have given all three designations to them. Again, how did the changing character of village organization during the Heian period relate to changes in the structure of local government and to the evolution of land institutions?

For the Kamakura period there is still a host of subjects requiring further research. Much more needs to be known about the decline of the Kamakura bakufu and the character and range of the Hōjō hegemony. Why at a time of apparent ascendancy in virtually all aspects of government did the Hōjō collapse so totally? At another level, despite the work of Kan'ichi Asakawa, there is still need for a full-scale study of medieval proprietorships and how they operated. With the influence of the warrior aristocracy clearly on the rise during the Kamakura period, how is one to account for the remarkable resilience of certain great shōen, especially those under religious ownership? Much work needs to be done to clarify how the disruptions that affected local areas during the brief Imperial Restoration of the 1330s helped to change the structure of power-holding within the civil and military elite. To what extent, for example, did the short-lived investiture of central proprietors with military titles serve to sweep away Kamakura period shugo and jitō and pave the way for the many new names that appeared under the Muromachi bakufu?

The Muromachi period has barely begun to be studied, and vast areas of ignorance remain to be illuminated. To cite only two of these, we still know very little about the phenomenon of the daimyo, how they came into being, and how they differed from region to region. Despite the work of J. W. Hall on the Bizen region, we need portraits of the great military houses from all major areas. Balancing such regional studies, we clearly require further work on medieval Kyoto and vicinity. For given the state of countrywide warfare and advanced decentralization, the question still remains as to how the capital region retained its position of economic and even political influence. How was it possible, for example, that Kyoto played such a crucial role in the first stage of the unification drive? Finally this brings us to the great unifiers themselves. Nobunaga and Hideyoshi still await their biographers.

In light of what is yet to be discovered about medieval Japan, the essays in this volume can claim to have made only a modest contribution. They have been brought together, however, in hopes that they will stimulate a greater interest in Japan's pre-Tokugawa age.

Glossary

andojō 安堵狀
Document confirming rights over land.

azukari dokoro 預所
Manager, or "custodian," of *shōen*. Often the title received by the major commender of a *shōen's* land; other times, centrally dispatched.

bettō 別當
Director of a noble house (or religious) administrative headquarters.

buke 武家
Generic term for military houses.

bushi 武士
Armed fighter; warrior.

chigyō-koku 知行國
Province held as a "proprietorship" by a central noble house or religious institution.

Chinzei bugyō 鎮西奉行
Kamakura *bakufu* commissioners for Kyushu before 1290s.

Chinzei tandai 鎮西探題
Kamakura *bakufu* deputies for Kyushu, established in 1290s, with full powers of jurisdiction over that island.

chō 町
Unit of land area: 2.94 acres until 1594 when Hideyoshi at the time of the national land survey (*kenchi*) reduced the size to 2.45 acres.

Chōdōin 朝堂院
The government office compound of the Imperial Palace Enclosure.

chokushiden 勅旨田
Imperial edict lands; imperial *shōen*.

Daidairi 大内裏
The Great Palace Enclosure.

Daigokuden 大極殿
The Audience Hall of the Imperial Palace Enclosure.

daimyo 大名
Regional military lord.

Dairi 内裏
The Imperial Palace.

dairyō 大領
District magistrate; *gunji*.

Dajō Tennō 太上天皇
Honorific title for an abdicated emperor.

Dazaifu 大宰府
Government-general for Kyushu under the imperial system.

gesu 下司
Resident estate manager.

Giyōden 宜陽殿
Office building for the *kugyō* in the Imperial Palace Enclosure.

goin 後院
Imperial retirement palace.

go-ke'nin 御家人
Shogunal vassal.

gun 郡
District, administrative division of a province. Sometimes translated "county."

han 藩
Tokugawa period daimyo domain.

hanzei 半済
　Income division system in which
　fourteenth-century Muromachi *shu-
　go* assigned to vassals half the pro-
　duce of "centrally owned" estates;
　soon became a veritable division
　of *shōen*.

hatamoto 旗本
　"Bannerman"; commander of
　military *kumi* organization.

Heian-kyō 平安京
　Heian period name for Kyoto.

Hikitsukeshū 引付衆
　Board of Coadjutors, a judicial
　agency of the Kamakura *bakufu*.

honjo 本所
　A *shōen*'s managerial office; often
　simply "central proprietor."

honke 本家
　"Patron" or "protector" of *shōen;*
　the highest *shiki* level.

Hyōjōshū 評定衆
　Council of State; central admini-
　strative agency under the Kamakura
　bakufu.

hyōrōryōsho 兵粮料所
　Temporary grant area (fourteenth
　century) for the support of troops
　in the field.

ichinomiya 一宮
　Literally, "the first shrine." First
　among the state-supported shrines
　within a province.

ie 家
　Household.

ikki 一揆
　Originally a form of organization
　for military purposes; later a revolt
　or rebellion (or general pattern of
　autonomous organization) by pea-
　sants and lower-grade warriors.

Ikkō-ikki 一向一揆
　A type of provincial *ikki* directly

associated with the Honganji Buddhist sect of Jōdo Shinshū.

In 院
　Retired emperor.

In-no-chō 院庁
　Administrative office of a retired
　emperor; sometimes also of a
　court lady or imperial temple.

In-no-kinshin 院近臣
　The advisers and ranking private
　officials of retired emperors.

insei 院政
　Traditional designation for the form
　of government of the late Heian
　period, postulating control over
　affairs of state by retired emperors.

inshi 院司
　Officials of the retired emperor's
　administrative house office.

inzen 院宣
　Retired emperor's directive.

jin no sadame 陣定
　Formal meeting of the Council of
　Nobles (*kugyō*) to decide matters
　of state.

jitō 地頭
　Estate steward, appointed by Kama-
　kura *bakufu;* major local figure
　during Kamakura times.

kan 貫
　Unit of cash; equivalent to 1000
　mon.

kanmon 貫文
　Unit of cash; *kan* plus *mon*.

kanshōfu 官省符
　A government charter of tax im-
　munity for a *shōen*.

kebiishi 検非違使
　Originally a policing office for the
　central capital, it later also became
　a designation for provincial enforce-
　ment officials.

keishi 家司
Household officials of ranking nobles.

kemmon seika 權門勢家
The civil and religious elite of Kyoto; central proprietary institutions.

ke'nin 家人
Private vassal; "houseman."

keryō 家令
Household officials of ranking nobles; later designated as *keishi*.

kirokujo 記録所
Central office for the screening and review of *shōen* charters.

kishin 寄進
Upward commendation—or endowment—of land, preparatory to *shōen* establishment.

koku 石
A measure of rice by volume; about 44.8 gallons (180 liters).

kokubunji 國分寺
State-supported provincial temple.

kokuga 國衙
Provincial administrative headquarters.

kokugaryō 國衙領
Lands still subject to public taxation; "public" counterpart of "private" *shōen*.

kokujin 國人
General designation for local warriors during the Muromachi period.

kubunden 口分田
Cultivators' allotment fields as authorized by the eighth-century imperial codes.

kudashibumi 下文
An edict of permanent application issued from a higher to a lower authority.

kuge 公家
The traditional court nobility.

kugyō 公卿
The highest ranking of courtier officials; sat in council during Heian times and "governed" the country.

kumi 組
Subdivision of a *kuni-ikki* organization; a form of military organization during Sengoku times.

kumon 公文
Local officer of a *shōen;* duties undefined, but generally below the *gesu* in rank.

kuni-ikki 國一揆
Provincial organization of local warriors and peasants; a provincial uprising.

mandokoro 政所
Family administrative headquarters.

Midō 御堂
Administrative agency of Honganji in Kaga Province during the sixteenth century.

Miyako 都
An early name for the imperial palace or court; medieval name for the city of Kyoto.

mokudai 目代
Deputy in residence for provincial governors.

mon 文
Unit of cash; 1000 equal one *kan*.

monzeki jiin 門跡寺院
An imperial residence temple.

myō 名
Unit of local cultivator's tenure.

myōden 名田
Rice fields in local possession.

myōshu 名主
Local landholders.

nengu 年貢
Annual land tax owed to proprietor of *shōen*.

ōban-yaku 大番役
Kyoto military guard service performed by vassals of the Kamakura *bakufu*.

onchi 恩地
Lands granted to vassals out of the largess of a lord.

Rakuchū 洛中
Medieval name for the city of Kyoto.

ritsuryō-sei 律令制
System of administrative and penal law, and state-controlled land tenure, established in the early eighth century.

Rokuhara tandai 六波羅探題
Kamakura *bakufu* deputies for central and western Japan, based in Kyoto.

rōtō 郎従
Generic name for retainers or servants, either civil or military.

ryō 両
Unit of cash, usually in gold.

ryōke 領家
Central proprietor of *shōen*.

ryōshu 領主
Generic term for "local lord" over land.

samurai-dokoro 侍所
"Board of Retainers," utilized by major Heian period court families, Kamakura *bakufu*, and Muromachi *bakufu*.

sangi 参議
Imperial court councillor.

satodairi 里内裏
Unofficial imperial residence.

sekkan 摂関
Sesshō and *kampaku*.

Sekkanke 摂関家
Sublineage of the northern branch of the Fujiwara house, which came to hold in heredity the posts of "imperial regent" (*sesshō*) and "civil dictator" (*kampaku*).

shiki 職
Originally, a specific function or office; later, a right to designated income under title of an "office," but with duties (if they existed at all) that might be only incidentally defined.

shinshi 進止
The right of legal jurisdiction over land, even when the formal title (*ryōke shiki*) lay with a central owner.

shiryō 私領
Literally, "private landed possession"; a term (late Heian and Kamakura) used to designate the hereditary landholding of a local person.

Shishinden 紫宸殿
Throne Hall of the imperial palace.

shitaji chūbun 下地中分
Territorial division of a *shōen* between competing central and local (*jitō*) claimants.

shōen 荘園
Private landed estate.

shōkan 荘官
Generic term for *shōen* officials.

shōke 荘家
General term referring to the influential families resident in a *shōen*.

shōmin 荘民
Generic term for the nonofficial class of *shōen* residents; hence local agriculturalists.

shoryō 所領
Landholdings of an individual.

shōshi 莊司
General term meaning local officers or managers of a *shōen*.

shugo (Kamakura) 守護(鎌倉)
Province-level "constable" appointed by Kamakura *bakufu*; liaison officer between *bakufu* and its vassals in a province.

shugo (Muromachi) 守護(室町)
Provincial military governor, appointed by the Muromachi *bakufu*.

shugodai 守護代
Deputy appointed by a *shugo*.

sō-gesu 總下司
Provincial recruitment officer established by the Taira in 1181.

sō-kan 總官
Commander–supervisor for central Japan and environs, established by the Taira in 1181.

sōryō-sei 惣領制
System of divided inheritance of family property; used by warrior houses in late Heian and Kamakura periods; designation also for a pattern of warrior organization in which, despite divided inheritance, general leadership over the extended family was retained by the house head.

sōtsuibushi 總追捕使
Police officer of a *shōen;* provincial constable during late Heian.

tokusei 德政
Bakufu legislation of 1297 limiting or nullifying certain commercial transactions involving lands that had been lost or sold by housemen; subsequently, a general term for any debt or sale cancellation decree whether civil or military.

tokusō 得宗
Designation for the head of the

Hōjō house during Kamakura times.

toneri 舍人
Servants and attendants of a high noble household.

tsubowake chūbun 坪分中分
Division of a *shōen* by component units of production; generally, a less drastic measure than a "territorial division" (*shitaji chūbun*).

tsuchi-ikki 土一揆
Regional peasant combination organized to protest (or rebel) against the economic demands made by higher civil or military authority.

tsuika-hō 追加法
"Supplementary legislation," added to the main bodies of law under both the Kamakura and Muromachi *bakufu* regimes.

uji 氏
The largest familial unit; clan.

ujigami 氏神
Chief clan deity.

uji no chōja 氏の長者
Clan chieftain; highest-ranking official in the clan.

uji no kami 氏の上
Clan chieftain; predecessor term for *uji no chōja.*

ukesho 請所
Contractual agreement between a central proprietor and (usually) a *jitō* authorizing the latter to assume full responsibility for collecting and delivering the annual tax. During Muromachi times *ukesho* arrangements were made between central owners and *shugo* (called *shugo uke*).

wayo 和與
Compromise agreement between central and local (usually *jitō*)

interests leading to an adjustment of rights over *shōen*.

yoriai 寄合

Hōjō family council; general term for meeting, as of *ikki* leaders.

za 座

Trade or craft guild.

zaichō kanjin 在聴官人

Resident provincial official.

zasshō 雑掌

Centrally appointed *shōen* administrator; also a nonresident legal-affairs expert relating to *shōen*.

zuryō 受領

"Tax manager"; mid–late Heian designation for provincial governor class official (*kokushi*).

Index